C000050895

Landscape and Settlement in Medieval Wales

Edited by Nancy Edwards

Oxbow Monograph 81
1997

Published by
Oxbow Books, Park End Place, Oxford OX1 1HN

© Oxbow Books and the individual authors, 1997

ISBN 1 900188 36 8

This book is available direct from
Oxbow Books, Park End Place, Oxford OX1 1HN
(Phone: 01865-241249; Fax: 01865-794449)

and

The David Brown Book Company
PO Box 511, Oakville, CT 06779
(Phone: 860-945-9329; Fax: 860-945-9468)

*Front cover: Newport in Pembrokeshire, from the north
(Copyright: Dyfed Archaeological Trust)*

Printed in Great Britain by
The Short Run Press, Exeter

Contents

Contributors

MARY ARIS
Anglesey Museums Service,
Oriel Môn,
Llangefni,
Anglesey, LL77 7TQ

PROFESSOR CHRISTOPHER DYER
School of History,
The University of Birmingham,
Edgbaston,
Birmingham, B15 2TT.

DR NANCY EDWARDS
School of History and Welsh History,
University of Wales Bangor,
Gwynedd, LL57 2DG.

DR DELLA HOOKE
Department of Geography and Geology,
Cheltenham and Gloucester College of Higher
    Education,
Francis Close Hall,
Swindon Road,
Cheltenham,
Gloucestershire, GL50 4AZ.

CHRISTOPHER HURLEY
17 Gifford Close,
Longlevens,
Gloucester, GL2 0EL

NEIL JOHNSTONE
Gwynedd Archaeological Trust,
Craig Beuno,
Garth Road,
Bangor,
Gwynedd, LL57 2RT.

DR JONATHAN KISSOCK
Faculty of Education,
Humanities and Science,
University of Wales College, Newport,
Caerleon Campus,
PO Box 179,
Newport, NP6 1YG.

DAVID LONGLEY
Gwynedd Archaeological Trust,
Craig Beuno,
Garth Road,
Bangor,
Gwynedd, LL57 2RT.

KENNETH MURPHY
Dyfed Archaeological Trust,
The Shire Hall,
Carmarthen Street,
Llandeilo,
Dyfed, SA19 6AF.

ROBERT SILVESTER
Clwyd-Powys Archaeological Trust,
7A Church Street,
Welshpool,
Powys, SY21 7DL.

DR STEPHEN RIPPON
Department of History and Archaeology
University of Exeter,
Queen's Building,
The Queen's Drive,
Exeter, EX4 4QH.

DR ANTHONY WARD
School of Continuing Education,
University of Kent at Canterbury,
Keynes College,
Canterbury,
Kent, CT2 7NP.

Preface

The main aim of this volume is to bring together the results of a wide variety of recent research and fieldwork on the landscape and settlement of medieval Wales, *c* 400–1500. Although the emphasis is archaeological, the contributers also make use of other evidence, including documents, maps and place-names as well as morphological analysis. These papers demonstrate an upsurge of interest, especially amongst archaeologists and historical geographers, in medieval settlement in Wales, particularly from the eleventh century onwards. Almost half the papers are concerned directly or indirectly, with the extensive survey work, funded by Cadw, Welsh Historic Monuments, which has recently been conducted on the historic settlements of Wales by the Welsh Archaeological Trusts, some of which is still ongoing. Much of this has been prompted by the needs of planning and development control, but the results have also illuminated important aspects of Welsh settlement history for the first time. The rest of the papers demonstrate that a considerable amount of complementary research is also currently being carried out by others.

The book is based on papers given at the eleventh Welsh Archaeological Conference fostered by Cadw which was held in December 1994 and hosted by the School of History and Welsh History, University of Wales, Bangor. All but two of the papers given at the conference are included here.

It is hoped that the publication of these papers will bring this work to the attention of others, historians as well as archaeologists and historical geographers, not just in Wales, but elsewhere. It is also hoped that the volume will stimulate further interest in all aspects of the landscape and settlement of medieval Wales and result in more new work, and particularly interdisciplinary research, on a national, regional and local level.

It should be noted that, following the precedents of the Royal Commission inventories and *Archaeology in Wales*, the pre 1974 system of Welsh counties is used throughout the text. It is hoped that this will avoid confusion, especially in the light of the 1996 local government reoganization which has banished Clwyd, Dyfed and Powys and significantly reduced the size of Gwynedd, resurrected some old counties, such as Anglesey, but also introduced many completely new authorities.

Papers carry their own acknowledgements. In additon the editor would like to thank Frances Lynch, who shared the organization of the original conference, and Dr A D Carr, David Longley, Huw Pryce and K Rees for help in various ways. The conference would not have been possible without the generous financial assistance of the Countryside Council for Wales.

Professor Glanville Jones died as this book was going to press. The bibliographies of the papers in this volume testify to the great contribution which Professor Jones made to the study of medieval settlement in Wales and it was decided to dedicate this volume to his memory.

Nancy Edwards   September 1996

Chapter 1

Landscape and Settlement in Medieval Wales: An Introduction

Nancy Edwards

The settlement of Wales and its evolution during the course of the middle ages is inextricably bound up with the landscape and its exploitation. Although the concept of Wales as an entity had emerged by the eleventh century (Davies, R R 1987, 3–4), its geography, dominated by a central mountainous massif with largely isolated pockets of more fertile coastal lowland, makes it predisposed towards political and cultural fragmentation. Early kingdoms and later Anglo-Norman and English domination may have waxed and waned, but in such a landscape regional identity on both a local and larger scale remained of vital importance (Davies, R R 1987, 13–14). The south and south east, Glamorgan and Gwent, were open to influences from across the Severn Estuary and England. The rich agricultural lowlands of this region were already marked out in the Roman period as part of the civil zone with a town at Caerwent and a sprinkling of Roman villas; in the eleventh century the Normans established themselves and their settlement possibly had more impact here than in any other part of Wales. To the north the central borderland, essentially Powys, which lay between the Wye and the Dee, was open to English penetration along its fertile river valleys, but its rounded hills, mountains and bleak moorland are enclosed and difficult of access. Offa's Dyke stands as testimony to relations between the Welsh and English in this strategic area in the late eighth century and the large number of earthwork and timber and later stone castles, many with small boroughs clinging to them, indicates the fluidity of the border before the Edwardian conquest in the late thirteenth century. The north east, Clwyd, bounded by the Dee and the Conwy, with its narrow coastal plain set against a mountainous backdrop, provides a ready means of access from the east. The Anglo-Saxons were already raiding as far as the Conwy in the early ninth century and the area changed hands several times before its final subjugation by Edward I. In contrast the north west, the heartland of Gwynedd, with its coastal lowlands and Anglesey protected by the mountainous girdle of Snowdonia, was, until the Edwardian conquest, much more open to western influence, including at least some settlers, Irish and Viking, coming from across the Irish Sea. This is also true of the south

west, Dyfed, which stretches between the Dyfi and the Nedd, a region of varied coastal scenery and rich lowlands with the Cambrian Mountains beyond. In the fifth and sixth centuries the south-western peninsula was ruled by the Irish and there is also some evidence for contacts with Dumnonia; later Scandinavian place-names testify to some Viking settlement. Despite the initial conquest of much of the area by the Anglo-Normans in the late eleventh and early twelfth centuries, only southern Pembrokeshire and south-west Carmarthenshire remained consistently in their hands until the Edwardian campaign of 1277.

Clearly the inhospitable mountainous core resulted in settlement being concentrated in the coastal lowlands and river valleys, as it still is today. Throughout the middle ages a mixed farming economy was paramount. There were few restrictions on the rearing of livestock but areas suitable for tillage, and especially for the growing of wheat rather than oats and barley, were severely limited, not just by the availability of good soils, but also by climate and altitude. A climatic deterioration in the fifth and sixth centuries, aided by the vacuum caused by the Roman withdrawal, seems to have precipitated an economic downturn, which led to the abandonment of reclaimed farmland on the Gwent Levels (see Rippon, Ch 2) and probably some retreat from the uplands. Although some agricultural continuity, at least in the south east (Davies, W 1978) is suggested, and sufficient surplus must have been produced for the payment of food renders, the overall impression of the Welsh economy up until the eleventh century, especially when compared with England, was of poverty, backwardness and underdevelopment (Davies, R R 1987, 161). However, the climatic upturn of the eleventh to thirteenth centuries presented opportunities for agricultural and economic growth including the foundation of towns. An increase in the native population bolstered by Anglo-Norman plantation led to some shortages of agricultural land with a consequent need for more marginal areas to be brought into cultivation. The Gwent Levels were again reclaimed (see Rippon, Ch 2) and there are signs of movement into permanent settlements on the uplands where oats were grown in addition to livestock farming (see Hooke, Ward, Chs 7–8; Davies, R R 1987,

139–71). As elsewhere in the early fourteenth century the climatic improvement was reversed bringing animal disease and plague in its wake leading to an economic downturn, depopulation and the shrinkage and sometimes desertion of settlements, and an increase in livestock farming at the expense of arable (Davies, R R 1987, 425–30).

The papers in this volume demonstrate the range of research and excavation which has recently been carried out on the landscape and settlement of medieval Wales. The purpose of this introduction is to provide a context for this work.

Early Medieval Settlement c 400–1070

The main problem which archaeologists still face in attempting to understand settlement in Wales in this period is the identification of diagnostic site types. Some 40 years ago Leslie Alcock (1963; 1987) excavated the hillfort at Dinas Powys, Glamorgan. It consisted of a small promontory (0.1 ha) enclosed by four banks and ditches on the landward side, one, or more likely all of which are of fifth- to seventh-century date (Edwards & Lane 1988, 59–61; Dark 1994, 67–72), fragmentary structures and industrial hearths. Its wide-ranging artefactual assemblage which includes exotic items such as imported pottery from the Mediterranean and Gaul (Campbell 1988, 127–30, figs 27–30), Germanic glass (Campbell 1989a) and metalwork (Graham-Campbell 1991, 221–3), not only dates the occupation of the site from the fifth to the seventh centuries, but also suggests that it was a high-status settlement of some importance, most likely a royal or aristocratic stronghold.

Dinas Powys remains of seminal importance and high-status hillforts, although they do not form a homogenous group, are still recognized as the only characteristic settlement type of the period c 400–700 so far discovered, and indeed of the early medieval period as a whole in Wales. In 1988, in addition to Dinas Powys, four other hillforts, Coygan Camp, Carmarthenshire, Degannwy and Dinas Emrys, Caernarfonshire, and Dinorben, Denbighshire, were definitely identified as having early medieval occupation on the basis of imported pottery, Germanic glass, ornamental metalwork, documentary evidence or radiocarbon dating (Edwards & Lane 1988). Two further definite examples, both found by chance while investigating later medieval castles, may now be added to the list. At Carew Castle, Pembrokeshire, four substantial rock-cut ditches spanning the promontory were partially excavated (Gerrard 1987) and radiocarbon dates (pers comm Q Drew) and a dozen sherds of E ware (Campbell 1990; Campbell & Lane 1993, 40, fig 6) suggest occupation during the fifth to seventh centuries. At Hen Gastell, Briton Ferry, Glamorgan, a precipitous rocky eminence which until recently dominated the west bank of the River Nedd at the ferry crossing point about 1km for its mouth, traces of structures were uncovered, together with B, D and E ware, Germanic glass and a Type G penannular brooch suggesting occupation during the fifth to seventh centuries. Later activity is suggested by a fragmentary bead of a type usually found in Hiberno-Norse contexts and two archeomagnetic dates centering on the late ninth century (Wilkinson 1995).

The fact that hillforts can be identified with relative ease because of their substantial defences, and those occupied c 400–700 may be regarded as high status on the basis of their comparatively rich artefactual assemblages which contain exotic imports, has understandably led to a considerable amount of research on the topography and typology of hillfort sites (Dark 1994), continued in this volume (see Longley, Ch 3), with the hope of isolating criteria which would aid prediction of other early medieval examples. Such work now needs to be backed up by geophysical survey and exploratory excavation.[1]

It has also become clear that not all high-status settlements c 400–700 were defended. Longbury Bank, Pembrokeshire, is a lowlying limestone promontory overlooking the River Ritec which was formerly navigable. The site was discovered only because of interest in prehistoric activity in the cave below the promontory which also brought to light sherds of imported pottery which had fallen in from above. Recent small scale excavation on this important site has suggested that it was of a similar size to Dinas Powys but *without* any traces of an enclosure or defences. Although there was severe plough damage and only fragmentary structures were found, the artefactual assemblage is of considerable interest. It included A, B, D and E ware, Continental glass and evidence of fine metalworking, all comparable with Dinas Powys, and suggests that the site was occupied for at least 100 years between the late fifth and seventh centuries (Campbell & Lane 1993). Like Dinas Powys it may best be interpreted as a royal or aristocratic settlement and it may also have acted as a focus for long-distance trade and exchange.

The realization that not all high-status sites c 400–700 were defended makes their discovery much more difficult, but concentrations of stray finds, particularly of imported pottery, glass or decorated metalwork, such as penannular brooches or pins, offer one way forward. In 1988 it was suggested that early medieval artefacts possibly associated with occupation debris might denote settlements on land engulfed by sand at Kenfig and Twlc Point, Glamorgan (Edwards & Lane 1988, 9, 85, 117). Linney Burrows, Pembrokeshire, where finds from sand-blow include E ware, a Type G penannular brooch similar to that from Longbury Bank and an antler comb, may now be added to the list (Campbell & Lane 1993, 33, 70, fig 6; Redknap 1991, 32). Similarly E ware from Caldey Island, Pembrokeshire, could point to settlement and trading activity (Campbell 1989b, 62–3). In fact a picture is emerging during the fifth to seventh centuries of a variety of high-status sites, both defended and undefended, located on or near the coast or with easy access to navigable rivers thereby emphasizing the importance of contact by sea in the post-Roman period.

After the seventh century archaeological evidence for the continuing high-status occupation of most hillforts and undefended sites such as Longbury Bank ends. However there is some evidence to suggest activity on hillforts after this, but whether occupation was continuous is unclear. Degannwy was burned in 812 and destroyed by the Anglo-Saxons in 822 (Williams ab Ithel 1860, 11–12); Castle Hill, Tenby, Pembrokeshire, is identified as a royal settlement on the basis of a poem, *Etmic Dynbych* ('In Praise of Tenby'), the origins of which have been dated to the ninth or tenth centuries (Williams, I 1980, 155–72); and the ninth- or tenth-century evidence for activity at Hen Gastell, Briton Ferry, has already been mentioned. In this volume (see Longley, Ch 4) the possible continuation of hillfort use in Gwynedd is put forward on morphological grounds as a hypothesis in need of testing by excavation. Nevertheless, as far as the majority of excavated examples is concerned, unless such sites continued, but without the deposition of any recognizably later artefacts, the evidence at present points to a distinct change in the focus of high-status settlement sometime during the eighth or possibly the ninth centuries. What might have precipitated this is unclear. The demise of the trade in imported luxury goods may have played a part (Campbell & Lane 1993, 71) and a less immediate need for defence; but other, less tangible reasons may be implicated, such as changes in the organization of society. Indeed, there seems to have been a more widespread move away from hillfort sites, not just in Wales, but elsewhere in Celtic Britain in this period. In Scotland the undefended site at Forteviot (Alcock & Alcock 1992, 218–42; Forsyth 1995), which was important in the ninth century, may provide a lead. In Wales, however, we remain almost totally ignorant of high-status settlement sites, or indeed *any* secular settlement sites, between the eighth and late eleventh centuries.

It is possible that some high-status settlements remained in the vicinity of hillforts but moved away from the exposed rocky knolls to more sheltered ground nearby. For example, although there is no proof of continuity, David Longley (see Ch 4) has drawn attention to the association of Degannwy with the *maerdref* located on the saddle of land between the two rock outcrops which may have continued to offer shelter in time of attack. Equally, the cross at Carew erected by the king of Deheubarth (1032–5) (Nash-Williams 1950, no 303) suggests continued or renewed activity in the vicinity. As both Longley and Johnstone have indicated (see Chs 4, 5), an important question needs to be addressed regarding the origins of the royal courts (*llysoedd*) and their dependent bond settlements (*maerdrefi*), not just in Gwynedd, but in Wales as a whole. *Llysoedd* and *maerdrefi* and the attendant commotal system emerges in documentary evidence during the twelfth and thirteenth centuries and can certainly be traced back into the eleventh. But to what extent do at least some of these sites go back further, perhaps to a time before the evolution of the commotal system? Further exploratory excavation may be able to tell us.

One of the major breakthroughs over the last decade has been the investigation of Llangorse crannog, Breconshire. Although no buildings have survived, details of the crannog make-up have been excavated. Two plank pallisades and other vertical piles around the island have also been recorded as well as traces of a causeway to the shore. Part of a logboat was discovered and a rich array of artefacts, including evidence for fine metalworking and a unique embroidered textile, confirms the high-status nature of the site. Timbers from the palisades have been dated dendrochronologically and indicate a late ninth- or early tenth-century phase of construction. In addition documentary evidence, in the form of two Llandaff charters and an entry in the Anglo-Saxon Chronicle, has provided a historical context for the site suggesting that it was the home of the kings of Brycheiniog and that it was attacked by Aethelflaed, 'Lady' of the Mercians, in 916 (Lane & Campbell 1988; Campbell & Lane 1989; Redknap, Campbell & Lane 1989; Campbell, Lane & Redknap 1990; Redknap 1991a, 16–17; 1991b; 1992; 1993). The problem is that no other crannogs have been found in Wales (Roberts & Peterson 1989). The closest parallels are Irish and it is possible that the crannog was constructed in order to emphasize the Irish ancestry of the kings of Brycheiniog.

It has been suggested (Edwards & Lane 1988, 8) that large square or rectangular enclosures may have been a characteristic high-status settlement type of the latter part of the early medieval period in Wales. This was based primarily on the site of Cwrt Llechryd, Radnorshire, a defended rectangular enclosure with a natural mound in the centre. A single radiocarbon date from under the enclosure bank provided a *terminus post quem* of cal AD *c* 750–1040 (2 sigma) for its construction (Musson & Spurgeon 1988). Various possible parallels have been cited including Mathrafal, Montgomeryshire, which may now be discounted (Arnold & Huggett 1995).

It has also been suggested that fragments of a rectangular enclosure at Aberffraw, Anglesey, are of significance (Edwards & Lane 1988, 18–21) and a recent reinterpretation of the bank and ditch sequence suggests two phases, the first Roman and the second post-Roman (White & Longley 1995). As Longley (Ch 4) suggests, Aberffraw and its environs remain of crucial importance since this area is associated with a royal settlement of the kingdom of Gwynedd from the early seventh century onwards. As Johnstone (Ch 5) has shown by the thirteenth century the *llys* seems to have been located to the south west of the village and was probably destroyed by development during the 1950s and 60s. But whether the *llys* was always in that location is unclear; it remains possible that at some stage it was sited within the rectangular enclosure and/or somewhere in the hamlet of Henllys to the north.

A second major breakthrough has been the discovery of archaeological evidence for Viking settlement. Place-names suggesting Viking activity have long been recognized (Richards 1962) and Wendy Davies (1990, 51–6) has emphasized the likelihood of settlement in north-west Wales on other grounds. But it is now clear that at least some Vikings settled near Red Wharf Bay, Anglesey, in the late ninth and early tenth centuries. At Glyn, Llanbedrgoch, a

'D' shaped enclosure has been discovered with three rectangular buildings marked by stone footings for timber walls and diagnostic artefacts, including coins and hacksilver, lead weights and a ringed pin, both of which suggest contacts with Ireland (Redknap 1994; Denison 1995). During the eleventh and twelfth centuries the kings of Gwynedd, particularly Gruffudd ap Cynan (d 1137), continued to have links with the Vikings of Dublin and the Isle of Man and occupation of a small coastal promontory fort at Castell, Porth Trefadog, Anglesey, would seem to fit best into this milieu. Excavation showed the promontory was defended by a substantial rampart and ditch with a rectangular stone-built house 10.5 × 5.5m inside; it had later been used for ironworking. There were few artefacts and none was closely datable. However, a series of radiocarbon determinations from the ironworking hearths and house collapse suggests occupation during the eleventh and twelfth centuries and the closest parallels are with Viking promontory forts on the Isle of Man (Longley 1991).

The ninth century onwards also witnessed increased English penetration, especially into north-east Wales, where there was also Scandinavian settlement. Excavations at Rhuddlan have confirmed that this was the site of the Anglo-Saxon *burh* of *Cledemutha* founded by Edward the Elder in 921 but which probably failed around the middle of the century. Although there has been some dispute about the line of the *burh* defences, it is most likely that they formed a large rectangular enclosure, the area of which, some 30 ha, is comparable with some of the Wessex *burhs* rather than others in the north west (Manley 1987). Traces of Anglo-Saxon structures, including three sunken floored buildings, have also been identified, together with some tenth-century artefacts, within the area of the later Norman borough (Quinnell & Blockley 1994). One other possible Anglo-Saxon site on the borders may be of significance. It is located adjacent to the Roman fort at Forden Gaer, Montgomeryshire, and consists of a timber aisled hall *c* 40 × 15m, the closest parallel for which is at the Anglo-Saxon palace of Cheddar (Blockley 1990).

Very little recent progress has been made in the identification of early medieval lower status settlements in Wales; their recognition is still dependent upon radiocarbon dates and occasional diagnostic artefacts (Edwards & Lane 1988). In the south east the site of Trostrey Castle, Monmouthshire, with its isolated church nearby is potentially of great interest. Multiperiod occupation has been uncovered including Roman military activity, a Norman ring-ditch and a later stone castle. In addition five oval post-and-wattle structures have been excavated, three of which would appear to be of early medieval date on stratigraphic grounds. S16 is 5.75 × 5.25m with a doorway on the south east. The walls were constructed of a double line of posts and wattles with a cavity between and there were also traces of internal arrangements. The only scientific dating evidence is a radiocarbon date of cal AD 439–634 (2 sigma) from a stake hole to the west of the house. S1 and S5 are similar in plan and construction but may be

considerably later. Two further, slightly larger oval houses, N4 and N6, also with double walls of posts and wattles and internal partitions may date to the period 1138–84 when this area was back in native control. A radiocarbon determination from N4 gives a date of cal AD 1024–1209 (2 sigma) (Mein 1993; 1994). Full evaluation of these structures must await the final report, but they may be of considerable importance. This appears to be the first discovery of early medieval oval post-and-wattle buildings in Wales and it is interesting to note the double post-and-wattle walling is characteristic of early medieval round houses of similar size in Ireland (Edwards 1990, 22–5). Secondly, the excavation of similar structures in the ?twelfth century might suggest that this was a native house type used over several centuries. Furthermore this would support Gerald of Wales' description (1193 × 4) of native houses as 'wattled huts' (Thorpe 1978, 252). If this is a characteristic Welsh house type and the settlements were unenclosed apart, perhaps, from fences, it would explain why they have been so difficult to locate. Our understanding of early medieval Irish houses has only expanded as a result of modern excavations of structures in ringforts such as Deerpark Farms, Co Antrim, which was partially waterlogged.

Turning to the south west, early medieval reoccupation of Iron Age and Roman-British enclosed farmsteads remains likely. At Drim, Pembrokeshire, the presence of a double-walled wattle round hut has also recently been suggested in addition to radiocarbon dates of cal AD 613–871 (2 sigma) and a penannular brooch similar to a G2 form (Edwards & Lane 1988, 68–9; Mytum 1995, 22, fig 5). In the north west, although archaeological work has continued on prehistoric and Romano-British hut groups which survive mainly in the uplands, no further evidence of early medieval activity (Edwards & Lane 1988, 5–6) has come to light. This is not surprising because work has been concentrated on survey in order to facilitate the management and conservation of the hut groups (Gwynedd Archaeological Trust 1994–5, 17–18) rather than on excavation. However this should result in a greater understanding of the typology of these monuments and, combined with a similar survey which has just begun of long huts and platform houses generally regarded as medieval (Gwynedd Archaeological Trust, 1994–5, 20–1), it may prove possible to pinpoint examples where further exploratory work should be concentrated because of their potential for early medieval occupation (Crew 1984).

Another recent approach has been to study the morphology and evolution of settlements which still survive today. In this volume Jonathan Kissock (Ch 10) suggests, as a result of research in south Pembrokeshire, that not all pre-Norman settlement was dispersed; there were also villages of radial form clustering round churchyards and important secular centres. In the latter it is possible that we can detect sites which, in areas which remained outside Anglo-Norman control, for example Gwynedd (see Johnstone, Ch 5), developed into *llysoedd* and *maerdrefi* with their surrounding farmland (*tir cyfrif*). Nucleated settlements clustered round churches are also identifiable in other parts of Wales. In a recent survey of *The Historic Settlements of Dinefwr* (Sambrook & Page 1995, 6–10), an area which in contrast to south Pembrokeshire retained its Welshness, it is suggested that several medieval parish churches with Celtic dedications which are now the foci of villages, may have had their origins in the early medieval period. Comparable villages, for example Llanfechell, have also been noted in Anglesey (Carr 1982, 32–3) and the classic site is Llanynys, Denbighshire (Jones, G R J 1972, 343–9). Similarly, in the Historical Settlement Surveys in Clwyd and Powys (see Silvester, Ch 9) an attempt was made to distinguish between early medieval Welsh foci and Anglo-Norman settlements. In the areas of Brecknock Borough and Radnorshire, where Welsh settlement is traditionally perceived as dispersed, it was noted that, in contrast to churches with curvilinear enclosures and Celtic dedications, Anglo-Norman churches were much more obvious as nucleations. Indeed, the relationship of church sites which may be securely identified as early medieval foundations (Edwards & Lane 1992, 3–11) to the surrounding settlement pattern and farming landscape needs to be more systematically investigated using air photography (James 1992), documentary evidence and morphological analysis followed up by geophysical survey and exploratory excavation. Such work, not only has the potential to throw light upon early medieval settlement and land exploitation, but also its subsequent evolution.

Work on reconstructing the early medieval landscape of Wales and determining how it was exploited is still in its infancy. This is partly because of the difficulty in identifying a range of characteristic settlement types and the dearth of documentary evidence, as well as the need for more work on place-names and pollen evidence. Wendy Davies' (1978) research on the landscape, exploitation and evolution of the estates in the Llandaff charters in south and south-east Wales remains of seminal importance and others are now beginning to build upon it. In this volume Christopher Hurley (Ch 3) sets out to compare the farming potential of estates in the Llandaff charters with those described in charters belonging to the bishops of Worcester. Ewan Campbell and Alan Lane have also used estates described in the Llandaff charters to provide a context for excavated sites at Longbury Bank (Campbell & Lane 1993, 55–60) and Llangorse crannog (Campbell & Lane 1989, 679, fig 1). A morphological approach combined with documentary analysis also has the potential to be of assistance. This has been adopted in Stephen Rippon's study (Ch 2) of the Gwent Levels.

Settlement in Wales c 1070–1500

Despite the fact that the settlement archaeology of Wales from the coming of the Normans to the end of the middle ages is very much more visible than that of the previous period, it has received surprisingly little attention, especially when compared with the amount of research, survey and excavation which has been carried out on both rural and urban settlements of the same period in England over the last 50 years. There would seem to be a variety of reasons for this. It is notable that what is now the Medieval Settlement Research Group has been very largely concerned with England. During the same period in Wales, because of their great numbers and commanding presence in the landscape, the emphasis has been on the study and to a lesser extent excavation of castles as well as their presentation to the public (RCAHMW 1991; Barker & Higham 1982; Avent 1995), though there has been a tendency to neglect their surroounding territories. While the survey of both rural and urban medieval settlements (RCAHMW 1956; 1960; 1964; 1982; Soulsby 1983) and houses (Smith 1975) has advanced our knowledge significantly, there has been comparatively little excavation to back it up. There have been few major excavations of deserted rural settlements and this is equally true of towns where, apart from Monmouth, the redevelopment of medieval urban settlements with the consequent need for rescue excavation has played a far less significant role when compared with the richness of urban excavations in many English historic towns and cities such as York, Norwich and London.

In Wales also the emphasis has largely been on historical research. The work of T Jones Pierce (1972), which drew on the native law books in conjunction with the fuller documentation available after the Edwardian conquest of Gwynedd, to try and reconstruct the form and evolution of medieval Welsh rural society, remains of great significance. This has been built upon by others: most significantly by Glanville Jones (eg 1972; 1973; 1985), who has combined documentary evidence with historical geographical approaches; but also by Colin Gresham (1954; 1973)and Lawrence Butler (1971; 1988), who have made use of both historical research and archaeological fieldwork; and more recently by Thomas Charles-Edwards (1993, 226–56, 364–411). Many archaeologists, however, seem to have been reluctant to grasp the potential of such research and there has been little attempt recently to investigate how the evidence of the documentary record measures up with that on the ground. In this volume we can begin to see more use of such historical research in conjunction with archaeological fieldwork (eg Johnstone, Ch 5; Hooke, Ch 7; Ward, Ch 8). In the future there needs to be more emphasis on combined historical amd archaeological research projects which might, for example, investigate the medieval landscape and settlement alluded to in the *Survey of the Honour of Denbigh* (Vinogradoff & Morgan 1914; Jones, G R J 1973, 448–9, 465–71). It is such interdisciplinary research which has advanced medieval settlement studies in England as, for example, at Wharram Percy (Beresford & Hurst 1990) and Shapwick (Aston 1993b), and in the recent medieval settlement and landscape project in the East Midlands (Lewis & Mitchell-Fox 1993).

Rural Settlement

Anglo-Norman settlement made its greatest mark on the

lowland areas of Gwent, the Vale of Glamorgan, Gower, parts of coastal Carmarthenshire, south Pembrokeshire and the borders, where conquest came early and the land was retained. In addition to the castles and adjacent boroughs of the Norman barons and their vassals, these parts of Wales were parcelled out into knights' fees, English settlers – and in south Pembrokeshire Flemish colonists (see Kissock, Ch 10) – brought in, and a manorial structure imposed with its consequent impact on the pattern of rural settlement and exploitation of the landscape (Davies, R R 1987, map 3, 82–100). In the Vale of Glamorgan it has been suggested that the origins of most nucleated villages can be traced back to the manorial settlements of the late eleventh century, though some may be part of secondary colonization in the twelfth (RCAHMW 1982, 215). It is in this area that the greatest effort has been made in Wales to study deserted and shrunken villages. There were several small scale excavations in the 1960s and 70s (RCAHMW 1982, 218–43), including the shrunken village at Barry, where excavation of various phases of houses demonstrated their occupation *c* 1100–1350 (Thomas & Dowdell 1987). The only significant work since has been at Cosmeston, Penarth, where excavation since 1982 has been followed up by reconstruction of parts of the medieval village on its original site, a project currently unique in Britain. There is documentary evidence to link the foundation of the village with the de Costenin family in the twelfth century and pottery has been discovered to support such a date, though no structures earlier than *c* 1300 have been recovered. Domestic and agricultural buildings have been excavated on three tofts as well as some investigation of the manor house, garden and dovecote to the north east (Parkhouse 1984; 1985; Coles *et al* 1986; Newman & Farwell 1993).

In lowland Gwent Paul Courtney (1983; 1986) has traced the course of Anglo-Norman rural settlement in the late eleventh and early twelfth centuries with the establishment of the manorial system and the foundation of nucleated villages with open fields. Building upon this Stephen Rippon (Ch 2), using morphological analysis combined with documentary research, charts the differing Anglo-Norman impact on the Gwent Levels, the likely role of the Lord of Caerleon in overseeing reclamation on the Caldicot Levels, and the foundation of the planned settlement at Whitson.

In south-west Wales it is likewise possible to trace the impact of the conquerors on the settlement pattern. In this volume Jonathan Kissock (Ch 10) studies the morphology of existing village forms in south Pembrokeshire. Villages, such as Templeton, Angle and Letterston, with their clearly planned layouts, may be compared, for example, with planned villages founded by Norman lords after the 'Harrying of the North'. In this part of Wales Flemish colonization in the early twelfth century was of some importance and at least some of these planned villages are likely to have been founded as rural boroughs by Flemish *locatores*.

Anglo-Norman settlements can also be recognized in the Welsh borderland of Brecknock Borough and Radnor-shire and here it has been noted (see Silvester, Ch 9) that some nucleated settlements with Anglo-Norman character-istics, such as Alexanderstone, have relict earthworks suggesting shrinkage. Such earthworks offer the opportunity for future archaeological investigation which could tell us something of their origins, development and decline.

Even less has been done to identify rural settlements in the lowland areas of Wales which remained largely in native control before the Edwardian conquest and to determine the impact of the conquest on them. As has already been noted the origins of at least a proportion of such settlements, whether dispersed or nucleated, may lie in the early middle ages. But the most important recent breakthough has been the identification, using documentary, place-name and topographic evidence, of the locations of many of the commotal courts (*llysoedd*) of the princes of Gwynedd from the eleventh to thirteenth centuries (see Johnstone, Ch 5). The ongoing excavation of the *llys* complex at Rhosyr, Anglesey, with its enclosing wall, hall and other buildings, is of tremendous interest, since there is the potential to illuminate the daily lives of members of the royal house of Gwynedd and their retinues. The locations of some of the adjacent bond settlements (*maerdrefi*) have also been identified and those which survive as greenfield sites, such as Neigwl, Caernarfonshire, and Ystumgwern, Meirioneth, cry out for further archaeological investigation. Outside Gwynedd there is an urgent need to employ similar techniques to try and locate the sites of *llysoedd* and *maerdrefi* and their subsequent archaeological sampling to determine comparisons and contrasts. Some research has already been conducted in the vicinity of Dinorben, Denbighshire (Jones, G R J 1973, 465–71), and as part of *The Historic Settlements of Dinefwr* survey where the castle at Dinefwr with its adjacent old town have been identified as the likely sites of the *llys* and *maerdref* of the commote of Dinefwr; the castle of Carreg Cennen and the nearby estate of Ferdre (from *maerdref*) as the commotal site of Iscennen; and the motte and bailey of Castellmeurig as the possible *llys* of the commote of Perfedd with the *maerdref* located at Felindre Sawdde, where an approximately rectangular nucleated settlement with an irregular pattern of dwellings and gardens has been noted together with an adjacent unenclosed field system (Sambrook & Page 1995, 13–14).

At present we know very little indeed about the settlements of the ordinary people, whether free or bond. In Gwynedd the documentary evidence suggests that by *c* 1100 the land, which was divided into townships (*trefi*), was mainly held by groups of free kin (*gwelyau*) who seem to have lived in scattered farming settlements. At the same time there were unfree bondmen (*taeogion*), such as those who lived in the nucleated *maerdrefi*. During the twelfth and thirteenth centuries the population was rising and it has been suggested that the numbers of freemen increased and consequently the lands they held expanded, some at the expense of the bondmen, and more land was brought into production (Charles-Edwards 1993, 226–39).

The problem is that there has only been one major modern excavation of a lowland settlement of this period in

Gwynedd: the farmstead at Cefn Graeanog, near Clynnog, Caernarfonshire, which may be broadly dated to the twelfth and thirteenth centuries (Kelly 1982). The farmstead was located on relatively good land and was set at right-angles to a low ridge to provide protection from the weather. The earlier phase consisted of a single rectangular, timber-framed bulding delineated by postholes. This was later replaced by four rectangular buildings with stone sills which would have supported wooden walls and a cruck-roof structure. The buildings were identified as a house, a barn, a byre and a stable. The change from wooden earth-fast posts to stone foundations has been commonly identified in England during the same period (Dyer 1986, 34–40). There were notably few artefacts and bone did not survive, but the recovery of charred crop remains indicated that both oats and wheat were grown. Richard Kelly suggested that this was a prosperous mixed farm sited on land alienated from the nearby *clas* at Clynnog Fawr. The difficulty is that at present the evidence for this farmstead is almost unique. No similar sites have been recently excavated in Gwynedd or in other native held areas. There is therefore no way of knowing how typical it may have been and how it fitted into the broader range of settlements which must have existed in this period.

The farmstead at Cefn Graeanog was probably abandoned before the Edwardian conquest. It is however clear that the crisis of the fourteenth century, with its climatic downturn, animal disease and plague, followed by the Glyndŵr rebellion must have affected the lowland settlement pattern of Gwynedd, just as elsewhere in Wales, causing desertion and shrinkage. Using documentary evidence A D Carr (1982, 32–5; 300–30) has studied the impact of these disasters on Anglesey and has noted in particular the abandonment of nucleated bond townships such as Deri, where now only two farms survive. It may be possible, using estate maps and other documents, to locate such settlements with more precision and this should be followed up by archaeological investigation. In addition the current settlement surveys by Clwyd-Powys, Dyfed and Gwynedd Archaeological Trusts embrace a broad range of both lowland and upland sites in different parts of Wales including farmsteads, dispersed and nucleated settlements and deserted villages (Gwynedd Archaeological Trust 1994–5, 20–1), which, if it is followed up by excavation, has the potential to increase greatly our understanding of medieval settlement throughout Wales.

The fourteenth-century crisis can also be traced at Llanelen in the Welshry of northern Gower where a prosperous farmstead built in the ruins of a church has been excavated. Documentary evidence, hedgerow dating and the pottery sequence suggest that the farm was assarted during the late thirteenth or early fourteeenth centuries but deserted in the years following the Black Death (Kissock 1991, 139, 143–4; Schlesinger *et al* 1995, 68–71). Carbonized grain indicates that oats and barley were cultivated, fragmentary bone that sheep and cattle were probably kept, and slag demonstrates that iron was being smelted, perhaps to provide an additional source of income.

Not surprisingly, there has been more archaeological work on settlements in the uplands, which remained very largely under native control, simply because on such marginal land more has survived. The pioneering research by Aileen and Cyril Fox in the uplands of Glamorgan on Gelligaer Common, which included the excavation of a late thirteenth- and early fourteenth-century farmstead consisting of three rectangular houses set on platforms at right-angles to the slope (Fox 1939), is well known, as is the complementary survey work carried out in Caernarfonshire, though there has been little follow-up excavation (Gresham 1954; RCAHMW 1956; 1960; 1964; usefully summarized in Butler 1971). It has now been realized that the present classification of these upland settlements, in the past mainly designated as platform houses and long huts, is confusing. In this volume (see Ward, Ch 8) a simpler classification is proposed for structures on the Black Mountain in the Brecon Beacons based on the character of the superstructures rather than their orientation in relation to the slope or the presence or absence of platforms. Such structures may also be set singly or in groups and related to yards, enclosures and sometimes field systems (see Aris, Ch 6). It is also clear that more archaeological excavation is required to determine when such rectangular structures originated and how long they remained in use. The excavations at Cefn Graeanog indicate that they were in existence by the twelfth century and they certainly continued into the post-medieval period. In fact both Della Hooke and Anthony Ward (Chs 7, 8) have drawn attention to the expansion of upland grazing towards the end of the middle ages, perhaps partly in response to lowland enclosure, with the likely establishment of permanent farms which may have been preceded by seasonal dwellings. This raises the whole question of transhumance and the extent to which it was practised and whether seasonality and permanence can be recognized in the archaeolgical record (see Ward, Ch 8). Again, much more excavation is required to answer such questions, in conjunction with more documentary and place-name research (see Hooke, Ch 7), to determine the changing exploitation of both upland and lowland environments and the relationship between the two. Such work would also enable comparison between different upland areas in Wales and with other parts of upland Britain such as Cumbria, Dartmoor and Bodmin Moor (Austin 1985; 1989; Johnstone & Rose 1994).

In England there has long been an interest in the archaeological evidence for field systems (Taylor 1975) and an increasing awareness of how the medieval landscape was exploited in other ways, for example hunting and woodland management, and the archaeological evidence which may have been left behind (Astill & Grant 1988). In Wales, however, although there has been quite a lot of documentary research (Davies, M 1973; Jones 1972; 1973; Jack 1988, 412–32; Williams, D H 1984, vol 2), there has yet to be extensive archaeological investigation. In areas early settled by the Anglo-Normans traces of open field sytems have been recorded, for instance in Glamorgan, and a particularly fine example has survived in working use on Rhosili Down in the Englishry of Gower (RCAHMW 1982, 307–12). In this volume (see Rippon, Ch 2) the process of land reclamation, field-names, field patterns and their changing exploitation are explored on the Gwent Levels and it is suggested that the eastern part of the Caldicot Levels had the largest influx of English settlers.

The study of fields in native areas of Wales has centred on the interpretation of systems of land tenure as described in the documents, particularly the Welsh laws (Jones 1972, 320–58; 1973). *Tir gwelyog* ('hereditary land') was held by a free kin group and consisted of unenclosed arable fields with scattered strips held by male members of the kin and periodically divided and reapportioned according to the customs of partible inheritance. Pasture, woodland and other waste were held in common. *Tir cyfrif* ('reckoned land') also consisted of unenclosed arable fields with scattered strips which were, however, worked by bondmen who were together responsible for paying certain dues to their lord, while *tir corddlan* ('nucleal land') consisted of plots of cultivated land set, radial fashion, around focal settlements, whether ecclesiastical or secular (see Kissock, Ch 10). Glanville Jones has also attempted, using air photographs and documentary evidence, to record survivals of such unenclosed field systems divided into strips with their attendant settlements, notably in the free township of Bryngwyn, Caerwys, Denbighshire, and Llan-non, Cardiganshire, an estate of the bishops of Dt David's (1985, 162–7). A similar unenclosed field system with strips and adjacent common associated with a bond settlement has been noted on the site of the *maerdref* of Felindre Sawdde, Carmarthenshire (Sambrook & Page 1995, fig 11). In addition Jones (1972, 343–8; 1973, 471–6) identified *tir corddlan* around the church of Llanynys, Denbighshire, with strips of *tir gwelyog* (now ploughed out) beyond. In this volume Mary Aris (Ch 6) uses aerial photography to record a series of relict field systems on the Great Orme, Llandudno, and suggests that some of them may be associated with the free township of Cyngreawdr. Further investigation making extensive use of air photography combined with documentary research is essential to record what remains of medieval field systems elsewhere in Wales.

Apart from the investigation of pillow mounds indicative of rabbit farming (RCAHMW 1982, 327–45; Austin 1988; Silvester 1995), there has been remarkably little archaeological research on other aspects of the exploitation of the medieval landscape in Wales despite the survival of landscape features such as deerpark enclosures and droveroads. However, there has been some interesting documentary research, for example D H Williams' work (1984, vol 2) on the exploitation of the landscape by the Cistercian order who held considerable lands in Wales. Detailed records, such as the Margam charters, provide a vivid picture of the monastic estates and the various farming and industrial activities. Although much has inevitably been destroyed by later industrial development, some granges, such a Monknash, Glamorgan, have extensive remains (RCAHMW

1982, 262–5), and such estates clearly deserve more archaeological investigation (Aston 1993a, 136–9).

Urban Development

Although the Roman towns of Caerwent and Carmarthen became ecclesiastical foci during the early medieval period, they were no longer urban. The Anglo-Saxon *burh* at Rhuddlan likewise failed. It is therefore not until the Anglo-Norman conquest that we can begin to trace the permanent development of towns in Wales. Documentary evidence makes it possible to chart the progress of castle foundation followed by the establishment of boroughs. For example, the town of Chepstow had been founded by 1075; Prestatyn and Rhuddlan by 1086, though they did not remain in English hands; Cardiff in the 1080s; Pembroke by *c* 1100 and Carmarthen by 1109 (Soulsby 1983, 7–11). There was less town foundation during the following century, but Usk, Monmouthshire, for example, which was probably established *c* 1174 after the recapture of the area from the Welsh, was the last of the major boroughs in Gwent (Courtney 1994, 98). The small borough of Llandovery, Carmarthenshire, was in existence by 1185 (Soulsby 1983, 162) and Newport, Pembrokeshire, was founded in the wake of the English recapture of the lordship of Cemais *c* 1197 (see Murphy, Ch 10). However during the reign of Henry III (1216–72) a new impetus was brought to town foundation and urban expansion in Wales (Soulsby 1983, 12–13). On the Borders, for example, Montgomery received its charter in 1227 and Painscastle in 1230 (see Silvester, Ch 9). Likewise in the south Trelech, Monmouthshire, was probably laid out in the 1230s and Laugharne, Carmarthenshire, was incorporated 1278–82. Because of the ebb and flow of Anglo-Norman control in many parts of Wales the foundation of some towns was faltering. At Aberystwyth, for example, at least two earlier castles on different sites were developed and destroyed before the final foundation of the Edwardian borough in 1277 (Griffiths 1978, 19–32). In north Wales, while the English attempted to found boroughs at Degannwy and Diserth during the mid thirteenth century, the general economic expansion of the period meant that in Gwynedd some of the native *maerdrefi*, such as Llan-faes, Anglesey, began to take on an urban aspect (see Johnstone, Ch 5). The Edwardian conquest had a profound effect on the urban landscape of north Wales with the plantation of castles with walled boroughs such as Conwy (1283) and Caernarfon (1284). The foundation of Beaumaris (1296) resulted in the destruction of Llan-faes and removal of the inhabitants to Newborough, but some other native towns, such as Nefyn and Pwllheli, continued to prosper. Other small Welsh towns include Lampeter, Cardiganshire, (1285) and Llanidloes, Montgomeryshire (1292), both of which developed around churches. Urban development peaked in the early fourteenth century, but after this the Black Death, castle abandonment and economic downturn followed by the Glyndŵr rising, caused many instances of urban decline, and in extreme cases, most notably Trelech, a gradual but dramatic contraction (Soulsby 1983, 13–19, 24–7, 256–9).

The documentation and topography of medieval towns in Wales has received considerable attention (eg Griffiths 1978). However, in the late 1970s the investigation of the material remains was still in its preliminary stages (Griffiths 1978, 10). An Urban Archaeology Rescue Unit had been established in University College Cardiff (1973–8) to collate what was known of the medieval towns of Wales and assess their archaeological potential (Soulsby 1983). But almost no excavations had taken place (Delaney 1977, 42–5); the most significant were at Usk (Courtney 1995) and Rhuddlan (Quinnell & Blockley 1994). The most extensive excavations since have been in Monmouth where a large number of burgage plots along Monnow Street have been investigated prior to redevelopment (Clarke 1987; 1990; Clarke *et al* 1993; 1994; Jackson & Jackson 1991; Maylan 1987; 1989). Excavation elsewhere has been mainly small scale and piecemeal, and apart from a regional survey of towns in Gwent (Courtney 1994, 111–31), there has been no recent attempt at synthesis, which is now overdue.

In this volume Kenneth Murphy (Ch 11) considers the results of various excavations and other archaeological work over the last twenty years in the small boroughs of Dyfed and Robert Silvester examines New Radnor (Ch 12) and some other small planted towns in Powys (Ch 9). These studies highlight the continuing need for documentary and topographical research, combined with archaeological excavation, to gain insights into the sometimes complex origins and evolution of such planted boroughs, their interaction with other towns in the region, and with their rural hinterlands and further afield. The fact that so many declined leaving vacant plots which have yet to be redeveloped indicates their archaeological potential, recently well demonstrated by excavation of burgage plots in Newport (see Murphy, Ch 11), Montgomery (Britnell & Jones 1989) and Trelech (Howell 1990; 1991; 1992; 1993; 1994). There has as yet been very little work on the native towns, though the recent geophysical survey of the greenfield site at Llanfaes (see Johnstone, Ch 5) has revealed considerable archaeological potential.

Conclusion

The aim of this chapter has been to provide a broad synthesis of our current understanding of archaeological and complementary work on the landscape and settlement of medieval Wales in order to provide a context for the chapters which follow. It has also served to demonstrate how little we know, even now, of settlement archaeology in the period before the coming of the Anglo-Normans. In the subsequent centuries, though the evidence is much more readily recognizable, it has not received the attention it deserves and the need for much more work, especially excavation, is self-evident. It is only then that we will be able to answer some of the broader questions which have been raised (see Dyer, Ch 13).

Acknowledgements

I am very grateful to Heather James and Huw Pryce for reading a draft of this chapter and for their helpful comments and suggestions.

Notes

1 This has already been done at Brawdy, Pembrokeshire, a promontory enclosed by three banks and three ditches, where a fifth- to seventh-century date has been claimed for Phase 7 (Dark 1994, 141–3). There was a lack of unequivocal dating evidence and we must await the final excavation report for a detailed discussion of phasing and chronology. Continuing excavation at Castell Henllys, Pembrokeshire, on an Iron Age promontory fort with Iron Age and Romano-British activity in the adjacent annexe, may also be noted. There is artefactual evidence in the annexe for occupation late in the Roman period and at some point the hillfort defences were refurbished but this is currently undated (pers comm, K Murphy). At Caergwrle Castle, Flintshire, radiocarbon dates from a section across the outer enclosure suggest third- or fourth-century AD activity on the site but the full range of the radiocarbon determinations and the fact that they came from large timbers means that a post-Roman date is possible (Manley 1992, 16).

References

Alcock, L, 1963, *Dinas Powys*, Cardiff

Alcock, L, 1987, *Economy, society and warfare among the Britons and Saxons*, Cardiff

Alcock, L, & E, 1992, Reconaissance excavations on early historic fortifications and other royal sites in Scotland, 1974–84: 5: Excavation and other fieldwork at A, Forteviot, Perthshire, 1981; B, Excavation at Urquhart Castle, Inverness-shire, 1983; C, Excavation at Dunottar, Kincardinshire, 1984, *Proc Soc Antiq Scot*, 122, 215–87

Arnold, C J, & Huggett, J W, 1995, Excavations at Mathrafal, Powys, 1989, *Montgomeryshire Collect*, 83, 59–74

Astill, G, & Grant, A, (eds) 1988, *The countryside of medieval England*, Oxford

Aston, M, 1993a, *Know the landscape, monasteries*, London

Aston, M, 1993b, Report on the Shapwick project 1993, *Medieval Set Res Group Ann Rep*, 8, 15–17

Austin, D, 1985, Dartmoor and the upland village of the south-west of England, Hooke (ed), 71–9

Austin, D, 1988, Excavation and survey at Bryn Cysegrfan, Llanfair Clydogau, Dyfed, 1979, *Medieval Archaeol*, 32, 130–65

Austin, D, 1989, The excavation of dispersed settlement in medieval Britain, in M Aston *et al* (eds), *The rural settlements of medieval England*, Oxford, 231–46

Avent, R, 1995, Laugharne Castle, Cardiff

Baker, A R H, & Butlin, R A (eds), 1973, *Studies of field systems in the British Isles*, Cambridge

Barker, P, & Higham, R, 1982, *Hen Domen, Montgomeryshire: a timber castle on the English/Welsh border*, London

Beresford, M, & Hurst, J, 1990, *The English Heritage book of Wharram Percy*, London

Blockley, K, 1990, Excavation in the vicinity of Forden Gaer

Roman fort, Powys, 1987, *Montgomeryshire Collect*, 78, 17–46

Britnell, J, & Jones, N, 1989, Pool Road, Montgomery: excavations within the medieval town, *Montgomeryshire Collect*, 77, 41–72

Butler, L A S, 1971, The study of deserted medieval settlements in Wales (to 1968), in M Beresford & J G Hurst (eds), *Deserted medieval villages*, Guildford, London, 249–69

Butler, L A S, 1988, Wales, in Hallam (ed), 931–65

Campbell, E, 1988, The post-Roman pottery, in Edwards & Lane (eds), 124–38

Campbell, E, 1989a, A blue glass squat jar from Dinas Powys, South Wales, *Bull Board Celtic Stud*, 36, 239–45

Campbell, E, 1989b, New finds of post-Roman imported pottery and glass from South Wales, *Archaeol Cambrensis*, 138, 59–66

Campbell, E, 1990, Carew Castle, *Archaeol Wales*, 30, 69

Campbell, E, & Lane, A, 1989, Llangorse: a 10th century royal crannog in Wales, *Antiquity*, 63, 675–81

Campbell, E, *et al*, 1990, Llangorse crannog, *Archaeol Wales*, 30, 62–3

Campbell, E, & Lane, A, 1993, Excavations at Longbury Bank, Dyfed, and early medieval settlement in south Wales, *Medieval Archaeol*, 37, 15–77

Carr, A D, 1982, *Medieval Anglesey*, Llangefni

Charles-Edwards, T M, 1993, *Early Irish and Welsh kinship*, Oxford

Clarke, S, 1987, Recent discoveries in Monmouth, Gwent, *Archaeol Wales*, 27, 30–1

Clarke, S, 1990, Recent archaeological work in Monmouth, Gwent, *Archaeol Wales*, 30, 25–7

Clarke, S, *et al*, 1993, Monmouth, *Archaeol Wales*, 33, 80–1

Clarke, S, *et al*, 1994, Monmouth, *Archaeol Wales*, 34, 69–70

Coles, N, *et al*, 1986, Cosmeston, *Archaeol Wales*, 26, 53–5

Courtney, P, 1983, *The rural landscape of eastern and lower Gwent AD 1070–1750*, unpublished PhD thesis, Univ Coll Cardiff

Courtney, P, 1986, The Norman invasion of Gwent: a reassessment, *Medieval History*, 12, 297–316

Courtney, P, 1994, *Medieval and later Usk*, Cardiff

Crew, P, 1984, Rectilinear settlements in Gwynedd, *Bull Board Celtic Stud*, 31, 320–1

Dark, K R, 1994, *Discovery by design. The identification of secular élite settlements in western Britain A.D. 400–700*, Brit Archaeol Rep, Brit ser, 237, Oxford

Davies, M, 1973, Field systems of south Wales, in Baker & Butlin (eds), 480–510

Davies, R R, 1987, *Conquest, coexistence, and change, Wales 1063–1415*, Oxford

Davies, W, 1978, *An early Welsh microcosm, studies in the Llandaff charters*, London

Davies, W, 1990, *Patterns of power in early Wales*, Oxford

Delaney, C, 1977, The present state of Welsh urban archaeology, in M Barley (ed), *European towns their archaeology and early history*, London, 35–46

Denison, S, 1995, First Viking settlement in North Wales, *Brit Archaeol*, 10, 5

Dyer, C, 1986, English peasant buildings in the later middle ages, *Medieval Archaeol*, 30, 19–45

Edwards, N, 1990, *The archaeology of early medieval Ireland*, London

Edwards, N, & Lane, A (eds), 1988, *Early medieval settlement in Wales AD 400–1100*, Bangor, Cardiff

Edwards, N, & Lane, A (eds), 1992, *The early church in Wales and the West*, Oxbow Mon 16, Oxford

Forsyth, K, 1995, The inscriptions on the Dupplin cross, in C Bourke (ed), *From the Isles of the North, Early medieval art in Ireland and Britain*, Belfast, 237–44

Fox, A, 1939, Early Welsh homesteads on Gelligaer Common, Glamorgan, *Archaeol Cambrensis*, 94, 163–99

Graham-Campbell, J, 1991, Dinas Powys metalwork and the dating of enamelled zoomorphic penannular brooches, *Bull Board Celtic Stud*, 38, 220–32

Gresham, C, 1954, Platform houses in north-west Wales, *Archaeol Cambrensis*, 103, 18–53

Gresham, C, 1973, *Eifionydd: a study in landownership from the medieval period to the present day*, Cardiff

Griffiths, R A, 1978, *Boroughs of medieval Wales*, Cardiff

Gwynedd Archaeological Trust, 1994–5, *The work of Gwynedd Archaeological Trust 1994–95*, Bangor

Hallam, H E (ed), 1988, *The agrarian history of England and Wales Vol II 1042–1350*, Cambridge

Hooke, D (ed), 1985, *Medieval villages*, Oxford

Howell, R, 1990, Trelech, *Archaeol Wales*, 30, 68

Howell, R, 1991, Trelech, *Archaeol Wales*, 31, 48

Howell, R, 1992, Trelech, *Archaeol Wales*, 32, 82–3

Howell, R, 1993, Trelech, *Archaeol Wales*, 33, 79

Howell, R, 1994, Trelech, *Archaeol Wales*, 34, 70–1

Jack, R I, 1988, Farming techniques, H) Wales and the Marches, in Hallam (ed), 412–96

Jackson, R & P, 1991, Archaeological work in Monmouth in 1991, *Archaeol Wales*, 31, 7–9

James, T A, 1992, Air photography of ecclesiastical sites in South Wales, in Edwards & Lane (eds), 62–76

Johnstone, N, & Rose, P, 1994, *Bodmin Moor. An archaeological survey, Vol 1: the human landscape to c 1800*, London

Jones, G R J, 1972, Post-Roman Wales, in H P R Finberg (ed), *The agrarian history of England and Wales Vol I part 2, AD 43–1042*, Cambridge, 283–382

Jones, G R J, 1973, Field systems of North Wales, in Hallam (ed), 430–79

Jones, G R J, 1985, Forms and patterns of medieval settlements in Welsh Wales, in Hooke (ed), 155–69

Jones Pierce, T, 1972, *Medieval Welsh society*, J B Smith (ed), Cardiff

Kelly, R S, 1982, The excavation of a medieval farmstead at Cefn Graeanog, Clynnog, Gwynedd, *Bull Board Celtic Stud*, 29, 859–908

Kissock, J, 1991, Farms, fields and hedges: aspects of the rural economy of north-east Gower, *c* 1300 to *c* 1650, *Archaeol Cambrensis*, 140, 130–46

Lane, A, & Campbell, E, 1988, Llangorse crannog, *Archaeol Wales*, 28, 67–8

Lewis, C, & Mitchell-Fox, P, 1993, The Leverhulme medieval settlements and landscape project: report on site selection for future fieldwork in the East Midlands, *Medieval Set Res Group Ann Rep*, 8, 27–35

Longley, D, 1991, The excavations at Castell, Porth Trefadog, a coastal promontory fort in North Wales, *Medieval Archaeol*, 35, 64–85

Manley, J, 1987, *Cledemutha: a late Saxon burh in North Wales, Medieval Archaeol*, 31, 13–46

Manley, J, 1992, The outer enclosure on Caergwrle Hill, Clwyd, *Flint Hist Soc J*, 33, 13–20

Maylan, C N, 1987, Monmouth, 82–85 Monnow Street, *Archaeol Wales*, 27, 61

Maylan, C N, 1989, 41 Monnow Street, Monmouth, *Archaeol Wales*, 29, 61

Mein, A G, 1993, Trostrey Castle, Trostrey, *Archaeol Wales*, 33, 52

Mein, A G, 1994, Trostrey Castle, Trostrey, *Archaeol Wales*, 34, 71

Musson, C R, & Spurgeon, C J, 1988, Cwrt Llechryd, Llanelwedd: an unusual moated site in Central Powys, *Medieval Archaeol* 32, 97–109

Mytum, H, 1995, Across the Irish Sea – Romano-British and Irish settlements in Wales, *Emania*, 13, 15–22

Nash-Williams, V E, 1950, *The early Christian monuments of Wales*, Cardiff

Newman, C, & Farwell, D, 1993, Penarth, Cosmeston medieval village, *Medieval Set Res Group Ann Rep*, 8, 65

Parkhouse, J, 1984, Cosmeston, *Archaeol Wales*, 24, 67–9

Parkhouse, J, 1985, Cosmeston, *Archaeol Wales*, 25, 38–41

Quinnell, H, & Blockley, M, 1994, *Excavations at Rhuddlan, Clwyd 1969–73, Mesolithic to Medieval*, CBA res rep 95, York

RCAHMW, 1956, *An inventory of the ancient monuments in Caernarvonshire, Vol I: East*, London

RCAHMW, 1960, *An inventory of the ancient monuments in Caernarvonshire, Vol II: Central*, London

RCAHMW, 1964, *An inventory of the ancient monuments in Caernarvonshire, Vol III: West*, London

RCAHMW, 1982, *An inventory of the ancient monuments of Glamorgan, Vol III: Medieval secular monuments, Part II: Non-defensive*, Cardiff

RCAHMW, 1991, *An inventory of the ancient monuments of Glamorgan, Vol III: Part 1a Medieval secular monuments, The early castles from the Norman Conquest to 1217*, London

Redknap, M, 1991a, *The Christian Celts*, Cardiff

Redknap, M, 1991b, Llangorse crannog, *Archaeol Wales*, 31, 38–9

Redknap, M, 1992, Llangorse crannog, *Archaeol Wales*, 32, 76

Redknap, M, 1993, The Llangorse landscape project, *Archaeol Wales*, 33, 36–7

Redknap, M, 1994, Glyn, Llanbedrgoch, Anglesey, *Archaeol Wales*, 34, 58–60

Redknap, M, *et al*, 1989, Llangorse crannog, *Archaeol Wales*, 29, 57–8

Richards, M, 1962, Norse place-names in Wales, *Proc Int Congress Celtic Stud*, Dublin, 51–60

Roberts, J G, & Peterson, R, 1989, Possible crannog sites in Wales and the Marches, *Archaeol Wales*, 29, 40

Sambrook, R P, & Page, N A, 1995, *The historic settlements of Dinefwr*, Dyfed Archaeol Trust, Project Record No 29799 (unpublished)

Schlesenger, A, *et al*, 1995, Excavations at Llanelen, Llanrhidian: an early church and medieval farmstead site, *J Gower Soc*, 46, 58–79

Silvester, R J, 1995, Pillow mounds at Y Foel, Llanllugan, *Montgomeryshire Collect*, 83, 75–91

Smith, P, 1975, *Houses of the Welsh countryside*, London

Soulsby, I, 1983, *The towns of medieval Wales*, Chichester

Taylor, C, 1975, *Fields in the English landscape*, London

Thomas, H J, & Dowdell, G, 1987, A shrunken village at Barry, Glamorgan, *Archaeol Cambrensis*, 136, 94–137

Thorpe, L (trans), 1978, *Gerald of Wales. The journey through Wales/The description of Wales*, Harmondsworth

Vinogradoff, P, & Morgan, F (eds), 1914, *Survey of the Honour of Denbigh*, London

White, R B, & Longley, D, 1995, Excavations at Aberffraw, *Trans Anglesey Antiq Soc*, 13–21

Wilkinson, P F, 1995, Excavations at Hen Gastell, Briton Ferry, West Glamorgan, 1991–2, *Medieval Archaeol*, 39, 1–50

Williams, D H, 1982, *The Welsh Cistercians*, 2 vols, Tenby

Williams, I, 1980, Two poems from the Book of Taliesin, in R Bromwich (ed), *The beginnings of Welsh poetry, Studies by Sir Ifor Williams*, Cardiff, 155–80

Williams ab Ithel, J (ed), 1860, *Annales Cambriae*, London

Chapter 2

Wetland Reclamation on the Gwent Levels: Dissecting a Historic Landscape

Stephen Rippon

This paper examines the reclamation of an area of coastal alluvium in south-east Wales, known as the Gwent Levels. The area is used as an example of the complex processes by which the present, or 'historic', landscape has come into being. Methodologies used to study the landscape are described and some of the events which led to its creation examined. The context of large scale landscape modification is considered, both in terms of the Norman marcher lords and monastic institutions. The role of peasant farmers, though poorly documented, should not be underestimated.

The Origins of Historic Landscapes

This paper is concerned with the origins of an important and distinctive 'historic landscape' on an area of reclaimed coastal alluvium between Cardiff (Glamorgan) and Chepstow (Monmouthshire) in south-east Wales. The term 'historic landscape' refers to the pattern of settlement, roads, fields and modified natural landforms, such as canalized rivers, which makes up the present countryside. In order to appreciate how these landscapes have come into being, emphasis must be placed upon understanding the processes of creation and change. In particular, the landscape should be thought of as a series of layers which may be peeled off one by one.

Most of the British landscape is a complex palimpsest, which has gradually built up over several millennia. Occasionally functional elements in the present countryside can be traced back to at least the Bronze Age, as, for example, the patterns of 'co-axial' fields around the fringes of Dartmoor and Bodmin Moor (Fleming 1988, figs 15, 73), and those recently identified in Pembrokeshire (Kissock 1993). In Essex and East Anglia a small number of field-systems are pre-Roman, probably Iron Age in date (eg Drury 1978, fig 74; Williamson 1987). The Roman contribution to our landscape is even greater, including the origins of many towns and major roads, though curiously, there are, at present, few identifiable examples of Roman field-systems still in use today (but see below).

It was largely during the medieval period that the present landscape came into being, either gradually, through many generations of work by farming communities, or rapidly, due to large scale reorganizations of landscapes, something traditionally attributed to seigniorial lords (Austin 1985, 204). Most areas saw some modification during the post-medieval period, notably an expansion in settlement, improvement in transport facilities and the piecemeal enclosure of common land. Certain areas saw more extensive remodelling, particularly through Parliamentary enclosure, though even here, elements from the earlier landscape usually survived (eg the village and basic road framework).

Therefore, the 'historic landscape' represents an amalgam of elements of many different periods; even when extensive reorganization occurred, features from earlier periods were often retained. In order to unravel such complex histories, we need to understand the processes of landscape change, and peel off the cultural layers one by one.

We also need to be able to identify what are the distinctive characteristics of landscapes of a particular date. One way in which this can be achieved is by studying places where the processes of creation were relatively unhindered by pre-existing features. Such places include those which have only seen intermittent occupation, areas which in the past have been called 'marginal' (Bailey 1989; Dyer 1990, 42–7; Rippon 1997, 4–8, 263–7 for a critique of this phrase). The main examples are the highest uplands and lowest lowlands, in which land was enclosed and cultivated only at times of high population pressure. During periods of expansion, new landscapes could be laid out just as their designers intended, on a 'blank sheet' largely unaffected by existing settlements, boundaries and patterns of land tenure. This is the ideal situation in which to study the mechanisms of how landscapes were created.

The Gwent Levels

There are *c* 111.2km² of reclaimed estuarine alluvium

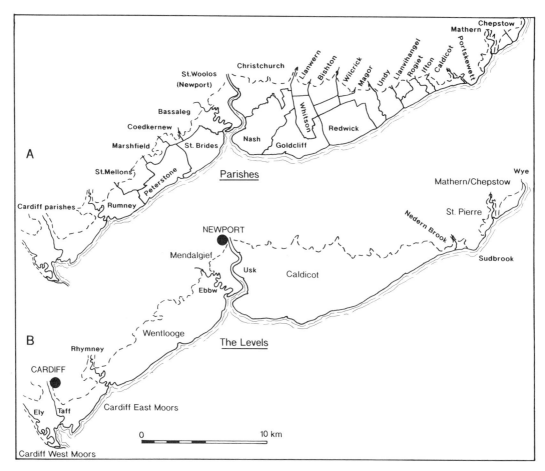

Fig 2.1 The Gwent Levels.
A: parishes wholly on or partly extending onto the levels. B: topographical divisions and major rivers.

between the Rivers Ely and Wye in south-east Wales, collectively known as the Gwent Levels (Fig 2.1). Together they form a coastal plain up to 6km wide fringing the northern side of the Severn Estuary. The two largest Levels are Wentlooge, between the Rivers Rhymney and Ebbw, and Caldicot between the River Usk and the bedrock promontory at Sudbrook. Smaller areas of alluvium are: Cardiff West, Leckwith and Penarth Moors between the Ely and Taff; Cardiff East and Pengam Moors between the Taff and Rhymney; the Level of Mendalgief between the Ebbw and Usk; and St Pierre and Mathern Levels between Sudbrook and the River Wye.

Like all the reclaimed wetland landscapes around the Severn Estuary, the Gwent Levels have been totally handcrafted by man (Rippon 1993; 1994; 1995; 1996a; 1997). They were created through the enclosing and draining of intertidal saltmarshes and are still dominated by the need to manage water. At just *c* 6m OD, all the Levels would be frequently inundated by the tide if it were not for the sea walls, and, without a network of drainage ditches, they would be flooded by freshwater run-off from the adjacent uplands. The process of reclamation, which started during the Roman period *c* 1700 years ago, represents a deliberate decision by man to alter his environment. It

marks a change from the previous 6000 years when he simply exploited a natural environment.

The Levels can be thought of in terms of alternating layers of intertidal and freshwater wetland landscapes formed during the post-glacial rise in sea level (Rippon 1996a, 14–24). During the last 'Devensian' ice age, what is now the Severn Estuary was a relatively dry flood plain and the herds of wild animals that it attracted were hunted by Palaeolithic man (Green 1989). This landscape was inundated during the Mesolithic by the rising sea levels, which deposited a thick layer of alluvium in the context of an intertidal saltmarsh. During the Neolithic and Bronze Age this phase of marine transgression came to an end and freshwater vegetation colonized the former saltmarsh. The peat that subsequently formed contains abundant, well preserved wooden structures which relate to the exploitation of this more terrestrial environment. There were occasional episodes of marine flooding, but the peat bog largely survived until the start of the Iron Age when there was a return to saltmarsh conditions (eg Bell 1993).

The Romano-British period saw extensive reclamation, when the marine influence was removed through the construction of sea walls; the earliest parts of the present 'historic landscape' date to this period (Allen & Fulford 1986; Fulford *et al* 1994; Rippon 1996a, 25–38). During the post-Roman period these walls partially broke down leading to further flooding, before a recolonization during the medieval period; the rest of the 'historic landscape' dates to this period with subsequent post-medieval modifications.

The Gwent Levels Historic Landscape Study

This paper reports on some of the research carried out for the *Gwent Levels Historic Landscape Study*, funded by Cadw and the Countryside Council for Wales (CCW), and undertaken by the author at the Department of Archaeology, University of Reading. Cadw and CCW had already been collaborating in the compilation of a *Register of Landscapes, Parks and Gardens of Special Historic Interest in Wales*, under the direction of Richard Kelly. That study identified the Gwent Levels as of exceptional importance; yet the area is under enormous pressure from a wide range of developments; around 40% of the formerly reclaimed coastal wetland between Cardiff and Chepstow has already been destroyed.

The Levels are important for a number of reasons: as a landform (the largest reclaimed wetland in Wales); in terms of their ecology (they are designated as a Site of Special Scientific Interest); and for their exceptionally well preserved archaeological remains. Recent finds include Bronze Age (Nayling 1993) and Roman boat fragments (Nayling *et al* 1993) and a series of rectangular Iron Age buildings, some complete with their floors (Bell 1993). Finally, the Gwent Levels are one of the few British wetlands that retains its traditional drainage system and field-boundary pattern.

The *Gwent Levels Historic Landscape Study* aimed to increase awareness of the area's importance as a historic landscape. Key organizations in this respect are the local authorities, which prepare development plans and grant or withhold planning permission, and those that advise them, such as Cadw, CCW and the Glamorgan Gwent Archaeological Trust. Another important group of organizations are those which manage the landscape including the Environment Agency and the Internal Drainage Board.

A multi-disciplinary methodology was used to examine the history of this landscape integrating palaeoenvironmental, archaeological, documentary, cartographic, place-name and field-name evidence. This has resulted in a detailed understanding of how the present landscape has come into being, and will be fully published elsewhere (Rippon 1996a; 1996b). This paper will focus upon certain aspects of the methodology and some of the results that relate to medieval settlement in Wales.

The Dissection of a Historic Landscape

One of the aims of this research was to establish the sequence in which the reclamation of different areas had taken place. Along with simple morphological and metrical analysis, the landscape was subjected to a 'retrogressive' study, a methodology described in detail elsewhere (Rippon 1991; Williamson 1987). Work on the analysis of field-boundary patterns

can be traced back to pioneering studies in Essex and East Anglia during the 1970s and 1980s (Drury 1978; Rippon 1991; Rodwell 1978; Williamson 1987). This was largely restricted to planned layouts, dating from the pre-Roman through to the late Saxon periods. Such regular landscapes are present on the Gwent Levels, where they date to the Roman and medieval periods, but large areas have a highly irregular pattern showing little sign of any planning. However, the same basic methodology for their study can be applied.

The approach developed involves firstly taking a detailed map of an area and gradually removing elements of a known age. The examination of air photographs and historic cartographic sources can also add ancient features that have been lost from the landscape in recent times. Secondly, a relative sequence then has to be established for what remains, using techniques and knowledge assimilated during the first stage. For example, when a railway is built, it slices through the landscape, sometimes cutting fields in half; a rectangular field can become two triangular fields if the railway cuts across the field's diagonal. Thus, the railway can be identified as stratigraphically later than the fields. Any field boundaries that post-date the railway will be aligned perpendicular to it, so as not to create further inconvenient and inefficient triangular fields. This is observed by examining a sequence of maps of the same area pre- and post-dating the construction of the railway. Therefore, during a retrogressive analysis, the railway is removed, along with any later field boundaries that were aligned upon it.

It might be asked whether this process is really necessary; why not simply go straight to the earliest available cartographic source we have pre-dating the railway? The answer is simple: by gradually working back through a series of maps of the same area, peeling off the layers one by one, a detailed insight can be gained as to how landscapes change over time, and why. For example, one will see that, while there are constant minor changes in the fields, the overall pattern, and particularly major elements such as roads, are remarkably stable. Thus, when a farmer decides to divide a rectangular field, he does not draw a line across its diagonal; triangular fields with awkward corners do not make for efficient farming. Instead, the new boundary will be perpendicular to or parallel with the others thereby maintaining the overall rectilinear pattern.

Therefore, when one looks at the field-boundary pattern on the Gwent Levels and sees a series of *triangular* fields behind the sea wall, a clear anomaly can be identified that needs to be explained. In this case, the original sea wall was set back in the late medieval period, resulting in it cutting across the grain of the landscape, in the same way as a modern railway or motorway does (Fig 2.2, I–III).

Therefore, by careful examination of a sequence of maps, a greater understanding can be achieved of how and why landscapes change in the way that they do. This understanding is then increased by integrating documentary and archaeological data. Finally, the empirical observations lead to a series of models as to how a landscape might have evolved (eg Figs 2.2, 2.7). These principles can then be applied to the earliest pattern of field-boundaries that exists (eg Figs 2.4–2.6).

One of the major techniques used in this study was the analysis of form. Patterns of field-boundaries, roads and settlements were found to be of great significance, particularly when used in conjunction with a wide range of other sources. To a certain extent, this involves developing a typology of the use and delimitation of space. Austin (1985, 203) has identified three main problems with such morphological analysis: firstly, that it is easy to reconstruct simple patterns from the complex, but almost impossible to reconstruct complex ones; secondly, that the processes of change themselves are seldom explored methodologically and critically; and thirdly, that dating is difficult to achieve, since it cannot be implied simply from morphology and typology. All of these issues are addressed elsewhere (Rippon 1996a; 1997); suffice it to say that complex patterns can indeed be reconstructed, understood and dated, if a sufficient range of data and methods are applied. The examples in this paper should illustrate this.

The attributing of absolute dates to particular landscape features is difficult. Documentary sources are of some use, though, perhaps surprisingly, major transformations are often undocumented; once again a multi-disciplinary approach is required. For example, in the late medieval period, the whole sea wall along the Gwent coast appears to have been set back but there is no documentary evidence for this. However, in 1590/1, a further retreat along one short stretch of wall south of Newton Farm on Wentlooge is recorded (Fig 2.3):

> 'There is a wall between the sea and the lordship, for the defence of the same, which wall being about two years in great decay, why by commission new made and placed more into the land that before it was, by reason where of there was cut out and left between the sea and sea-wall 28 acres most part meadow and pasture' (Lewis & Davies 1952, 455–6).

This gives a *terminus ante quem* for the first retreat of 1590/1 (Allen 1988). In the present intertidal zone there is a double row of stakes, which originally appears to have been filled with stone rubble; a radiocarbon date suggests a late fifteenth-century date (410±40 uncal BP; SRR 2699: Allen & Fulford 1986, 107–8). This structure may be a revetment along a small creek, in which case it must originally have been in an intertidal context; thus, the sea wall must have retreated to its present location by that date.

Several fragments of archaeological and documentary evidence give *termini post quem*. An intertidal spread of pottery at Rumney Great Wharf, probably derived from an eroded settlement, contains no material later than the fourteenth century (John Allen, pers comm 1994). This suggests that the settlement was abandoned then, so that the sea wall retreat occurred at some time after that date. In 1415, there is reference to a piece of land in St Brides parish with Key Gowte and a road called 'Muddlewalle' on the east, and 'Herbardis' Warth [saltmarsh] *outside the sea wall* to the south (italics added; NLW Tred 67/25). If the setting back of the sea wall had occurred shortly before 1415, the reference might be expected to have run 'outside the new sea wall'. Therefore, it appears that the sea wall retreated after 1415 and before the late fifteenth century. The final stage on the development of this sea defence came in 1970, when the original late medieval line was re-established.

Landscape Creation in a Coastal Wetland

The Gwent Levels never appear to have been protected by a natural coastal barrier, such as a belt of sand dunes. Thus, if flooding is to be prevented, artificial mechanisms have to be developed. Once the decision had been taken to drain the marsh, a sea wall was constructed along the coastline and major tidal rivers (Fig 2.2, 2). A rudimentary system of drainage then had to be established to enable minor upland streams and rivers to discharge their waters without flooding the area now protected from tidal inundation by the sea walls. This was achieved through the canalization and embanking of watercourses and former tidal creeks.

Settlements were then established on the now protected higher coastal areas (Fig 2.2, 3). In many cases they appear to have lain on the edge of small, roughly oval-shaped areas of *c* 20–40 acres termed 'infields'. They were carved out of an open landscape and so adopted the most economical shape, an oval. Such features are found throughout the Gwent Levels and elsewhere around the Severn Estuary (eg Rippon 1994, fig 4; 1997, 172–3). These and other early settlement foci were linked by trackways, which also allowed the driving of livestock from the permanently occupied higher lands by the coast, to seasonal pastures in the back-fen and on the remaining intertidal saltmarshes.

Land around the infields was subsequently enclosed and drained by ditches in a piecemeal fashion. In the earliest enclosed areas, small, irregularly shaped parcels of land were enclosed, often lobe shaped in plan (Fig 2.2, 4). An overall framework for this gradually emerging landscape was provided by the infields, the rudimentary drainage system, the pattern of trackways, and also the former tidal creeks which became fossilized in the field-boundary pattern. As the open moor was eaten away, the droveways were left at the centre of long sinuous strips of land. These linear, often funnel shaped, street commons are a distinctive part of landscapes on the higher coastal areas. This complex type of landscape is termed 'irregular'.

In contrast, the lower lying back-fen was left as an open moor used for common grazing. Freshwater run-off from the uplands would flood this area, and threaten the enclosed fields towards the coast. To combat this, banks were constructed along the landward/northern edge of the enclosed land; these earthen 'fen-banks', known locally as 'walls', can still be traced as sinuous field-boundaries roughly parallel to the coast. At some stage a very rudimentary system of enclosure and drainage was developed on the back-fen involving a handful of major banks and ditches known as 'reens' (Figs 2.2, 5–6).

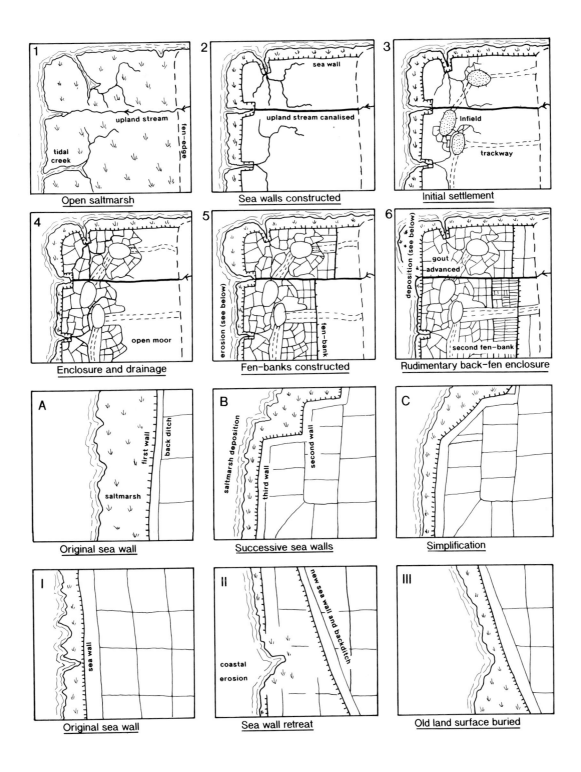

Fig 2.2 Modelling the creation of a wetland landscape.

1–6: the sequence of sea wall construction, initial colonization and expansion from the higher coastal lands into the lower lying backfens.
A–C: the advance of a sea wall through further saltmarsh reclamation. This process can be seen using recent, mapped, examples.
I–III: the retreat of a sea wall due to coastal erosion. Note how the new wall cuts across the grain of the landscape, creating triangular fields.

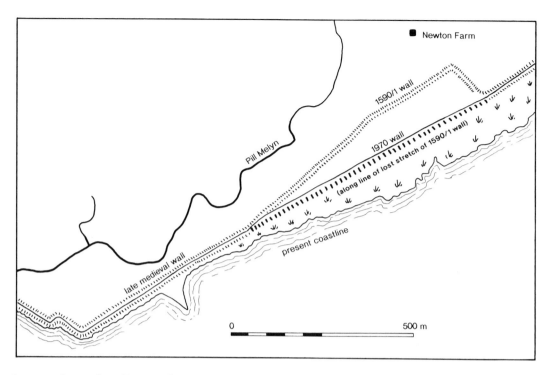

Fig 2.3 Sequence of sea walls at Rumney Great Wharf, south of Newton Farm, Rumney, Wentlooge. The sea wall was set back in the late medieval period. Part of this was then lost when a short stretch was moved back again in 1590/1. However, the late medieval line was re-established in 1970 when that short stretch of wall was moved forward (based on Allen 1988).

Over time, as population increased, more land was required, and parts of the open moor adjacent to the old lands were drained. As the enclosures moved into the ever lower-lying back-fen areas, sequences of fen-banks were constructed. Eventually, the surviving areas of unenclosed moor were in the minority and came to be a valued resource. These common pastures survived as late as the nineteenth century, when many of the street commons and small parcels of roadside waste were also enclosed. These areas tend to have planned or 'regular' landscapes. This was the last major period of 'historic landscape' creation; since then, the story has been one of loss and destruction.

Along the coast, saltmarshes in front of the sea wall were either eroded away, or grew through gradual accretion. If the latter process was dominant, then eventually the sea wall might be moved forward, so enclosing more land (Fig 2.2, A–B). However, if the saltmarsh was completely eroded away, the base of the sea wall would be undermined. In these cases, if wooden revetments could not halt the erosion, the sea wall would have to be moved back to a new location cutting across the line of earlier fields and leaving some previously reclaimed lands in the intertidal zone (Fig 2.2, I–III). If a phase of erosion was subsequently replaced by one of deposition, the old ground surface would then be buried under a saltmarsh.

It looks as if the whole of Wentlooge and at least part of the Caldicot Levels were enclosed by sea walls and drained during the Roman period. In terms of the subsequent *c* 1700 years, the Levels can be divided into two very broad

landscape types: firstly, those areas showing continuity between the Roman period and the present day; and secondly, landscapes of discontinuity, which saw flooding in the post-Roman period and the burial of the Roman landscape under alluvium. This meant that recolonization was necessary in the medieval period.

This represents the process of reclamation, but does not explain why it happened. Some of the critical factors can be summarized. Though the intertidal wetlands were rich in natural resources, their value was greatly increased through drainage since the fertile soils produced rich pasture and high arable yields. In times of rising population, reclamation on the Levels provided a source of much needed new land, and in the medieval period the Levels supported a mixed economy. Though arable yields were high, success depended upon a huge input of labour to maintain the drainage system, and the risk of destruction was very high. Pastoralism was, however, a more conservative choice. In the late medieval period a gradually rising sea level, increased storminess and high rainfall made arable farming on the Levels increasingly difficult. Thus, as national trends in population declined and led to a decreased demand for grain and increased demand for meat and dairy produce, aided by the growth of local and regional markets, there was a shift to what the Levels were more suited to, pastoralism. This range of inter-related factors led to the development of specialized meat and dairy production. Later changes in the national economy also had an impact upon the Levels, notably affecting the amount of arable. Peaks in cultivation during the Napoleonic and Second World Wars were due to increased demand and a need for self-sufficiency in food production.

A Case-Study: the Wentlooge Level (Figs 2.4–2.6)

During the late Iron Age, all the Gwent Levels, including Wentlooge, were intertidal saltmarshes, crossed by tidal creeks such as that recorded at Rumney Great Wharf (Fulford *et al* 1994); this was the penultimate marine transgressive phase (Fig 2.5, 1). The major rivers must always have flowed across the Levels, in the same broad 'corridor' as today, since they drain extensive areas of upland. However, their exact lines have changed through meandering, so in Figures 2.5–2.6 they are shown schematically.

During the Roman period (Fig 2.5, 2) a sea wall was constructed (since lost to erosion) and the higher coastal areas at least were enclosed and drained to create a remarkable planned landscape. This can be termed the penultimate marine regressive phase; it is unclear the extent to which there actually was a fall in relative sea level at this time, though terrestrial as opposed to marine influences certainly dominated after reclamation due to man's intervention in the landscape.

In the late Roman/post-Roman period the Roman landscape was flooded to the north east and south west

which led to the deposition of alluvium and the re-establishment of tidal creeks preserved today as earthworks, vegetation marks and fossilized in the later field-boundary pattern (Fig 2.5, 3). This was the last transgressive phase, though another was narrowly avoided during the late medieval/early post-medieval period when there was increased coastal erosion and flooding leading to the sea wall having to be moved back (see above).

During the medieval period, communities were attracted back to the Levels (Fig 2.6, 4). The Roman sea walls and river floodbanks were either repaired or new ones constructed, as the areas that had been smothered in alluvium were re-enclosed and drained. Thus, two quite distinct processes were at work: in the area previously flooded, there was recolonization of a largely open and 'blank' landscape. In the central area, where the flooding was limited and the Roman pattern of fields survived, a process of rehabilitation took place, restoring the drainage system to good working order. The major rivers started to assume their present locations and were flanked by sea walls.

The reoccupation of the previously flooded areas led to the creation of an 'irregular' landscape, probably in the late eleventh or early twelfth century. One settlement focus appears to have been an 'infield' to the south of St Brides' church; the church itself may lie in a second, smaller enclosure (Fig 2.6, 4). To the east of the 'infield' the field-

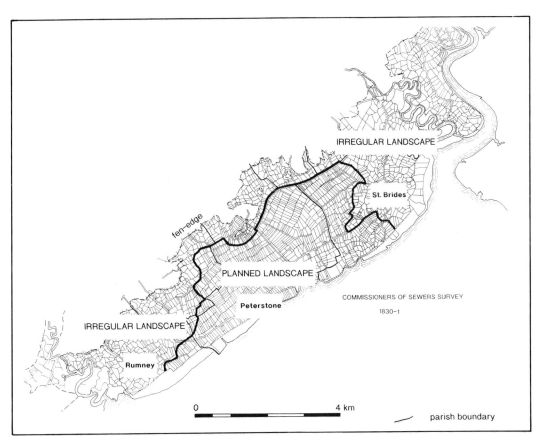

Fig 2.4 Broad landscape divisions on the Wentlooge Level, distinguishing areas with an 'irregular landscape' of small irregularly shaped fields and sinuous roads with an abundance of roadside waste (around Rumney and St Brides), and regular 'planned' landscapes showing evidence of planning, with rectilinear patterns of fields and long, straight narrow roads (around Peterstone).

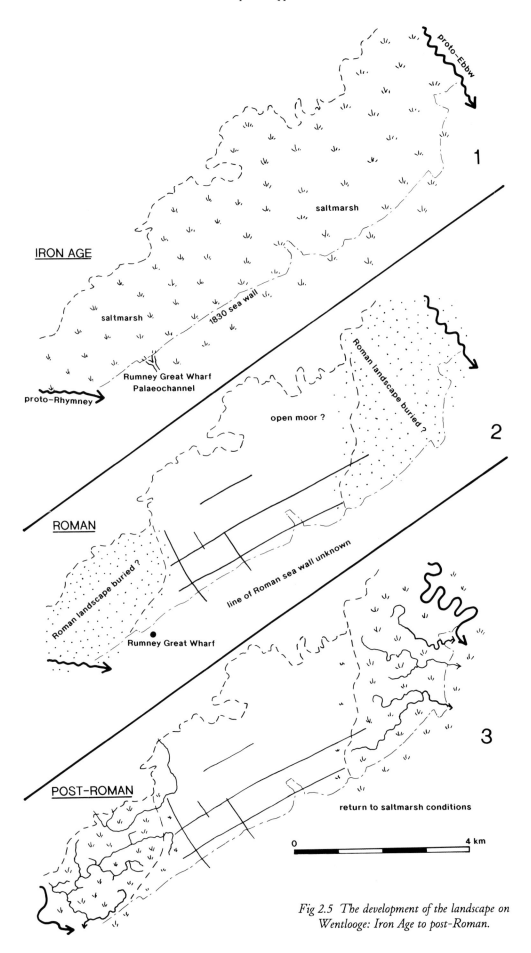

Fig 2.5 The development of the landscape on Wentlooge: Iron Age to post-Roman.

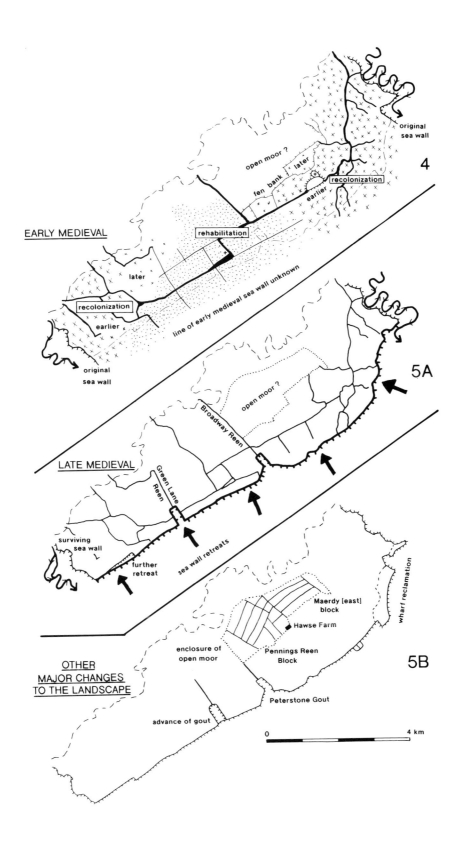

Fig 2.6 The development of the landscape on Wentlooge: medieval and later.

boundary pattern consists of small, irregularly shaped fields partly derived from former saltmarsh creeks which were pre-existing features in the landscape. There were also occasional blocks of more regular fields.

To the west of the St Brides' 'infield' there is a very different landscape, comprising numerous small blocks of rectilinear fields. There is an overall regularity provided by a number of relatively straight south-west/north-east oriented alignments of roads and fields; in several cases these appear to line up with elements of the Roman landscape in the neighbouring parish of Peterstone. Therefore, though individual Roman fields did not survive in this area, the major drains and roads did, to give a basic framework to the medieval recolonization. To the north and west of St Brides' church there are a number of fen-banks which enclosed these reclaimed lands representing a sequence of intakes from the open moor as the population and pressure for land increased.

During the late medieval period, the sea wall was moved back in response to coastal erosion (see above; Figs 2.3, 2.6, 5A). In the post-medieval period, there were further modifications to the landscape (Fig 2.6, 5B). The last areas to be drained and enclosed lay to the north of Hawse Farm. The area was divided into a number of blocks of carefully laid out fields. The two main planned units each had three south-west/north-east oriented boundaries, *c* 80m, *c* 95m, and *c* 80m apart. Though superficially similar to the Roman fields of Peterstone, these were much shorter and the longitudinal boundaries are noticeably curving. There were also other changes to the landscape in the post-medieval period: saltmarsh reclamation took place off St Brides and the formerly recessed gout at Green Lane Reen was moved forward, a common trend throughout the Severn Estuary in the post-medieval period (Allen & Rippon 1994; 1995).

The Context for Recolonization: the Marcher Lordships

The north-eastern part of Gwent was conquered by the English during the Late Saxon period, possibly with a *burh* being established at Monmouth (Courtney 1994, 111). There is also some evidence for late Saxon penetration in south-east Gwent. Llandaff charters dated to the tenth and eleventh centuries mention some 50 English names in south-east Wales as a whole (Davies, W 1979, 145; Williams, A G 1993, 448), including a King Edwin who appears to have had land at Undy (Davies, W 1979, no 249b). In 1063 Harold Godwinson (later King Harold) defeated King Gruffudd ap Llywelyn of Gwynedd and built a hunting lodge at Portskewett (Courtney 1983, 47; Knight 1993, 7; Williams, A G 1993, 449). R R Davies (1987 6, 9) argues that this suggests the annexation of south-east Gwent was imminent, though it is equally possible that the construction of the hunting lodge followed on the conquest of an area (Davies, R R 1987, 26).

The initial Norman advance into south-east Wales took place in the early 1070s led by William FitzOsbern, Earl of

Hereford (Davies, R R 1987, 24–9). Courtney (1986) argues that the initial occupation of Gwent was very partial, and possibly limited to territories previously claimed by Harold. A G Williams (1993, 451) also sees a limited conquest in this early period with Gwent being a 'military subjugated zone intended to support imminent advance further along the Welsh littoral'. The area occupied appears to have been limited to that east of the Usk (Davies, R R 1987, 34).

The advance faltered *c* 1075, though an enclave was established at Cardiff in *c* 1081, as Morgannwg, west of the Usk, became a client kingdom (Davies, R R 1987, 29–43; Lightfoot 1992, 157). The advance resumed in the 1090s with the whole of south-east Wales conquered in the following fifteen years (Davies, R R 1987, 29–43). The newly occupied territory remained in royal hands until the early twelfth century, by which time it was divided into Lordships (Courtney 1983, 59–63). The Lordship of Caerleon was established by Domesday, but was seized by the Welsh *c* 1155 during the anarchy of Stephen's reign. Part of the lordship was recovered by the English in 1217, but the rest was held by Welsh lords until 1270 including the area of demesne at Liswerry (Courtney 1983, 61–3, 177). The original eastern boundary of this demesne may have been the artificial watercourse called Monksditch, whose early outfall lay to the east of Goldcliff Point (Fig 2.9).

The English had occupied Newport by 1107 when, along with Gwynllwg between the Rivers Usk and Rhymney, it became part of the new Lordship of Glamorgan; in 1317 it became a lordship in its own right (Lightfoot 1992, 157; Reeves 1979, 6).

It is difficult to determine the pattern of estates that the Normans inherited. For several reasons, the traditional Welsh system of land organization based on *trefi* and commotes may never have existed or may not have survived much beyond the conquest. Firstly, it is possible that a Roman estate structure survived in south-east Wales until around the eighth century, when it began to fragment (Davies, W 1978, 62–4). Secondly, in the late eleventh or early twelfth century, the new English lords reorganized the landscape creating nucleated villages and a feudal manorial system of tenure; it is not clear if this was carried out within an existing tenurial framework, or whether they imposed a totally new structure.

The English Colonization

South-east Gwent forms part of a broad belt of English settlement in south Wales covering the lowlands of Pembrokeshire, Gower, Glamorgan and Gwent (Courtney 1983; Davies, M 1973, 488–9; 1975, 57–9; Davies, R R 1987, 93–100). The main English immigration was in the late eleventh and early twelfth century. Within the English lordships the general pattern was for the fertile lowland areas to be exploited directly through the establishment of English-style manors; such areas were known as 'Englishries' (Reeves 1979, 8; Sylvester 1969, 116–17). The upland areas took longer to conquer and, when finally subdued, they tended to keep their Welsh customs and be exploited less directly, for example through the payment of food renders instead of rent; they were known as 'Welshries'.

The English subjugation of south-east Wales was firmly based upon feudalism; it was a 'joint stock enterprise by barons and vassals, under the ultimate control of the king' (Davies, R R 1987, 93). Each Englishry was divided into manors or 'knights' fees' (Davies, R R 1987, 94). By the thirteenth century all the coastal zone of southern Gwent was divided into manors. East of the Usk there was generally a fairly simple pattern, often with coterminous townships, manor and parish (eg Ifton, Llanvihangel, Rogiet, Undy), though some parishes contained several manors, occasionally discrete but often with scattered holdings. For example, Caldicot appears to have fragmented into at least four manors: Caldicot, Westend (or Caldicot by Caerwent), Priory (or Eastend) and Dewstow (GwRO D.668/25; Bradney 1929, 110–15; Birbeck 1970, 14).

An even more complex pattern is seen in Wentlooge. For example, the four parishes of Coedkernew, Marshfield, St Brides and Peterstone were divided by 1700 between fourteen small manors, which bore no relationship to the parish structure (GwRO D.43/5397; GwRO D.668/1; Thomas, V 1987, 4, 15). These included St Brides, Sutton, and FitzJohn de la Moor all wholly in St Brides' parish, St Peters in the Moor wholly in Peterstone, while Cogan Pembroke, English Dowlais and Ebboth/Greenfield had land in both. Cogan Fleming had land in St Brides, Peterstone, Marshfield and Bassaleg parishes. This fragmentation, or 'sub-infeudation', was due to the division of knights' fees, each fraction becoming an independent manor; for example, Cogan Fleming was regarded in 1658 as a tenth of a knights' fee (Thomas, V 1987, 16).

The most Anglicized area of the Gwent Levels appears to have been in eastern Caldicot. Whitson was the most westerly knight's fee in the lordship of Caerleon, lying in a complex transitional zone in the feudal/tenurial structure, between an area dominated by Anglo-Norman peasant plantation to the east (with nucleated villages and open fields), and an area to the west in which Welsh traditions survived under a thin veneer of Anglicization and manorialization.

The new Norman overlords seized the pre-existing estates, established English-style manors, and exercized control through a series of castles located at strategic points and in areas of the greatest agricultural potential, including Chepstow, Newport, Rumney and Cardiff. They proceeded to establish nucleated villages and common-fields, both of which were alien to the Welsh. These two elements are closely linked as communal agriculture requires the population to be concentrated in one location allowing the rest of the available land to be laid out systematically as common-fields. This gave the lord much greater control over both human and landed resources.

Unenclosed fields were familiar to the Welsh, as described in twelfth- and thirteenth-century law books and court rolls, but these lacked the communal cropping, rotations and fallowing that characterized English common-fields (Courtney 1983, 45, 277–9). The field-systems established by the English lords appear much closer to those found in England. There is no evidence for communal cropping in any of the common fields on the Levels, though this merely reflects the lack of suitable medieval documentary records (especially manorial court rolls), and the predominant land use of meadow in the better documented post-medieval period. However, field-names do include typically English terminology such as 'acre', 'furlong' and 'land'.

The distribution of known common-fields is concentrated to the east of Monksditch on the Caldicot Level, though there are examples to the west, including the common meadow of Broad Mead in Christchurch, first documented in 1375 (NLW Bad D. 1839). In 1398, Goldcliff was granted 58 acres of arable land and 5½ acres of meadow called 'Durrantesfeld', between 'Gillangespulle' to the south, 'Blanchispulle' to the east, and the Usk to the north and west (ECR 64/5); proximity to the Usk implies that this area was in western Nash. Several field-names might indicate the presence of English-style common-fields on Wentlooge, notably in St Brides. References include 'Gretebrodefelde', 'Lytylb de felde' [Little Field] and 'Revenfurlonge' in 1408 (Courtney 1983, 283), 'churchfield' in 1629 (NLW Tred 54/16), and 'Nawes [Hawse?] filde' in 1669 (Courtney 1983, 283).

The new manors and villages were partly settled by English tenants, though the proportion of English to Welsh is unclear (Davies, R R 1987, 93–100). English place- and field-names could have been imposed by the new Norman lords and their officials, but personal names should reflect the ethnic origins of the population. Using medieval estate documents, it can be seen that the greatest proportion of English personal names was in the extreme south east of Gwent. The further west one moved, the fewer English names are found; Wentlooge had a predominance of Welsh personal names (Courtney 1983, 209, 233; Thomas, V 1987, 5).

A similar trend can be seen in field-names. In most of the Caldicot Levels there were very few Welsh field-names. The number increased significantly as one moves west of Monksditch, particularly in Christchurch parish, though even here English names were predominant (eg in 1585: NLW Powis 12657; and in 1654: NLW Llang A.1060). Welsh was far more common on the Wentlooge Level and was used in the vast majority of field-names (eg in 1625: NLW Tred 56/240).

The Responsibility for Reclamation

Episodes of reclamation on the Gwent Levels are rarely documented and the initial sea wall construction is totally unrecorded. The earliest secure reference to the creation of a drainage system and the division of land into fields is an agreement between Urban, Bishop of Llandaff, and Count Robert of Gloucester in 1126, concerning 100 acres in the marsh between the Rivers Taff and Ely [Cardiff West

Moors] (Boon 1980, 33). The area could have been used for ploughing or pasture and so, even though there is no reference to sea defences, they must have been undertaken for arable cultivation to have been possible.

It is unclear when the recolonization of the Wentlooge and Caldicot Levels began, though in the case of Caldicot at least it must pre-date *c* 1113 when the Lord of Caerleon granted Nash and Goldcliff to the new Priory of Goldcliff (Williams, D H 1970–1, 39; Crouch & Thomas 1985, 155). The gift included chapels at these two places, indicating that this was neither a regularly flooded saltmarsh nor unpopulated wasteland. Thus, by that time, either the Roman sea walls had been repaired, or new ones constructed; as they have since been lost to erosion it is impossible to tell which.

A critical question is who was responsible for this undertaking? In the Roman period, we can be reasonably confident that only the legionary authorities would have been capable of such an enormous task as the drainage of Wentlooge and possibly Caldicot. As described above, it is tempting to see the later resettlement of the Levels in the context of the general process of Anglo-Norman colonization. The new English lords often planted migrant settlers on virgin lands or in areas not hitherto intensively or permanently cultivated (Davies, R R 1987, 98). However,

the Levels were divided between numerous estates. Was there a co-ordinated effort, or did the different estates work separately?

Some communities and/or landowners certainly did have different policies towards reclamation and this is seen most clearly either side of Collister Pill on Caldicot. To the east, in Llanvihangel, there was almost no attempt at reclamation, whereas to the west, in Undy, a sea wall ran from the fen-edge to the sea and hence along the coast; clearly these two communities managed their parts of the Levels entirely separately. Later erosion has caused the loss of the twelfth-century coastal wall, so we do not know whether the whole of Caldicot west of Collister Pill was enclosed by a single sea bank, implying that all the communities and/or landowners with land on this part of the Levels worked together. If individual communities had operated separately, we would expect to see the same situation as already described on the east side of Undy, with sea walls running from the fen-edge down to the sea, along the coast and then back to the fen-edge in which case there would not have been a continuous sea wall along the coast.

Figure 2.7 presents a model for the construction of sea walls on Caldicot and Wentlooge. The Iron Age open saltmarsh was enclosed in the Roman period, though these

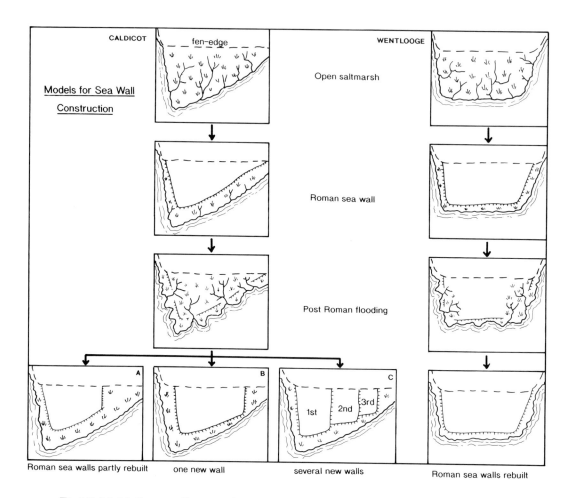

Fig 2.7 Models for sea wall construction, giving the three possible scenarios for the Caldicot Level.

defences later broke down. On Wentlooge the Roman drainage system, and so possibly the sea walls, were restored. However, on Caldicot three possibilities present themselves. The first scenario is that the old Roman sea wall survived and simply needed repairing; this would have required some degree of co-operation between the various estates/communities as there is no point in one community maintaining a strong wall if its neighbour did not.

Secondly, there is the possibility that a single new sea wall was constructed around all the reclaimed lands, either implying that one authority was responsible or that many communities/manors must have co-operated. It has already been stated that Goldcliff Priory was granted with its church and Nash with its chapel in *c* 1113, suggesting that the sea wall must have been in place by then. It therefore seems most plausible that the wall was constructed under the authority of the Lord of Caerleon who granted these lands to Goldcliff, or possibly under the authority of the king who initially held them. It is therefore interesting to note that the eastern boundary of Caerleon Lordship was Collister Pill which also formed the edge of the reclamation.

The third possibility is that these early estates did indeed work separately, and that sea walls originally ran north-south, from fen-edge to the coast, along the estate boundaries. No such walls survive today, though the possibility cannot be ruled out that they once existed; the line of Monksditch provides one possible line (Fig 2.9). Thus, on balance, the second scenario might be favoured, suggesting a major role for the marcher lords in the reclamation of the Gwent Levels.

The Monastic Landlords

The church was a major landowner in medieval Britain and took a leading role in improving its estates through drainage. The Gwent Levels were no exception, though it should be stressed that particularly on Wentlooge, by far the greatest proportion of land on the Levels was owned by secular lords. The two main ecclesiastical holdings were those of Goldcliff Priory, concentrated in Goldcliff and Nash, and

Tintern's granges in Magor and Redwick, all on Caldicot. Llantarnam Abbey also held a grange with significant amounts of meadow at Pwll-Pan (Williams, D H 1990, 30). Keynsham Abbey in Somerset also held lands on the Wentlooge Level (Gray 1990, 186–7), while St Augustine's Abbey in Bristol owned lands in Peterstone (GwRO D.302/0007; NLW Tred 110/121; Sabin 1960).

The Granges of Tintern Abbey (Fig 2.8)

Tintern had two granges on the Levels, and one on the adjacent uplands. Lower or 'Moor' Grange in Magor was a discrete block of land, focused upon a small oval 'infield' type enclosure. Between *c* 1114 and 1150 the monks of Tintern received the land on Magor moor 'divided by ditches' implying at least rudimentary enclosure and drainage (*CChR* III, 88–9; Boon 1980, 34). In 1245 Tintern was given permission by Walter, Earl of Pembroke and Lord of Strigoil (Chepstow), to enclose the land of Moor Grange at Magor by a ditch, and to make consequential arrangements for enclosure and drainage within it (*CChR* III, 88–97; Boon 1980, 34). In 1291 the Moor Grange comprised 50 acres of meadow valued at twice the normal rate for pasture compared with Tintern's holdings (*Taxatio*, 282b). It also contained two carucates of ploughland; the value was half as much again as arable on other granges (Boon 1980, 34; Williams, D H 1984, 225).

'New Grange' was a moated farmstead responsible for managing Tintern's lands in Redwick parish (Williams, D H 1965, 25). These included a tenement close to the church, several parcels in a large open-field called 'Broadmead' and land in 'Burdimesmead' to the north. Land in other parishes included 30 acres in Berland in Magor to the north of Green Moor, 40 acres on Llanwern Moor and 50 acres at Porton in Goldcliff (*CChR* III, 96–100; Williams, D H 1965, 26).

A moated site lies in the north-west corner of Redwick parish by Grangefield Farm. The modern place-name, 'Grangefield', first recorded in 1687 (Bradney 1932, 239) suggests that this is the location of the 'New Grange'

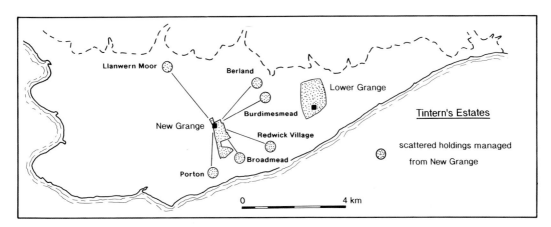

Fig 2.8 The estates of Tintern Abbey on the Caldicot Level.

recorded in 1572 (NLW Bad D.254; Rippon 1996a, 79–81; Williams, D H 1984, 278; 1990, 31). The moat consists of an inner enclosure, *c* 20 × *c* 25m, on a slightly different orientation to the surrounding outer enclosure (*c* 40 × *c* 5m) and adjacent field boundaries. This suggests that the original moat was built in an area of open moor with no pre-existing boundaries to constrain its shape. By the time that the outer moat was dug, the surrounding area had been divided into fields, causing it to be on a different orientation to the inner enclosure. The approximate extent of the land of New Grange can be determined by tracing the ownership of land since the dissolution. The estate included all the land in north-west Redwick beyond the open-field at Broadmead and its northern boundary 'Mere Reen' (GwRO D. 1365/1–2). It seems, therefore, as if Tintern was granted the waste ground beyond the common-fields, that they constructed the grange, and then enclosed the surrounding land.

Goldcliff Priory (Fig 2.9)

Goldcliff Priory was founded in *c* 1113 when Robert de Chandos, Lord of Caerleon, granted land to the Abbey of Bec, near Rouen, in France. The place-name is derived from the bedrock outcrop at Goldcliff Point which was described by Gerald of Wales in 1188 as a 'golden rock' (Bradney 1932, 272). The foundation charter refers to the church of Goldcliff, chapel of Nash (*Fraxino*), and moorland in Nash and Goldcliff (Crouch & Thomas 1985, no 1). These lands were probably carved out of the Lord of Caerleon's large putative demesne estate of Edlogan and Lebenith (see above). Further grants added more land and in 1291 Goldcliff held most of the higher coastal land in

Nash and Goldcliff, along with a large part of the back-fen. Its estates comprised 7 carucates of land, 100 acres of meadow, 3 mills and tanneries in Goldcliff, Nash and Whitson; 13 acres of meadow in Magor; 21 acres of land and 2 mills in Undy; 2 mills in St Brides; and a water-mill at Milton (*Taxatio*, 281; Williams, D H 1984, 205).

However, in the late medieval period the priory fell on bad times. As an alien priory (one attached to a foreign monastery), the outbreak of war in 1295 led to royal interference in its affairs and regular demands for payments to the exchequer (Cowley 1977, 221; Graham 1929; Williams, D H 1970–1). The payments Goldcliff made steadily declined throughout the fourteenth century (*CPR* Edward I, 1292–1301, 175; *CFR* V, 49). In 1324 serious flooding is recorded and as a result payments to the exchequer were reduced; during 1351 there was a further reduction because of pestilence (Graham 1929, 112). In 1424 low-lying land was flooded and storms caused the parish church, situated in the priory nave, to be destroyed, and a new parish church was built inland (*CPR* Henry IV, 1422–1429, 265). Around 1440, the priory's assets were granted to Tewkesbury Abbey, and then in 1450 to Eton College (Graham 1929, 119).

The present village of Goldcliff is located at the head of Goldcliff Pill. It lies in a relatively regular block of tenements with a planned appearance (Fig 2.9, inset). Metrical analysis suggests that a very tentative planning unit of 8 perches (16ft 6in) might have been used.

Whitson (Fig 2.10)

Whitson is the smallest parish on the Levels, occupying just 800 acres on the edge of the low-lying back-fen on

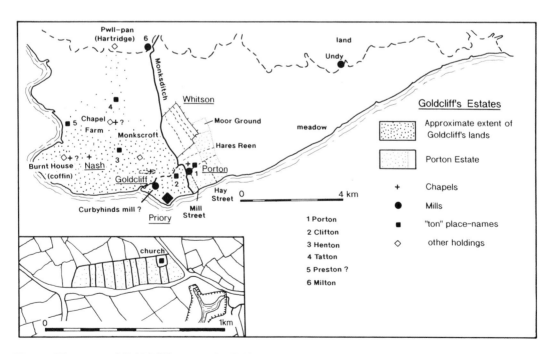

Fig 2.9 The estates of Goldcliff Priory on the Caldicot Level, with the possibly planned village at Goldcliff (inset).

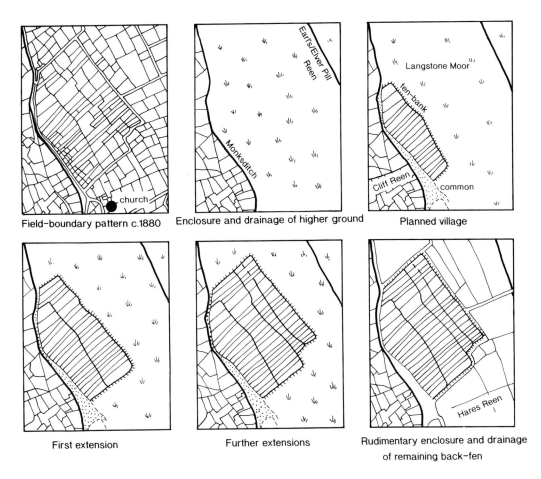

Fig 2.10 The development of Whitson. The higher coastal land west of Monksditch appears to have been reclaimed first. The village was then planned out to the east, and the long narrow tenements and fields were extended several times. Each time the enclosed area was surrounded by a 'fen-bank' to prevent flooding from the east.

Caldicot. Monksditch, on its western edge, lies on the 5.5m contour which marks the approximate edge of the 'irregular' landscape in Goldcliff. Whitson has a highly distinctive morphology but unfortunately it is poorly documented.

Figure 2.10 shows the field-boundary pattern *c* 1880 (based on the first edition 6in Ordnance Survey maps) and suggests a model for how it came about. Morphologically, the landscape is dominated by the planned village consisting of a block of very long, narrow fields running at right angles to a funnel shaped common. Though longitudinally these strips extend for 1km, they are divided laterally by three boundaries; the westernmost at least was formerly a lane.

The sequence appears to be as follows. The earliest area to be enclosed and drained in this part of the Caldicot Level was the higher ground west of Monksditch. The area between Monksditch and Elver Pill Reen, the only other drainage channel existing at this time, was an open moor. The settlement of Whitson was then laid out along the edge of a street common across this relatively featureless landscape. A fen-bank prevented flooding from the back-fen while Cliff Reen took water from the village, under Monksditch, to the coast. The open moor to the north east was known as Langstone Moor. The long narrow

strips of land were subsequently extended several times, with a new enclosing fen-bank each time. By the eighteenth century the remaining areas of open moor were enclosed with larger and more rectangular fields. The common was the last area to be enclosed, in 1870.

The closest parallel for a settlement of Whitson's morphology is in Holland, where it was known as the 'cope' system (Besteman 1986, 338). Settlements of this pattern occurred when a great landowner appropriated the 'regality', or rights of exploitation of wilderness areas, and leased them to colonists for a minimal rent in order to have them reclaimed. A settlement was strung out along a street on the highest ground with long narrow tenement strips laid out at right angles to that street, extending away from the highest ground. This reclaimed area was surrounded by an embankment. Over time the area of drained land needed to expand so the tenement strips were extended, and a new embankment constructed. This pattern is matched at Whitson and other planned settlements in south-west Wales, as for example, at Templeton (Kissock 1992, fig 5; see Kissock p 124–6). Slight changes of orientation in the tenement boundaries, along the line of the lateral lanes, do indeed suggest a phased development.

Some of the planned villages in south-west Wales were the work of Flemings who settled during the twelfth century, as described by Gerald of Wales (Richter 1976, 18–21; see Kissock p 131). Specialist 'village founders' called *locatores*, including a Fleming called Wizo, are known to have founded planned settlements there, including Wiston (Kissock 1992, 39, 42). This was done through the king, who also held the Gwent Lordships at this time. There is, however, little evidence for Flemings on the Gwent Levels, though there is a village called Flemingston *c* 20km west of Cardiff, and a manor called Cogan Fleming of unknown antiquity on Wentlooge. Hassall (1815, 282) describes a local tradition that the Levels were drained by Dutchmen, but this was regarded by him as supposition. Therefore, although there are intriguing Flemish connections in Whitson, no firm conclusion can be reached.

There is little independent evidence as to when the settlement was founded. Moore (1982) identifies Whitson as one of the un-named vills in Domesday, though this is pure supposition (Courtney 1986). The earliest documentary reference to Whitson is actually in 1314 when it is recorded as part of Langstone Manor in the Lordship of Caerleon held by Gilbert de Clare (*CIPM* V, 336; the name Langstone Moor was inherited from this). The possibility that settlement in Langstone Manor could have been replanned into the present village after this date cannot be ruled out, but such an upheaval in the late medieval period is unlikely. Furthermore, there are earlier, more plausible, contexts. By 1291 Goldcliff owned land at Whitson (*Taxatio,* 281; Williams, D H 1970–1, 51), though it is not referred to in the foundation charter. If Monksditch was indeed the boundary of the demesne estate of the Lordship of Caerleon, from which Goldcliff's lands were carved, Whitson must have been a later addition. Goldcliff Priory was part of the Benedictine order, who managed their estates like secular lords, for profit. They rented lands out, and so it would not be impossible for them to have created a planted settlement (Cowley 1977, 62). Since the settlement appears to have been created in an area of open landscape after the higher coastal land was enclosed and drained, a date after the early twelfth century is most likely. Assets of the priory were seized by the Crown in 1295, meaning that, if it was responsible for founding Whitson, it must have been before this date. Thus, if Goldcliff was responsible for creating Whitson, a mid twelfth- to late thirteenth-century date seems likely; this would therefore seem too late to be the work of Flemish settlers.

By 1314, Whitson was once again part of the Lordship of Caerleon, being held off the manor of Langstone. If we postulate its earlier ownership by Goldcliff, then the obvious context for its loss is during the late thirteenth century, when, as an alien priory dependent on a foreign superior, it became increasingly harassed by the English Crown; following France's invasion of Aquitaine, Edward I seized the property of alien priories (Graham 1929, 111). In 1289 Goldcliff was also suffering from deteriorating relations with its patron, Gilbert de Clare, Lord of Caerleon (and Langstone); he even seized the liberties of the priory for a year or so (Williams, D H 1970–1, 42). There is no reference to Goldcliff losing lands in 1289, nor any indication of how de Clare acquired Whitson, but its seizure from the Priory cannot be ruled out. However, it is impossible to say whether de Clare seized an area of land and planted a settlement, or seized the settlement itself.

Overall, therefore, it is frustrating that we cannot come to a firm conclusion about Whitson's origins. Morphologically, there are possibly Dutch parallels, though the most likely contexts would seem to be later, either as the work of Goldcliff Priory or its patron the Lord of Caerleon.

Conclusions

This paper has examined the origins of one small part of the Welsh landscape. It has shown how rigorous analysis of the present 'historic' landscape, integrated with a range of documentary, archaeological and other evidence, can reveal the relative sequence in which a landscape was formed. Landscapes can be thought of as a series of layers, which can be peeled off one by one. Some areas have been created gradually over a long period of time, while others have seen extensive remodelling in one particular period. In both instances, later changes in the landscape, often imposing identifiable culturally and/or chronologically specific features, can be identified and removed, allowing one to move closer to the original pattern.

In order to understand the processes of creation, the physical laying out of drainage systems, roads and fields must be understood. The construction of models is also important, in order to appreciate the range of possibilities for how a particular landscape might have come about. To understand a landscape, the causes of change must also be appreciated, ranging through environmental, demographic, social, political and economic factors. Certain positive factors 'pull' or encourage communities to exploit an environment: fertile soils, rich natural resources, a marine regression. Other factors 'push' communities into that area because of population pressure and a shortage of resources elsewhere. Equally, certain events 'push' people out of an area, such as rising sea levels and increased flooding.

Major institutions have clearly been instrumental in creating the Gwent Levels historic landscape. The legionaries at Caerleon were probably responsible for draining the Levels during the Roman period. The marcher lords, notably of Caerleon, were of great importance in the aftermath of the Norman conquest. In the succeeding centuries monastic landlords managed large areas, particularly of the Caldicot Level. However, we should not ignore the all important role that the ordinary peasant farmer played. It was he who cultivated the land and maintained the drainage system. In areas which lacked strong manorial controls, notably western Caldicot and Wentlooge, the communal actions of peasant farmers must have been instrumental in shaping their environment. However, such are the vagaries of the documentary record, we have little or no record of their achievement, other than the landscape which they created.

Acknowledgements

The research which forms the basis of this paper, the *Gwent Levels Historic Landscape Study*, was funded by Cadw, Welsh Historic Monuments and the Countryside Council for Wales; however, all the views expressed here are those of the author. I would like to acknowledge the help of all those who assisted with the research, and particularly Rick Turner of Cadw on whose initiative it was carried out. Finally, I would like to thank my former colleagues at Reading for all their help, advice and inspiration.

References

Unpublished sources

Eton College Records (ECR), 64/5

Gwent Records Office (GwRO), D.43/5397; D.302/0007; D.668/1–2; D.668/25; D.1356/1–2

National Library of Wales (NLW)
> Badminton Collection (Bad) D.254; D.1839
> Llangattock Collection (Llang) A.1060
> Powis Collection (Powis) 12657
> Tredegar Collection (Tred) 54/16; 56/240; 67/25; 110/121

Published Sources

Allen, J R L, 1988, Reclamation and sea defence in Rumney parish, Monmouthshire, *Archaeol Cambrensis*, 137, 135–40

Allen, J R L, & Fulford, M G, 1986, The Wentlooge Level: a Romano-British saltmarsh reclamation in south east Wales, *Britannia*, 27, 91–117

Allen, J R L, & Rippon, S, 1994, Magor Pill, Gwent: the geoarchaeology of a Late Flandrian tidal palaeochannel, *Archaeology in the Severn Estuary 1994*, 41–50

Allen, J R L, & Rippon, S, 1995, The historical simplification of tidal flood defences: four case histories from the Severn Estuary, south west Britain, *Trans Bristol Gloucester Archaeol Soc*, 113, 73–88

Austin, D, 1985, Doubts about morphogenisis, *J Hist Geog*, 11 (ii), 201–9

Bailey, M, 1989, *A marginal economy? East Anglian Breckland in the later middle ages*, Cambridge

Bell, M, 1993, Field survey and excavation at Goldcliff, Gwent, 1993, *Severn Estuary Archaeology 1993*, 81–101

Besteman, J, 1986, The history of medieval settlement in north Holland and the reclamation of peat areas in archaeological perspectives, in P Murphy & C French (eds), *The exploitation of wetlands*, Brit Archaeol Rep, Brit ser, 186, Oxford, 327–69

Birbeck, T T, 1970, Medieval Caldicot, *Severn and Wye Review*, 1 (i), 11–16

Boon, G C, 1980, Caerleon and the Gwent Levels in early historic times, in F H Thompson (ed), *Archaeology and coastal change*, Soc Antiq Occ Papers, new ser, 1, London, 24–36

Bradney, J, 1929, *History of Monmouthshire: Volume 4 Part 1. The Hundred of Caldicot Part 1*, London (reprinted 1994, Cardiff)

Bradney, J, 1932, *History of Monmouthshire: Volume 4 Part 2. The Hundred of Caldicot Part 2*, London (reprinted 1994, Cardiff)

Bradney, J, 1993, *History of Monmouthshire: Volume 5. The Hundred of Newport* M Gray (ed), Cardiff

CChR, Calendar of Charter Rolls, London, 1903–27

CFR, Calendar of Fine Rolls, London, 1911–

CIPM, Calendar of Inquisitions Post Mortem, London, 1904–

CPR, Calendar of Patent Rolls, London, 1891–

Courtney, P, 1983, *The rural landscape of eastern and lower Gwent*, unpublished PhD thesis, Univ of Wales Cardiff

Courtney, P, 1986, The Norman invasion of Gwent: a reassessment, *J Medieval Hist*, 12, 297–312

Courtney, P, 1994, *Report on the excavations at Usk 1965–1976: medieval and later Usk*, Cardiff

Cowley, F G 1977, *The monastic order in South Wales 1066–1349*, Cardiff

Crouch, D, & Thomas, G, 1985, Three Goldcliff charters, *Nat Lib Wales J*, 24 (ii), 153–63

Davies, M, 1973, Monmouthshire, in M Davies, Field systems of south Wales, in A R H Baker & R A Butlin (eds), *Studies of field systems in the British Isles*, Cambridge, 488–97

Davies, R R, 1987, *Conquest, coexistence and change, Wales 1063–1415*, Cardiff

Davies, W, 1978, *An early Welsh microcosm: studies of the Llandaff Charters*, Cardiff

Davies, W, 1979, *The Llandaff Charters*, Aberystwyth

Drury, P J, 1978, *Excavations at Little Waltham 1970–71*, CBA res rep 26, London

Dyer, C, 1990, The past, present and the future in medieval rural history, *Rural Hist*, 1 (i), 37–50

Fleming, A 1988, *The Dartmoor Reaves: investigating prehistoric land divisions*, London

Fulford, M G, Allen, J R L, & Rippon, S J, 1994, The settlement and drainage of the Wentlooge Level, Gwent: survey and excavation at Rumney Great Wharf, 1992, *Britannia*, 25, 175–211

Graham, R, 1929, Four alien priories in Monmouthshire, *J Brit Archaeol Ass*, 35, 102–21

Gray, M, 1990, The administration of monastic estates in Gwent in the sixteenth century, *Bull Board Celtic Stud*, 47, 177–90

Green, S, 1989, Some recent archaeological and faunal discoveries from the Severn Estuary Levels, *Bul Board Celtic Stud*, 36, 187–99

Hassall, C, 1815, *A general view of the agriculture of the county of Monmouth: with observations on the means of its improvement*, Board of Agriculture, London

Kissock, J, 1992, Planned villages in Wales, *Medieval World*, 6, 39–113

Kissock, J, 1993, Some examples of co-axial field systems in Pembrokeshire, *Bull Board Celtic Stud*, 40, 190–7

Knight, J, 1993, The early church in Gwent, II: the early medieval church, *Monmouthshire Antiq*, 9, 1–17

Lewis, E A, & Davies, J C, 1952, *An inventory of the early Chancery Proceedings concerning Wales*, Board of Celtic Studies History and Law Series 3, Cardiff

Lightfoot, K W B, 1992, Rumney Castle: a ringwork and manorial centre in South Glamorgan, *Medieval Archaeol*, 36, 96–159

Moore, J, (ed), 1982, *The Domesday Book, Gloucestershire*, Chichester

Nayling, N, 1993, Caldicot Castle lake, *Archaeology in the Severn Estuary 1993*, 77–80

Nayling, N, Maynard, D, & McGrail, S, 1993, Barland's Farm, Magor, Gwent: a Romano-British boat find, *Antiquity*, 68, 596–603

Reeves, A C, 1979, *Newport Lordship 1317–1536,* Newport

Richter, M, 1976, *Giraldus Cambrensis: the growth of the Welsh Nation,* Aberystwyth

Rippon, S, 1991, Early planned landscapes in south east Essex, *Essex Archaeol Hist,* 46–60

Rippon, S, 1993, *Wetland reclamation and landscape evolution around the Severn Estuary,* unpublished PhD thesis, Univ Reading

Rippon, S, 1994, Medieval wetland reclamation in Somerset, in M Aston & C Lewis (eds), *The medieval landscape of Wessex,* Oxford, 239–53

Rippon, S, 1995, Human/Environment relations in the Gwent Levels: archaeology and ecology in a coastal wetland, in M Cox, V Straker & D Taylor (eds) *Wetlands: archaeology and nature conservation,* Norwich

Rippon, S, 1996a, *The Gwent Levels: evolution of a wetland landscape,* CBA res rep 105, York

Rippon, S, 1996b, *The Gwent Levels historic landscape study: characterisation and assessment of the landscape,* Report prepared for Cadw/CCW, Cardiff

Rippon, S, 1997, *The Severn Estuary: landscape evolution and wetland reclamation,* Leicester

Rodwell, W, 1978, Relict landscapes in Essex, in H C Bowen & P J Fowler (eds), *Early land allotment in the British Isles: a survey of recent work,* Brit Archaeol Rep, Brit ser, 48, 89–98

Sabin, A, 1960, *Some manorial accounts of St. Augustine's Abbey, Bristol,* Bristol Records Society 22

Sylvester, D, 1969, *The rural landscape of the Welsh borderland,* London

Taxatio, Taxatio ecclesiastica Angliae et Walliae, auctoritate Pope Nicholai IV., circa A.D. 1291, Record Commission, London, 1802

Thomas, V, 1987, *Communities of the Wentlooge Levels, Monmouthshire 1650–1800,* unpublished MA dissertation, Univ Wales Cardiff

Williams, A G, 1993, Norman lordship in south east Wales during the reign of William I, *Welsh Hist Rev,* 19 (iv), 445–66

Williams, D H, 1965, Tintern Abbey: its economic history, Monouthshire Antiq, 2 (i), 1–32

Williams, D H, 1984, *The Welsh Cistercians,* Tenby

Williams, D H, 1990, *Atlas of Cistercian lands in Wales,* Cardiff

Williams, M, 1975, *The making of the South Wales landscape,* London

Williamson, T, 1987, Early coaxial field systems on the East Anglian boulder clay, *Proc Prehist Soc,* 53, 419–31

Landscapes of Gwent and the Marches as seen through Charters of the Seventh to Eleventh Centuries

Christopher Hurley

This study explores aspects of the relationship between estates dated to before the middle of the eleventh century, claimed by the bishops of Worcester and Llandaff, and the landscape in which they are found. In particular, the study focuses on the distribution of these estates and their relative agricultural value. By studying the estates of two distinct regions which are close to each other, one Celtic, the other Anglo-Saxon, areas which are quite different in terms of physical geography, it is possible to compare and contrast the way in which the estates of the two regions relate to the physical surroundings in which they occur. Ultimately it may be possible to gain a greater understanding, not only of the patterns of land ownership in this area of south-west Britain, but also of the way in which land organization elsewhere can be affected by both physical and non-physical factors.

The overall intention of my research is to arrive at a fuller understanding of the nature of the location, organization and management of estates referred to in charters purportedly datable to before the middle of the eleventh century, belonging to the charter collections of the bishops of Llandaff and Worcester, as preserved in the Liber Landavensis (Evans 1979)[1] and the manuscript BL Cotton Tiberius A xiii, sometimes referred to as 'Heming's Cartulary'. In order to achieve this, two approaches which have hitherto been somewhat overlooked have been focused upon. The first is an attempt to consider the whole area of the piece of land referred to in the charter text. It is necessary, if we are to reach a fuller understanding of the estates of the early medieval church, to look at the whole unit and not just the various landscape features that are referred to within the various forms of boundary clauses which occur at the edges of such estates. This is especially important in the case of the Llandaff charter material since the boundary features defining estates in this collection refer to noticeably fewer agricultural indicators than do examples in English collections. As Oliver Rackham, overstating the case perhaps, remarks, 'In South Wales there are charters . . . but I shall use these less because they are short and deal in features such as streams and mountains.' (1986, 10).

The second aspect of this study is to take and compare the charter collections of two distinct centres and consequently regions. Without some means of comparison it would be difficult to interpret the significance of whatever results were forthcoming. It is fortunate that two of the three most complete charter collections in Britain (the

third is at Christchurch, Canterbury) belong to centres almost adjacent to each other, Llandaff and Worcester, separated only by the territory of the bishops of Hereford, the early charters of which are lost. This situation presents us with an area some 90km east/west and 70km north/south, within which the estates of two distinct charter collections can be analysed, compared and contrasted (Fig 3.1).

It is important to state at the outset that this study is primarily geographical and environmental. In using the charter material I have not concerned myself in any great depth with issues of authenticity and the reliability of using charter texts as indicators of actual situations described at the dates given or inferred from within the charter texts themselves. In this matter I have followed the views expressed by other scholars, notably Wendy Davies (1978; 1979) and H P R Finberg (1961).

Methodology

In order to discover the range of sources available and which of these would be most valuable to a survey of this kind, it was decided to begin with a pilot study. This would take a small number of sites and consider all of the available information for each, before making any judgements regarding which sources were most valuable and should be applied to a greater number of sites. Estates for the pilot study were chosen using the following criteria. First, the charter texts in which they are referred to must be regarded as authentic by Davies and Finberg. Secondly, it should be

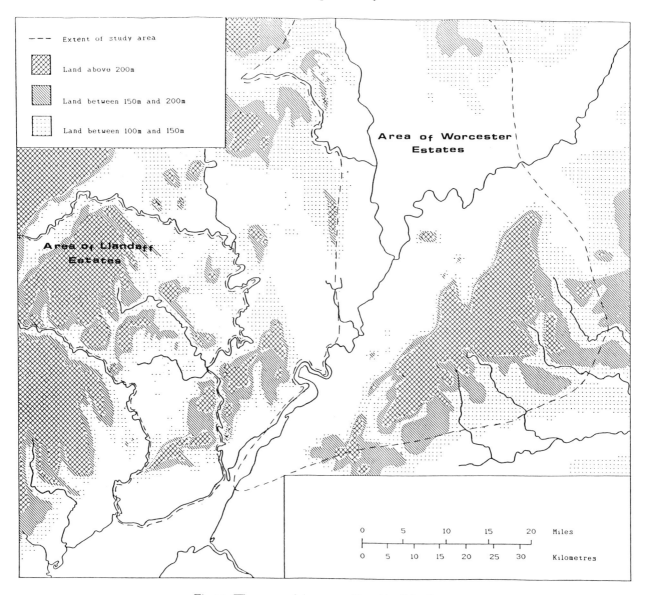

Fig 3.1 The extent of the survey either side of the Severn.

possible to map the bounds of the estates with a particularly high degree of accuracy. Thirdly, in the applicable area the estates should occur in conjunction with a church surrounded by an enclosed churchyard, as presented in Diane Brook's list of such churches (1992, 88-9); but in the area to the east of Brook's research the estate should be referred to in what was clearly a foundation charter or else refer to a church with Anglo-Saxon architecture remaining (though, the latter did not occur).

Having applied the above criteria nine estates were found to meet the desired qualifications. However, at this stage of the research the exact limits of the survey had not been established and as a result two of the nine estates lie to the west of the study region as shown in Fig 3.1: these were Ewenny (LL176a) and St Brides-Super-Ely (LL263), both in Glamorgan. Only one estate belonging to the Worcester collection was included in the pilot study: Daylesford (BL Cotton Tib A xiii, fos 31–2, 99–100) in Gloucestershire.

The remaining estates were Ballingham (LL164, 171b) and Llanwarne (LL174, 200) in Herefordshire; Itton (LL171b), Llanbedr (LL261) and Wonastow (LL201) in Monmouthshire and Tidenham (LL174b, 229b) in Gloucestershire.

A series of maps was then created for each of the nine estates, using all the available evidence relating to aspects of the land and its exploitation. Each of these aspects is briefly outlined below presenting those maps created for the estate at Ballingham (Fig 3.2) as an example. The bounds of the estate are as follows:

> 'From above the Selinam ford, crossing as far as the great river [until] next to the stream *circhan*. The whole angle has been given to God . . .' (LL164).

The ford is indicated on Fig 3.2 and the dashed line gives the approximate route from it to the Wye, 'the great river'. The dashed line is present on all the maps to illustrate the

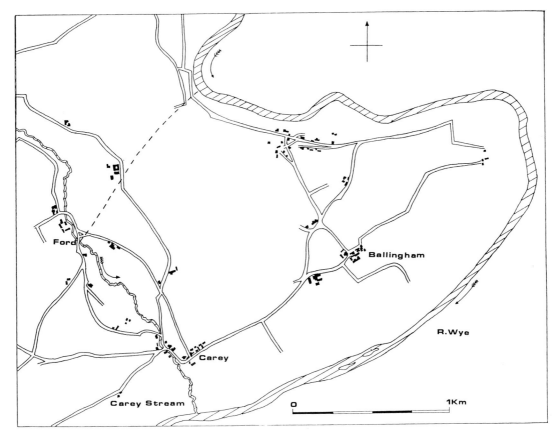

Fig 3.2 The area around Ballingham, Herefordshire. The bounds of the estate are the River Wye and the Carey Stream, with the dashed line indicating the remaining limits.

extent of the estate, which is also bounded by the Carey Stream south of the ford to the Wye.

Topography

Contour lines were added to the base maps, with 10m intervals being chosen as the most convenient to record. This immediately gives a third dimension to the estate and begins to define distinguishable zones within the area (Fig 3.3). We can see the area consists mostly of gentle, south facing slopes with a narrow strip in the north made up of a very steep, north facing slope. In the west a valley containing the Carey stream opens out to the south at the stream's confluence with the Wye. Two prominent but gently rising hills can be distinguished either side of this valley to the west and north of Carey village.

Geology

Maps illustrating the underlying rocks were created for those areas with any discernible geological variation. Ballingham, however, lying wholly within the great expanse of the Devonian Old Red Sandstone outcrop in this region, did not require such a map.

Soil coverage

Soil associations were mapped (Fig 3.4) following the series of maps published by the Soil Survey for England and Wales (1983). This exercise was undertaken in conjunction with reference to descriptions of the various soil groups which are published in a series of regional surveys accompanying the maps. Soil 571b, for example, is identified as the Bromyard association, a loamy/silty argillic brown earth, moderately good for mixed farming, though tending to be droughty on shallower soils and with a slight acidity towards the surface; 541c indicates the Eardiston 1 association, a collection of reddish, well drained, coarse loamy and fine silty soils better suited to arable as it can suffer drought under grass; 561b is the Teme association, a deep and permeable alluvial brown soil associated with river flood plains which, due to high degrees of flooding, is dominated by permanent grass.

Modern land classification

The Ministry of Agriculture, Fisheries and Food (MAFF) produce two key maps relating to the modern landscape. The first is a land quality classification map (1968). This classification consists of a five point scale with grade 1 being the best agricultural land and grade 5 the worst. For example, land of grade 1 quality will have no or only very minor physical limitations to agricultural use. The soils

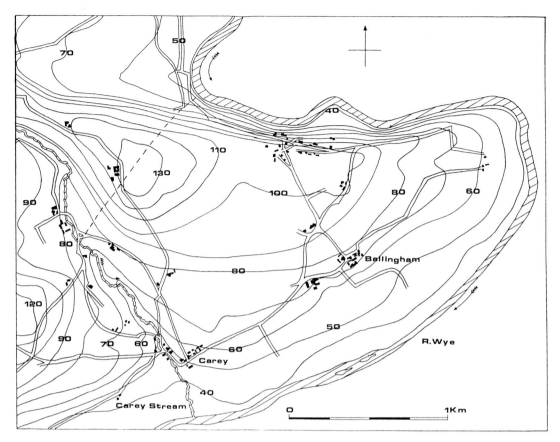

Fig 3.3 Topography of the Ballingham area.

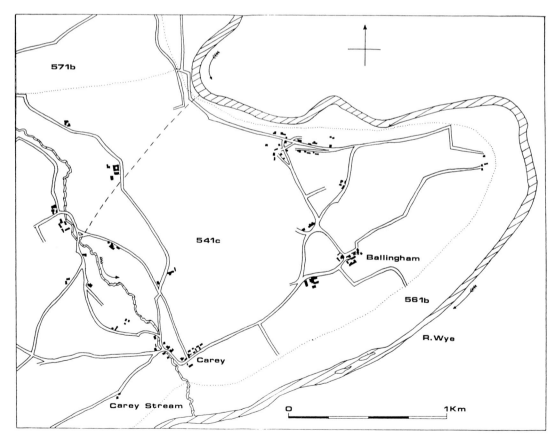

Fig 3.4 The soils of the Ballingham area.

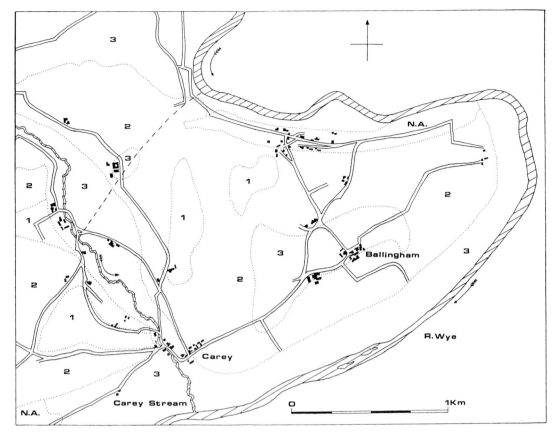

Fig 3.5 Land classification of Ballingham in the modern era (after MAFF, grade 1 = best, 5 = poorest).

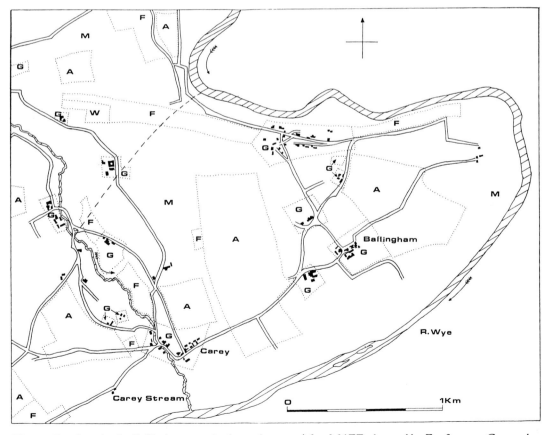

Fig 3.6 Land use in the Ballingham area in the modern era (after MAFF, A = arable, F = forestry, G = gardens and orchards, M = meadow and pasture, W = waste land and heath).

will be well drained, loamy or peaty and occur on gentle slopes. They will be well supplied with nutrients and highly responsive to fertilizers, thus giving high yields (MAFF 1968, 2). The classification of Ballingham is shown in Fig 3.5.

Modern land use

The second map produced by MAFF presents modern land use (1961–77). This map (Fig 3.6) presents a useful compliment to the land classification map, allowing for comparison between the two, and from this a greater understanding of the link between land potential and use in the modern world.

Tithe map

In order to begin to project the agricultural landscape backwards reference was made to the tithe maps (Fig 3.7) which were produced during the 1830s and 40s. These maps present a landscape where, though field boundaries demonstrate a significantly different field pattern from their modern counterpart, recorded land use seems to have changed relatively little over the last 130 or so years. Fieldwork was also undertaken, though with generally poor results due to the difficulty of dating features encountered.

By the end of the pilot study two significant points were

clear. First, in all but one example the location of a pre-Norman church site could not be established and as a result aspects of church location within the estate and any links with the nature of the landscape were pursued no further. Secondly, it was established that there were two fundamental problems regarding the use of the modern land classification map series in a study of this kind. One, the classification is wholly skewed towards arable and vegetable cropping; thus land which is given a low grade is done so because it is not suitable for arable crops, though it may yet be of good potential for pasture or meadow. Such a bias is the result of modern economic factors which cannot be assumed for this early period. Two, the classification includes the large scale use of and the response of the land to lime and fertilizers, for which there is no evidence of use on anything approaching the present scale during the early medieval period.

Approach for the Remainder of the Study

Given that the modern land use classification referred to above is not appropriate, it was necessary to devise a land classification that was. The three principle factors in any land classification are topography, soil type and hydrology. Taking into account these three factors with regard to the suitability of the land to produce specific vegetation, a five point system was developed featuring the following classifications:

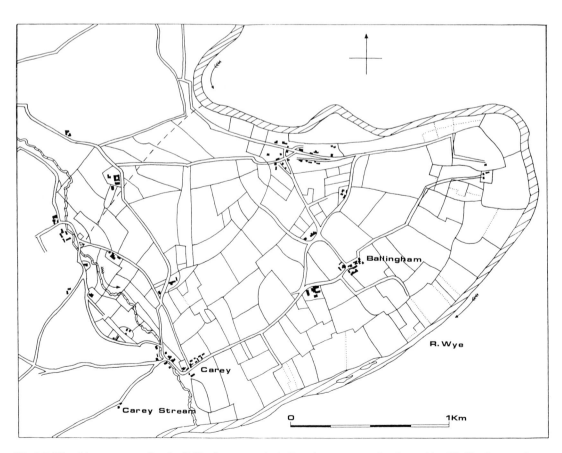

Fig 3.7 The tithe assessment for the Ballingham area: including the assessment for the parish of Ballingham and part of Little Dewchurch.

1　*Good*: Land capable of producing both high crop and grass yields.

2　*Moderately Good*: Land capable of producing one of either good grass or crop yields, with the remainder capable of moderate, but not poor yields.

3　*Moderate*: Land where moderate yields of both grass and crops could be sustained or a good yield of one with only a poor yield for the other.

4　*Moderately Poor*: Land where one of either crops or grass might be expected to provide a moderate yield, whilst the other would only give up a poor yield.

5　*Poor*: Land only capable of producing a poor yield of either crops or grass.

Where applicable other factors were taken into account, notably opportunities for fishing or the mention of ship mooring facilities. For example, fish weirs and ship mooring are referred to in the charters pertaining to Caldicot of supposedly late ninth-century date (LL235b) and to Chepstow of supposed seventh-century date (LL165).

Such a scale removes any inordinate bias towards arable based production and gives equal standing to quality grassland. As regards the potential of the soil, recourse was made to publications of regional soil surveys by the British Soil Survey (Findley *et al* 1984; Ragg *et al* 1984; Rudeforth *et al* 1984), in which it is possible to assess the value and versatility of a given soil before fertilizers and lime are added. This system was then applied to a greater corpus of estates, which, though not meeting the strict criteria outlined for the pilot study, were still the subject of charters dated to before the mid eleventh century, in the area outlined in Figure 3.1. This larger corpus contains 73 estates (35 claimed by Llandaff and 38 claimed by Worcester), as presented in Figure 3.8.

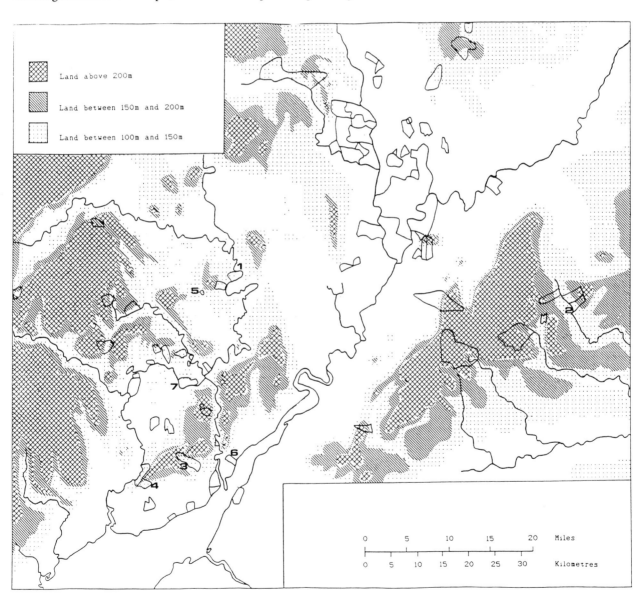

Fig 3.8 Map showing all estates included in the survey. Those belonging to the pilot study are indicated as follows: 1 Ballingham, 2 Daylesford, 3 Itton, 4 Llanbedr, 5 Llanwarne, 6 Tidenham, 7 Wonastow. Ewenny and St Brides-Super-Ely lie to the west of the area shown.

Results

In general the Llandaff estates are small and considerably less consolidated than those of Worcester. This possibly reflects different strategies of acquisition by the respective ecclesiastical centres, in which the differing extent of suitable land may well play a part. The amount of lowland to be found between the Usk and the Wye is tiny compared with the area of the Worcester properties. Not only is there less lowland, but as a result of greater altitudes, rainfall and a greater proportion of steeper slopes in the western region, the uplands within the area in which the Worcester estates occur are of considerably greater potential for agriculture than their western counterparts. It is unfortunate that the extents of non-ecclesiastical properties in the two areas are unknown, since this would make our understanding of the relationship between properties in general and landscape somewhat clearer.

There is a distinguishable concentration of ecclesiastical estates on land below 150m. This feature appears to be largely a result of the estates being located in river valleys. This phenomenon cannot be easily seen in any of the maps presented here, since only the largest rivers are shown, but the link is obvious when the estates are considered on a smaller scale. It should be pointed out, however, that there are conspicuous exceptions to this in the examples of properties in the Cotswolds and two estates in the vicinity of Trelleck, Trelleck itself (LL199b) and Llandogo (LL156).

This relationship can be presented by means of the following statistics: 33% of the Llandaff estates have no land over 100m, with 56% of the Worcester estates having no land above the same height. In total, then, over half of the estates encountered lay completely at altitudes less than 100m. Considering the amount of land above 100m found within the estates we find that 54% of Llandaff estates and 64% of Worcester estates have less than 25% of their area over 100m. Thus 59% of the total number of estates possess at least 75% of their area below the 100m contour. Lastly, it is the case that only 12% of Llandaff estates lie wholly above 150m, and none of the Worcester properties meet this qualification.

The constant difference between Llandaff and Worcester figures is not unexpected since, whilst only 33% of the land found between the Usk and the Wye occurs below 100m, 63% of the area in which the Worcester properties occur is below 100m; almost double the proportion. The comparative lack of lower, and apparently more desirable land between the Wye and Usk may well be a factor in the smaller size of the estates of Llandaff and their less consolidated nature.

There is also a notable lack of any supposed upland/lowland division within the estates of the two regions. This can be illustrated in the following way. Four altitude bands were created, with the lowest band consisting of land below 100m, the second of land between 100m and 150m, the third of land between 150m and 200m and the last of land above 200m. Then each estate was considered and any significant amount of land occurring in any of the four bands noted: for example the estate at Ballingham contains land in the two lowest bands only.

The result of this exercise was that only 24% of the estates claimed by Llandaff and 33% of the Worcester estates possess land in three or more of the altitude ranges, and can thus be divided into what may be termed upland and lowland divisions. Such a feature does, however, occur in isolated cases: for example a small number of estates in the Brecon upland region, where deeply incised river valleys provide a wide range of altitudes over relatively short distances. The estate at Bishops Cleeve, Gloucestershire (BL Cotton Tib A xiii, fo 116), half of which lies in the Severn Vale and half above the Cotswold scarp slope, is also a good example where an upland/lowland division is clear, but in all only 10 estates (7 belonging to Llandaff) fit this pattern.

Lastly, the relationship between the size of an estate and its overall agricultural potential can be shown to be significantly different when comparing the estates of the two land owners. There is a clear and direct link between the size and quality of estates held by Llandaff (Fig 3.9): estates of good quality tend to be smaller in size with the estate's size increasing as quality deteriorates. There are, as can be seen, three notable exceptions to this, which are of high quality and of greater than average size: Ballingham (1127 acres), Chepstow (1275 acres) and Llanarth (1560 acres). This link does not, however, appear in those estates owned by Worcester (Fig 3.10). Any possible link between size and quality in this area is far less clear. Thus, in the case of the Worcester properties, the size of the individual estate is considerably less closely linked to its natural agricultural potential. The exact reason for the difference between these two regions is unclear, though one possible explanation may be suggested. This is that the Llandaff estates were less intensely managed, whereas the Worcester estates may have been more aggressively managed, perhaps with a greater number of workers (possibly slaves) capable of greater manipulation of the natural resources available. Thus more effective drainage, greater manuring, and possibly liming, and more strictly controlled crop management, perhaps involving some form of rotation system, may have combined to raise the soils beyond their natural potential, as many soils today are changed, albeit to a much greater extent, by modern farming methods. This could have resulted in the overall value attached to any given piece of land being less directly related to its natural potential than to its worked quality.

Further Questions

A number of questions arise from the research conducted thus far, two of which are of particular interest and are given here, since it is intended to attempt to answer them later in the research programme.

The first question relates to whether there is any direct link between the different terms used for churches in the charter texts and the size and quality of their associated

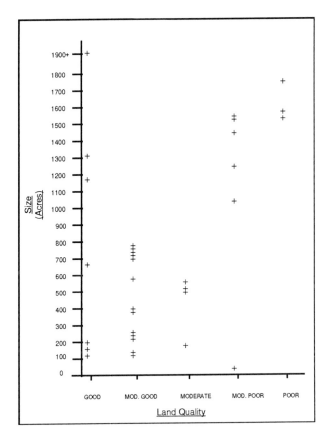

Fig 3.9 *Graph illustrating the relationship between land quality and estate size for the estates claimed by Llandaff.*

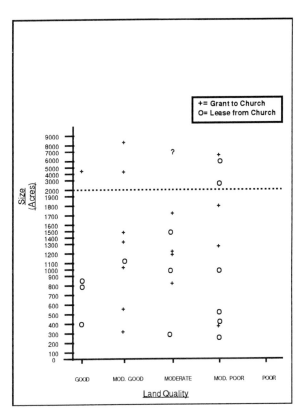

Fig 3.10 *Graph illustrating the relationship between land quality and estate size for the estates claimed by Worcester (+ = grant of land to the church, 0 = lease of land from the church into private hands for a set period, ? = a boundary clause detached from its relevant charter).*

land. For example, *podum* is applied to some churches and this term has been thought to refer to centres of a more monastic nature than the term *ecclesia*. The early church associated with the estate at Ballingham is one such example of a *podum,* and it is the case that the estate to which it is linked is comparatively large in size and high quality within the Llandaff corpus of properties. It would be interesting to know whether other estates linked with *poda* are also larger than average.

The second question asks whether ecclesiastical estates occupy significantly superior or inferior land within the local region in which they are found. Thus, whilst it is possible to point to estates which are of greater agricultural potential than other ecclesiastical estates, it would also be possible to discover, for example, whether any estate was of greater or lesser agricultural potential than the surrounding 10km or 20km. This exercise would allow us to make conclusions, not only about the relative values of ecclesiatical estates, but also about the relative values of secular estates, and to determine whether there are any differences in the quality of land between the two.

Notes

1   References to charters in the *Liber Landavensis* are given here by number referring to the page number in Evans' (1979) transcription preceded by the abbreviation LL. The same numbering is used in (Davies 1979).

References

Unpublished sources
British Library (BL) Cotton Tiberius A xiii

Published Sources
Brook, D, 1992, The early Christian church east and west of Offa's Dyke, in N Edwards & A Lane (eds), *The early church in Wales and the West*, Oxbow mon 16, Oxford, 77–90

Davies, W 1978, *An early Welsh microcosm: studies in the Llandaff Charters*, London

Davies, W, 1979, *The Llandaff Charters*, Aberystwyth

Evans, J G (ed), 1979, *The Book of Llan Dav: Liber Landavensis*, Aberystwyth

Finberg, H P R, 1961, *The early charters of the West Midlands*, Leicester

Findley, D C, *et al*, 1984, *Soils and their use in south west England*, Harpendon

Rackham, O, 1986, *The history of the countryside*, London

Ragg, J M, *et al*, 1984, *Soils and their use in Midland and western England*, Harpendon

Rudeforth, C C, *et al*, 1984, *Soils and their use in Wales*, Harpendon

Maps

MAFF, 1961–77, Ministry of Agriculture, Fisheries & Food, 1961–77 *Land use maps*, 1:25000, The Second Land Utilisation Survey of Great Britain

MAFF, 1968, Ministry of Agriculture, Fisheries & Food, 1968 *Agricultural land classification maps for England and Wales*, 1:63360

The Soil Association of England and Wales, 1963, *Soil map series of England and Wales*, 1:25000

Chapter 4

The Royal Courts of the Welsh Princes of Gwynedd, AD 400–1283

David Longley

The pattern of llys, maerdref *and commote in Gwynedd represents a snapshot in time of what was an essentially evolving process. Three stages of development are proposed. In the first, 'high-status' settlement is characterized principally by fortification. Some locations identified as power bases later acquired the status of* maerdref. *Other fortifications are considered on the basis of morphology and layout. Secondly, during the twelfth century, the disposition of royal sites reflects an emphasis on accessibility; fortification is not a regular component. Thirdly, by the late twelfth century, new castles were built – often on the king's* ffridd – *for strategic reasons. The court resorted to these as often as the traditional* maerdrefi, *the character of which was evolving. Some* llysoedd *ceased to be maintained but some* maerdrefi *developed a proto-urban function.*

The decline of centralized Roman government in Britain at the turn of the fourth and fifth centuries allowed the emergence of an independent British kingdom in north-west Wales. The English conquest under Edward I in 1283 marked its eclipse. Over nine centuries fortunes and boundaries ebbed and flowed, but Gwynedd was always one of the most powerful kingdoms of western Britain. For the purposes of this paper the boundaries of Gwynedd are taken to be the lands held by the native Welsh kingdom in the area north west of a line from the Dyfi to the estuary of the Dee (Fig 4.2). This territory approximates to the extent of the kingdom in the mid thirteenth century.

It can reasonably be argued that the royal administrative centres of the successive kings and princes of Gwynedd have a claim to be considered as the most important secular complexes in the north Welsh landscape in the centuries before the Edwardian conquest. The most recent survey of the available evidence (Edwards & Lane 1988) can only point to three sites, Degannwy, Dinas Emrys and Rhuddlan, which can be described with any certainty as both high status and secular in the period before AD 1100. In the later period, the twelfth and thirteenth centuries, a royal administrative complex could comprise a *llys* (royal court) and *maerdref* (the royal estate which incorporated communities of the king's bond tenants who worked the royal demesne) (Stephenson 1984, 57–8). The names and general locations of over twenty such *maerdrefi* can be deduced from documentation of the thirteenth and fourteenth centuries. But, with the possible exception of Degannwy, it has not, until very recently (see Johnstone Ch 5) been

possible to pinpoint these locations accurately; nor to describe the structural characteristics and organization of these sites from the evidence of the tangible remains. The questions which will be addressed in this paper concern the degree to which it might be possible to identify these high-status political foci on the ground: where were they, what were they like and how did they evolve through time?

Llysoedd *and* Maerdrefi

The Welsh lawbooks provide us with a theoretical model for the administrative organization and subdivision of regional units (Jenkins 1986, 120–2). This is useful as a starting point and as a framework for discussion, but to what extent the reality of the situation ever conformed to the ideal is a debatable point. Stephenson (1984, xli) reminds us that 'although the lawbooks may elucidate or complement the evidence obtained from other sources, no attempt should be made to force such evidence into a framework created by reference to the lawbooks alone'. With this caveat we may analyse the jurists' exemplar. The important administrative unit in a kingdom is the commote (*cwmwd*) although there is continual reference to the archaic larger unit of the *cantref* (literally 100 rural townships). It is assumed that commotes are paired and that each pair of commotes constitutes a *cantref*. Logically, each commote in a pair should contain 50 *trefi* (townships) giving 100 townships in the parent *cantref*. Each commote should comprise twelve *maenolau* (large estates) and each *maenol* should encompass four *trefi*. From this calculation it can be seen that each commote is

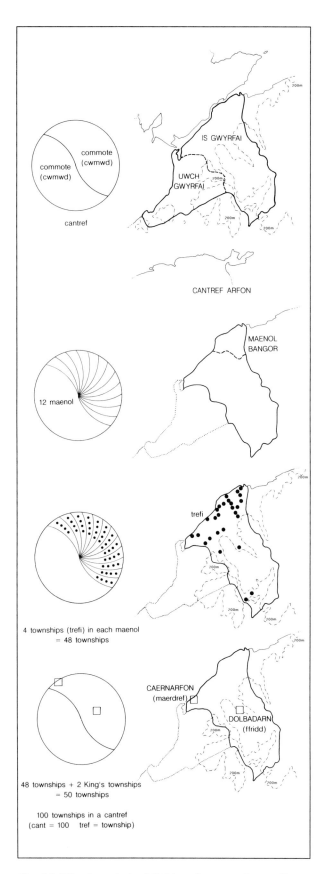

Fig 4.1 The theoretical subdivision of a cantref *according to Welsh law; and a documented example: Cantref Arfon and the commotes of Is Gwyrfrai and Uwch Gwyrfai.*

two townships short of the requisite 50. The deficiency is reconciled with the realization that two additional townships are set aside in each commote for the king's use. One of these is the *maerdref* (literally, the *tref* of the king's administrator); the other is the king's *fridd,* his waste or summer pasture in the commote (Fig 4.1).

The *maerdref* comprised land held in demesne by the king and the hamlet or hamlets of the king's bond tenants who worked the demesne in support of the *llys.* A particularly restrictive form of bond tenure, *tir cyfrif,* is frequently associated with *maerdref* tenants (Ellis 1838, *passim*; Carr 1972, *passim*). There would also have been other renders and services due from other townships in the commote.

The *llys* was the complex of buildings, which could include a hall or halls, food-house, stables, a porch etc, and which may or may not have been enclosed (Jenkins 1986, 41; Carr 1982, 143). The *llys* stood at the nucleus of the *maerdref* and provided a base for the administration of the commote and a siphon for the collection of taxes in kind owed to the king from the commote. The king would periodically visit his *llysoedd,* meeting the people he needed to meet, doing business, dispensing justice and, with his retinue, eating his way through his taxes.

In practice the *actual* political geography of the kingdom might depart, to a greater or lesser degree, from this ideal. Some *cantrefi* might comprise more than two commotes, for example, and the complement of townships would vary from commote to commote, determined by considerations other than mathematical symmetry. Nevertheless, by the thirteenth century, the commote had become the unit of regional administration and, in general, one *maerdref* could be found within each commote as the focus of that administration. The names and general locations of most of the *maerdrefi* are known to us through documentary sources of the thirteenth century and later (see Johnstone p 57–60). Place-names can also be useful clues in narrowing the search. Corruptions of *maerdref,* as in the form Vardre at Degannwy, for example, or *tre'r gyfrif,* designating a community under *tir cyfrif* tenure, as at Trefriw in the Conwy Valley, occur.

An immediate difficulty presents itself, however, in that the pattern of Welsh royal administration in Gwynedd was summarily eclipsed in 1283. The royal lands were forfeit to the English Crown and the administrative centres and demesne lands ceased to be maintained or to perform their functions in the traditional way. To some extent our loss of information arising from this discontinuity in settlement history is counterbalanced by a particularly detailed set of records compiled for the English Crown during the late thirteenth and fourteenth centuries by surveyors whose business it was to assess the newly annexed lands for taxes due (Stephenson 1984, xxxv–xxxviii; in particular Ellis 1838; Vinogradoff & Morgan 1914).

The Chronological Dimension

An initial question which must be addressed concerns the

degree to which the identifiable pattern of *llysoedd* and *maerdrefi* in the thirteenth century can be seen to have an earlier origin, and the extent to which this pattern can be used as a model for an earlier period.

Thirteenth-Century Decline

The administrative framework based on *maerdrefi* was, to some extent, in decline by the thirteenth century. At some locations the labour services owed to the prince had been commuted to money payments, particularly where the opportunities for commerce existed, and it seems unlikely that the royal estates and court buildings in these townships continued to be needed or maintained in the traditional way (Jones Pierce 1972, 278–80, but see Stephenson 1984, 59–63). Llan-faes, for example, developed a proto-urban function and, during the reign of Llywelyn ap Gruffudd, accounted for 70% of Gwynedd's trading revenues (Carr 1982, 232). For other reasons certain *llysoedd* were no longer being resorted to. For example, in the Conwy Valley, the rents due to the *llys* of Arllechwedd Isaf were payable at the *llys* of Aber in the next commote. Similarly, when English surveyors made their assessments of former Welsh royal lands after the conquest, virtually all record of the *maerdref* of Llifon on Anglesey had been lost (Carr 1982, 134). There are other examples of this trend and it would seem that, as the governance of Gwynedd was becoming more centralized, fewer of the traditional foci of peripatetic kingship were being utilized. A system in decline presupposes an earlier origin.

Earthwork Castles

The motte is a particular Norman form of castle building. There is a striking correspondence between the distribution of earthwork castles in Gwynedd, particularly west of the Conwy, and the possible sites of *maerdrefi*. There are at least two ways of interpreting this association. Johnstone has argued that a number of these castles may have been built by Welsh lords as component parts of *llysoedd*, copying Norman prototypes (see p 61). On the other hand, it is possible to argue that the motte is a more generally intrusive Norman form which was only subsequently and occasionally taken up by the Welsh as, for example, at Owain Gwynedd's castle at Tomen-y-Rhodwydd, built in 1149. As the construction of the majority of Gwynedd mottes remains undocumented, this question may only be resolved by excavation. The distinction has chronological significance, however, in that the earliest mottes in North Wales were certainly built during the Norman intrusive campaigns and settlement in the late eleventh century, whereas Welsh imitation was necessarily later. It is of anecdotal interest that in 1094 Gruffudd ap Cynan is credited by his biographer with 'delivering Gwynedd from castles' (Evans 1977, 20–1).

It is possible to identify a number of mottes which were built by campaigning Normans in the late eleventh century as they pushed across the Clwyd and Conwy into heartland Gwynedd (Fig 4.2). In 1073 Robert built a motte at Rhuddlan at King William's command to control the Welsh. He may also have established his *caput* at Denbigh and built the possible motte there at this time (Spurgeon 1991, 159). During the next decade Robert of Rhuddlan and Hugh of Chester built castles at Degannwy, Bangor, Aberlleiniog and Caernarfon (Davies 1991, 90). The motte at Aber may also have been built by Robert, although this cannot be proven. These early Norman castles, symptomatic of territorial expansion rather than consolidation, appear to have been erected on, or near, locations which were already politically important Welsh centres which we can later recognize as the sites of *maerdrefi*. Rhuddlan was the royal seat of Gruffudd ap Llywelyn by 1063 (Whitelock 1961, *sub anno* 1063); Degannwy is recorded as *arx Decantorum* in the ninth century and the association of imported Mediterranean pottery of the fifth-sixth century suggests a longer chronology (Morris 1980, *sub anno* 812; Alcock 1967). Rhuddlan, Denbigh, Degannwy and Caernarfon could all be regarded as *maerdrefi* by the thirteenth century (Jones, G R J 1991, 202; Ellis 1838, *passim*); Aberlleiniog is close to the *maerdref* of the commote of Dindaethwy at Llan-faes and Aber, which is unlikely to have been bypassed in the Norman coastal advance, was the *maerdref* of Arllechwedd Uchaf. The recurring conjunction of motte and *maerdref*, particularly west of the Conwy (but noticeably absent from most of Anglesey which barely came under Norman control) and the demonstrable associations of these sites with documented eleventh-century Norman campaigns suggests that earthwork castles may be one indicator of *maerdref* locations and that a number of our known *maerdrefi* were functioning in this capacity as early as the eleventh century.

The Normans were pushed back across the Conwy in the last decade of the eleventh century. It is probable that some intrusive earthwork castles continued to be used by the Welsh in areas recovered from the Normans, both west of the Conwy and to the east in the debated Perfeddwlad, and it is possible that a number of mottes were subsequently raised by the Welsh in imitation of the Norman model. However, only three mottes are of documented Welsh construction: they are Cymer, near Dolgellau, Cynfal, near Tywyn and Tomen-y-Rhodwydd on the furthest eastern boundary of Gwynedd's expansion. All were built in the twelfth century (Jones, T 1955, 45–6, 56, 57). Only Tomen-y-Rhodwydd can be shown to have been *built by the Welsh* on a *maerdref*, although it is possible that a proportion of those mottes lacking documentation, and which correspond to the locations of *maerdrefi*, are Welsh rather than Norman. In particular two locations should be noted in the context of possible early Welsh castles. Both are close to the king's *ffridd* in their respective commotes. At Dolwyddelan, close to the river below the castle, the rocky motte-like knoll of Tomen Castell may have supported a precursor to the thirteenth-century keep (RCAHMW 1956, 83). In Cwm Prysor a motte has been created by the modification of a natural boss of rock. Traces of a possible hall and other

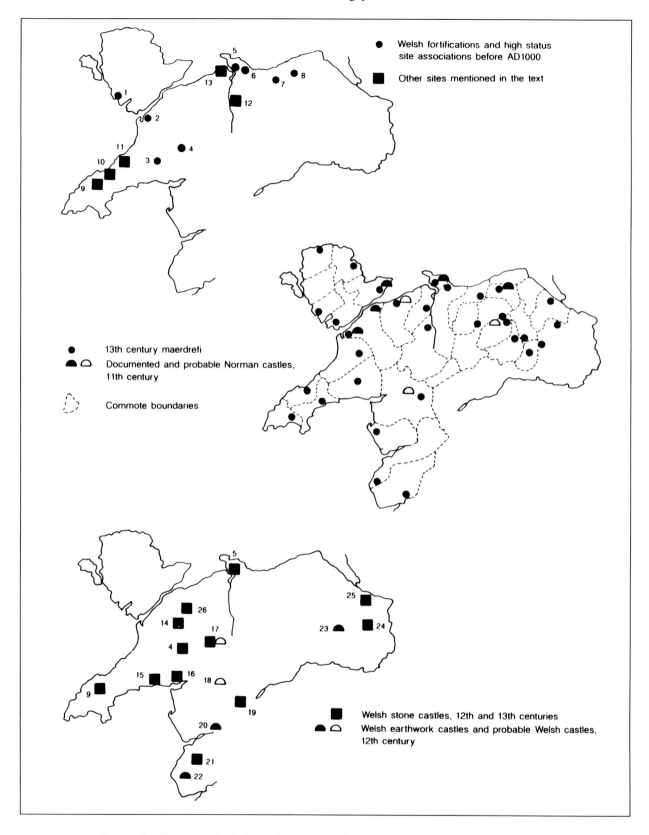

Fig. 4.2 Fortifications and administrative centres in Gwynedd, fifth to thirteenth centuries: key sites.

1 Aberffraw	7 Dinorben	13 Caer Lleion, Conwy	18 Prysor	24 Caergwrle
2 Caernarfon	8 Rhuddlan	Mountain	19 Carndochan	25 Ewloe
3 Pen Llystyn	9 Carn Fadrun	14 Dolbadarn	20 Cymer	26 Tŷ'n Tŵr, Bethesda,
4 Dinas Emrys	10 Garn Boduan	15 Cricieth	21 Bere	a possible site.
5 Degannwy	11 Tre'r Ceiri	16 Aber Iâ	22 Cynfal	
6 Bryn Euryn	12 Pen-y-Castell, Carreg Olau;	17 Dolwyddelan	23 Tomen-y-Rhodwydd	

structures survive at the base of the mound. It would seem that Prysor operated as *maerdref* of the commote of Uwch Artro at the time of the conquest (Johnstone forthcoming; Ellis 1838, 285, 292). There are obvious implications for the degree to which Welsh administrative centres were traditionally fortified.

Early Royal Associations at the Sites of Later Maerdrefi

There are a small number of sites which can, either on direct evidence or by association, be considered as significant power bases during the early centuries of the kingdom of Gwynedd and which can, later, be documented as *maerdrefi*.

Degannwy provides the best evidence. Two precipitous hillocks and an intervening saddle dominate the east bank of the Conwy estuary. Roman pottery of the first to fourth centuries and a third- to fourth-century coin series indicate occupation of the westernmost of the two hills. One sherd of class Bi imported eastern Mediterranean wine amphora and several other possible sherds suggest post-Roman activity (Alcock 1967, 190–201; Campbell 1988, 126). A persistent local tradition associates the early sixth-century king, Maelgwn, with Degannwy. This, in itself, of course, is only significant as evidence that later generations considered Degannwy an appropriate location for an early royal association. But the tradition finds some tenuous support in a parenthetical comment on the reference in the *Annales Cambriae* to the death of Maelgwn 'in the *llys* of Rhos' (Morris 1980, *sub anno* 547). His death or 'long sleep' had achieved proverbial status by the thirteenth century and Degannwy is almost certainly implied as the location (Bromwich 1978, 437–9). Mentions of the burning and siege of *arx Decantorum* in the ninth century also probably refer to Degannwy. Robert of Rhuddlan built a castle there *c* 1080 following which the hill was held alternately by the Welsh and Anglo-Normans until 1263. Llywelyn ap Iorwerth and Henry III both built stone castles there (RCAHMW 1956, 152–4). Degannwy was obviously an important political and strategic focus controlling the Conwy estuary over a very long period of time. It is one of the few centres of commotal administration in Gwynedd which can be shown conclusively to have had a native, rather than intrusive, fortification and post-conquest surveys confirm its *maerdref* status (Ellis 1838, 2).

Aberffraw, on the west bank of the Ffraw near its estuary on the west coast of Anglesey, has sometimes been styled the capital of the independent kingdom. It is recognized in bardic tradition as one of the three tribal thrones of the island of Britain and is consistently equated with the symbols of kingship (Bromwich 1978, 228–9). These are not in themselves evidence of antiquity in that function. However, 2.5km to the east, at Llangadwaladr, a seventh-century memorial stone commemorates Cadfan, 'wisest and most renowned of all kings' (Nash-Williams 1950, 55–6), father of Cadwallon, the victor over Edwin's Northumbria, and

grandfather of Cadwaladr whose dedication the church bears. English and Welsh traditions conspire to suggest that during Edwin's years of exile he spent some time on Anglesey, perhaps at the court of Cadfan, perhaps in the company of Cadwallon (Bromwich 1978, xcvii–xcviii). Later, before his final defeat at the hands of the Gwynedd and Mercian alliance, Edwin returned to harass the island bringing 'Anglesey and Man under English rule' (Shirley-Price 1968, 108). It has been argued that a two-phase bank and ditch defence in the area of the present village might be dated, in its first phase, to the Roman period and, in its second phase, to the early middle ages (White & Longley 1995). Aberffraw was ravaged by Vikings in 968 (Jones, T 1952, *sub anno* 966). Llywelyn ap Iorwerth took the unique title 'Prince of Aberffraw, Lord of Snowdon' in the last decade of his reign (Davies 1991, 247). Thirteenth-century sculptured masonry has been recovered from the present village (White 1977) and in 1317 198 lengths of timber were removed from the buildings of the court for reuse in the construction of Edward I's castle at Caernarfon (Carr 1982, 123n). When English surveyors assessed the former Welsh royal lands after the conquest, Aberffraw could clearly be seen to have been an exceptional *maerdref* with seven dependent bond hamlets under *tir cyfrif* tenure (Carr 1972, 172–6; 1982, 132–4).

Caernarfon Here, on an elevated ridge overlooking the Seiont, near its estuary, the Roman auxiliary base of Segontium took its name from the river and, in turn, gave a descriptive colour to the medieval focus which succeeded it: *Caer Segeint* (Morris 1980, 65) which became *Caer Seint yn Arfon* (Williams 1982, 38, 189). Regular references to, and the location of traditional stories at, Caernarfon are no confirmation of its antiquity although these, and an evolving form of the name, do suggest a continuing familiarity with the place in popular perception. Adjacent to the fort on the south-east side stands the parish church of Llanbeblig, sharing a name with the bond township which supported the king's *llys* at Caernarfon and raising the possibility that the nucleus of the Welsh administrative centre may originally have been close by. Two coins, an early ninth- century Northumbrian styca and an eleventh-century penny of Cnut, have been found in stratified contexts within the Roman fort (Edwards & Lane 1988, 115–16). Four penannular brooches from the site are possible but not certain indicators of post-Roman activity. By the thirteenth century the *llys*, and timber buildings of the *maerdref*, appear to have been sited on the estuary itself. Here, a Norman earthwork was built in the late eleventh century and this was the location Edward I finally chose for his idiosyncratic and politically symbolic castle and frontier capital after the conquest of Gwynedd in 1283. *Maerdref* houses were demolished by Edward to build his town walls (RCAHMW 1960, 115).

Rhuddlan was an important strategic location on the Clwyd, more obviously so in antiquity, when marshes extended between the site and the sea. A battle (at *Rudglann*) is recorded in the late eighth century (Morris 1980, *sub anno* 797) and in 921 the Anglo-Saxon *burh* of *Cledemutha* was established (Whitelock 1961, *sub anno* 921). It is the Welsh name which persists, however, and by the eleventh century Rhuddlan was back in Welsh hands. In 1062 Harold Godwinson drove Gruffudd ap Llywelyn from Rhuddlan and burnt his estate and his ships (Whitelock 1961, *sub anno* 1063). Ten years later Earl Robert built a motte close to the site. By the mid twelfth century Owain had regained Rhuddlan, and much more, for Gwynedd, but in 1277 work had begun on Edward I's masonry castle (Jones, T 1952, 119).

Dinorben This limestone promontory with its strong natural defences to the west, north and south, was in later prehistory the site of a major hillfort with multiple ramparts protecting the easier approach from the south. A significant quantity of late Roman artefacts suggests occupation to the end of the fourth century. Animal bones from the upper fills of the main outer ditch have produced radiocarbon dates which centre on the fifth and sixth centuries (Guilbert 1980, 336–8) and a fragment of Anglo-Saxon metalwork of seventh-century date was found within the fort (Gardner & Savory 1964, 162–3, fig 16.3). This material, however, does no more than hint at continued occupation. By the fourteenth century the *llys* of the commote of Is Dulas and *maerdref* of Dinorben were located a short distance to the south of the hillfort (Edwards & Lane 1988, 65–6). A reference to the hearth of Dinorben in *Englynion y Beddau* is significant only in identifying that the site had, by the thirteenth century, or perhaps as early as the tenth, become a landmark of the *ancient* landscape (Jones, T 1967, 53).

Sites with Early Medieval High-Status Associations

In addition to sites which might be argued to be the precursors of *maerdrefi*, a number of settlements might, on circumstantial grounds, be considered to have high-status associations in the early middle ages. Alcock (1987, 168–71) and Alcock and Alcock (1990 130–8) have compiled gazetteers of fortified sites which include those of early medieval Wales. Edwards and Lane (1988) have produced a more general gazetteer of secular settlement in Wales. Dark (1994) has analysed secular 'elite' settlements in western Britain from AD 400 to AD 700 and has suggested a methodology for identifying previously unrecognized sites. From these surveys may be abstracted a recent broad consensus on the location of possible and probable early medieval high-status sites within Gwynedd. Figure 4.3 summarizes a sample of current opinion. The degree of confidence with which sites have been assigned to the period has been assessed by the researchers against different criteria and has been expressed by them in different ways. A 'probable' categorization in the table would mean a 'definite' site to Edwards and Lane, 'more certain' to Alcock and Alcock and 'very probable' to Dark. A 'possible' site in the table would mean a 'possible' site to Edwards and Lane,

DEGREES OF CONFIDENCE	EDWARDS & LANE 1988	ALCOCK & ALCOCK 1990	DARK 1994
Probable Site	Degannwy Dinas Emrys Rhuddlan	Degannwy Dinas Emrys	Carn Pentyrch Degannwy Dinas Emrys Tre'r Ceiri Pen Llystyn
Probable Site	Aberffraw Bryn Euryn Dinorben Pen Lystyn Segontium	Aberffraw Bryn Euryn Carreg-y-Llam	Bryn Euryn Camp Hill (Bangor) Carn Fadrun Dinorben Pen-y-Corddyn
Dark's Group 1			Bryn Euryn Craig-y-Deryn Creigiau Gwineu Dinas Gynfor Moel-y-Gest Tal-y-Garreg

Fig 4.3 Table showing fortified and high-status sites of possibly early medieval date according to recent assessments.

'less certain' to Alcock and Alcock and 'probable' to Dark. Dark's optimistic analysis has identified a further 26 sites within the wider boundaries of Gwynedd which might be regarded as 'possibles' but as the 'positive' evidence in these cases rests on less secure grounds it has not been considered feasible to take the majority into consideration in this discussion. Some of these 'possible' sites, however, fall within Dark's morphological classification of 'citadel and ward type' which, he argues, may not be represented in the earlier Iron Age landscape (Dark 1994, 135). As some aspects of the citadel-and-dependent outwork disposition of defences is discussed in more detail below, Dark's Group 1 sites have been included in the table.

The list includes Degannwy, Aberffraw, Dinorben and Rhuddlan, which have been discussed above, and Carreg-y-Llam, Pen Llystyn, Bryn Euryn and Dinas Emrys. In addition Dark (1994, 134) would suggest Carn Pentyrch and Tre'r Ceiri as 'very probable' and Camp Hill (Roman Camp, Bangor), Carn Fadrun and Pen-y-Corddyn as 'probable' sites. However Campbell (1988, 125) has discounted the pottery evidence from Carreg-y-Llam and Edwards and Lane would regard only Degannwy, Dinas Emrys and Rhuddlan as 'definite' identifications.

The chronology and nature of the postulated palisaded enclosure on the site of the Roman auxiliary fort at Pen Llystyn (Edwards & Lane 1988, 102–4) is very uncertain although late Roman activity at both Segontium and Canovium must encourage consideration of the possibility of continued occupation of an indeterminate nature at these former Roman military sites. A number of Dark's 'possible' identifications also rest on the presence of late Roman pottery. This, on current evidence, is the status of Pen-y-Corddyn, despite the recent discovery of an early medieval penannular brooch from the foot of the hill (Dark 1994, 128).

Roman Camp, Bangor, is a rectilinear earthwork with a prominent internal boss-like expansion in the southern angle. Doubt has been cast on the authenticity of the association of a late Roman coin found on the site (Lynch 1986, 81). The site must therefore be regarded as undated. The ridge on which Roman Camp stands overlooks the early monastery of Bangor, an important centre of ecclesiastical lordship, and commands extensive views down the Menai Straits and across Conwy Bay. Rather than, as Dark suggests (1994, 124), the monastic site providing a context by association for the earthwork, it has always seemed to this observer that the earthwork might represent the documented Norman campaign base of the late eleventh century. On this interpretation the relevant association between the earthwork and the township of Bangor is that the Normans sought to control the existing lordship as they did other administrative foci.

Tre'r Ceiri The defences extend over 2 ha and enclose 150 huts on an exposed peak of Yr Eifl which rises to 485m OD. In places the ramparts still stand over 4m high. A cairn, recently excavated and almost certainly of Bronze Age date, caps the summit. The structures within the ramparts include large round houses, subdivided round houses, cellular agglomerations of polygonal structures and large rectangular structures set against the rampart. Not all the houses are contemporary as compartmentalization and cellular accretions appear to supersede the larger round houses. It is presumed that the defences are Iron Age in origin. Roman pottery of the second to late fourth century is present (RCAHMW 1964, lxxiv-lxxv). However, during 1993, 24 sherds from a single Severn Valley jar of second- or third-century date were recovered from low in the core of a refacing of the main (west) entrance (Hopewell 1993, 49). The pottery occurred in front of an original facing to the entrance passageway in circumstances which strongly suggest that the entrance was being refurbished during, or after, the Romano-British occupation of the site. The location of fifth-sixth century memorial stones at Llanaelhaearn, below the hill, has been remarked upon (Nash-Williams 1950, 87–8; Dark 1994, 126) but an association with Tre'r Ceiri cannot be demonstrated.

As Alcock's gazetteer and his published analyses of site location techniques demonstrate (Alcock 1987, 153–67), in default of documentary testimony, the only proof of early medieval occupation is the evidence of datable stratigraphic associations obtained through excavation. Site morphological analysis is strewn with pitfalls (Alcock 1987, 154–5). In disregard of this good advice and in cognisance of Dark's analysis, the following observations are offered for consideration concerning the morphology and circumstantial associations of a small group of fortified sites including those listed by Edwards and Lane and Dark.

Dinas Emrys is a prominent igneous intrusion rising steeply through 84m from the floor of Nant Gwynant, a major north-south routeway through Snowdonia. Access from the base of the rock on the west side is channelled through a series of entrances, up terraces to the summit. The summit, enclosing an area of around 1.2 ha, and a dependent terrace to the west, are enclosed by weak ramparts. The highest point is crowned by a rectangular masonry keep of probable late twelfth- or early thirteenth-century construction (RCAHMW 1960, 25, n 742). The disposition has the appearance of a nucleated fort except that it lacks the essential prerequisite: a nucleus, a deficiency which the keep does not remedy. Interpretation is further complicated by uncertainty regarding the chronology of the component parts of the complex. The keep is medieval; the ramparts post-date deposits containing fourth-century artefacts. Whether the ramparts are contemporary with the keep, or whether they indicate an early medieval fortification of the rock is debatable. Numerous sherds of a single imported eastern Mediterranean amphora of fifth/sixth century date and a fragment of a stamped plate base of the sixth century (Campbell 1988, 126–7), together with a strong tradition that the site had developed a reputation as a fortress before the construction of the keep (Bromwich 1978, *passim*), strengthens the argument for an early medieval fortification.

Bryn Euryn is a prominent, but low, terraced hill commanding the north-eastern access to the Creuddyn peninsula, as Degannwy does the southern. (It should be noted that two recent published plans of the site (Edwards & Lane 1988, fig 3; Dark 1994, fig 43) are reproduced at in incorrect scale which magnifies the area enclosed by a factor of 4.) The small summit area, 30m across, is enclosed by a drystone rampart with a rubble core and a terrace below the summit is partially enclosed by an earthwork on its western side and by precipitous cliffs on the south (Fig 4.4). This arrangement of defences was sufficiently reminiscent of a motte and bailey for the Ordnance Survey to designate it such on the 25in map. The designation is incorrect, but the overall impression is of a strong citadel with a dependent outwork. Unfortunately the contemporaneity of the summit fort and the more extensive outwork cannot be demonstrated. Nevertheless, the nucleated composite plan should be noted. A debate has developed as to whether Bryn Euryn can plausibly be associated with a sixth-century reference by Gildas to Cuneglasus 'driver of the chariot of the bear's refuge' (Winterbottom 1978, 31, 101; Jackson 1982, 33–4; Dumville 1984, 57–9). The arguments in favour of such an association are that 'the bear's refuge' *(receptaculum ursi)* reasonably paraphrases the British *Dineirth* ('citadel of the bear'); that the medieval township, within which the site lies, was so named Dineirth; and that the Cuneglasus, who precedes Maelgwn in Gildas' list of tyrants, and who Gildas dubs 'red butcher' *(lanio fulve)* is no other than Cynlas Goch ('the red'), cousin of Maelgwn and king in Rhos – the Creuddyn and its hinterland. If the association is correct, then Bryn Euryn is one of the very few identifiable royal sites of early Gwynedd, although it is unclear whether Dineirth was the *maerdref* of Uwch Dulas, as Glanville Jones has suggested (1991, 202).

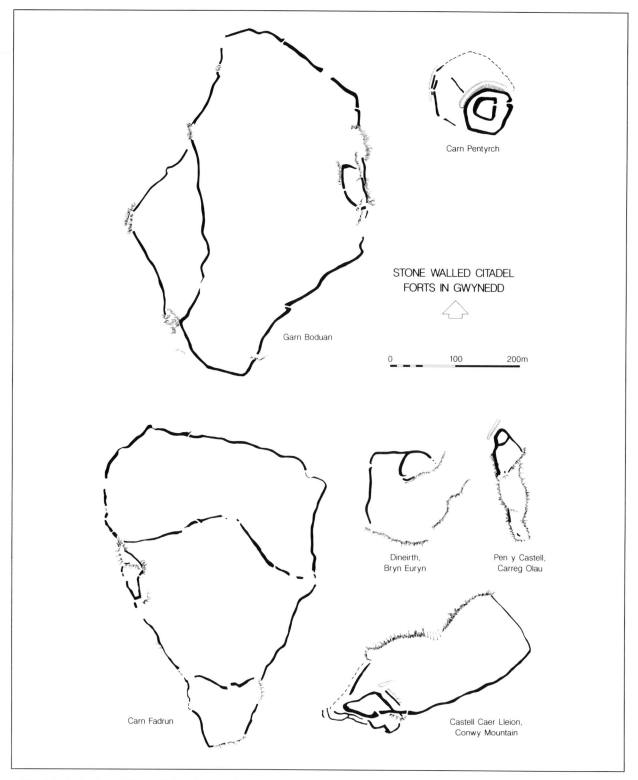

Fig 4.4 A selection of Gwynedd fortifications sharing the morphological characteristic of a strong 'citadel' and dependent outwork.

Carn Fadrun is a large sprawling hillfort occupying 10 ha of the summit plateau of a prominent hill of the same name in the southern part of the Llŷn peninsula. It is possible that two prehistoric phases are represented and the ramparts which outline these are in a dilapidated condition. Close to the summit crag, however, a small polygonal fortification, 57m by 7m, defines a more regular, better faced and

apparently better built fort (Figs 4.4–4.6). This construction has been identified with Gerald of Wales' description in 1188 of a stone castle recently built on the Llŷn peninsula by the sons of Owain Gwynedd and called *Karnmadrun* (Thorpe 1978, 2.6). Among the jumble and succession of round, subrectangular and rectangular stone structures and enclosures which occupy the area, both within and outside

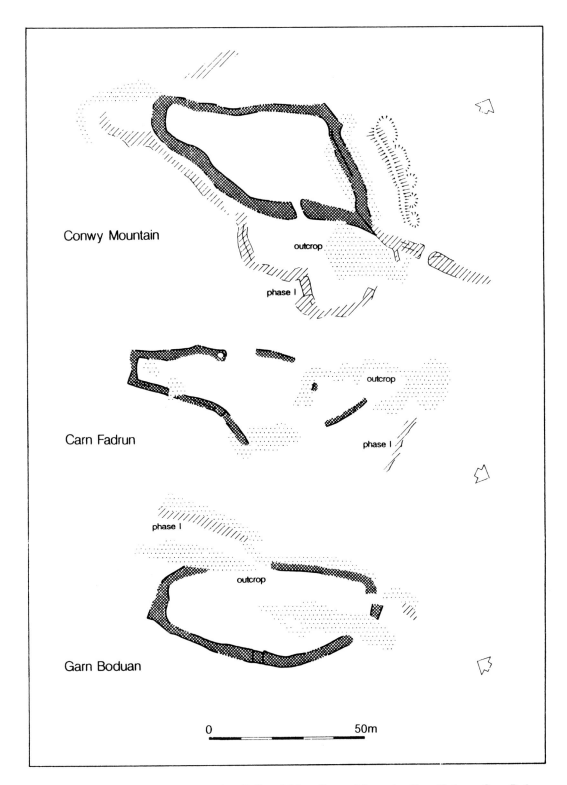

Fig 4.5 Three stone-walled 'citadels': Castell Caer Lleion, Conwy Mountain; Carn Fadrun; Garn Boduan.

the larger defences below the summit, are those which belong to the earlier occupation and those which almost certainly belong to a later phase. These later structures might arguably be associated with the summit fort (RCAHMW 1964, 69–70).

Garn Boduan lies some 5km to the north east of Carn Fadrun. This equally prominent hill rises above the *maerdref* of the commote of Dinllaen at Nefyn and the presumably Iron Age promontory fort of Porth Dinllaen. The summit plateau is defended, as Carn Fadrun is, by extensive ramparts of more than one phase, in this case enclosing a maximum area of around 11 ha. The footings of over 170 circular

Fig 4.6 Carn Fadrun, 'citadel' wall (photograph: author).

Fig 4.7 Garn Boduan, 'citadel' wall (photograph: author).

houses are visible and the fort is thought to be of Iron Age date (RCAHMW 1964, 22–4). On the highest point on the hill is a conspicuous boss of rock crowned by a small (66m by 25m) but very strongly built 'citadel' with walls surviving in a better state of preservation than the main fort (Figs 4.4–4.5,4.7). At Garn Boduan there is no documentary evidence of date. Excavations within the small fort in 1954 identified Iron Age VCP ('very coarse pottery') within a round house and Roman pottery and beads overlying tumbled material from the rampart. None of this can be used to argue for early medieval occupation and Garn Boduan, despite previous serious consideration by Alcock (1971, 217), has been excluded from recent gazetteers. Nevertheless, the arrangement of a strong summit fort within the remains of a much more extensive fortification bears close comparison with Carn Fadrun and, at one stage removed, with Castell Caer Lleion on Conwy Mountain.

Castell Caer Lleion occupies the summit of Conwy Mountain, a ridge rising to 244m, precipitous on the north side which overlooks the Conwy Bay coastline, less so on the landward side. It does not feature in any gazetteer of early medieval fortification. An area of 3 ha is defended by a seriously denuded stone rampart, enclosing about 50 round houses. At the western end, just below the summit knoll, the presence of a small (60m by 25m), strongly defended

'citadel' presents a number of problems of interpretation (Figs 4.4–4.5, 4.8). Griffiths and Hogg (1956) believed the first phase of the small enclosure to be Iron Age, contemporary with the main fort and that it incorporated an impressive entrance on the south side. A second phase of this 'citadel' would then involve a reduction in area. This second phase now presents itself as a strong, well built enclosure with a significantly greater level of preservation than the remainder of the large fort. In places the wall is 5m thick and revetted both front and back. It might be possible to accept one or both phases of the small fort as contemporary though anomalous components of the prehistoric defences were it not for two significant points of detail. Firstly, the main fort and the small fort appear, in both phases, to have had their own completely separate access with no direct communication between the two. Secondly, a bank and ditch earthwork was constructed immediately to the east of the small fort with the effect of enhancing the segregation of the two enclosures. This earthwork was erected over occupation surfaces of an earlier phase.

Pen-y-Castell, Carreg Olau, occupies a rocky ridge rising some 170m above the east bank of the Conwy. The highest end to the north (Fig 4.4) is defended by a strong, drystone ringwork approximately 20m across with walls up to 5m thick. A ditch cuts off the base of the ridge on the north

Fig 4.8 Castell Caer Lleion, Conwy Mountain, 'citadel' wall (photograph: author).

side. To the south, three terraces, dependent on the ringwork, are defended by intermittent stretches of drystone walling. This arrangement, in recognition of the citadel and outwork plan, has been described as 'the adaptation of a motte and bailey layout to an unusual site' (RCAHMW 1956, 168). Both Avent (1983, 7–8) and the Royal Commission (1964, cxliv) compare it with the summit 'castle' on Carn Fadrun.

The suggested chronology of the forts described above spans a very wide range. Griffiths and Hogg argued that the entire complex at Conwy Mountain was Iron Age, at least in phase 1, with the 'citadel', although the term is disputed, contemporary with the main fort. The small fort at Garn Boduan, which structurally and in its relationship to the larger enclosure can be compared to both Conwy and Carn Fadrun, has been variously assigned to the pre-Roman and post-Roman periods. Bryn Euryn or *Dineirth* may be the location of Cynlas Goch's citadel in the sixth century, although Dumville (1984, 57–9) argues for caution in acceptance of this identification. The defences of Dinas Emrys, stratigraphically post-Roman, have been associated by some with the sixth-century occupation, by others with the later stone keep. The ringwork at Pen-y-Castell has been described as an undocumented Welsh castle and comparison has been drawn with the summit fort on Carn Fadrun, which has itself been associated with castle building by the sons of Owain Gwynedd in the late twelfth century. At none of these has the dating been established and the majority of these chronological associations are circumstantial or inferred. If it can be suggested to the point of general acceptance (Avent 1983, 7–8) that the summit fort

at Carn Fadrun, on the one hand, is the documented twelfth-century castle of the sons of Owain Gwynedd, while on the other that the small fort at Castell Caer Lleion, in phase 1, is contemporary with the 'otherwise perfectly normal' main Iron Age fort (Hogg 1975, 180), then the implications have to be addressed. In this respect the circumstantial and relative dating indicators, together with shared morphological characteristics, of the forts described above suggest the potential for considering further the possibility of early medieval activity at these sites.

With the exception of Dinas Emrys, which lacks a nucleus, all these sites share the characteristic of a spatial disposition which incorporates a strong citadel associated with a dependent outwork or an association with a potentially earlier enclosure which creates this impression (Fig 4.4). This morphological characteristic has been noted by the present writer in respect of Caernarfonshire and by Dark as his Group 1, citadel and ward type (1994, 135). It also appears to fall within Alcock and Alcock's class of hierarchically organized fortifications (1991, 103, 130–8). In addition Carn Pentyrch, though lacking any dating evidence whatsoever and omitted from Dark's Group 1 list, would fit within this group, although it would seem hard to justify the inclusion of Dinas Gynfor which *is* on the list. These sites should not automatically be equated with the Pictish and North British series of nuclear forts, although Dark does draw such a comparison (1994, 135). Rather, the significant feature appears to be the focus created by the presence of a small strong 'citadel' regardless of topographic potential or constraints. It is even debatable whether the 'outwork' need necessarily be of contemporary construction or be maintained as an organic unit with the fort. In this respect (though, of course unrelated) the siting of the Norman motte within the earthwork of the Roman fort at Tomen-y-Mur is possibly relevant (Jarrett 1969, 111–13).

Discussion

It is reasonable to see fortification as an indication of status in early British society. Fortifications on 'high hills, steep and menacing, and the cliffs of the sea coast' were common in Iron Age Wales but extending the chronology of such sites into the early middle ages has proved remarkably difficult. This is in contrast with the situation in north Britain where the Picts and *Gwŷr y Gogledd* beyond Hadrian's Wall held their citadels. As both Irish and Welsh law texts make clear, however, it is through access to the labour services of tenants that status was made manifest in building works which could, when circumstances allowed, include the ramparts of a fortification (Kelly 1988, 30; Jenkins 1986, 124–5). In fact early Irish law, in describing the court of a tribal king, specifies the character and dimensions of the earthwork which was theoretically his by right of status (MacNeill 1923, 305; Binchy, 1970, 22, 38). It may be that, in Wales, the top-slicing effect of Roman central government taxation had a greater limiting effect on the maintenance of defences than any prohibition on the continued occupation of previously defended sites. But with the collapse of central government and the devolution of power to regional dynasties in the post-Roman period a local taxable resource in the form of labour once again became available for more complete exploitation. It is tempting to consider whether the availability of this non-monetary resource became the basis for the regional exploitation of tenants and the collection of dues through the maintenance of royal estates for the periodic use of a peripatetic court. It is clear that, in various Anglo-Saxon kingdoms, arrangements were in place, by the seventh century, for the assessment of land for taxation and that, in Northumbria for example, the collection of dues and renders was based on a network of royal vills (Campbell 1982, 58–61). Alcock has seen, in Bede's and Eddius' descriptions of Northumbrian royal progresses, the same kind of 'administrative organisation based on the collection of taxes in kind at royal centres where they would be utilised by the king and court in periodic circuits' (Alcock 1981, 179) that we can perceive, in a later period, at the Welsh *maerdrefi*. When Bede provides us with an assessment of the carrying capacity of Anglesey in the seventh century it is evident that the infrastructure must already have been in place for calculating what is, in effect, a tax assessment (Sherley-Price 1968, 114). It is also tempting to wonder, on the analogy of contemporary power bases in north Britain and Ireland, whether new fortifications might have been constructed in Wales between the fifth and the ninth centuries.

Of defended sites in Gwynedd, Degannwy and Aberffraw are sufficiently close to later documented *maerdrefi* to be regarded as their locational precursors but the status of the

Dinorben hillfort is less certain in relation to the *maerdref* of the same name. The other fortifications are not on the sites of documented *maerdrefi*. Alcock, drawing on extensive analysis of North British high-status sites during this period, has discerned a hiatus in the occupation of hillfort locations: early historic fortifications appear to have been abandoned by the ninth or tenth century and not reoccupied until the thirteenth century when some forts were overlaid with stone castles. This was the case with ten out of sixteen sites in Alcock's 1981 gazetteer. In the meantime, kings may have used unfortified, low lying centres such as Scone (Alcock 1981).

It would seem, in Wales as in Scotland, that, as a pattern of administration evolved, the disposition of sites and the requirements of defence changed. During the twelfth and thirteenth centuries, by which time it is possible to identify true castles in the North Welsh landscape, there are only two documented instances of Welsh castle building on a *maerdref* at Degannwy and Tomen-y-Rhodwydd. The latter is a significant exception in that it could be considered intrusive in so far as it represented an attempt, by Owain Gwynedd, to regain and consolidate control of Gwynedd Is Conwy. When new stone castles were built from the late twelfth or early thirteenth century onwards, the considerations of their disposition were strategic rather than administrative. They are frequently found on the king's *ffridd*, as at Dolbadarn, Dolwyddelan and Bere, where extensive cow pastures were maintained, and it is no coincidence that these castles also control the mountain passes through Snowdonia (Jones, G R 1969, 35–9). In this respect the siting and status of the castle at Cwm Prysor might be significant. The location is *ffridd* (Ellis 1838, 292) but, by 1283, it would appear to be a *maerdref* (Johnstone forthcoming). The motte is undocumented, but could as well be Welsh as intrusive Norman given the proximity of Tomen-y-Mur where William Rufus campaigned in the 1090s. The commote of Ardudwy Uwch Artro lacks a lowland *maerdref*. Harlech on the coast was, however, a township under *tir cyfrif* tenure and in tradition, if nothing else, an appropriate place for the seat of kings (Williams 1982, 29). One wonders whether Prysor, on the *ffridd*, was an early manifestation of a trend towards strategically sited fortification at new locations which is more clearly represented in the thirteenth century at, for example, Dolbadarn and Cricieth, where new castles had begun to utilize the resources and take on many of the administrative functions of traditional *maerdrefi*.

A Hypothesis

On the basis of the preceding consideration of status sites the following working hypothesis proposes three stages of development. In a first period we might perceive a miscellany of 'royal' or 'high-status' sites of secular character. Some are fortified, occupying naturally defensible locations; Bryn Euryn and Dinas Emrys might be examples. Others, if the evidence of Aberffraw is accepted, could involve the enclosure of sites which are not inherently natural fortifications. Still others might not have been enclosed or fortified at all. This possibility remains to be demonstrated in the early period as it is the field evidence of fortification that, in default of other evidence, commands our attention in the identification of high status. The sites singled out for discussion are not all obviously linked to the pattern of commotal administration that is discernible by the thirteenth century, although some are. Is it possible to suggest a greater degree of diversity linked to political units which had not yet achieved that later coherence?

In our hypothetical second period, the disposition of royal sites reflects an emphasis on communication and accessibility in the way in which royal estates became established as foci of commotal administration and the exploitation of a taxable resource. These *llysoedd* with their associated *maerdrefi* appear, in general, not to have been fortified until the superimposition of intrusive earthwork castles during the Norman campaigns of the late eleventh century. Where Welsh fortifications *are* employed their disposition is determined by strategic rather than administrative considerations.

By the late twelfth century, stone castles were being built at Carn Fadrun and at Deudraeth (Thorpe 1978, 2.6) and possibly elsewhere. The recognition, in our final period, of the need for fortification must have occasioned a review of the role and siting of power bases. The new Welsh castles of the thirteenth century were predominantly on new sites which came to usurp the functions of the *maerdrefi* while they continued to exploit their resources. Indeed, the court came to spend as much of its time at the new castles as it did at the *maerdrefi*. Demesne lands continued to be exploited for the maintenance of the court at some traditional *maerdrefi*, but in some instances services had been transferred for the support of castles, and in others renders had been commuted for money payments.

In proposing this hypothesis the following questions, which might inform further research, suggest themselves. Firstly, if we are able to perceive some evidence for early medieval fortification, to what extent does this reflect a more extensive occurence in situations which are, in some cases, on the one hand morphologically indistinguishable from traditionally accepted Iron Age fortifications and which, on the other hand, reoccupy traditional 'Iron Age' locations? Conwy Mountain and Garn Boduan, for example, might be candidates for investigation. Secondly, to what extent is there a dislocation between forts of the early period and castles of the later period? We might put this question another way and ask whether the apparently accepted identification of Carn Fadrun as a twelfth-century castle represents the tail end of the stone fort tradition, encompassing Garn Boduan and others, or whether it marks the first phase of stone castle building?

Thirdly, we may wish to ask whether the sparse evidence for native fortification at the *maerdrefi* is genuine or illusory. Is the appearance of earthwork castles at *maerdrefi* a largely intrusive and short lived phenomenon or did the Welsh continue to use these mottes and build their own? Following this line of enquiry we might ask whether the distribution of *maerdrefi* (Fig 4.2) and the apparent absence of pre-Norman fortification genuinely characterizes a *maerdref* or whether it represents a stage in the continuous evolution of centres of power and authority? The increasing centralization of the functions of government, the increasing use of strategically sited castles as the focus of the court supported by money rents and the transfer of services from commotal centres, while retaining the maintenance of the royal estates at a reduced number of traditional *maerdrefi* (Stephenson 1984, *passim*), far from representing the decline of the *maerdref* system, characterized its maturation. The process was cut short in the late thirteenth century. Our perception of a traditional *maerdref* may be no more than a snap-shot in time of an evolving system. To understand the process of development and its culmination we must now seek evidence of its origins.

References

Alcock, L, 1967, Excavations at Degannwy Castle, *Archaeol J,* 124, 190–201

Alcock, L, 1971, *Arthur's Britain,* London

Alcock, L, 1981, *Early historic fortifications in Scotland,* in G Guilbert (ed), *Hill-fort studies,* Leicester, 150–80

Alcock, L, 1987, *Economy, society and warfare amongst the Britons and the Saxons,* Cardiff

Alcock, L, & E A, 1990, Reconnaissance excavations on early historic fortifications and other royal sites in Scotland, 1974–84: 4 Excavations at Alt Clut, Clyde Rock, Strathclyde, 1974–5, *Proc Soc Antiq Scot,* 120, 95–149

Avent R, 1983, *Castles of the Welsh princes,* London

Binchy, D A (ed), 1970, *Críth Gablach,* Dublin

Bromwich, R (ed), 1978, *Trioedd Ynys Prydein,* Cardiff

Campbell, E, 1988, The post-Roman pottery, in Edwards & Lane (eds), 124–36

Campbell, J (ed), 1982, *The Anglo-Saxons,* London

Carr, A D, 1972, The Extent of Anglesey, 1352, *Trans Anglesey Antiq Soc,* 1971–2, 150–272

Carr, A D, 1982, *Medieval Anglesey,* Llangefni

Dark, K R, 1994, *Discovery by design: the identification of secular élite settlements in Western Britain, AD 400–700,* Brit Archaeol Rep, Brit ser 237, Oxford

Davies, R R, 1991, *The age of conquest,* Oxford

Dumville, D N, 1984, *Gildas and Maelgwn: problems of dating,* in M Lapidge & D Dumville (eds), *Gildas: new approaches,* Studies in Celtic History 5, Woodbridge, 61–84

Edwards, N, & Lane, A (eds), 1988, *Early medieval settlements in Wales AD 400–1100,* Bangor, Cardiff

Ellis, H (ed), 1838, *Registrum Vulgariter Nuncupatum 'The Record of Caernarvon',* Record Commission, London

Evans, D S (ed), 1977, *Historia Gruffud vab Kenan,* Cardiff

Gardner, W, & Savory, H N, 1964, *Dinorben,* Cardiff

Griffiths, W E, & Hogg, A H A, 1956, The hillfort on Conwy Mountain, *Archaeol Cambrensis,* 105, 49–80

Guilbert, G, 1980, Dinorben C14 dates, *Current Archaeol,* 70, 336–8

Hogg, A H A, 1975, *A guide to the hill-forts of Britain,* London

Hopewell, D, 1993, Tre'r Ceiri conservation project, *Archaeol Wales*, 33, 49–50

Jackson, K, 1982, Gildas and the names of the British princes, *Cambridge Medieval Celtic Stud*, 33, 245–65

Jarrett, M G, 1969, *The Roman frontier in Wales*, Cardiff

Jenkins, D (trans), 1986, *The Law of Hywel Dda*, Llandysul

Johnstone, N, forthcoming, Llys *and* maerdref: *the royal courts of the princes of Gwynedd*

Jones, G R J, 1969, The defences of Gwynedd in the thirteenth century, *Trans Caernarvonshire Hist Soc*, 30, 29–43

Jones, G R J, 1991, Medieval settlement, in Manley *et al* (eds), 186–202

Jones, T (trans), 1952, *Brut y Tywysogion, Peniarth MS 20*, Cardiff

Jones, T (ed & trans), 1955, *Brut y Tywysogyon; the Red Book of Hergest version*, Cardiff

Jones, T, 1967, Englynion y beddau, *Proc Soc Brit Acad*, 53, 97–137

Jones Pierce, T, 1972, *Medieval Welsh society: selected essays by T Jones Pierce*, J B Smith (ed), Cardiff

Kelly, F, 1988, *A guide to early Irish law*, Dublin

Lynch, F, 1986, *Museum of Welsh Antiquities Bangor, Catalogue of archaeological material*, Bangor

MacNeill, E, 1923, The law of status or franchise, *Proc Roy Irish Acad*, 36C, 265–311

Manley, J *et al* (eds), *The archaeology of Clwyd*, Mold

Morris, J (ed & trans), 1980, *Nennius: British history and the Welsh annals*, London, Chichester

Nash-Williams, V E, 1950, *The early Christian monuments of Wales*, Cardiff

RCAHMW, 1956, *An inventory of the ancient monuments of Caernarvonshire, Vol I, East*, London

RCAHMW, 1960, *An inventory of the ancient monuments of Caernarvonshire, Vol II, Central*, London

RCAHMW, 1964, *An inventory of the ancient monuments of Caernarvonshire, Vol III, West*, London

Sherley-Price, L (trans), 1968, *Bede: A history of the English church and people*, Harmondsworth

Spurgeon, J, 1991, Mottes and moated sites, in Manley *et al* (eds), 157–72

Stephenson, D, 1984, *The governance of Gwynedd*, Cardiff

Thorpe, L (trans), 1978, *Giraldus Cambrensis: The journey through Wales/The description of Wales*, Harmondsworth

Vinogradoff, P, & Morgan, F (eds), 1914, *Survey of the Honour of Denbigh, 1334*, London

White, R, 1977, Sculptured stones from Aberffraw, Anglesey, *Archaeol Cambrensis*, 126, 140–5

White, R, & Longley, D, 1995, Excavations at Aberffraw, *Trans Anglesey Antiq Soc*, 13–22

Whitelock, D (ed), 1961, *The Anglo-Saxon Chronicle*, London

Williams, I (ed), 1982, *Pedeir keinc y Mabinogi*, Cardiff

Winterbottom, M (ed & trans), 1978, *Gildas: The ruin of Britain*, London, Chichester

An Investigation into the Location of the Royal Courts of Thirteenth-Century Gwynedd

Neil Johnstone

*Until recently comparatively little was known of the commotal courts (*llysoedd*) of the thirteenth-century princes of Gwynedd and their adjacent bond townships (*maerdrefi*). This study explores the nature of the evidence, documentary, antiquarian, place-name and topographical, for the locations of the* llysoedd *of Gwynedd. Aberffraw, Aber and Rhosyr are then examined in more detail to show how the locations of the* llysoedd *have been identified. Follow-up excavations on the sites identified at Aber and particularly at Rhosyr have uncovered important and extensive evidence for buildings and artefacts datable to the thirteenth and fourteenth centuries.*

By the twelfth and thirteenth centuries the administration of the kingdom of Gwynedd was based on a network of local foci serving an itinerant royal court. Gwynedd was divided into administrative areas known as commotes, each with a centre containing a local court or *llys* (Fig 5.1). The bond township in which the commotal *llys* was located was referred to as the *maerdref* ('reeve's township'). The component parts of a *llys* and *maerdref* complex included the *llys* itself, with its royal hall and other buildings, the royal demesne (*tir bwrdd*) worked by bond tenants and the settlement of the tenants, the *maerdref*, which might be close to the *llys*, and which is generally thought to have been nucleated.

Before this investigation began the names of most of the *llysoedd* of Gwynedd were known, but the precise locations of their buildings, with perhaps the sole exception of Degannwy, were yet to be securely identified. In the past the failure to locate these sites has rendered them vulnerable to a range of inadvertent threats, including agricultural, commercial and residential developments. For instance, at Aberffraw (Anglesey) a housing estate built in the 1950s and 60s now sprawls over the probable location of the court complex (see below) and at Llan-faes (Anglesey) an oil pipeline constructed in the 1970s cuts a 30m swathe through the fields where evidence of the pre-conquest town has recently been identified.

The Gwynedd Archaeological Trust's *Llys and Maerdref* Project, funded by Cadw, Welsh Historic Monuments, developed out of a rapid survey of the historic towns of Gwynedd. That survey, undertaken in 1991–2, highlighted the potential for investigating the pre-Edwardian settlements of Gwynedd. In 1992–3 the six *llys* sites in Anglesey were investigated. This work showed the value of using documentary evidence to trace landholdings, land transfers and property boundaries associated with the royal past (Figs 5.2, 5.3). Landscape features which might be indicative of *llys* locations were also considered, such as castles, churches and surviving settlements. The study was then extended to Caernarfonshire and Meirioneth and the documentary research was followed up by fieldwork, comprising field walking, geophysical survey and trial excavation at Aber (Caernarfonshire), Llan-faes and Rhosyr (Anglesey). In 1994 and 1995 extensive excavations were conducted at Rhosyr leading to the identification of several components of a *llys* complex.

This paper will begin by discussing current perceptions of the form of the commotal centres in thirteenth-century Gwynedd. Secondly, it will outline the methodology and the sources used in the identification and topographical reconstruction of the commotal centres. Finally, it will consider the results of research done to locate the site of the commotal centre at Aberffraw and of excavations at Aber and Rhosyr.

The Form of the Commotal Centres in Thirteenth-Century Gwynedd

By the thirteenth century the essential administrative subdivision of the kingdom was the commote. Each commote was divided into townships (see Longley, Fig 4.1), the basic unit of both settlement and taxation. One of these townships contained the royal court or *llys* with its associated *maerdref*, a nucleated settlement of bondmen whose services and renders maintained the court (Jones Pierce 1962, 39).

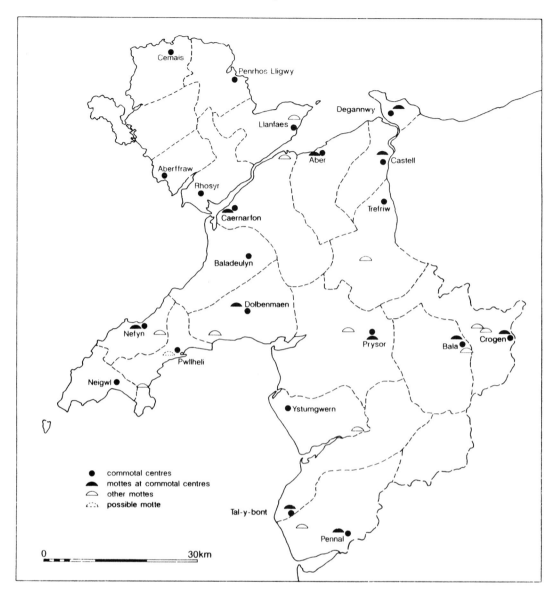

Fig 5.1 Commotes of Gwynedd and their llysoedd.

The Buildings of the Court Complex

The Welsh law books of the late twelfth and thirteenth centuries refer to the layout of the *llys* in which up to ten buildings were maintained by the bondmen of the commote. These included a hall, a chamber, a kitchen, a stable, a granary or barn, a kiln, kennels and a privy (Butler 1987, 49). The number of buildings varies according to the text: in *Llyfr Iorwerth*, for example, there are only seven, but in a revised version of that lawbook there are ten, two of which are located in the *maerdref*. It should be remembered that the laws may depict an ideal rather than the reality and for this reason the Edwardian extents, compiled after the conquest of 1282 possibly provide a truer account of the court buildings. Some court buildings were maintained by the English Crown into the early fourteenth century; others, however, were dismantled. Llywelyn's Hall at Conway was

repaired in 1302–6, but dismantled and moved to Caernarfon Castle in 1315 (Taylor 1974, 354). The hall at Ystumgwern was dismantled and moved to the inner ward of Harlech Castle in 1307 (Davies 1987, 355). In 1317 198 pieces of assorted timber from the court buildings at Aberffraw were also removed to Caernarfon Castle (Taylor 1974, 386). Court buildings at Aber were repaired in 1304 (PRO E101 485/30), and at Nefyn and Pwllheli in 1306 (Jones Pierce 1930, 150) probably in preparation for Prince Edward's intended visit in that year. But as A D Carr has said, 'There was really little use for the court buildings after 1282' (1982, 152). Indeed, there is no evidence to show that there was any attempt to maintain the buildings beyond the fourteenth century and most of the labour services owed on the court buildings appear to have been fairly quickly commuted to money payments (Carr 1982, 133, 152).

The Maerdref

In medieval documents the term *maerdref* is used to describe the legal status of the tenants and associated land. It has been used more recently to describe the actual settlement adjacent to the *llys*. Details in the law books throw some light on the layout of the *maerdref* and refer to the accommodation of the king's retinue within certain houses adjacent to the court. For example, the head of the household was to be accommodated in the largest and most central house in the settlement (*tref*) and the steward was expected to reside in lodgings nearest to the court (Wiliam 1960, 5–16, 20). All the available evidence suggests that the bond settlement of the court would have been nucleated; the *maerdref* was therefore in all probability a village (Jones, G R J 1985, 161).

'The existence of a nucleated settlement and the demands of a royal court provided a favourable context for urban growth' (Davies 1987, 165). Indeed, by the thirteenth century several *maerdrefi* seem to have achieved something equivalent to borough status. In Gwynedd the most successful of these emerging towns were Llan-faes, Nefyn and Pwllheli. Llan-faes, the largest of these settlements, had 120 tenements at the eve of the Edwardian conquest (Soulsby 1983, 166) and may have been granted a charter in the pre-Conquest period (Lewis 1912, 10). Burgesses of Nefyn are also mentioned in a late twelfth-century charter (Rees 1985, no 787). Small proto-urban communities were also beginning to emerge elsewhere, at Caernarfon and Trefriw, for instance (Carr 1992, 23). At Rhosyr a fair and market had been established prior to the foundation of the Edwardian borough of Newborough in 1303 (Carr 1982, 259). After the Edwardian conquest the trading monopolies and status of a number of these settlements were confirmed. Markets and fairs were given legal recognition at Aber and Aberffraw from the 1330s (Lewis 1912, 180). Nefyn and Pwllheli both received borough charters in 1355 (Lewis 1912, 31).

Tenurial Arrangements

There were two main types of bond tenure in pre-conquest Gwynedd; *tir gwelyog* and *tir cyfrif* (alternatively referred to as *maerdref* tenure). Originally *tir gwelyog* tenure was normal free tenure and was therefore the least restrictive form of bond tenure; bondmen who held land by it enjoyed the same rights of inheritance as freemen. *Tir cyfrif* (lit 'reckon land') was more restrictive than *tir gwelyog* tenure, since land held thus could not be inherited; instead bondmens' holdings under *tir cyfrif* were liable to be reallocated by the prince's officials. The *tir cyfrif* community was also liable for the whole burden of dues, even if there was a fall in the number of tenants. Bondmen in the *maerdref* owed the highest amount of labour services on the prince's demesne or *tir bwrdd* (Stephenson 1984, 58).

Some changes in the composition of the commotal centres can be seen to have occurred after the Edwardian conquest as, for example, the evolution of a class of tenants known as *gwŷr tir bwrdd* (lit 'men of the table land' or 'men of the demesne') who emerged 'as the result of demesne leasing after the Conquest' (Stephenson 1984, 59). Forms of tenure within the townships other than *tir cyfrif* were probably present prior to the Edwardian conquest. Jones Pierce believed that the appearance of newer settlements or tenures within the townships containing the *llys* came about as a result of the prince's right to exploit the waste (unenclosed land) (Jones Pierce 1972, 278). At Aberffraw for instance there were both bond and free tenants within the township (Seebohm 1904, 8).

Demesne Lands

The demesnes at five of the Anglesey *llysoedd* together amounted to 36 carucates (2160 acres) with appurtenant meadows and gardens (Jones Pierce 1972, 277). Even where a borough had evolved, the demesne was still a 'directly exploited resource of the princes' (Stephenson 1984, 57). At Llan-faes there were thirteen carucates of demesne and three at Pwllheli. There are a number of factors which suggest that there may have been little intention on the part of the new Edwardian administration to maintain any direct demesne farming following the conquest. From early in the fourteenth century demesne lands were farmed out to English officials or leased to various tenants. In addition the commutation of labour services into cash payments 'brought to an end the situation still just visible in the Edwardian extents, where the bondmen and demesne had maintained the ruler and his court' (Carr 1992, 16).

Edward I's boroughs also had an effect on the layout of the commotal centres. They were almost all built on Welsh royal bond townships. At Llan-faes the town and demesne lands were absorbed within the new borough boundary of Beaumaris and the residents of Llan-faes were forcibly resettled on the old demesne lands at Rhosyr (Carr 1982, 258). A further six carucates of demesne at Caernarfon and two at Conway were incorporated into the two newly created boroughs (Lewis 1912, 44–9). Further afield parts of the demesne at Ystumgwern were acquired by the burgesses of Harlech (Gresham 1988, 221–2). At Bala the new borough was established partly on the old royal demesne (Lewis 1912, 55).

Sources for the Identification and Topographical Reconstruction of the Commotal Centres

Documentary Sources

There are a range of documentary sources which provide information on both the location and composition of the *llysoedd* and *maerdrefi* of Gwynedd. The earliest sources consulted include: the letters and charters of the Welsh princes, the post-conquest itineraries of Edward I, and the Edwardian extents.

Owing to the paucity of documentary evidence prior to the Edwardian conquest, it is seldom possible to chart the progress of the prince's court and where it stayed. However,

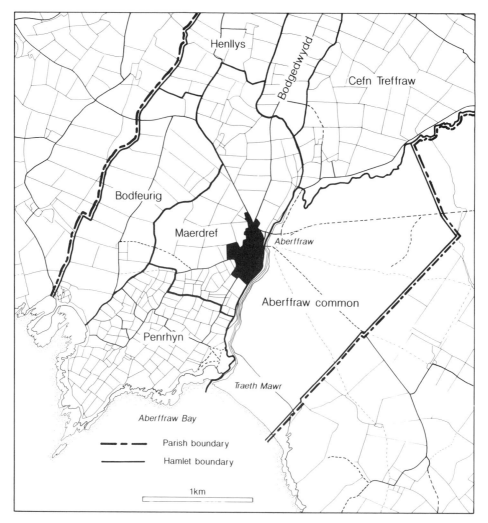

Fig 5.2 Reconstruction of the hamlets within the medieval township of Aberffraw. The shaded area indicates the present extent of the village.

some letters and charters were written at the commotal centres during the reigns of both Llywelyn ap Iorwerth (1190-1240) and Llywelyn ap Gruffudd (1255–82) (Edwards, J G 1940; Maund 1996, *passim*). Furthermore, Stephenson (1984, 233–4) has tentatively plotted the movements of the court for the period between July 1273 and January 1277, which included stays at the *llysoedd* of Aber, Penrhos and Tal-y-bont. The court also visited the prince's stone castles at Dolwyddelan and Cricieth, and monastic granges, including Abereiddon and Dinasteleri which belonged to the Cistercian Abbey of Cymer.

The itinerary which Edward I undertook of his newly conquered territories following the defeat of Llywelyn ap Gruffudd in 1282 is rather more useful because it is more complete. It included the majority of the commotal centres and a number of sites known on other grounds to have been pre-conquest royal sites are mentioned for the first time, for example Castell Prysor (1st July 1284) and Dolbenmaen (13th August 1284) (*CChW* 1927).

Following the defeat of Llywelyn ap Gruffudd in 1282, the English Crown acquired all the bond townships which

had previously been the exclusive property of the Welsh princes (Williams 1958, 38). Jones Pierce (1972, 274) has calculated that on Anglesey alone this must have been as many as 40 townships. Among the properties now administered by the Crown were all the old commotal centres which had formed the basis of the pre-Edwardian administration. The rents for the bond vills, including the commotal centres, were now paid to the Caernarfon Exchequer; however the commotal centres were often farmed out to royal favourites and local *uchelwyr* ('gentry') (Carr 1982, 85).

As already indicated the Edwardian extents (Carr 1972; Jones, M C 1867, 184–92) of the late thirteenth and mid fourteenth centuries are of great interest for the details they give of the former Welsh administrative system and they also include important information on land tenure. Furthermore, information regarding the duties owed by the inhabitants of the commotes to work on the court buildings provides a realistic account of those buildings in the immediate post-conquest period. The information contained in the Edwardian surveys is also crucial in attempting any topographical reconstructions of the town-

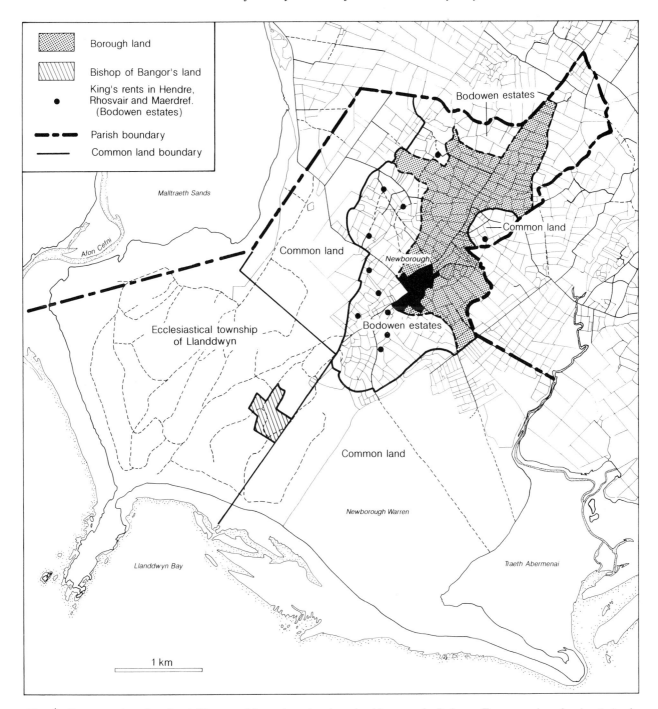

Fig 5.3 Reconstruction of medieval Rhosyr and its environs based on the tithe map, the Bodowen Estate rentals and a description by Henry Rowlands of the borough estate boundaries. The land indicated by the Bodowen Estate rentals is the area of the former bond lands of the maerdref *of Rhosyr. The black area indicates the extent of the present town of Newborough.*

ships. Other Crown administrative records have also proved useful: the ministers' accounts, for instance, provide information on expenditure on repairs to court buildings in the fourteenth century (Jones Pierce 1930, 149–55).

Despite a decline in the number of bond tenants following the effects of the plague in the mid fourteenth century and a resultant loss of revenue, by the end of the century there had been an improvement in the returns from bond townships (Jones Pierce 1972, 44). However the unsettled

conditions of the fifteenth century, commencing as it did with Owain Glyndwr's rebellion, precipitated the demise of the bond vills: 'by the end of the fifteenth century bond land in many parts of the county lay untenanted and desolate' (Williams 1958, 41).

Even in the late fifteenth century and despite the decline in the bond population, the bond townships were still in theory *tir caeth* 'bond land', and for that reason were not attractive to the landed gentry, although 'the outskirts of many of the bond vills had been absorbed into adjoining freeholds' (Jones Pierce 1972, 47) by this period. Possibly in order to facilitate the exploitation of bond land, in 1507 the bondmen of the Principality of North Wales were granted a charter of emancipation (Smith, J B 1966–7, 157–9, 162–6). Following the charter, leases of the bond townships by the Crown were granted on a far larger scale than had previously been the case. This resulted in a series of disputes between the new lessees, usually the local gentry, and the tenants of the bond vills. These disputes can be followed in the Records of the Court of Augmentations (Lewis & Davies 1954) and subsequently in the Exchequer Proceedings Concerning Wales (Jones, E G 1939). Both sources often provide valuable information on the identity of the Crown lessee and frequently contain useful information about internal arrangements within the townships. It is often the case that the Crown properties are retained and subsequently incorporated within the estates of the earliest lessees; their later history can therefore be found in the surviving estate papers.

From the reign of Henry VII the Crown appointed special surveyors to supervise the granting of leases of Crown land; subsequently Thomas Cromwell extended the use of auditors and surveyors. Records relating to this period of the administration of Crown lands are to be found in the Public Record Office in the Land Revenue Collection. Among these one particular Land Revenue survey dated 1608 stands out for the wealth of information it contains on Crown lands in Anglesey (PRO LR 2/205). During the reign of Charles I and the Commonwealth there were extensive sales of Crown land in north Wales (Williams 1958, 34). In 1628 a large amount of the Crown lands in both Anglesey and Caernarfonshire was obtained by the Corporation of London in lieu of a debt owed by Charles I (CLRO Research Paper 2.29). This was fairly soon sold to local landowners in north Wales, and several hamlets at Aberffraw and Rhosyr were included among the transactions (CLRO Royal Contract Estates Sales Contracts 114d).

References to, or the original documents of, the purchase of Crown lands are occasionally to be found amongst estate records. Many of the new proprietors continued to refer to their new acquisitions as manors in their estate rentals. Indeed, three of the sites on Anglesey, Aberffraw, Cemais and Penrhosllugwy, held manorial courts in the eighteenth and nineteenth centuries, although this does not imply any continuity of this practice (for a discussion on the manorial courts prior to the Act of Union, see Williams 1958, 29). Such estate records are valuable because they may include documentation such as inquisitions into manor boundaries. Estate papers may also contain detailed maps, though for Gwynedd these are usually no earlier than the late eighteenth century; these provide the earliest cartographic sources for the former *maerdrefi*. A full list of field-names also occurs for the first time in this source providing further possible evidence. Where estate maps are unavailable the tithe maps *c* 1840 may also provide the means to plot the extent of a particular estate's property within a parish.

Antiquarian Evidence

A fairly extensive search was also made of antiquarian material because, in many instances, it provides the only references to the possible locations of some of the *llys* sites. Among the more useful of these sources were the accounts of John Leland (Smith, L T 1906), Thomas Pennant (1883) and Richard Fenton (1917); local commentators, such as Henry Rowlands (1846), Angharad Llwyd (1833) and Lewis Morris (1878) also refer to a number of the *llysoedd*. Some sites, Aberffraw and Aber, for example, were on popular antiquarian itineraries and received a considerable amount of comment, while some of the less well known sites, such as Penrhosllugwy, are only mentioned once (Fenton 1917, 350). While such references need to be treated with caution, in several instances it is clear that the observations derive from local traditions about the supposed site of the *llys* and such accounts are therefore potentially of some importance.

Place-name Evidence

Place-names may provide further vital information on the location of a *llys* and *maerdref* complex. Sources consulted include the Melville Richards place-name archive, University of Wales, Bangor, the medieval documents referred to above and cartographic sources. The name *maerdref* in its various forms is of considerable importance; it is still used at Degannwy and Neigwl for the former demesne and was used at Aberffraw and Rhosyr until the seventeenth century. Other place-name indicators, such as *Henllys* ('former court') and *Gadlys* ('camp' or 'headquarters') (*Geiriadur Prifysgol Cymru*) have also been considered. Of these, *Gadlys* often appears in association with supposed *llys* locations, as for example, at Penrhosllugwy, Nefyn, and Pwllheli, and also adjacent to the bishop of Bangor's *maerdref* at Treffos (Anglesey). *Gadlys* can however be a notorious red herring as it is often interchangeable with *gadlas* ('rickyard').

Topographic Evidence

The notion that a *llys* might, in some instances, be based at a castle is unpopular among some archaeologists who tend to see the *llys* as 'lightly protected within an enclosure, perhaps surrounded by a palisade or stone wall' (Avent 1983, 6). The problem may be caused by the rigidity of the terminology employed. A *llys* could be a defended or non-defended residence with administrative functions. At Degannwy, for example, it would be perverse to argue that the *llys* in the thirteenth century was anything other than the castle located on the two hillocks on the east bank of the Conwy estuary. Cricieth Castle may also have taken over the administrative functions of the *llys* at Dolbenmaen where there is a motte (Gresham 1973, 372). However, on the whole, the thirteenth-century stone castles were sited away from the commotal centres (Jones, G R J 1969, 35), but the relationship between *llysoedd* and earthwork castles is more telling. The motte-and-bailey complex at Marford

(Flintshire), described by Pratt under the heading 'Castle, Court and *Llys*', is a tacit recognition of the problem of terminology. Here the eleventh-century motte, possibly the site of the court of Osbern Fitztesso, was 'rebuilt to become the new *llys* of Madog ap Maredudd (d 1160) (Pratt 1992, 35). But speculation concerning the relationship between mottes and *llysoedd* is not entirely new; the Royal Commission referred to fortified *llysoedd* (RCAHMW 1964, cxliii) as did Stephenson (1984, 4) in the context of Aber, Caernarfon and Nefyn.

The initial report on the *Llys* and *Maerdref* project drew attention to the correlation between the siting of Norman earthwork castles and the location of *llysoedd* in Gwynedd. The Royal Commission had already noted that 'there was a basic pattern of one castle (motte) to each commote in Caernarvonshire' (RCAHMW 1964, cxli). The resulting distribution of mottes further emphasizes the relationship between *llys* locations and earthwork castles (Fig 5.1). With the exception of the six Anglesey *llysoedd*, and four other sites, Baladeulyn, Neigwl, Trefriw and Ystumgwern, all the commotal centres appear to have been located in the vicinity of a motte. The fact that there are no mottes associated with the *llysoedd* on Anglesey is an exception which requires further explanation.

That a number of the mottes in the vicinity of *llysoedd* may originally have been Norman constructions is not in doubt: Degannwy, Caernarfon, and possibly Bala fall into this category (see Longley p 43). However the evidence clearly suggests that several other mottes associated with *llysoedd,* such as Dolbenmaen and Nefyn, were constructed in areas outside Norman influence and are therefore almost certainly Welsh. Avent also noted that, although there were hardly any references in the *Brut y Tywysogyon* to castles being built by the Welsh, there were plenty of references to Norman castles being captured and occupied by them (Avent 1994, 11). The association of mottes with commotal centres is a phenomenon also present beyond Gwynedd: of the 154 *maerdrefi* identified on the *Ordnance Survey Map of Britain before the Norman Conquest* the majority have castles in their vicinity.

The construction and use of mottes in Wales into the thirteenth century is well documented. There appears, however, to be a remarkable reluctance to acknowledge a similar pattern within Gwynedd, despite numerous contemporary references. Llywelyn ap Iorwerth's predecessors Owain Gwynedd and his brother Cadwaladr were active in raising new earthwork castles as well as occupying those of the enemy. Owain built the motte at Tomen-y-Rhodwydd (Denbighshire) in 1149 and captured the motte at Basingwerk (Flintshire) in 1166, and those at Prestatyn and Rhuddlan (Flintshire) in 1167. He is also credited with building a motte at Corwen (Merioneth) in 1165. It has also been suggested that Cadwaladr built two ringworks, one at Castell Cynfal (Merioneth) in 1147, and the second at Llanrhystud (Cardiganshire) in 1149 (Spurgeon 1987, 31). In 1202 the mottes at Bala and Crogen were both captured by Llywelyn ap Iorwerth (Jones, T 1952, 82) and

probably retained in use (Johnstone forthcoming).

The relationship between motte-and-bailey castles and commotal centres is particularly evident in Meirioneth where, with the exception of the *llys* at Ystumgwern, there is a motte in the immediate vicinity of each of the commotal centres (Smith, L B 1975, 34). While we may accept that both Llywelyns were primarily engaged in the construction of stone castles in locations away from the commotal centres, we cannot ignore the possibility that a number of the *llysoedd* were already fortified with earthwork castles. At what point the motte ceased to be of any military importance is another matter. The available evidence does however suggest that if a *llys* was originally fortified, the residence remained focused on the motte even if this no longer had any defensive capability. This must be true at Crogen, where the fourteenth-century hall house is located adjacent to the motte (RCAHMW 1949) and at Tyn-y-Mwd, Aber, where the recently excavated medieval hall is also situated next to the motte (see below).

Very few of the *tir cyfrif* and lay *tir gwelyog* townships had their own church (this information is provided in relation to Anglesey in Carr 1982, 38). However there were royal chapels at most of the *maerdrefi*. On Anglesey, apart from the commotal centres, Llanllibio was the only *tir cyfrif* township with a church; however this may not be an exception as there is reason to believe that Llanllibio had once been the location of the *llys* of the commote of Llifon (Johnstone forthcoming). These royal chapels were served by a household priest and 'presumably resembled royal chapels in medieval England . . . [which] included churches on estates visited by the itinerant court' (Pryce 1993, 148).

Some of the royal chapels had been granted in the time of the princes to monastic houses, for instance Llywelyn ap Gruffudd granted the chapels at Llanbadrig (Cemais) and Llanbeblig (Caernarfon) to Aberconwy (Stephenson 1984, 204). Others were subsequently granted by the English Crown, for example Llan-faes and Penrhoslugwy were acquired by Penmon Priory in 1394 (Carr 1982, 273). At the remainder presentments were made by the Crown on a regular basis after 1282 (Carr 1982, 282). Many royal chapels subsequently became parish churches as territorial parishes developed; but others went into decline after the abandonment of the court, including the probable royal chapels at Ystumgwern, known as Capel y Temlwydd, and Capel Halen at Penrhoslugwy (Johnstone forthcoming). In a number of instances, where the exact location of the *llys* is known or suspected, it would appear that the chapel was located immediaetly adjacent to the *llys*, for example at Aberffraw, Rhosyr and Trefriw. However this does not appear to have been so in every case; the *llys* at Caernarfon (if it was indeed based at the motte located within the later Edwardian castle) would have been 1km north west of the church at Llanbeblig. The new borough which replaced the Welsh settlement did not establish a church within the town walls until 1307 (RCAHMW 1960, 123). At Trefriw tradition records that Llywelyn ap Iorwerth established a church there because of the inconvenience of attending the existing church at Llanrhychwyn 1.7km to the south east suggesting that the village and royal hall were not originally located adjacent to a convenient place of worship (Pennant 1883, 155). At Pwllheli the medieval borough and *llys* was 0.6km south of the church of St Beuno which is located near a *Henllys* place-name.

The provision of royal chapels at each *llys* may have been a fairly late development (or alternatively they may be contemporary with the foundation of the network of royal courts at each commote which may itself be a late occurrence). There are few instances where the foundation date of a chapel is known, although there is some slight indication that the royal chapels may have been late foundations. The life of Gruffudd ap Cynan (d 1137) claims that he was responsible for building chapels in all the major courts (Evans 1990, 50), while the church at Trefriw is associated with Llywelyn ap Iorwerth. It is possible therefore that in the early medieval period the needs of the royal courts could have been provided by the nearest mother church. As such the court at Degannwy would have been served by the important church of Eglwys yn Rhos (Carr 1992, 7) and Aberffraw by the royal foundation of Eglwys Ail, Llangadwaladr, which may be traced back to the seventh century (Nash-Williams 1950, no 13).

The location of *llysoedd* and their relationship to surviving settlements and their medieval predecessors is of significance. 'Why do villages die? In fact most bond communities which existed in medieval Wales have vanished, they only survived where there were conditions conducive to their survival' (Carr 1982, 33). It is the relationship between the modern villages and their medieval predecessors that may be of particular importance when considering the location of the *llys*. Aberffraw, Aber, and Trefriw provide examples. It should already be apparent that many of the commotal centres already possessed a number of characteristics of small nucleated centres: the *llys*, the bond settlement with its market and fairs, and perhaps a royal chapel. Many were also located near the coast, locations which were conducive to commerce; the villagers were therefore not wholly dependent on agricultural activities. Several of these sites were officially recognized by the English Crown as market towns in their respective localities during the fourteenth century, for example Aber, Trefriw, Dolgellau and Aberffraw (Lewis 1912, 175). If these are indeed surviving medieval settlements, as they almost certainly must be, then the growth and expansion of these villages (massively accelerated since the mid nineteenth century) forms the main threat to the site of the *llys*. In some instances these settlements may have expanded in the postmedieval period. At Pwllheli, for example, the probable location of the *llys* may long since have been overwhelmed by later development. But at Aberffraw the probable site of the *llys* was only built on in the 1950s and 1960s. At Aber and Trefriw, where the *llysoedd* may remain unencumbered by village expansion, both locations have been subjects of recent planning applications as such open spaces become more sought after for housing development.

In several instances, where there is sufficient documentation, attempts have been made to reconstruct the medieval township boundaries. The success of such an approach often depends on the amount of information contained in the Edwardian extents. In many respects it is the relationship of the modern parish boundary to the earlier secular township boundary which provides the most accessible link between the medieval and modern landscapes.

It is generally agreed that ecclesiastical parish boundaries in Gwynedd, which were only accurately mapped for the first time on the mid nineteenth-century tithe maps, had undergone numerous alterations since the twelfth and thirteenth centuries (Gresham 1987, 137; Richards 1969). The ecclesiastical parish did not acquire any civil administrative functions until the Tudor period when it became increasingly important in, for example, the relief and maintenance of the poor. Even after the establishment of the new political order in 1536 and 1542 the Court of Quarter Sessions, which replaced the county court of the medieval period, continued to record details of an indicted person according to the township in which he resided and not the parish. 'Medieval townships were referred to in the records of the Crown auditors and other records relating to Crown revenues until much later, since Crown rents and dues continued to be based upon the economic system of the medieval principality' (Williams 1958, 43). It is for this reason, perhaps, that references to townships are often found in eighteenth-century land tax records, in particular for Anglesey. The continued use of the township as a meaningful unit is also apparent in many estate records, in rentals and land transactions well into the nineteenth century.

A number of simple rules have been observed in the original relationship between parish and township boundaries. Parishes could be coterminous with townships while a larger parish might contain a number of smaller townships exactly within its boundary (Gresham 1987, 141). On the other hand a single township could not normally extend into more than one parish. Where these simple rules are not followed, this is usually believed to be a result of later reorganization. A number of the *maerdref* townships were among the bond townships which were coterminous with single parishes, as for example at Penrhosllugwy and Dolbenmaen.

While it is impossible to be certain in all instances, it does appear that there has been little adjustment to the original parish/township boundaries in the case of many of the commotal centres. In many instances the medieval layout seems to have been fossilized into the modern period. Where information contained in the Edwardian extents is particularly detailed it has proved possible to reconstruct the internal arrangements of the townships, as for example, at Aberffraw and Rhosyr (Figs 5.2, 5.3). This may in part be due to the continuous administration of these units by Crown officials and to continuity of ownership.

Case Studies

Aberffraw

Figure 5.2 shows a topographical reconstruction of the separate hamlets within the township of Aberffraw. This is based on evidence contained in the extent of 1352 (Carr 1972) together with later Crown surveys (PRO LR 2/205) and eighteenth- and nineteenth-century documentation (in particular GRO Llangefni MS LIQ+/1/1 and the late eighteenth-century estate map, UWB Llys Dulas MS 53). The reconstruction clearly shows *maerdref* to have been a term specific to the central part of the township rather than a general term for the whole area. The *maerdref* boundary follows natural and man-made features such as streams and roads.

There is still some doubt as to the precise location of the *llys* complex at Aberffraw. A number of locations have been proposed. The most recent suggestion considers that the centre of the present village lies on the site formerly occupied by the *llys* (Edwards, N & Lane, A 1988, 21). This interpretation is based on a consideration of excavations conducted in the 1970s (White 1979). The excavations revealed a complex sequence of banks and ditches which appear to form a rectangular enclosure, but there was insufficient evidence to allow for any certainty in the date of the two or possibly three phases of construction (Edwards, N & Lane, A 1988, 21; White & Longley 1995). White suggested (1978, 355) that the earliest phases were related to a Roman fort subsequently reused in the post-Roman period; however others have argued that the entire sequence is post-Roman and the enclosure has been accepted as the site of the early medieval *llys* (Edwards, N & Lane, A 1988, 21; Jones, G R J 1985, 161). But current research has shown that there is another more likely location for the *llys*. This is supported by specific antiquarian observations, by logical deductions concerning the *llys* and its topographical setting in relation to the bond settlement which existed there in the thirteenth century, and by the likely fate of the *llys* location once it had been abandoned.

There are numerous antiquarian references which mention remains of the *llys* located at the west end of the village near the church (Edwards, N & Lane, A 1988, 20). The most specific of these is the legend printed on a late eighteenth-century estate map:

> 'Here about antiently stood the Royal Palace of the Princes of North Wales of the Welch Blood of which at present nothing remains the stones have been carried for making Hedges and for Building Houses about 30 years ago'.
>
> (The original map is located at Bodorgan Hall, estate survey 1773, but there is a later copy, UWB, Llys Dulas MS 53.)

If we are to accept that the rectangular enclosure identified in the 1970s relates to the location of the *llys* in the thirteenth century, this implies that the medieval village has been relocated on the site of the former *llys*. It is however far more logical to expect that the eventual expansion of the village would at some stage have overwhelmed the former site of the *llys*. Indeed, the remains of the court complex are likely to have discouraged any building on the site for some time. As indicated above, antiquarian and cartographic evidence strongly suggests that remains of the *llys* were still visible in the mid eighteenth century. The area in question was only developed in the 1950s and 60s when the housing estate called Maes Llywelyn was built.

Aber

Aber is often referred to as one of the favourite residences of the princes of Gwynedd in the thirteenth century (Davies 1987, 119). Both princess Joan, the wife of Llywelyn ap Iorwerth, and Dafydd ap Llywelyn, his son, died there in 1237 and 1246 respectively (Jones, T 1952, 104, 107). After the Edwardian conquest there are references to repairs to the buildings of the *llys* in both 1289 and 1303; the latter is reproduced below:

> 'In preparing the site of the Hall and Chamber [at Aber] at task 8/- To Masons supplying carriage of stone, setters, porters, and in carriage of sand at task by William of Kyrkby and Ithell of Bangor masons in the 3rd year of Prince Edward £17. 9s. 3d.
>
> Total £17. 17s. 3d.'

> 'Further expenses laid out on the works of the Hall and Chamber of the Lord Prince at Aber in the 6th year of Prince Edward, by the hands of Richard of Hokenhall (? Hucknall), namely:-
>
> In carriage of 4 boatloads of stone from the sea to Aber at task, at (several) times 4/- And to hiring 2 carts with 2 horses and 2 boys (or grooms) for carrying stones of freestone, lime and sand, for 57 working days 28/6d. That is each taking 3d. a day.'

(PRO E101/485/30)

There are numerous antiquarian accounts which refer to remains associated with the *llys* at Aber being visible near the motte at Tyn-y-Mwd. The earliest is Leland's of 1530 (Smith, T L 1908, 84). While it is often considered that this reference could be applied to a number of locations in Aber a recent analysis of the account and its context supports the idea that Leland is referring to the motte (RCAHMW 1993). Pennant and others certainly believed that remains associated with Llywelyn ap Iorwerth were still visible at Tyn-y Mwd (Pennant 1883). However, by the second half of the nineteenth century, speculation concerning the site of the *llys* had turned to the late medieval house known as Pen-y-Bryn to the east (eg Hughes & North 1924, 154–5).

In January 1993 Gwynedd Archaeological Trust undertook a small assessment excavation in the field immediately adjacent to the motte occasioned by a planning application for residential development. The assessment identified the foundations of a large building in association with thirteenth- and fourteenth-century pottery. In November 1993 a further excavation was conducted as part of the *Llys* and *Maerdref* project. This was intended to clarify the nature of the structure recognized in the earlier excavation. A rectangular stone structure 26m long × 10.2m wide and aligned north/south was uncovered (Fig 5.4). It may be suggested that

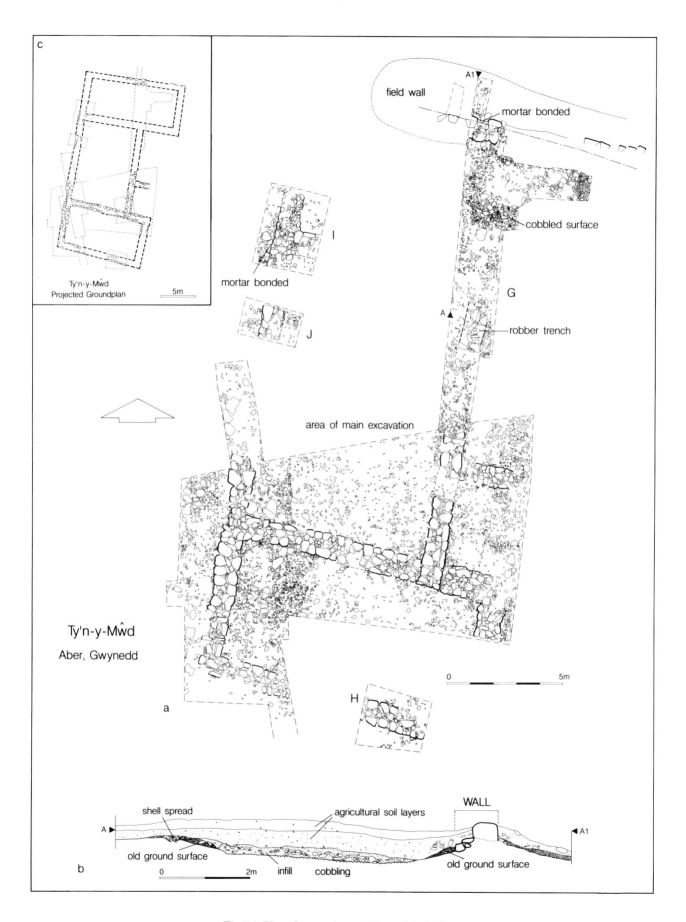

Fig 5.4 Plan of excavations at Tyn-y-Mwd, Aber.

internally it was divided into three units with projecting wings at the north and south ends. The central hall unit measured 11.2 × 8m internally; the southern wing 10.8 × 5m internally and the northern wing less certainly 13 × 5m internally. The structure had been robbed leaving only a single course of its foundations and the northern limit of the building had been incorporated into a later field boundary. The width of the foundations was generally 1.1m and they were typically composed of an inner and outer face of large, rounded boulders with a rubble infill of brown silty clay. There was also evidence of modifications to the original structure in two instances. First, the south end of the east wall of the central unit had been truncated and the north wall of the south wing butted this wall at this point. Second, the use of mortar in the north wing also implies a later alteration. The artifacts recovered included over 30 sherds of thirteenth- and fourteenth-century pottery and a decorated bronze ring brooch of similar date. It may therefore be suggested that the building was probably the main hall of the *llys* complex, which had undergone a number of alterations during its use.

Rhosyr

Rhosyr was the administrative centre of the commote of Menai. A charter of Llywelyn ap Iorwerth was issued there in 1237 (*CChR* 1257–1300, 460; Maund 1996, no 140)

and a fair and market were well established before the conquest (Carr 1982, 267). The pre-conquest demesne extended over 600 acres and in 1303 the new borough of Newborough was established on these lands (Lewis 1912, 52). Fourteenth-century documents refer to some elements of the pre-conquest *llys* including the hall of the manor, the fence around the lord's manor, a chapel, the steward's hall, the privy and the stable (Carr 1972, 247). In 1332 over 200 acres of land were lost as the result of a sand storm (Carr 1982, 262) and blown sand must have been a persistent problem. In the eighteenth century Henry Rowlands (1846, 311) referred to the sand-covered walls of the former *llys* a short distance south of the church, but by the twentieth century nothing was visible.

The local place-name, Cae Llys ('Court Field'), together with the generalized locational information provided by antiquarian sources, the topography and the apparent association with the adjacent church recommended the site for limited trial excavation during 1992–3. Structural debris, including stone walling and stratified pottery of the thirteenth and fourteenth centuries confirmed the potential of the site for further work.

There have subsequently been two seasons of excavation at Cae Llys resulting in the identification of a number of buildings and the extent of the site is now more fully understood (Fig 5.5). Within the perimeter wall of the *llys* three buildings have been investigated. The largest (Building

Fig 5.5 The llys *at Rhosyr, view from the south with Building B in the foreground and Building A behind (photograph: author).*

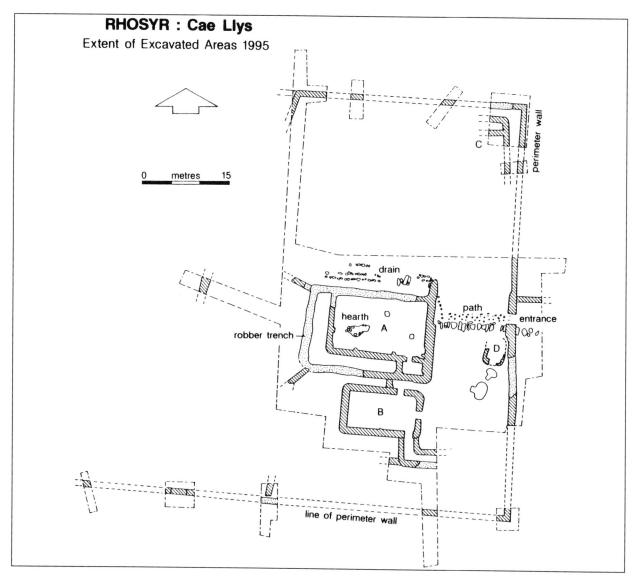

Fig 5.6 Plan of excavations at Cae Llys, Rhosyr.

A) measures 20 × 14m and it appears to have been of at least two phases. The first phase comprised a rectangular block 15m long by 9m wide internally. This building may have subsequently been enlarged with the addition of ranges on the south and west sides forming additional rooms 2m wide with a further division at the south-east corner forming a small room measuring 2m by 4m internally. There had been a considerable amount of stone robbing: the north side of the building was defined by a robber trench, as was the range on the west side. An external stone surface laid to the north of the structure had been provided with a drain. Towards the east end of the building the drain had a number of large capping stones, some of which probably also served as a laid path leading into the structure. A number of internal features were excavated including the probable hearth, which consisted of an oval stone plinth located slightly off centre at the west end of the building.

A second building (B) was identified in 1995. It was located to the south of Building A parallel to and almost immediately adjoining it. This structure measured 13m long by 7.5m wide and the stone walls survived in places to a height of 1m. There were three entrances into the building, one in the eastern gable end and the other two towards the eastern end of the north and south walls respectively. A substantial corridor led away from the south entrance and may have acted as a pentice connecting this building to another structure to the south east. A third substantial and well preserved building (C) has also been recognized in the north-eastern corner of the enclosure, although its complete plan has yet to be uncovered.

The line of the perimeter wall around the site has now been recovered on the north, south and east sides and, while there has been significant stone robbing, the walls still stand up to eight courses high (up to 1.1m) in places. Two entrances, one on the east and the other on the south, have also been located; the southern entrance has dressed sandstone blocks still *in situ*. A path lead from the eastern entrance in the direction of Building A. The southern side of the path was flanked by a series of large flagstones and led to a well-laid surface of flat stones below the east end of Building A which pre-date the floor levels of the building thereby suggesting an earlier phase. An area with evidence for some form of specialized production, either industrial or domestic, has also been recognized, together with the remains of a small building (D) to the south of the eastern entrance through the perimeter wall. Artifacts recovered include a spur and pottery and coins of the thirteenth and fourteenth centuries; slags suggest the presence of metal-working on the site.

On the basis of the evidence retrieved to date it is tempting to see Building A as a hall, probably the main hall of the *llys*, and Building B as a private chamber. Differences in the quality of the foundations of the hall and ranges of Building A might also suggest that the hall was of timber construction on stone footings. At present there are no immediate parallels for the ground plan of Building A with other known medieval buildings in Gwynedd, although a similar arrangement of rooms occurs at the much larger early thirteenth-century aisled hall at Tintern Abbey, Monmouthshire (Courtney 1989, 105). The dimensions of the hall without the ranges are comparable to the dimensions of the largest known medieval hall in Gwynedd, that of the bishop's palace at Gogarth (RCAHMW 1956, 113).

Conclusions

This paper has demonstrated how, through a detailed analysis of documentary, antiquarian, place-name and topographical evidence, it has proved possible to locate a number of the *llysoedd* of Gwynedd and their adjacent *maerdrefi* on the ground. Reconstructions of the tenurial basis of the medieval landscape, as for instance at Aberffraw and Rhosyr, have shown how former administrative divisions can be traced and still influence the layout of the modern landscape. Excavations at Aber and Rhosyr have recovered important evidence of the halls and other buildings of the *llys*.

It has also been shown that agricultural, commercial and residential developments have all had a detrimental affect on the locations of the *llysoedd* and *maerdrefi* of Gwynedd. Village expansion, in particular over the last century, has proved the most damaging, with the possibility that several *llys* locations may have been destroyed.

Much work still remains to be done. Where the exact location of a *llys* complex has yet to be established with certainty, this should be resolved. There are several avenues which might be pursued in order to pinpoint exact locations. At Nefyn, for instance, the construction of new ovens for the royal tournament held in 1284 (Jones Pierce 1957) would appear to offer an ideal opportunity for a magnetometer survey of the target area followed up, if successful, by a small scale assessment excavation; such trial excavations at Cae Llys, Rhosyr and Tyn-y-Mwd, Aber provided

worthwhile results which were subsequently followed up by larger excavations. Where recent village expansion may already have proved destructive retrospective evidence might be forthcoming from aerial photographs taken during the 1940s by the RAF.

The archaeology of the dependent *maerdref* has been as neglected as that of the *llys* itself. In Gwynedd, for instance, only at Aberffraw has there been any archaeological investigation in advance of development, and this was conducted in the mistaken belief that such investigation would provide information about the *llys*. Evidence for the origins and form of *llysoedd* and *maerdrefi* will only be forthcoming if there is more excavation. Sites where the medieval settlement has failed such as Llan-faes (Anglesey), Neigwl (Caernarfonshire) and Ystumgwern (Meirioneth) could yet provide a full picture of a royal *llys* and its bond settlement or *maerdref*.

Almost 30 years ago Beresford concluded that too little was known of the topography of the pre-Edwardian boroughs to 'reveal whether the arrangements of streets and burgages were those of a planned addition or an organic transformation of rural holdings' (Beresford 1967, 528). Geophysical survey results obtained at Llan-faes may finally have begun to shed some light on the layout of the pre-conquest settlement there (Johnstone forthcoming). More information might be obtained from analysis of historical data and detailed surveys. Jones Pierce suggested that Pwllheli might have been a new planned settlement of the thirteenth century with regular burgage plots located away from the original focus at Henllys to the north (Jones Pierce 1972, 144). The layout of the village of Nefyn is also intriguing, as it has an oval area to the east of Stryd-y-Ffynnon between the church and the motte has all the appearance of a planned settlement.

More work on the relationship between mottes and *llysoedd* is also required. That earthwork castles were utilized throughout the thirteenth century is not in doubt; the occurrence of so many at the commotal centres implies that in some instances the *llys* by this date was fortified. Other than at Tyn-y-Mwd, Aber, there has yet to be any extensive archaeological investigation of earthwork castles and their immediate environs in Gwynedd. Neither, should it be said, has statutory protection been extended beyond the immediate castle mound in most instances. A programme of geophysical survey and limited trial trenching would provide valuable additional data.

There are a number of other areas where further research might prove beneficial. *Henllys* place-names in Gwynedd, such as those to the north of Aberffraw (Fig 5.2), those to the north of Pwllheli and those in the vicinity of Llan-faes may represent the locations of early medieval *llysoedd*. The *hen* element indicates not 'old' but 'former', an important distinction (Roberts, T 1992, 43). Geophysical survey and excavation could provide important new data on such sites. The identification of township boundaries on maps might be taken further through fieldwork and trial trenching and provide valuable information on the form and date of landscape divisions in the medieval period. Finally, there is an urgent need to study comparable *llys* and *maerdref* settlements in Wales as a whole, to provide contrasts and comparisons, to mitigate against any further losses on the scale suggested in Gwynedd and to provide statutory protection wherever possible.

Acknowledgements

The author wishes to thank Dr A D Carr for his help with several unpublished sources; Tomos Roberts, the archivist at the University of Wales, Bangor, for access to his own notes on Aberffraw and for his help when consulting documents in his care; and David Longley and George Smith for helpful comments on an earlier version of this paper. The final version has however benefited enormously from the patient help and guidance given by the editor, Dr Nancy Edwards. The drawings are the work of Helen Riley and L A Dutton.

References

Unpublished Primary Sources

Corporation of London Record Office (CLR)
    Research Paper 2.29;
    Royal Contract Estates Sales Contracts 114d
Gwynedd Record Office (GRO) Llangefni MS LIQ+/1/1
Public Record Office (PRO)
    Land Revenue L.R. 2/205
    E101/485/30
University of Wales, Bangor (UWB)
    Llys Dulas MS 53
    Melville Richards Place-name Archive

Published Sources

Avent, R, 1983, *Castles of the princes of Gwynedd*, Cardiff
Avent, R, 1994, Castles of the Welsh princes, *Chateau Gaillard*, 16, 11–20
Beresford, M W, 1967, *New towns of the middle ages*, London
Butler, L A S, 1987, Domestic buildings in Wales and the evidence of the Welsh laws, *Medieval Archaeol*, 31, 47–58
CChR, Calendar of Charter Rolls 1257–1300, London
CChW, Calender of Chancery Warrants preserved in the Public Record Office, 103, Itinerary of Edward I 1272–1290
Carr, A D, 1972, The Extent of Anglesey, 1352, *Trans Anglesey Antiq Soc*, 150–272
Carr, A D, 1982, *Medieval Anglesey*, Llangefni
Carr, A D, 1992, The medieval cantref of Rhos, *Trans Denbighshire Hist Soc*, 41, 7–24
Courtney, P, 1989, Excavations in the outer precinct of Tintern Abbey, *Medieval Archaeol*, 33, 99–143
Davies, R R, 1987, *Conquest, coexistence and change, Wales 1063–1415*, Oxford
Edwards, J G (ed), 1935, *Calander of ancient correspondence concerning Wales*, Cardiff
Edwards, N, & Lane, A (eds), 1988, *Early medieval settlements in Wales AD 400-1100*, Bangor, Cardiff
Evans, D S (ed & trans), 1990, *A mediaeval prince of Wales: The life of Gruffudd Ap Cynan*, Lampeter

Fenton, R, 1917, *Tours in Wales (1804–1813)*, J Fisher (ed), Cambrian Archaeological Association
Geiriadur Prifysgol Cymru 1950–67, *A dictionary of the Welsh language, I, A-Ffysur*, Cardiff
Gresham, C A, 1973, *Eifionydd: a study in landownership from the medieval period to the present day*, Cardiff
Gresham, C A, 1987, Medieval parish and township boundaries in Gwynedd, *Bull Board Celtic Stud*, 34, 137–49
Gresham, C A, 1988, Addendum: *Vairdre* alias *Vaildre, J Meirioneth Hist Soc*, 10 (3), 221–6
Hughes, H H, & North, H L, 1924, *The old churches of Snowdonia*, Bangor
Johnstone, N, forthcoming, *Llys and Maerdref: The royal courts of the princes of Gwynedd*
Jones, E G (ed), 1939, *Exchequer proceedings (equity) concerning Wales. Henry VIII - Elizabeth: Abstracts of bills and inventory of further proceedings*, Cardiff
Jones, T (trans), 1952, *Brut y Tywysogyon (Peniarth MS 20 version)*, Cardiff
Jones, G R J, 1969, The defences of Gwynedd in the thirteenth century, *Trans Caernarvonshire Hist Soc*, 30, 29–43
Jones, G R J, 1985, Forms and patterns of medieval settlement in Wales, in D Hooke (ed), *Medieval villages*, Oxford, 155–69
J[ones], M C (ed), 1867, Extent of Merionethshire *temp.* Edward I, *Archaeol Cambrensis*, 3rd ser, 13, 184–92
Jones Pierce, T, 1930, Two early Caernarvonshire accounts, *Bull Board Celtic Stud*, 5 (2), 142–55
Jones Pierce, T, 1957, The old borough of Nefyn, 1355–1882, *Trans Caernarvonshire Hist Soc*, 28, 36–53
Jones Pierce, T, 1962, Aber Gwyn Gregyn, *Trans Caernarvonshire Hist Soc*, 23, 37–43
Jones Pierce, T, 1972, *Medieval Welsh society*, J B Smith (ed), Cardiff
Lewis, E A, 1912, *The mediaeval boroughs of Snowdonia*, London
Lewis, E A, & Davies J C (eds), 1954, *Records of the Court of Augmentations relating to Wales and Monmouthshire*, Cardiff
Llwyd, A, 1833, *A history of the island of Mona*, Ruthin
Maund, K L, 1996, *Handlist of the Acts of native Welsh rulers, 1132–1283*, Cardiff
Morris, L, 1878, *Celtic Remains*, Cambrian Archaeological Association, London
Nash-Williams, V E, 1950, *The early Christian monuments of Wales*, Cardiff
Pennant, T, 1883, *Tours in Wales*, J Rhys (ed), Caernarfon
Pratt, D, 1992, Fourteenth century Marford and Hoseley: a maerdref in transition, *Trans Denbighshire Hist Soc*, 41, 25–69
Pryce, H, 1993, *Native law and the church in medieval Wales*, Oxford
RCAHMW, 1949, Report on Crogen (unpublished)
RCAHMW 1956, *An inventory of the ancient monuments in Caernarvonshire Vol I: East*, London
RCAHMW 1960, *An inventory of the ancient monuments in Caernarvonshire Vol II: Central*, London
RCAHMW 1964, *An inventory of the ancient monuments in Caernarvonshire Vol III: West*, London
RCAHMW 1993, Report on Pen y Bryn Aber Caernarfonshire (unpublished)
Rees, U (ed), 1985, *The cartulary of Haughmond Abbey*, Cardiff
Richards, M, 1969, *Welsh administrative and territorial units*, Cardiff
Roberts, T, 1992, Welsh ecclesiastical place-names and archae-

ology, in N Edwards & A Lane (eds), *The early church in Wales and the West*, Oxbow Monograph 16, Oxford, 41–4

Rowlands, H, 1846, Antiquitates parochiales, *Archaeol Cambrensis,* 1, 305–17

Seebohm, F, 1904, *The tribal system in Wales*, London, 2nd ed

Smith, J B, 1966–7, Crown and community in the principality of North Wales in the reign of Henry Tudor, *Welsh Hist Rev*, 3, 145–71

Smith, L B, 1975, Cestyll a Thomennydd, in G Bowen (ed), *Atlas Meirionnydd*, Bala, 34–5

Smith, L T (ed), 1906, *The itinerary in Wales of John Leland in or about the years 1536–1539*, London

Soulsby, I, 1983, *The towns of medieval Wales*, Chichester

Spurgeon, C J, 1987, Mottes and castle-ringworks in Wales, in J R Kenyon & R Avent (eds), *Castles in Wales and the Marches* Cardiff, 23–49

Stephenson, D, 1984, *The governance of Gwynedd*, Cardiff

Taylor, A J, 1974, *The king's works in Wales 1277–1300*, London

White, R B, 1978, New light on the origins of the kingdom of Gwynedd, in R Bromwich & R B Jones (eds), *Astudiaethau ar yr Hengerdd*, Cardiff, 350–5

White, R B, 1979, Excavations at Aberffraw, Anglesey, 1973 and 1974, *Bull Board Celtic Stud,* 28, 319–42

White, R B, & Longley, D, 1995, Excavations at Aberffraw, *Trans Anglesey Antiq Soc,* 13–22

Wiliam, A R (ed), 1960, *Llyfr Iorwerth*, Cardiff

Williams, W O, 1958, *The Tudor Age in the Principality of North Wales*, Caernarvonshire Hist Soc

Chapter 6

Aerial Photography and Historic Landscape on the Great Orme Llandudno

Mary Aris

The overview offered by aerial photography is particularly useful for recording and comparing areas of relict agricultural landscape. On the Great Orme, Llandudno, there is evidence for quite intense arable cultivation in the medieval period on very marginal land including some evidence for an infield/outfield sytem on the plateau. In the later medieval period there are indications of agricultural expansion and increased economic activity, when marginal lands were brought within the permanently cultivated area. This landscape also has a time depth which can help to illuminate some of the processes of landscape change.

Introduction

Aerial survey offers a useful method for the investigation of past landscapes. It is a method which can complement other, more traditional approaches. It offers an effective, non-destructive technique. Aerial reconnaissance can increase understanding of earlier landscapes in a number of ways. It allows the historian and archaeologist, in a most effective way, to view the relict evidence and patterns of past landscapes, and visualize past geographies. But it has far more than illustrative value. In places air photography can allow the reconstruction or detailed mapping of former field systems and areas of cultivation. It can reveal new

information or provide additional detail about already well known landscapes. Sometimes it may contribute to the understanding of agricultural practices, landscape organization and the processes of landscape change.

This study is an investigation of one particular area, the Great Orme at Llandudno, Caernarfonshire, which has some well preserved examples of surviving historic landscape, some of which can be attributed to the medieval period. The Great Orme is a limestone promontory, which rises to 207m. In area it is little more than 2km wide by 4km in length (Fig 6.1). It thus offers a limited and well defined area for study. While there is valuable evidence for settlement

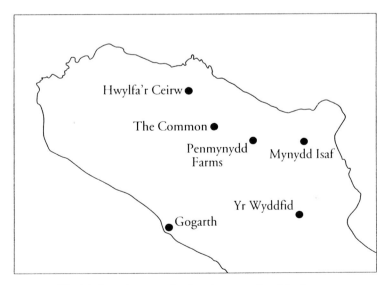

Fig 6.1 Location map showing places mentioned in the text.

and industrial activity, the present study will focus on the agricultural evidence. The plateau is marginal land in terms of present day agriculture and much of it is classed as grade 5, the poorest (Bassett & Davies 1977, 212). It was also a marginal, pastoral area in the eighteenth century when visitors such as Thomas Pennant described it as 'a beautiful sheepwalk' (Pennant 1883, 141). Yet, far from being an upland area given over entirely to animal husbandry, as might perhaps have been expected, aerial survey reveals extensive evidence for former arable cultivation on the plateau. This in itself makes it an interesting candidate for study. There is an added bonus in the quality and surviving detail of the relict landscape, which, in places, has escaped damage or obliteration by later agriculture. The surviving relict landscape also has a time depth which may offer some insights into landscape change over the centuries.

Methodology

This study utilizes oblique aerial photography for the investigation of historic landscape. Although there is valuable vertical air-photo coverage (the RAF has carried out three photographic surveys on a countrywide basis, and there has been later commercial coverage), much of this was flown at heights of 10,000 or 15,000 feet. There is therefore still an important role for oblique photography and lower level reconnaissance which is particularly valuable for highlighting archaeological detail. The amount of data recovered, and the sensitivity of the technique, can be enhanced by flying an area many times over in a range of lighting and climatic conditions (Wilson 1975, 12–31). Snow and low light conditions have proved invaluable for recording earthwork evidence. Information gathered can also be affected by the time of year in which the reconnaissance takes place. Some detail is highlighted by vegetational changes and on rare occasions by drought conditions. It should be emphasized that the data gathered is a synthesis of information gleaned from many sorties. No single aerial photograph can be expected to show up every detail.

Areas of extensive relict landscape can be plotted from data on aerial photographs. Three areas which probably saw use during the period *c* AD 500–1500 are discussed here. It should be stressed that there are other areas, some with more fragmentary evidence, which may also repay investigation.

The aerial viewpoint is particularly valuable for the overview it affords. It is possible to cover the ground quickly and to examine features which are not adjacent. It can be appreciated, for instance, that relict traces on one side of the plateau may be related to similar evidence elsewhere. From the air the detailed patterns and forms can be recorded, and different areas compared. It is possible to appreciate differences in width or alignment, which may be pointers to different phases of use. The degree of weathering of features, such as cultivation ridges or field boundaries, can also be appreciated. While assessment of weathering and

degree of preservation may to some extent be subjective, it is a yardstick that most archaeologists tend to use, and the overview provided by aerial survey allows detailed comparisons. It is also possible when flying to see which areas have been subject to modern farming practices, and why there are archaeologically 'blank' areas. Sometimes it is possible to identify areas of former ridge and furrow within modern farmland even when the detail has been obliterated. Importantly, in a limestone area, one can also identify the lie of natural ground-marking of the limestone strata and distinguish this from cultivation traces.

Oblique photography can be useful in investigating points of overlapping landscape. Relict landscape should not be viewed as a past 'geography' of a single era. There are many 'palimpsests' in the landscape. Practitioners such as Kissock (1993, 194) and Williamson (1987) have promoted the concept of topographic analysis or landscape stratigraphy, examining overlying landscape features, and features which cut into earlier landscape, which can be used to create a relative 'stratigraphy' of landscape change. Although these two writers were working on extensive areas, a similar approach can also be adopted on more limited areas.

The Field System on the Common (Figs 6.2–6.3)

One well preserved agricultural system, which is probably of medieval date, lies on the common not far from the church. A system of ridge and furrow (Fig 6.3, A), seemingly divided by low baulks, can be identified. The long ridges which cover the sloping ground are plough formed. The ploughing goes beyond the present track and the top and bottom of the ridges show the distinctive, reversed-S, aratral curves, which facilitated the turning of an ox team. Ridges of this sort may take several centuries to form. Ploughing occurred in a particular pattern, with the sod being turned in one direction on the outward leg, and in the opposite direction on the return. Parallel furrows followed the same pattern (Aston 1985, 123). Over centuries a high, broad-backed ridge would build up.

At the head of the relict field system the foundations and yards of two settlements (Fig 6.3, B-C) can be traced lying in the shelter of the slope. These are substantial homesteads with several buildings and would have been significant features in the landscape. One is a platform house of typical late medieval form, set into the slope, with a distinctive drainage hood. The habitation sites are almost certainly associated with the ridge and furrow and would therefore appear to be contemporary, though the origins of the cultivation are probably earlier. It would be incorrect to view the land below the two homesteads as belonging to particular compact 'farms' since medieval farmers owned lands of different qualities in dispersed strips scattered through a township. But the inhabitants of these two homesteads, located at the edge of the farmland, can reasonably be viewed as members of a later medieval community which farmed these township lands. The location of much of the settlement on the plateau is dispersed there are several upstanding field walls on the same alignment as the relict fields, fossilizing the earlier pattern. Thirdly, there is some evidence from the 1840 tithe apportionment for Llandudno (GAMS tithe), a survey which, unusually, preceded the Enclosure Award of 1847, that part of this system survived in use up to the nineteenth century. Within the farmland of what was then called Penmynydd, a system of parallel fields is depicted, divided only by low baulks which are shown on the tithe map as dotted lines. These are of similar width to the land divisions on the common and are on the same alignment. Although they have no solid boundaries and are divided by baulks rather than walls, judging from the manner of their depiction, the fields still have individual names. The two Penmynydd farms are located in one of the most fertile sectors of the plateau. Cultivation continued in the east after the land on the common was abandoned to pasture. There is a nineteenth-century place-name, Ty'n yr Hendre, in the area near Penmynydd Isaf farmhouse (Williams 1869, map frontispiece). This may imply that the Penmynydd farmland was the original 'core' of the township sharelands, with subsequent intakes of cultivation at greater distances, on more marginal lands.

In examining the landscape we need to break it down into its smallest units, and then see how these were organized. The question arises, therefore, as to whether the baulks which divide the ridges do in fact denote an allocation or ownership of land. (Alternatively the divisions could represent some pre-existing landform, still recognizable in the medieval landscape.) If they are units of land, then they are quite generous allocations (as will be seen when other systems are compared). These land allocations may link up with the suggestions of substance visible in the homesteads – their occupants can be viewed as quite prosperous farmers.

On the western edge of the system (Fig 6.3, E), the width of ridge changes. It may be that these areas were spade dug, or ploughed afterwards, because of the awkwardness of their shape. Just in the area where the modern field

Fig 6.2 Medieval cultivation on the common (photograph: author).

and it is often tucked into sheltered niches on what is a very exposed headland.

The field system probably extended eastwards (Fig 6.3, D) into what is now the farmland of the two farms, Penmynydd Uchaf and Penmynydd Isaf. There are three reasons supporting such a hypothesis. First, aerial photography suggests that the plough ridges continued. Secondly,

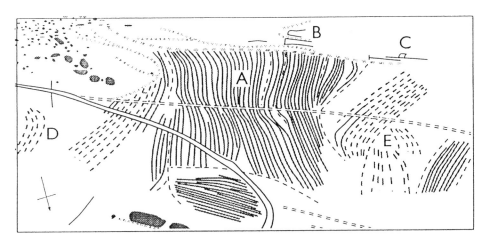

Fig 6.3 Sketchplan showing medieval cultivation on the common.

walls meet, however, there is a patch of very different ridges, and further west still the pattern changes again. While this may simply denote differences of geography, it could be that the field system just discussed sits on an earlier landscape, with a somewhat different organization. Another tenuous indication of a time depth to the landscape exists on lands towards the church. In one area a distinct overlap can be seen. Above the church there is a fragment of a curved bank, which may once have been part of an enclosure. Although the building of the Victorian cemetery has destroyed most of the evidence, it is clear that the enclosure had been cultivated. It is quite crisp and clear and the cultivation may even be contemporary with the ploughing on the common – perhaps an opportunistic outfield cultivation. However the curved bank predates at least one of the linear baulks or divisions on the common, itself now a relict boundary.

Fields and Cultivation near Hwylfa'r Ceirw
(Figs 6.4, 6.5)

The relict landscape near Hwylfa'r Ceirw is one of the most complicated and detailed to have survived around Llandudno. It is a fascinating area utilized in different ways over a long period. Some of the evidence is almost certainly prehistoric; it seems also to have been exploited in the middle ages and there was further use into the industrial period.

Hwylfa'r Ceirw, 'Highway of the Deer', is the name given to a double line of stones which runs from the cliffs towards a complex of small interlocking relict fields. While the stones may be an avenue, as suggested by the Royal Commission (RCAHMW 1956, no 380), it is more likely to be a lane or droveway between ancient fields. Traces of these (Fig 6.5, A), and faint indications of cultivation on them in places, can still be seen. At one time the field system may have extended almost to the cliff where the right-angle of an enclosing wall is clearly visible. This section of the fields may have prehistoric origins. (The assumption made by the compilers of the Royal Commission inventory about a prehistoric dating for the 'avenue' may have been correct even if the function they suggested for it is open to reinterpretation.) The degree of preservation is also an indicator of an early date. Superimposed on this landscape, above a scarp on a small plateau, is a tight grouping of rectangular fields (Fig 6.5, B). This 'core area' is itself complex and has a considerable time depth. Agriculture was organized into a neat system of plots with prominent cultivation ridges. These ridges may have been spade dug, for in places they fork around boulders. Indeed, there may be several layers or phases of land use since cultivation in one place seems to overlie earlier, broken-down terraces. There is also another patch of cultivation (Fig 6.5, C) set at a different angle to the neat plots. A later, rectangular structure (Fig 6.5, D) is cut into this cultivation. Whether this is associated with settlement or with mining activity cannot be determined from the air-photo evidence alone. It may be quite old for several late eighteenth- and early nineteenth-century visitors mention ruins near Hwylfa'r

Fig 6.4 Early cultivation and field systems at Hwylfa'r Ceirw (photograph: author).

Ceirw (Pennant 1883, 143; Caernarvon & Denbigh Herald 1849, 23 May, 8). However the entrance to this structure or enclosure is itself blocked with debris, probably from ore processing. There is some evidence that the spring, Ffynnon Rhufeinig, has been used for washing and separating copper ore (Caernarvon and Denbigh Herald 1849, 23 May, 8). By the late nineteenth century there was only one small enclosure or sheepfold (Fig 6.5, F) surviving at this spot (Ordnance Survey 25in map 1888) which indicates the final transition of this area from arable to pastoral usage, a situation which is mirrored in several other places on the Great Orme. The surviving evidence therefore offers a considerable time depth, suggesting many different phases of land use.

The surrounding area, which is rough ground today, carries further evidence (Fig 6.5, E). There are fainter cultivation ridges around the core complex of fields. At one time cultivation has spread over a large area of very marginal land. The cultivation is on several different alignments, and it is the suggestion of this author that the different alignments may represent different periods of use and phases of arable activity. In some outlying areas the evidence for cultivation is extremely faint. In one place there are suggestions of cross ploughing (only visible under snow conditions which highlight detail). The boundary of one

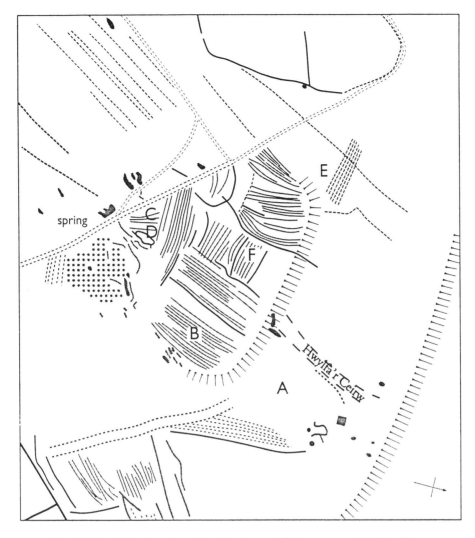

Fig 6.5 Sketchplan showing early cultivation and field systems at Hwylfa'r Ceirw.

area of cultivation is delineated by a line of marker stones. There are also traces of a D-shaped enclosure with cultivation inside. The phenomenon of outfield ploughing is well known in Scotland and in certain other areas of northern Britain (Whittington 1973, 552–67) and it may be that there is an instance of it here. Some of the outlying cultivation may represent the occasional breaking up and bringing into use of marginal surrounding areas. When yields fell because of soil exhaustion, the area was abandoned to waste for a long recovery period. Fertility in the core area, where cultivation and use over a long period seems to be indicated, could have been maintained by the usual practice of manuring the infield area by carting and spreading midden waste or by tethering, night-folding or pasturing livestock.

It must be pointed out that this is an extremely exposed, windswept location, which has long been outside the farmed area. The nineteenth-century tithe and enclosure maps show it as a blank and eighteenth-century antiquarian visitors commented on its bleak, inhospitable nature and the lonely area below, around the church (Pennant 1883, 144). On some exposed terraces there are some indications of soil erosion, which may be a result of breaking the ground for cultivation.

The Multi-Period Landscape below Mynydd Isaf
(Figs 6.6, 6.7)

In the remote north-eastern sector of the Great Orme, well outside the present day farmed area, a small but interesting landscape of multi-period agricultural use has survived. The most obvious archaeological remains are four small long huts (Fig 6.7, A) tucked against a cliff (RCAHMW 1956, no 371). These are most likely to be of medieval date, although no excavation has confirmed this. They contrast with the more substantial homesteads noted earlier elsewhere on the Orme and they also show greater evidence of nucleation, if indeed they were occupied at the same time. Two of them lie against an ancient bank (Fig 6.7, B) which seems to overlie other lines which appear to form a series of very small paddocks or enclosures (Fig 6.7C), in one of which small pits or circular features are visible. (However, the possibility that some of these may have a natural

Fig 6.6 Early cultivation at Mynydd Isaf (photograph: author).

explanation needs to be born in mind, because of the limestone geology.)

Further west are traces of early agriculture (Fig 6.7, D). This has been noted previously (RCAHMW 1956, no 371) and it has been assumed to be associated with the long huts. From the air, at certain times of the year when the vegetation permits, a greater complexity and time depth is revealed. This agricultural landscape seems to consist of a number of elements: there is a trace of an ancient field bank, and another parallel to it further west, underlying and at an angle to a later, fairly ruined wall, which however aligns with a modern field wall. Fragments of an earlier and a later system of land divisions (Fig 6.7, D) are therefore visible on different alignments. Inside one of the earlier land divisions, the area appears to have been subdivided into three narrow linear plots, which are reminiscent of the slender rectangular land divisions at Hwylfa'r Ceirw. These plots carry faint traces of narrow cultivation ridges. Adjacent and at one point overlying, where there is cross ploughing, is a freer form of cultivation (Fig 6.7, E), with broader ridges, and a suggestive curve that may indicate it is plough formed.

This evidence is not all of one period, and because of this there is a difficulty in deciding with which agricultural evidence the settlement is associated. There seem to be at least two phases of arable activity. The earlier cultivation, part of an ordered, partitioned landscape (Fig 6.7, D), may be related to the long huts, although this cannot be easily

proved. The overlying ploughing (Fig 6.7, E) may be an instance of an opportunistic outfield-type of land use (it is not within very clearly defined boundaries, as the other activity is). The latter may possibly be associated with those who farmed the lands of the Penmynydd farms and the common using an ox team.

There is a small scale mining area in a nearby field above Porth Helyg and a series of rectangular structures (yards and buildings) which could be associated with such activity. Alternatively they might be another homestead, set girdle pattern at the edge of the area thought to have been cultivated in the later medieval period.

The ground evidence here may be indicating sequences of activity and offering some sort of relative dating evidence, even if it is difficult to anchor them firmly in time. The identification of points of overlapping landscape is a useful contribution of aerial photography.

Evidence from Written Sources

The dearth of written sources prior to the Edwardian conquest is well known. The earliest relevant documentary evidence comes in a series of surveys known as the *Record of Caernarfon* ranging in date between 1294 and 1352 (Ellis 1838, l09–11). That which includes Llandudno is now ascribed to 1306/7 (Stephenson 1982, 95). By that time the Great Orme formed part of the manor of Gogarth, which

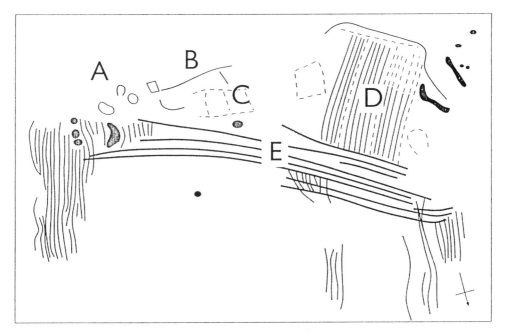

Fig 6.7 Sketchplan showing early cultivation at Mynydd Isaf.

had been granted by Edward I to the bishop of Bangor. (It was amongst the the lands ceded by Llywelyn ap Gruffudd after the war of 1277.) In the early fourteenth century three small townships existed in the area of Llandudno: Gogarth situated below the Great Orme beside the sea shore, Wyddfid in the eastern sector, and Cyngreawdr in the north. The survey offers some indications of the agricultural carrying capacity of the area, although one needs a multiplier to get from the number of holdings to a population estimate. Thirteen bond tenants and one free tenant are mentioned at Gogarth; nine, mainly bond, tenants held land at Wyddfid; and at Cyngreawdr the tenants included two free tenants, with under tenants, holding six houses and land.

Often medieval townships mentioned in the documentary sources prove extremely difficult to locate precisely on the ground. At Gogarth one can locate the township lands near the ruins of the bishop's palace (RCAHMW 1956, no 361). At Wyddfid a later eighteenth- and early nineteenth-century mining settlement developed on the site of the old strips of the township. Many of the strips of both these townships are recorded on the tithe map for 1840. In both cases a vestigial form of relict strip system survived into the nineteenth century. Some narrow strips were delineated on the tithe map only by dotted lines, suggesting they were still unenclosed in 1840. Others were fossilized by stone walls. All, however preserved the forms of strips, which were probably a relict feature from a far earlier, medieval system. Significantly, a different form of relict system was preserved at Gogarth and Wyddfid, compared with the relict system within the farm of Penmynydd in 1840. Strips in these two townships were extremely narrow, though they occurred in both long and short forms. Such a survival of relict systems is occasionally known in other places in Gwynedd. Sometimes these are royal *maerdref* sites (Jones

1973, 461–5, 471), or sites associated with ecclesiastical holdings (Jones 1972, 340–9), which preserved extremely conservative forms of land tenure. Relict forms of holding often survived where there was some other kind of subsistence to supplement that offered by the limited size of the holdings. At Llandudno fishing and copper mining may have offered a supplementary means of subsistence, and this may explain why fragments of earlier land systems survived to 1840 in all three townships.

The location of the Cyngreawdr township lands is more problematical. However, on top of the plateau most of the land is bare limestone pavement or extremely rough ground and there are very few cultivable areas. The farmland of Penmynydd is the most fertile and sheltered part and therefore seems the most likely area for the township's core. The relict fields on the common, the land around the church, the relict lands at Hwylfa'r Ceirw, and the present day farm of Parc, which was not formed until after enclosure in 1847, offer more marginal possibilities. As we have seen there is evidence of late medieval occupation on the common, probably extending into the Penmynydd lands. For a time the area formed part of the permanently cultivated land. It is therefore possible that the substantial homesteads (Fig 6.3, B-C) might correspond with some of the holdings of the free tenants of Cyngreawdr. The freemen were more privileged and less burdened than the bond tenants of Gogarth and Wyddfid, and many other tenants elsewhere; they also had subtenants. It is possible that greater privilege in the landscape (the substantial homesteads) corresponds with privilege in the record evidence. The lands on the common and in the Penmynydd farmland may therefore represent lands of the tenants of Cyngreawdr. Settlement in free townships was often ranged girdle-pattern around the sharelands (Jones 1959, 339) and there are suggestions of a corresponding distribution in a dispersed settlement pattern on the edge of the cultivated area.

There is substantial evidence for increasing numbers of free tenancies being established in Gwynedd after 1150, and considerable evidence of strategic land reorganizations elsewhere in the Creuddyn area *c* 1200 (Jones 1949, 37–55; 1969, 40–1; Lewis 1964, 63–4)). There may be the potential for further investigation in order to try and correlate further the documentary and landscape evidence for the very important period just before and just after the Edwardian conquest. Whether the signs of enterprise and economic activity and wealth that are visible in the medieval landscape (with the growth of substantial farms, intakes of marginal land, etc) are in some way related to the development of free tenancies at Cyngreawdr, is an interesting possibility. Free tenants seem to have been perceived as an asset and seem to have been involved in invigorating the economy of Gwynedd under the later Welsh princes. There may have been official encouragement of newer, freer forms of tenure. Whether a distinction between bond and free tenants may help to explain some of the landscape evidence also requires further investigation.

Expansion onto marginal lands, and the practice of outfield cultivation are activities that have taken place at several periods in the past on the Great Orme. This may have been forced upon the inhabitants, not just by factors such as population pressures, but by soil exhaustion and by very real problems of maintaining yields and soil fertility on such thin soils in such an exposed and marginal area. Climate may also have influenced periods of intake of more marginal lands. The benign climatic period before 1300 may have been favourable for expansion onto an area such as the common. But after 1300 a marked climatic deterioration began which culminated in the so-called 'Little Ice Age' in the sixteenth century. The wetter climate may have exacerbated problems of declining yields and soil exhaustion, particularly on the poorer soils. There may never have been a conscious decision to abandon lands on the common. But declining yields would have necessitated ever longer periods of fallow to allow the land to recuperate. Eventually, the land was not put back into production. Wider economic change in the sixteenth century also created new livestock markets and provided viable alternatives to arable cultivation.

The Way Forward

There is much surviving early landscape on the Great Orme and aerial photography can make an important contribution to its recording. Despite the wealth of vertical coverage there is a role for lower level oblique air reconnaissance under a range of conditions. Evidence from aerial photography raises many issues and suggests other avenues of enquiry. There is scope for further research to see if the documentary evidence that survives can be correlated with the equally detailed ground evidence. As well as more traditional approaches, however, an interesting way forward for the future would be to map all the landscape data onto a GIS (Geographical Information System) database. This relatively new technology has the ability to map disparate elements onto 'layers' of landscape data which can then be manipulated and interrogated in various ways. It is exciting to see that the Royal Commission at Aberystwyth, for example, have recently acquired this form of computer technology. Through such means, new technology could be utilized to analyse the data and to relate it to other factors such as soil quality and micro-climate, or produce various models. Aerial photography can offer some of the data for the ongoing investigation of former landscapes and of the processes of landscape change.

References

Unpublished Sources

Gwynedd Archives and Museums Service (GAMS),
    Aerial photograph collection, XD/80
    X/ Tithe / Llandudno
    Enclosure Award Llandudno, 1847
Mostyn Estates Office, Mostyn Estates map of Llandudno, 1828

Published Sources

Aston, M, 1985, *Interpreting the landscape*, London
Caernarvon and Denbigh Herald, 1849, 23 May
Baker, A R H, & Butlin, R A (eds), 1973, *Studies of field systems in the British Isles*, Cambridge
Bassett, T M, & Davies, B L (eds), 1977, *Atlas Sir Gaernarfon*, Caernarfon
Ellis, H (ed), 1838, *The Record of Caernarvon*, London
Jones, G R J, 1949, *The military geography of Creuddyn*, unpublished MA thesis, Univ Wales, Bangor
Jones, G R J, 1959, Rural settlement in Ireland and western Britain, *Brit Ass for the Advancement of Science*, 338–42
Jones, G R J, 1969, The defences of Gwynedd in the thirteenth century, *Trans Caernarvonshire Hist Soc*, 30, 29–43
Jones, G R J, 1972, Post-Roman Wales, in H P R Finberg (ed), *The agrarian history of England and Wales, Vol I, part II, AD 43–1042*, Cambridge, 283–382
Jones, G R J, 1973, Field systems of North Wales, in Baker & Butlin (eds), 430–79
Kissock, J A, 1993, Some examples of co-axial field systems in Pembrokeshire, *Bull Board Celtic Stud*, 40, 190–7
Lewis, C W, 1964, The Treaty of Woodstock, 1247, its background and significance, *Welsh Hist Rev*, 2, 37–65
Pennant, T, 1883, *Tours in Wales*, J Rhys (ed), Caernarfon
RCAHMW, 1956, *An inventory of the ancient monuments of Caernarvonshire, Vol I, East*, London
Stephenson, D, 1982, *The governance of Gwynedd*, Cardiff
Whittington, G, 1973, Field systems of Scotland, in Baker & Butlin (eds), 530–79
Williams, W, 1869, *Llandudno its history and natural history*, Llandudno
Williamson, T, 1987, Early co-axial field systems on the East Anglian boulder clay, *Proc Prehist Soc*, 53, 419–31
Wilson, D R, 1975, *Photographic techniques in the air, aerial reconnaissance for archaeology*, CBA Res Rep, 12, London
Withers, C J, 1995, Concepts of landscape change in upland North Wales – a case study of Llanbedr y Cennin and Caerhun parishes, c. 1560–c. 1891, *Landscape Hist*, 17, 35–47

Place-names and Vegetation History as a Key to Understanding Settlement in the Conwy Valley

Della Hooke

In both Llanaber on the west coast of Gwynedd (Merioneth) and in the parishes of Caerhun and Llanbedrycennin in the Conwy valley (Caerns) it is possible to analyse place-names, field-names and ancillary documentary evidence to explore the chronology of settlement and related land use. Areas of medieval arable cultivation can be identified, together with the development of pastoralism and the degeneration of woodland. The methodology is outlined and some of the specific problems encountered in the second region are discussed. It is possible to show that the area of cultivation in the lowlands expanded after the decline of native farming systems but that the complex relationship between the cultivated lowlands and the large tracts of upland pasture was constantly shifting.

Settlement Patterns and Environmental Change

The sequence of development which has moulded the landscape of parts of the Conwy valley is by no means unique. Certain areas have much in common with the coastal area of Merioneth in the ancient commote of Ardudwy Is Artro where, in the parish of Llanaber, an earlier study (Hooke 1975; 1983) showed how landscape change could be investigated by combining the evidence of field- and place-names with historical documentary and cartographic evidence, all closely related by fieldwork to the actual landscape and present day land use.

Above the valley proper, in the parishes of Caerhun and Llanbedrycennin, is a desolate plateau extending over a width of some 7km which runs down the western side of the Conwy valley between the Carneddau and the River Conwy (Figs 7.1, 7.2). It is drained eastwards by the Afon Roe, Afon Dulyn and Afon Porthllwyd which occupy wide, ill-drained valleys in their upper stretches before dropping steeply through deeply incised valleys to the flood plain of the Conwy. The upper plateau is some of the emptiest land in North Wales, yet it is only about 305m above sea level. In part this reflects the hostile environment provided by an underlying bedrock of Ordovician strata, but it also reflects the activities of man in a marginal zone. Historically, however, this is *not* an empty area: the remains of settlements and relict field systems litter the slopes and much of the land is, of course, still farmed from lower-lying settlements today.

The environment is not so very different to that of the west Merioneth coast along the valley of the Afon Ysgethin on the western side of the Rhinogau. Here Walker and Taylor (1976) were able to show that man had played a

major role in producing the landscape we see today - assisting nature, perhaps, in giving rise to the rather sterile ill-drained land now characteristic of this area. By soil-pollen analysis, taking samples from near Pont Sgethin and in Nantcol to the north, they were able to suggest that open woodland covered the area at the beginning of the prehistoric period, with an abundance of *Alnus* and *Quercus* (alder and oak).

Increasing interference with the woodland associated with pastoral farming gradually led to woodland degeneration, although this occurred in intermittent phases rather than in a steady decline, with local regeneration at intervals, shown particularly in *Betula* (birch) pollen. The culmination of woodland degeneration, they argued, took place in the Iron Age and Roman periods, when representation of herbaceous species increased and cereal pollen, together with the weeds of arable cultivation, made a significant contribution, although suggesting only small scale cultivation. *Quercus* never again reached its prior levels. It is possible that intensive fieldwork might have provided more information about historical land use. There is ample evidence of Romano-British settlement and associated field systems a few kilometres to the west but no systematic survey has been made of the Ysgethin valley itself, much of which shows little sign of land clearance. Peat began to form at this time and rendered the soil less and less suitable for cultivation. Pastoralism must have remained dominant from this period onwards and was already probably the dominant land use earlier. Only just over a kilometre from Pont Sgethin the hillfort of Craig y Dinas may have served as a focus of such activities. Thereafter, several periods of intensified human activity entailing cultivation can be

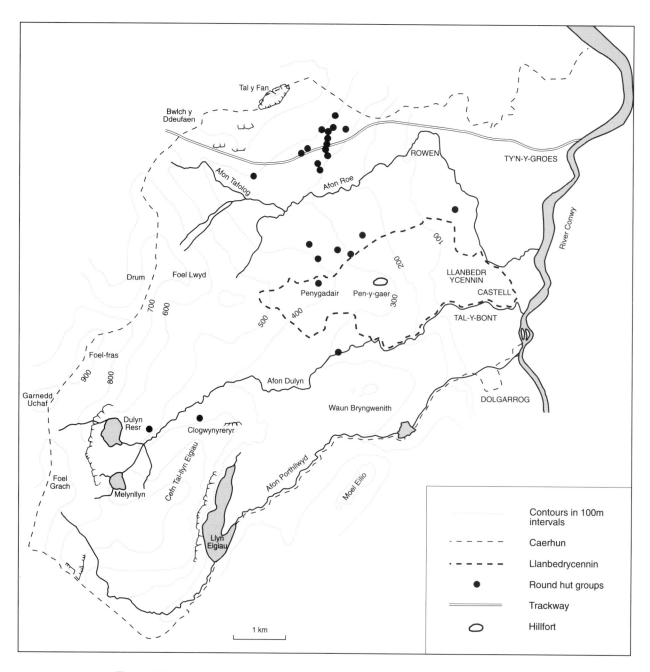

Fig 7.1 Topography and early settlement in the parishes of Caerhun and Llanbedrycennin.

detected, alternating with periods of diminished cultivation but continued pastoral activity. Cereal pollen, for instance, peaked in the medieval period but gave way to increased pastoral activity along the moorland edge at a stage they suggest may be identified as the sixteenth century when encroachment is known to have occurred; there was further small scale cultivation in the uplands during the Napoleonic Wars, although less here than might have been expected. This stage ends with rises in the pollen of *Gramineae* (grasses) and *Ericaceae* (heath), and a marked rise in *Sphagnum* (moss) indicative of renewed peat growth. This reflects a wetter phase but grazing pressure is also evidenced in the upper parts of the pollen sequence with a *Potentilla*

(cinquefoils, silverweed, etc) maxima (Walker & Taylor 1976, 330–3, 339).

Some concern may be expressed at the way Walker and Taylor have tied their results so closely to historical phases but this underlines a number of important conclusions: first, it does seem that man was a potent factor in producing landscape change: 'Palynological evidence for the upland peat site at Pont Scethin [Sgethin] reveals that cultivation had taken place since Iron Age times in association with a varying pastoral element' (Walker & Taylor 1976, 343); and, second, this study shows how selection of a marginal zone can provide particular evidence of changing vegetational conditions related to man's use of the land. Such a zone is one of perpetual bioclimatic marginality and responds clearly to both climatic fluctuations and changing land use. Above all, it underlines the necessity for further detailed studies of this nature.

In Caerhun, the landscape is similar in many ways to that of the Ysgethin valley. Wide expanses of treeless moorland and peaty, ill-drained valleys appear to present a hostile image to today's visitor. There is, however, ample evidence of early fields and dwellings on these apparently empty moorlands: such as the extensive settlement of roughly circular huts, some 28 in number, with associated cairns, which lie at Pant-y-griafolen on the north side of the Afon Dulyn between 472m and 524m (SH 708666; RCAHMW 1956, 27, no 115) upon the slopes below the Dulyn Reservoir (Fig 7.1). The largest number of these 'round huts' and associated oval enclosures which still survive are scattered over the lower slopes of Tal-y-fan between the 91m and 122m contours above the holding of Maen-y-bardd. These have obviously stood a better chance of survival on the more difficult upland terrain but chance survivals on much lower ground, such as the pair of round huts found at only 46m, on land near Maesycastell which remained wooded until recent times (RCAHMW 1956, 33, no 152), suggest that such dwellings were once more widespread. A more obvious landmark is the Iron Age hillfort of Pen-y-gaer in Llanbedrycennin which crowns a bold hill rising to 380m at the eastern end of a long ridge descending from

the Carneddau towards the Conwy valley (RCAHMW 1956, 100–1, no 315). Numerous hut circles have been identified within the ramparts, which are best preserved on the southern side. A sheepfold has been made near the western entrance which has damaged part of the site and tracks crossing the ramparts were probably made to take away stone for house and wall building, perhaps in the nineteenth century. None of these settlement complexes has been dated by excavation but the majority of round huts are probably of prehistoric date.

In the Roman period the focus appears to have shifted to the main corridor of the Conwy valley itself with the construction of the auxiliary fort of Canovium on the west bank in the first century AD. In North Wales, this was second only to Segontium in size and formed one of a network of forts controlling the valley routes through Wales (Fig 7.3) (Casey 1969, 56). It lay at the upper tidal limit of the Conwy, accessible to vessels of up to 100 tons burden, and controlled both the coastal road which crossed the Conwy near here, passing via the Bwlch y Ddeufaen westwards towards the north coast, and a secondary road leading south westwards towards the forts of Bryn y Gefeiliau and Tomen-y-mur. The date at which the fort was abandoned is unclear because the late coin evidence is now considered intrusive to the site (Casey 1969, 56; 1989). The fort was subsequently chosen as the appropriate site for the construction of the parish church of St Mary, part

Fig 7.2 Cwm Eigiau in Caerhun; an area of marginal land use, (Photograph: author).

of which dates from the thirteenth or fourteenth century. At Tal-y-cafn, the crossing over the Conwy, earlier made by a ford known as Cafn Gronant, is overlooked by a medieval motte, Bryncastell (RCAHMW 1956, 27, no 114).

In Ardudwy Is Artro, the focus of medieval development remained on the coastal zone with the royal *maerdref* located at Ystumgwern on the narrow coastal plain (see Johnstone p 57). Recent work has identified the actual position of the *maerdref* settlement, which was to be replaced by two or three farms, one named Faildref, as bond holdings were given to villein families displaced by the building of Edward I's borough at Harlech. Four such holdings were apparently to become the holding of Faildref, and the remainder of the demesne lands, supporting in total some 20 holdings, were to be appropriated in the same way (Gresham 1988). This kind of amalgamation probably explains why one of the neighbouring present day farms, Taltreuddyn, was entered in the *Extent of Merioneth* as a township of thirteen households in 1293 (PRO, E 179/242/53; Thomas, C 1970, 130, n 5), the original *tyddynnod* now lost without trace. This example shows the danger of reconstructing early settlement patterns too readily from present day evidence: the Upland regions of Britain are often cited as 'ancient landscapes' with little consideration of the hidden changes that may have occurred. In addition to the *maerdref*, other bond holdings can be identified to the south along the coastal strip in Ardudwy is Artro. *The Record of Caernarvon* (Ellis 1838) states that the inhabitants of eight free *gwelyau* in Llanaber, Llanddwywe and Llanenddwyn were unable to describe their boundaries to the commissioners. While this may betray a reticence to cooperate it also seems that some of their lands may indeed have been interlocking. Parcels of free land can also be identified, but the ancient system of land holding also combined use of the communities' arable on the coast with seasonal use of hill pastures and inland valleys: Ystumgwern was linked with pastures in Nantcol and the other summer pastures of the commote lay at Bryn Coch, Y Feidiog and Prysor.

As in Ardudwy, the lowland zone of Arllechwedd Isaf continued to be the focus of medieval settlement. This commote extended from the Conwy estuary to the confluence of the Conwy and the Afon Porthllwyd near Dolgarrog, covering the later parishes of Gyffin, Llangelynnin, Caerhun and Llanbedrycennin. It included the free township of Castell with its five hamlets: Bodidda and Cymryd (both in Gyffin); Merchlyn (Gyffin detached); Penfro in Caerhun between the Penfro (now known as the Afon Dulyn) and the Afon Porthllwyd but with extensions in Llanbedr and the Conwy marsh; and a fifth lying on both sides of the river Castell (now known as the Afon Roe) between Bwlch y Ddeufaen, Cafn Gronant and Castell village (Jones Pierce 1942; 1972, 200) (Fig 7.3). Glyn and Gronant had been other bond townships which 'were entirely denuded of villeins soon after the conquest' (Jones Pierce 1939; 1972, 41). The site of the medieval *maerdref* of Arllechwedd Isaf is unknown but a strong case has been made for a location in Gronant beside the Conwy and near

the Bryncastell motte (Gresham 1979). The late Professor Jones Pierce was able to identify most of the 22 free *gefaelion* which spread over the administrative vill of Castell, eight of which were confined to Castell but with the fourteen others which had their nuclei there spread out in the other hamlets: none formed distinct territorial units. The nearby bond *gafael* of Cwm Eigiau, however, similarly denuded of its occupants after the conquest, appears to have been demarcated by precise metes and bounds. The reconstruction of these units was only made possible because of the survival of documents relating how Bartholomew Bolde built up his estates by the leasing and purchase of land from former clansmen (eg UWB, MS 1939).

The core of medieval settlement was on the brown earth soils of the Conwy valley below 152m, an area initially covered with oak woodland. Some of the native *gefaelion* held portions of arable and meadow in Llwydfaen and Morfa an Llwydfaen and the situation resembles that of Ystumgwern in that the intermixed holdings came to be represented by consolidated farm holdings: largely those of Llwydfaenuchaf and Llwydfaenisaf. Some 69 tenant holdings identified at the close of the fourteenth century had become only nine just over 100 years ago, providing some clue to the heartland of medieval arable cultivation (Jones Pierce 1942; 1972, 203). In contrast, such detailed reconstruction was not generally possible in Ardudwy where, outside Ystumgwern, only farm names survive to suggest the location of the medieval hamlets and holdings. In Caerhun, Professor Jones Pierce was also able to identify two large areas of arable, one of twelve acres called *Hen Dir Adda*, and several smaller pieces. The significant feature is that where field-names are given, 'apart from an occasional *cae* and *tir*, the recorded field names are prefixed by the word *erw* . . . The only exception is a *dryll* called *Dryll y Golwydd*' (Jones Pierce 1972, 204).

No group held a single block of territory: all were fragmented in different parts of the hamlet and often intermingled with fragments of other *gefaelion*. It is hard to visualize the appearance of the landscape with its system of quilletted fields, but no hedges or walls appear to be recorded by this date. As Jones Pierce so graphically describes:

> 'The above reconstruction affords a glimpse of the scene which would meet the eye of the traveller landing at Cafn Gronant near the turn of the fifteenth century. During the first half-mile of his journey along the highroad towards Bwlch y Ddeufaen (*y ffordd fawr* from Cafn Gronant so often mentioned in the rental) he would see the *tyddynnod, erwau*, and *drylliau* of the vill of Gronant, once cultivated by the prince's bondmen and now held in villeinage by free tenants of Castell, covering the rises on either hand and merging imperceptibly, unbroken by wall or hedgerow, into the fields of Llwydfaen and, on the other side, into territory today occupied by the home-farm and plantations of Caerhun Hall' (Jones Pierce 1972, 209).

Methodology

The identification of medieval arable from the survival of such distinctive field-names as *dryll*, 'a strip or ridge', *talar*, 'a headland', *lleiniau*, 'quillets', and *cyfar* and *erw*, measures of land, formed the basis of part of the investigation of field-name evidence in the parish of Llanaber (Hooke 1975). More recently, Colin Thomas (1980; 1992) has used the same technique to propose a model of settlement development in the Welsh uplands. He notes how the arable-type names frequently refer to small parcels of land, infrequently more than two statute acres in size and rarely larger than four acres. In Llanaber there is a dramatic concentration of such names along the coastal strip below the 152m contour where a belt of well-drained loams surely represents the area preferred for crop growing in the early part of the medieval period (Hooke 1975, fig 2). It is significant that very few such names occur in the area along the estuary of the Mawddach, perhaps an area of later clearance.

The clear picture of landscape evolution presented by the Ardudwy study suggested that similar research might be instructive in other areas. However, the parishes of Caerhun and Llanbedrycennin are almost unique outside Anglesey in having no field-names entered in the tithe apportionment. This, with its accompanying plans, names and maps only individual holdings; it does not show internal field boundaries and only rarely names the fields themselves. So how does one proceed? The documentation for these parishes is exceedingly full due to the large number of estate deeds that have been preserved, especially in the Baron Hill documents (UWB). Most are, however, unaccompanied by maps and the identification of medieval holdings and fields is often difficult unless they can be related to later mapped evidence. Many early names refer to 'places' which are not necessarily settlements (for instance, references in the UWB, MS 1939 are to places called *mayn y berth* and *garth more c* 1450 which probably refer to settlements but this is difficult to prove). The plotting of holdings and their associated fields has been possible only by the slow piecemeal investigation of individual farm and estate records. Fortunately, there are such records for the Caerhun and Vaynol estates in the eighteenth and nineteenth centuries but these frequently refer to tiny holdings which are still difficult to identify, never mind to piece together. Obviously it is only when rentals etc, are accompanied by maps that they can be used satisfactorily. These do, however, reveal remarkable consistency in the naming of individual fields and suggest that confidence can also be placed in later Sales Catalogue records where they, too, are accompanied by plans. The dotted areas on Figure 7.3 show just how much of the parish has so far been investigated in this way. There is, however, an added bonus in that the documentation available for these parishes may ultimately permit the dating of field-names in a way that was quite impossible for Llanaber.

The commonest term relating to medieval arable cultivation occurring here is *erw,* although a few such names are associated with holdings not yet identified. The term is found most frequently in the north east of Caerhun parish (Fig 7.3). A cluster occur to the north of Llanbedrycennin. The majority occur in the main valley or valley side. Jones Pierce (1942; 1972, 210–11) identified a second core area

of *tyddynnod* and *erwau* on the banks of the Afon Castell where it drains southwards towards the Conwy, an area today containing the present Castell village and the farms of Ydrefechan, Maesycastell and Dolycastell. There are certainly a number of *erw* field-names surviving in this area and a further group are found to the south of Garth-mor where there is also a *dalar*, another area in which Bolde had been acquiring the holdings of the native *gafaelion*. The incidence of such names further up the Afon Castell valley on the holding of Maen-y-bardd at first gave rise to some concern but the Roman road through Bwlch y Ddeufaen opens up this area and Jones Pierce notes how a fifteenth-century traveller would 'still meet with many signs of agricultural activity even as far as Bwlch y Ddeufaen itself' (Jones Pierce 1972, 211). A parcel at Maen-y-bardd is referred to *c* 1450/65 and a specific house by 1546 (UWB, MS 1939, 1920). The ruins of the old house exist among the farm buildings (RCAHMW 1956, 26, no 96). To the south, the *erw* names are again confined to the valley area occupied by the majority of later farms. The two *gafaelion* of Llanbedr identified from the Bolde rental lay in the immediate neighbourhood of the church, with Penfro holdings extending to Tyddynrobin close to those of Castell, and this cluster is also represented by *erw* names. The majority of Penfro holdings appear to have lain along the north bank of the Afon Porthllwyd and on both sides of the Afon Dulyn. It seems that the individual *tyddyn* possessed little more than six acres of arable. Encroachments were also being made in the uplands, involving considerable inroads on the pastoral resources of the community. It is at this stage that we find the Conway burgesses buying up the ancient holdings to form the basis of their growing estates, including rights to the associated pastures in the uplands.

No medieval *tyddyn* site has been excavated in these parishes but the remains of a long hut, surviving in a poor state below a later sheepfold in the main Conwy valley above Llwydfaen, appear to be those of Bryn-cwn, a farm recorded by the mid fifteenth century (UWB, Bangor MS 1939; RCAHMW 1956, 33, no 161) (Fig 7.3). This was a house measuring 15 × 4.5m. The groups of long huts, some of them platform houses (averaging about 7–8m in length and about 3m in width), which are found to the east of Tyddyneithiniog on the brow of the valley side overlooking the Afon Dulyn are associated with small irregular fields; these are said to exhibit 'marks of the medieval plough' (RCAHMW 1956, 31–3, nos 138–150) but the date of the narrow ridge and furrow here is unknown and is found in later contexts higher up the valley. These settlements had apparently fallen out of use by the time that the farm of Tyddyneithiniog, first recorded in the sixteenth century (UWB, Baron Hill 2417), was established, its name referring to gorse and implying land that had by then become neglected and overgrown. Of the surviving house foundations, one near the modern leat which crosses the site may be the remains of the sixteenth-century house; it is considerably larger than the earlier long huts, measuring 11.5 × 5.3m (SMR, RCAHMW 1956, no 316).

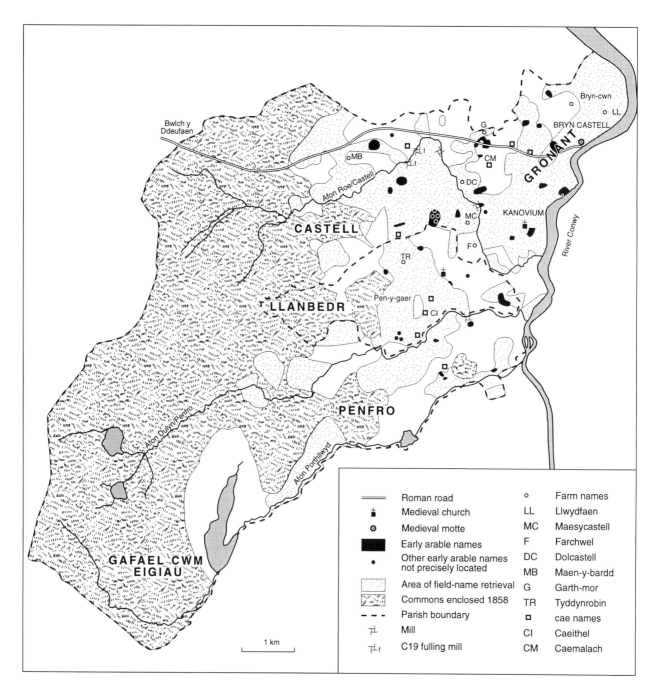

Fig 7.3 Medieval townships and field-name retrieval in Caerhun and Llanbedrycennin; areas of medieval cultivation and farms referred to in the text.

The fifteenth and sixteenth centuries were a crucial period for the emergence of the present day pattern of settlement. The parishes of Caerhun and Llanbedrycennin are so well documented that it may be possible to trace development here more fully than in many other areas through the large number of surviving rentals and deeds, building upon the work already carried out by Jones Pierce, Hughes and others. Jones Pierce has shown how the holdings of Llwydfaen, in particular, developed out of the native holdings in the fifteenth century (Jones Pierce 1942; 1972;

eg UWB, Baron Hill 2285, 2292, 2317). The documents suggest that many of the farms in the Conwy valley had been established by the end of the fifteenth century, although it is often difficult to distinguish between the names of messuages and those of parcels of land, while many bore the names of their contemporary owners and have subsequently been difficult or impossible to trace. The difficulty with the early documentation lies in the identification of holdings and fields; these can only be precisely located if they can be related to later cartographic evidence.

In the Llanaber study (Hooke 1975), it was suggested that *cae* as a field-name appeared to represent a period of enclosure after the demise of the shared clan lands. In Llanaberuwchmynydd the name often occurred just below the margins of the commons but below any *ffridd* names (see below). Some occurred as farm names such as Caegwian, Cae-mur Hywel and Caetudur, farms tucked in at the head of tributary valleys or in common-side locations. Caegwian was associated with an encroachment of fifteen acres in 1575 (Hooke 1975, 227). Others along the coastal zone seemed to be in secondary locations. Colin Thomas also found that *cae* as a field-name was 'by far the most frequent name associated with *tyddyn* in the rental of Crown lands in 1592' and *cae* with *erw* and *maes* 'were among the earliest enclosed territories to become intensively used before the need or desire arose to expand into the *ffridd* zone' (Thomas, C 1992, 44). However, the term *cae* may have continued to be used and implemented at a later date for almost any enclosed land.

Several *cae* names appear in Caerhun in the fifteenth century. Caeithel in Llanbedrycennin (Fig 7.3) is recorded as early as 1438 (UWB, Baron Hill 2290) when it was already divided between the two tenements of Caeithelisa and Caeithelucha; near Ty'n-y-groes, Cae-y-pin appears in the records in 1451 with a new house built in 1555 (UWB, Baron Hill 2335, 2423) and Caemalach in 1464 (UWB, Baron Hill 2358). Other holdings include Tyddyn-y-llwyn in Penfro, recorded in 1498 (UWB, Baron Hill 2659). Others appear in sixteenth-century records. Farchwel, beside the Afon Roe, is first named in 1518 (UWB, Baron Hill 2370) and it 'is probable that some fabric of the present house dates from the middle of that century' (RCAHMW 1956, 23, no 92). Garth-mor, in the far north of Caerhun parish, is recorded in 1520 (UWB, Baron Hill 2373). The earliest recordings do not, of course, necessarily indicate the date at which such holdings came into being and many remain unrecorded until a much later date. The records suggest, however, that many of the holdings were relatively limited in extent and eighteenth- and nineteenth-century estate deeds confirm that the large estates which had been established in this area continued to work the land, with a few exceptions, through quite small tenant holdings.

The Conwy valley, away from the marshes of the flood plain, was excellent crop growing land and Gareth Haulfryn Williams (1979) has analysed productivity in the seventeenth century on the Caerhun demesne, one of the major estates which was to acquire land in Caerhun and Llanbedrycennin. The Davies family, who lived at Caerhun, were descended from the medieval clansmen of Castell. The home estate lay around the present day nineteenth-century mansion beside the parish church but the estate in the seventeenth century was scattered over the old arable lands, administered as numerous individual farm holdings, as was common for the period. The Bulkeleys of Baron Hill also had land here and there were other substantial farm owners in addition. The seventeenth-century Caerhun rentals itemize oats, barley, rye and peas among the crops listed, but also show

that livestock comprised over half the value of the estate, referring to cattle, sheep, goats and horses but with cattle representing the greatest value. While the lush pastures along the Conwy offered hay and grazing, the upland *hafod* of Hafod-y-clawdd, above Ro-wen, was the breeding ground for horses and goats; cattle were pastured higher in the mountains.

The Use of Marginal Land

In an important study of the environment and human settlement in Arlechwedd Isaf published in 1940, R Elfyn Hughes related the documentary evidence to vegetation and soil type, attempting to show the progression of farming from the Conwy valley on to the higher land. It is in many ways the empty marginal land which is of such interest because it is here that the advances and recessions of settlement can still be identified on the ground. It was in the mid 1970s, when walking in Llanaber over the *friddoedd* above Egryn, that the present writer first became aware of the rich field remains that survived on the upper pastures: former house sites, the broken down walls of enclosures and tiny fields, with an occasional hint of terracing suggesting cultivation. These sites had hitherto been unrecorded. Sketch surveys showed that these collections of house platforms spread across the hillside mostly between the 183m and 228m contours. They are best preserved on the holdings of Egryn and Llwynwcws (Fig 7.4) but they occur, almost always in clusters, at intervals along the coastal strip, usually where water was available from a nearby spring or stream. They are not confined to the coastal strip and more have recently been identified on the estuary side of the Llawllech ridge.

A first reaction was to see these as the sites of medieval *hafodydd*. They are certainly older than the great intake fields which seem to represent Tudor encroachment on to the *ffriddoedd*, with house platforms often cut by the field walls, and some lie above today's mountain wall. Are these the summer dwellings of the clansmen, one of whom in 1326 was fined in Llanaber 'for keeping his animals "in the common pasture of the old settlement" (*in communi pastura del hendrevi*) after the community of the township (*communitas villate*) had moved, early in May of that year, with its animals to the mountains' (Jones, G R J 1972, 298; PRO SC 2/225/28)?

While the earlier sites appear to have left little impression on later field-names, this system was still continuing in Llanaber in 1687 and *hafod* field-names are recorded on several major holdings in the nineteenth-century records (Fig 7.5). By this date the upland *hafod* seems to have been appropriated to a specific lowland farm, often but not always termed a *hendref*, but field investigation has frequently failed to find evidence of the long huts found above Egryn where such later field-names occur. One *hafod* field-name above Llwynddu, *Cae hafod tŷ*, does contain a house platform but a second house site is cut by the field wall which it obviously pre-dates. The name was perhaps given to the field, an

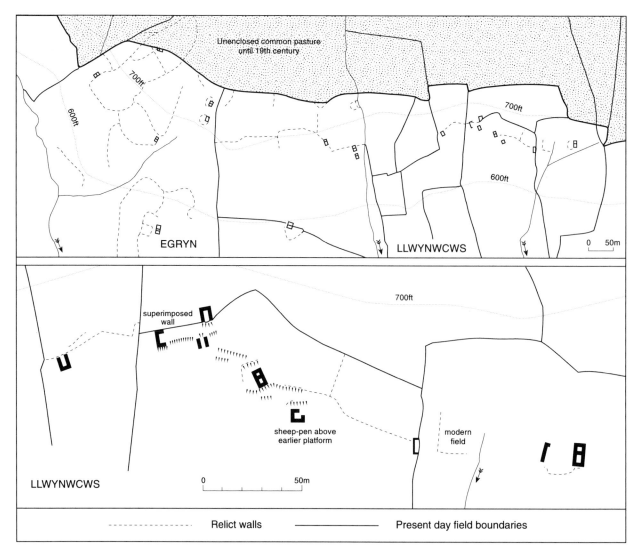

Fig 7.4 Hafod *sites and* friddoedd *in Llanaber, Merioneth, with a detail of those in Llwynwcws.*

intake above the *ffridd* fields, in recognition of its former use but the enclosure is likely to have served as a cattle yard, as the second small field, *Buarth bach,* suggests. In Llanaber several fields bearing *hafod* names contained the ruins of barns or byres; one *hafod* at 244m in St David's valley had become the site of a farmhouse known as Hafoduchaf that, once it came to be permanently occupied, had acquired another *hafod* higher up the valley at 282m; here *ffridd oddiar caeau y fotty* and *wern tan y fotty* record the upper *hafod* where there is today a ruined byre. The site lies below Craig Aderyn, a south-facing spur of Diffwys, where a summer house called *Havottu mownog carreg yr aderyn* was attached to the farms of Llechfraithuchaf and Llech-fraithisaf in 1687.

Certainly there were *hafodydd* in Caerhun. Cwm Eigiau was appropriated to a bond *gafael* of the township of Castell and had been an area of summer grazing for cattle. Increasing value was attached to such land in the sixteenth century and Hughes (1940, 22) notes how four small houses were built there at a height of 369m (he gives a date of 1554 but this

cannot be substantiated from the documents he cites) and about 100 cattle were kept there (UWB, Baron Hill 2718–2724) and in winter they were folded at Dolymarchog and Gronant in the main Conwy valley (UWB, Baron Hill 2637). In the mid seventeenth century the Bulkeley family asserted their rights to the Cwm Eigiau lands, then described as sheepwalks with the barn of Pant-y-pyrse (UWB, Baron Hill 2637). There were a number of other *hafodydd* near Cwm Eigiau, their names attached to later farm holdings: Hafodygarreg and Hafod-fach formed an island of enclosed land on the southern bank of the Afon Dulyn, Hafod Gors-wen lay to the north (Fig 7.6). In the same locality, however, Maeneira may have been permanently occupied for it was granted as a tenement as early as 1468 (UWB, Baron Hill 2654). Other *hafod* farm names include Hafod-y-rhiw which lay just over the boundary in Dolgarrog and is now used as a mountain rescue post; others are found to the north of the Afon Castell and include Hafotty-gwyn and Hafod-y-cae; Hafod-y-clawdd lay on the south bank a little to the east. The earliest recorded dates of these holdings have yet to be ascertained but seasonal settlements here can be traced back to the fifteenth century. Work on the original documents is not yet complete and there are many other Baron Hill manuscripts which warrant inspection.

Another term frequently applied to buildings used on a seasonal basis is *lluest, llety,* 'a lodging, a dairy house'. *Lletty y Marghet* is recorded in 1448–9 (UWB, Baron Hill 2530). *Lletty'rdderwen* (or Ddeufaen), recorded in 1598 (UWB, Baron Hill 2530), may have lain at a relatively high altitude on the commons and is, interestingly, associated with metal or ore that might be on the premises ('mynes called lead oare or ane other mettall') and with passage for horses and men to and from the mines, perhaps suggesting a further source of occupation for the inhabitants of these small difficult upland holdings. The possibility of finding ore on other *hafod* land also appears in a deed of 1614 (UWB, Baron Hill 2576). The shielings were, however, undoubtedly primarily concerned with the seasonal pasturing of stock. Llettytudor, situated in Bryn Gwenith in Penfro (in the far south of Caerhun to the north of Llyn Coedty), is mentioned *c* 1450 (UWB, Bangor MS 1939) and again alongside Ffridd-ddu and *Maes y Gwenydray* (*Maes y Gwyddfa*) in 1564 and 1574–5 when leased by Sir Richard Bulkeley; only at the

latter date was it specified that the land should be enclosed with fences within ten years, the waste to be 'cleansed and scoured off', the meres and bounds to be carefully maintained' (UWB, Baron Hill 2683, 2685). Another *llety* name occurs on the common of Allt Wyllt in the south of Caerhun parish and appears to refer to an encroachment cottage. Other *llety* names include *Llettu'r ddwy fuwch* and *Llettu'r un fwch* recorded in 1774 which related to tiny cottages near Garth-mor in the long settled zone. A field-name *lletty llwyd* also occurs on the valley holding of Pen-y-bryn-pedr in the nineteenth century while there is a Hafod house name near Tyn-y-groes. It may be that such names were affectionately transferred more readily to cottage dwellings without any implication of seasonal use.

All over the hillsides in Caerhun are the ruins which represent the foundations and lower walls of rectangular long huts: abandoned dwellings of various types, the construction of which the RCAHMW places between the middle ages and the eighteenth century (RCAHMW 1964, clxxviii). It is not clear how many features like this existed at lower levels, to be destroyed by subsequent farming, but some surviving examples have been discussed above. Some appear to have been permanently occupied homesteads but

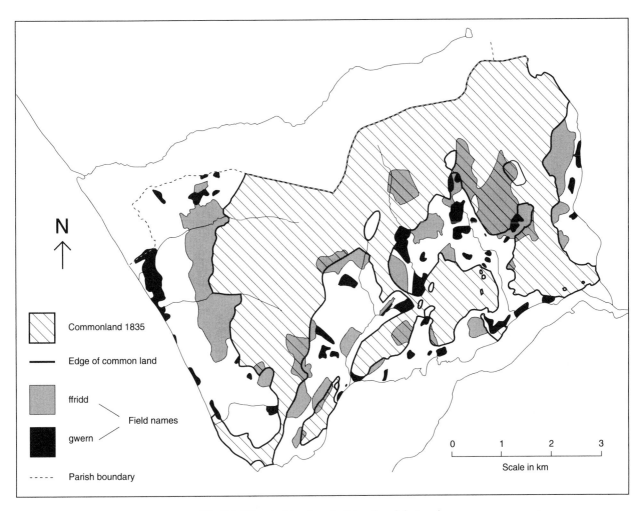

Fig 7.5 Historical land use in Llanaber, Merioneth.

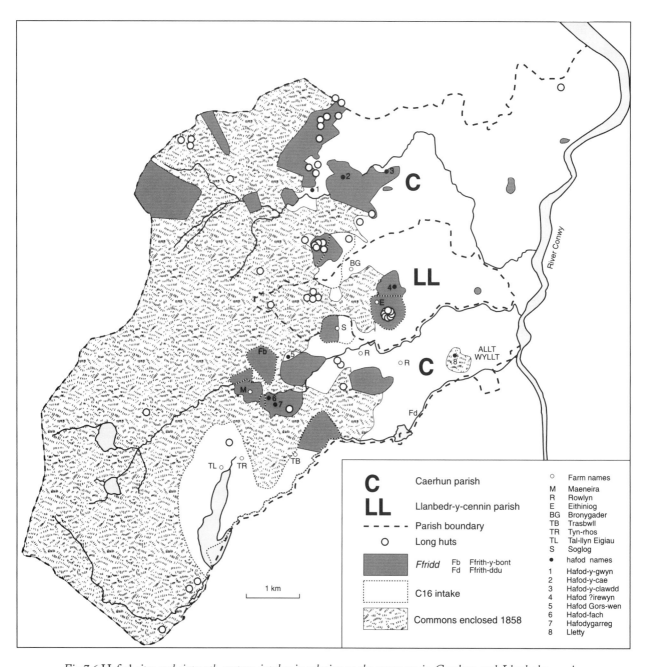

Fig 7.6 Hafod *sites and sixteenth-century intakes in relation to the commons in Caerhun and Llanbedrycennin.*

many others lie at high altitudes and may represent either movement onto marginal land at particular periods or settlements that were used on a seasonal basis (see Ward, p 104–7). Although they have been surveyed in the field no excavation has been carried out, and these sites cry out for environmental analysis which might provide evidence for the type of land use with which they were associated.

Today such sites show an upland bias, located generally between the 183m and 365m contours, as in the parish of Llanaber. Many of them are aligned at right angles to the contours, built into the hillside at the upper end with a platform or apron at the lower end. A large number of long huts lie in the same area as the previously noted round huts

above Maen-y-bardd (Figs 7.1, 7.6). One group, two rectangular huts within an enclosing wall faced with upright stone, are associated with lazy beds (SH 74097207, RCAHMW 1956, 31, no 129); another long hut in this area, representing the remains of a small cottage which contained a fireplace at its upper end, is associated with an enclosure and lies on top of a field terrace (RCAHMW 1956, 31, no 131). Another cluster lie at a similar height above Bronygader. Of those near the trackway leading to the Afon Ddu in Llanbedr, one site, at least, seems to be far too substantial to have been a temporary dwelling but the huts are characteristic platform houses, one with a hood wall; one a little to the west seems to be actually

Fig 7.7 Medieval settlements and fields on the holding of Tyddyneithiniog in Llanbedrycennin
(Copyright Mary Aris, Gwynedd Archives Service).

earlier than the present track, which swerves to avoid it. Many of the house sites have been reused for sheepfolds or byres which obscure the house remains below them. The groups noted on the holding of Tyddyneithiniog, probably of various dates, are, however, associated with a particularly well-preserved field system and a possible droveway (above p 83; Fig 7.7).

Permanent settlement undoubtedly reached higher levels at several periods in the past but few of the observed long hut sites can be correlated with documentary evidence. Neither do they bear any relationship to later field-names or references to later known *hafodydd*. It is entirely possible that a substantial number of such sites represent movement onto the margins of the commons for permanent occupation in medieval times. Some, however, lie at such heights and amidst such inclement terrain that it is difficult to believe that they can ever have been anything other than seasonal *hafodydd*. A small group lie high on the Bwlch y Ddeufaen at a height of 411m; others above 518m in the innermost recesses of the valley of the Afon Dulyn and yet others in a remote situation within Cwm Eigiau. Amazingly, one of the latter, a platform house measuring 9m by 3.7m, is situated at 518m but is associated with an enclosure which shows signs of plough-marks (RCAHMW 1956, 34, no 163).

Certainly assarts and encroachments were taking place along the moorland edge and in Llanaber some of these could be identified with a fair degree of precision because they had been entered in the Earl of Leicester's list of encroachments into his so-called 'Forest of Snowdon' in 1575. These were substantial intakes of as much as 20 acres in extent, usually on the edge of the upland commons, but could not be equated with settlement sites, being mostly additional intakes to established farms (Hooke 1975). In the Conwy valley, the Baron Hill manuscripts also show estate owners buying, leasing and enclosing sections of the mountain pastures, usually referred to, if named, as the *ffriddoedd*. Several near Llyn Eigiau are said to be bounded by or even to lie within the Forest of Snowdon in late sixteenth-century deeds (UWB, Baron Hill 2697–9). The next step in the Conwy valley has been to try to map these fields from contemporary and later documents.

The exact implications of the term *ffridd* are far from clear. It is usually interpreted as 'hill pasture, often marked out as summer pasture in the first instance' (Adams 1976, 95, citing Sylvester 1955–6, 21); the *Geriadur Prifysgol Cymru* gives 'rough mountain pasture, sheepwalk; woodland, forest, park'. Certainly, in the *Record of Caernarvon* (Ellis 1838) the *Havotreffrith* fulfilled the function of summer pasture in the commote of Ardudwy. The term here seems to have been attached initially to unenclosed land, only in Tudor times becoming attached to the large intakes that had then been newly enclosed. In Llanaber these formed a wide band above the arable lands but below the land still unenclosed in the nineteenth century, the characteristic land use illustrated in the *ffridd* names given to these intakes. The band was unbroken for some 3km along the coastal range but occurred intermittently at the valley heads and along the edges of the commons above the Mawddach (Fig 7.5). Here the *ffridd* name was also attached to part of the commons themselves, usually the area immediately adjacent to the enclosed land. The term may have been related to the Old English term *fyrhð* which is taken to mean 'wooded countryside' and often appears in later official or semi-official records as 'frith or forest', using the latter term 'in the older sense of game-preserve or woodland interspersed with scrub' (Richards 1967, 24), but again the exact implications are unknown. To return to the subject touched upon at the beginning of this paper, it is likely that woodland was much more extensive in these regions until the increase in grazing pressure in the fifteenth and sixteenth centuries added to the difficulties facing the natural regeneration of trees on these podzolised and waterlogged soils. Whole trunks of birch have been seen far above the present tree line a few feet down in the peat above the Afon Dulyn where it has been eroded by streams.

The *ffridd* names of Caerhun and Llanbedrycennin occur in a similar location to those of Llanaber and the nineteenth-century enclosure award frequently refers to *ffridd* intakes as 'old enclosed land'. They form islands in the commons around the farms of Hafod-fach and Hafodygarreg, around the upland farms of Ffrith-y-bont and Hafod Gors-wen, Hafod-y-gwyn etc (Fig 7.6). A further group of *ffridd* intakes lie, as in Llanaber, between the old enclosed lands and the common edge; these include the fields of Tyddyneithiniog and some of the fields of the Rowlyn farms. Ffrith-ddu farm stands on the margin of Waun Bryngwenith. To complicate matters, some of the *ffriddoedd* acquired different names: a deed of 1611 records the sale of various *ffriddoedd* in Penfro, namely *Afon Eigie, Rhos y Fengal, Llethr Glas, Allt Moel y Cesyg* and *Carreg yr Eigie*, and this deed defines the bounds of these (UWB, Baron Hill 2729). Some of the *ffridd* names were attached to land distant from their mapped holdings and have been difficult to identify. The term obviously conveyed a meaning of upland pasture but became attached to intakes from the commons made in the fifteenth and sixteenth centuries; as late as 1858 a newly enclosed area high on the upper flanks of Drum was given the name *Fridd Cwm Ithel*. In the same area, another enclosure of this date is named *Ffrith Bwlch y Ddeufaen* in 1919 (Gwynedd Co Arch, XSC0121), suggesting, perhaps, that the term had been attached to much of the commonland prior to enclosure.

There is documentary evidence of a number of new farms having been established beyond the ancient core areas by the end of the fifteenth century and during the sixteenth century. In this period grazing was intensified in the marginal zone as the newly emerging large estates took every opportunity to extend their holdings, largely at the expense of the common waste (Emery 1967, 377–81) usually, therefore, taking in part of the unenclosed land. Maen-y-bardd, recorded by the mid fifteenth century, is discussed above. In addition to the farms noted in Cwm Eigiau, Tyddyneithiniog appears in the Baron Hill manuscripts 2417 and 2449 as already in existence by the sixteenth century, occupying a shelf of land below Pen-y-gaer hillfort and above the Afon Dulyn (RCAHMW 1956, 100, no 314). It stands among the complex of possibly earlier long huts and small enclosures discussed above. New land on the edge of the commons appears to have been taken in beyond the Rowlyn farms in the sixteenth century, themselves first recorded at the beginning of the same century: Hughes (1940, 23) notes the enclosure of a holding called *Gwern fays y glog* (UWB, Baron Hill 2953; mapped in Emery 1967,148–9, fig 7), later known as Soglog, on the northern bank of the Afon Dulyn. Emery also notes large sixteenth-century intakes above the farms of Waunfechan and Bronygader (Fig 7.8). Significantly, five of the seven fields attached to Tyddyneithiniog in 1777 and 1832 bore *ffridd* names: *Ffrith uchaf, Ffrith newydd, Ffrith cefn tai, Ffrith ysgubor* and *Ffrith ganol* - only the field around the cottage and a cattle yard bore other names - suggesting that the land was uncultivated when enclosed. A substantial part of Bronygader land also bore this name. Some of the new farms themselves bore *ffridd* names: Fridd-ddu is recorded by 1564 (UWB, Baron Hill 2683) and Ffridd-bach and Fridd-y-bont are recorded later. Here the place-name index compiled by the late Professor Melville Richards (UWB) can offer invaluable assistance.

Some of the *hafod* settlements were also to become permanent farms in the sixteenth century: the farms of Trasbwyll, Tyn-rhos and Tal-llyn Eigiau are recorded in the Baron Hill manuscripts, (the last glossed as 'a cottage and a little percyll of land inclosed to it' (UWB, Baron Hill 2718). Earlier this had been a dairy house called *Tallyn Eigie* and adjoining *Tallyn Eigie* was *Rhose y Vengill* where Edward Williams had built several small houses (UWB, Baron Hill 2718–2724; Davies 1979, 31). These farms stand out as an enormous expanse of enclosed land in Cwm Eigiau on the nineteenth-century maps, their huge fields still largely undivided. Williams believes that seasonal use of the *hafodydd* was nearing the end of its existence by the last quarter of the seventeenth century on the Caerhun estates, when Hafod-y-clawdd (Fig 7.6) appears to have been abandoned for a period before becoming just another farm on the estate (Williams 1979, 44). Hafod-y-gwyn was permanently occupied in 1774 when its field known as *Ffrith newydd* was described as 'fenced out from the Common' (Gwynedd Co Arch, Caerhun estate papers CRO XM 437 3).

Vegetation Names

Field- and farm names were particularly illustrative of changing vegetational cover in Llanaber parish. Wood names occur thickly over the hills and valley sides of Llanaberuwch-

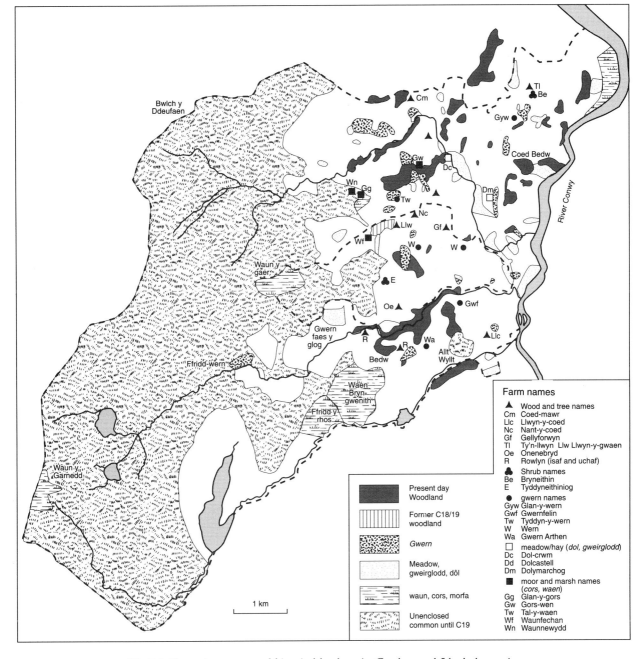

Fig 7.8 Vegetation names and historical land use in Caerhun and Llanbedrycennin.

mynydd beyond the Llawllech ridge and suggest much later clearance here than along the coastal zone. Settlement names contain the elements *goitre*, 'homestead in a wood', *gelli*, 'grove' and *coed*, 'wood', together with woodland recorded in nineteenth-century field-names. This side of the parish remains more heavily wooded today although the native deciduous woods have frequently been replaced by the ubiquitous conifer or, at best, by foreign species of oak.

In Caerhun and Llanbedrycennin, the valleys away from the river Conwy are still wooded where they carve their way down to the main valley and this is also reflected in some farm names (Fig 7.8). Llwyn-y-coed, combining the term *llwyn*, 'grove', with *coed*, stands beside the main north-

south valley road but had no surviving woodland by the nineteenth century; it did, however, have extensive hay meadows on the flood plain. Above the Afon Dulyn, Llwyn-on is 'ash grove' and Onenebryd also refers to the ash; the Rowlyn farms may take their name from *ywlwyn*, 'the yew grove' (UWB, Melville Richards' place-name index). Llwyn-y-gwaew/gwaen, Ty'n-llwyn and Gellyforwyn are other 'grove' names indicating pockets of woodland in the northern part of Llanbedrycennin parish. Tyddyn-y-coed stands a little further to the east. Other *coed* names are found in the north of Caerhun parish. Tyddyneithiniog, on the other hand (as noted above), on its shelf of higher land, refers to *eithin*, 'gorse'. It is likely that some deliberate tree planting took place on the main home estate of Caerhun Hall and perhaps around Gors-wen (now a National Nature Reserve). Coed Bedw above Caerhun Hall is the birch wood. There are also a number small plantations in the main valley, such as that to the north of Llwydfaen, but elsewhere the woodland mainly survives on the steeper slopes of the valley sides where farming was difficult, especially along the rivers Dulyn and Castell.

Cors, 'bog, marsh', occurs in the name of Gors-wen but does not seem to be common. Fridd y Rhos, referring to damp moorland, is the name for an extensive area on the northern side of the Afon Porthllwyd in Cwm Eigiau and gives a clear picture of the peaty areas of rough pasture found in this part of the parish. Ffridd-wern also occurs in the valley of the Afon Dulyn and Hughes writes of the upland alder and birch woods on peaty soils being enclosed and cleared during the sixteenth century for hay; he names _Rhos y wyngyll_ (elsewhere named _Rhos y Vengill_) and _Gwern y llyn_ (or _llwyn_) _bychan_ on the banks of the Afon Porthllwyd and _Gwern fays y glog_ enclosed in the same period on the banks of the River Dulyn (Hughes 1940, 23; UWB, Baron Hill 2688, 2718–2724). Wern as a farm name occurs on several occasions (Fig 7.8). On a smaller scale, waterlogged pockets often gave rise to small alder thickets and _gwern_ field-names are common for small enclosures near streams and rivers, mainly in the east of the parish; pockets are found on many farms in the eighteenth and nineteenth centuries. Low-lying marshy land may also bear names containing the term _gwaun_ but often this appears to describe rather drier upland moorland (Kelly, pers comm). Waun y Gaer was an extensive area of moorland on the edge of the commons near Penygadair in Llanbedrycennin, Waun y Garnedd the name given to the high northern slopes of Carnedd Llewelyn on the western boundary of Caerhun, and Waun Bryngwenith the moorland on the watershed between the Afon Dulyn and Afon Porthllwyd in Caerhun. Hughes (1940, 8–9) describes the high northern boundary as an area predominantly characterized by blanket peat but the lower _gwaun_ areas he classifies as areas where dwarf gorse (_Ulex galii_) and grasses such as mat grass and bent grass (_Nardus-Agrostis_) are the dominant species. Along the banks of the Conwy _morfa_ names indicate saltmarsh often enclosed and drained as late as the nineteenth century.

Hay meadows were of enormous value, whether upland or low lying, and were usually found alongside streams and rivers. Land set aside for hay meadow is shown by the frequent occurrence of _gweirglodd_ names (_gwair,_ 'hay', _clawdd,_ 'hedge, bank, boundary') all over the enclosed area of the parish, even on the lands of Soglog beside the upper waters of the Afon Dulyn, but these are most extensive on the flood plain of the Conwy itself. _Dôl,_ 'meadow, pasture', is less in evidence for hay meadows but is found in the farm names Dolcastell, Dolymarchog and Dol-crwm beside the Afon Roe.

Later Changes in the Landscape

There were other changes in the valleys of Caerhun which could be deciphered by field study. In the seventeenth and eighteenth centuries the land was farmed, as noted above, from myriad small holdings, part of much larger estates. Estate records occasionally include detailed maps of these holdings and their field boundaries can readily be traced on the ground. Usually there has been little alteration but occasionally whole field systems have been reorganized. These offer considerable scope for field wall analysis, especially when the documentary record has been fully analysed. The remnant walls of prehistoric farming can be identified, as can those associated with the long hut complexes, although detailed work where such sites intermingle, as around Tyddyneithiniog, might prove of considerable interest. Interestingly, Jones Pierce (1972, 209) suggests that most of the cultivated lands worked by the medieval native farmers were not marked by individual boundaries but consisted of intermingled quillets more akin to the English open-field system. Certainly the field walls of such farms as Llwydfaen cannot pre-date the amalgamation of these earlier holdings. Enclosures are increasingly referred to after the fifteenth century but differences can also be detected in later field walls and enclosures. In the valley region, for instance, hedges are commonly found. In part, this probably reflects a lack of suitable stone on the valley alluvium but also suggests that clearance had already been completed when the hedged boundaries were planted. On occasions, hedges accompany stone walls and detailed plotting, due to commence shortly, may provide further valuable evidence of the sequence of field enclosure. The nineteenth-century walls of parliamentary enclosure are again distinctive not only in their straightness but also in their method of construction. Analysis of these boundaries is now part of an ongoing project in these two parishes.

The duration of the Napoleonic Wars (1793–1815) was another period of intensified upland usage (Thomas, D 1963). Detailed studies have yet to be carried out for the parishes of Caerhun and Llanbedrycennin to clarify whether any upland farmsteads were erected or rebuilt at this time. However, some of the patches of narrow ridge and furrow which represent abandoned areas of cultivation, as observed along the flanks of the Dulyn valley, may date from this period of rising crop prices. Some new holdings were established as late as the mid nineteenth century, probably at the time of the enclosure of the upland commons: Tan-y-bwlch in Caerhun seems to be one such example, the large windows of its ruined shell betraying its late construction.

The common pastures of the parishes of Caerhun and Llanbedrycennin lay open at the time of the tithe award surveys. Just over 5,840 acres of land in Caerhun and just over 400 acres in Llanbedrycennin were affected by the award of 1858, most of this land on the mountain slopes on the east side of the Carneddau range. A small common in Caerhun at Yr Allt Wyllt had seen encroachment in tiny parcels since the sixteenth century. Elfyn Hughes (1940,

24) notes how many of these cottagers gained a living as fisherman on the Conwy and late nineteenth-century census returns reveal that a number of the occupants were then working as quarrymen or sulphur miners (an iron sulphide mine had been operating some years previously in the neighbouring parish to the south). This small common lay upon a steeply sloping hillside above the Afon Porthllwyd and was a maze of tiny enclosures and cottages in the nineteenth century (Hooke forthcoming). Elfyn Hughes notes encroachments still taking place in these parishes as late as the nineteenth century, commenting upon the construction of a *tyddyn* called Tal-y-braich below Bwlch y Ddeufaen: the then occupant of Tyddyn-du told how his grandfather 'worked at night by candle light building walls, clearing and cultivating the land' (perhaps continuing the tradition of the *tŷ unnos* cottage) (Hughes 1940, 24). Enclosure of the hillside commons was not effected without dissent and there were riots in Caerhun but it did eventually take place. Not all the projected boundaries were ever constructed but the substantial walls of nineteenth-century enclosure were eventually to subdivide the former open hillsides with, however, no great effect upon the moorland vegetation.

Drainage of the Conwy marshes by Lord Newborough in the nineteenth century probably had a more lasting effect on land use. Valuable hay and pasture land and additional arable land was obtained by the cutting of drains. The remaining small areas of *gwern* marshland were also reclaimed. But if land was being gained in the lowlands abandonment was to dominate in the uplands. It is not perhaps surprising that some of the small lowland farms should have been amalgamated into larger units. Pen-y-llan, named in 1832 as a 36–acre farm (Gwynedd Co Arch, Vaynol estate papers 4071), was taken into the Rowlyn farms; Tynewydd, with 30 acres in 1774 (Gwynedd Co Arch, Caerhun estate papers XM 437), became part of the main Caerhun estate. Desertion is, however, much more evident in the upland parts of these parishes and may have been helped by the break-up of the large estates. The abandonment of Hafod-fach, Hafod Gors-wen and Maeneira, in their islands on the commons, may not occasion surprise and several were unoccupied by the end of the nineteenth century. Similarly Hafod-y-clawdd and Hafod-y-cae on the southern bank of the Afon Roe are now deserted. Likewise, the Cwm Eigiau farms, two of which were occupied by shepherds with their families as late as 1881, are now abandoned, as are the sixteenth-century intakes identified by Elfyn Hughes (1940, 23) and Emery (1967, 148) above Rowlynuchaf (the dwelling of Soglog referred to as an 'old house' in 1920 (Gwynedd Co Arch, Caerhun estate sales cat) and the old sites near Bronygader and Rowlynisaf have been left in favour of new sites. But a further string of dwellings along the road into the valley above Pen-y-gaer also lie empty, their lands farmed only from below. Ffrith-y-bont, Tan-y-bwlch and Bwlch-y-gaer are falling into ruin. Tyddyneithiniog failed long ago but even Onenebryd, much closer to the main Conwy valley,

has been deserted in recent times. Further to the south, Rowlynisaf and Rowlynuchaf are no longer farmed, their fields used for the cattle of neighbouring farms. Sadly, many of these buildings may one day be features in the landscape little more intrusive than the platform sites of their medieval predecessors. They, will, however, be yet another overlay on the palimpsest that is Caerhun and Llanbedrycennin.

Mining has also left an impression in the area and abandoned workings can be seen at various locations. Slate was quarried at several places in Cwm Eigiau in the nineteenth century and a tramway was constructed to a wharf on the Conwy in the parish of Dolgarrog. Near Melynllyn, at the head of the valley of the Afon Dulyn, a small slate quarry which was initially opened in the 1860s later went over to the exploitation of a honestone vein, continuing in operation until 1908 (Jones & Gwyn 1989, 23); ruinous buildings still stand at the site. It is the collection and rerouting of water, however, that has made the most impact on the more remote parts of these valleys this century. With the establishment of aluminium refining at Dolgarrog at the beginning of this century, several of the upland lakes were dammed to provide a supply of water for the works: Llyn Eigiau was dammed in 1910. A continuing shortage of water led to an extension of the scheme and a tunnel to take water from the Afon Dulyn to Llyn Eigiau was constructed by 1916 (Jones & Gwynn 1989, 66–7). The Llyn Eigau dam was to be breached in 1925, bringing disaster to the village below, but the systems still provide water for the generation of hydro-electric power at Dolgarrog and the system of leats was extended in the late 1950s, drawing water from as far north as the valley of the Afon Roe. One prominent leat encircles the holding of Tyddyneithiniog, narrowly avoiding the long hut sites discussed earlier but cutting across early field systems and the possible droveway.

Future Research

The way forward is obvious; the parishes of Caerhun and Llanbedrycennin have seen a considerable degree of documentary study already. R Elfyn Hughes (1940) worked through the Baron Hill manuscripts and Frank Emery (1967) again referred to the sixteenth-century intakes of Waunfechan and Bronygadair and of the Rowlyn farms; Elwyn Davies (1979) to the farms within Cwm Eeigiau. Gareth Haulfryn Williams (1979) has examined estate management in Caerhun *c* 1685. More recently, Charles Withers (1995), from his years of experience with students in this area, has analysed the model of settlement proposed by Colin Thomas (1992). Field survey is also well advanced (RCAHMW 1956), augmented by sites recorded in the Gwynedd Archaeological Trust Sites and Monuments Record. Nevertheless, there still remains scope for these fields of study to be integrated more fully and, above all, to be more deeply investigated by modern methods of environmental analysis. Further field survey, as noted above, may permit a closer classification of boundary types.

Della Hooke

How far did crop cultivation spread into the upper valleys? Is it possible to ascertain the period at which the long hut settlements were in use and what were their functions? Just when did the tree cover diminish to leave the rather depressing peat-filled wastes of today?

The widespread presence of *gwaun* names over the upland plateau strongly suggests that moorland was dominant in this area by the sixteenth century but wood and tree names indicate that woodland was rather more plentiful than it is today in the valleys and along the eastern rim of the plateau into the later historical period. The uplands obviously experienced an ebb and flow of farming activity: prehistoric and medieval settlement on what was later open moorland is clearly attested by surviving field remains. The long huts are, as yet, undated but many seem to date from medieval times, pre-dating the later, sixteenth-century period of expansion and were perhaps associated with native farming systems. In the sixteenth century there was a deliberate attempt by estate owners to recolonize the uplands for financial gain although pastoralism no doubt represented the main source of income from these upland holdings. Many of the holdings that were established remained in use, if not financially viable as independent units, into the nineteenth century, when a further spate of opportunism associated with the enclosure of the commons led to the establishment of a small number of new farms. However, few remain occupied in this upland area today.

The excellent documentary and cartographic record demands that a study be made of the boundaries and field walls found in these parishes in order to examine further the chonology of settlement and land use. Relict field walls often accompany the groups of long huts and an earlier system can be seen in places beneath the modern field walls near Rowlynisaf; walls topped with hawthorn hedges or hedges alone can be found in the main valley; the walls of nineteenth-century parliamentary enclosure are distinctive. Obviously, an investigation of many of these points is proposed over the next few years and it is hoped that it will be possible to include soil studies in order to look more closely at some of the sites that can be selected upon the basis of further enquiry. In being one of the best documented areas in North Wales, embodying both excellent agricultural land and marginal land that has been subject to massive fluctuations in land use and settlement, this is an area with considerable potential for providing answers that underlie an understanding of landscape evolution throughout Wales.

Acknowledgements

I should like to thank Kathryn L Sharp for drawing the figures. I am grateful to Mary Aris of Gwynedd Archives Service for her superb air photograph of the medieval settlements and fields on the holding of Tyddyneithiniog, to Richard Kelly for his comments upon Welsh land use terms, to Gareth Haulfryn Williams and Tomos Roberts for their encouragement and archival assistance, and to the RCAHMW for up to date data on the settlements of Tyddyneithiniog. I should also like to thank Professor Charles Withers for reintroducing me to an area I had not studied for many years and the students who participated in much of the fieldwork.

References

Unpublished Sources

Gwynedd County Archives (Gwynedd Co Arch)
 XSC0121
  Caerhun estate papers, CRO XM 437 3
  Vaynol estate papers, 4071
Public Record Office (PRO) E 179/242/53
 SC 2/225/28
Univesity of Wales Bangor (UWB) MS 39
  Baron Hill 2285, 2290, 2292, 2317, 2335, 2358, 2370, 2373, 2417, 2423, 2449, 2530, 2576, 2637, 2654, 2659, 2683, 2685, 2688, 2697–9, 2718–24, 2729, 2953
  Melville Richards' place-name index

Published Sources

Adams, I H, 1976, *Agrarian landscape terms: a glossary for historical geographers,* London
Casey, P J, 1969, Caerhun, in V E Nash-Williams (ed), *The Roman frontier in Wales,* 2nd edn revised M G Jarrett, Cardiff, 56–9
Casey, P J, 1989, Coin evidence and the end of Roman Wales, *Archaeol J,* 146, 320–9
Davies, E, 1979, Hendre and hafod in Caernarvonshire, *Trans Caernarvonshire Hist Soc,* 40, 17–46
Ellis, H (ed), 1838, *The Record of Caernarvon,* London
Emery, F, 1967, The farming regions of Wales, in J Thirsk (ed), *The agrarian history of England and Wales IV, 1500–1640,* Cambridge, 113–60
Gresham, C A, 1979, The commotal centre of Arllechwedd Isaf, *Trans Caernarvonshire Hist Soc,* 40, 11–16
Gresham, C A, 1988, Addendum; 'Vairdre alias Vaildre', *J Merioneth Hist Rec Soc,* 10, 221–6
Hooke, D, 1975, Llanaber: a study in landscape development, *J Merioneth Hist Rec Soc,* 7, 221–30
Hooke, D, 1983, The Ardudwy landscape, relict landscape features in southern Ardudwy, *J Merioneth Hist Rec Soc,* 9, 245–60
Hooke, D, forthcoming, A 'lost' settlement on the common of Allt Wyllt in the parish of Caerhun
Hughes, R E, 1940, Environment and human settlement in the commote of Arllechwedd Isaf, *Trans Caernarvonshire Hist Soc,* 2, 1–25
Jones, E, & Gwyn, D, 1989, *Dolgarrog, an industrial history,* Caernarfon
Jones, G R J, 1972, Post-Roman Wales, in H P R Finberg (ed), *The agrarian history of England and Wales, I.II, A.D. 43–1042,* Cambridge, 283–382
Jones Pierce, T, 1939, Some tendencies in the agrarian history of Caernarvonshire during the later middle ages, *Trans Caernarvonshire Hist Soc,* 1, 18–36, repr in J B Smith (ed), 1972 *Medieval Welsh society, selected essays by T Jones Pierce,* Cardiff, 39–60
Jones Pierce, T, 1942, The *gafael* in Bangor manuscript 1939, *Trans Hon Soc Cymmrodorion,* 158–88, repr in *Medieval Welsh society,* 195–227

RCAHMW (Royal Commission on Ancient and Historical Monuments in Wales and Monmouthshire), 1956, *An inventory of the ancient monuments in Caernarvonshire, Vol I: East, the cantref of Arllechwedd and the commote of Creuddyn*, London

RCAHMW (Royal Commission on Ancient and Historical Monuments in Wales and Monmouthshire) 1964, *An inventory of the ancient monuments in Caernarvonshire, Vol III: West, the cantref of Lleyn*, London

Richards, M, 1967, *Fridd/ffrith* as a Welsh place-name, *Studia Celtica*, 2, 29–86

Sylvester, D, 1955–6, The rural landscape of eastern Montgomeryshire, *Montgomeryshire Collect*, 54, 3–26

Thomas, C, 1970, Social organisation and rural settlement in medieval North Wales, J *Merioneth Hist Rec Soc*, 6, 121–31

Thomas, C, 1980, Field name evidence in the reconstruction of medieval settlement nuclei in North Wales, *Nat Libr Wales J*, 21, 340–56

Thomas, C, 1992, A cultural-biological model of agrarian colonisation in upland Wales, *Landscape Hist*, 14, 37–50

Thomas, D, 1963, *Agriculture in Wales during the Napoleonic Wars*, Cardiff

Walker, M F, & Taylor, J A, 1976, Post-Neolithic vegetation changes in the western Rhinogau, Gwynedd, north-west Wales, *Trans Inst Br Geogr*, new ser 1, 323–45

Williams, G H, 1979, Estate management in Dyffryn Conwy, c. 1685: the Caerhun, Baron Hill and Gwydir estates, *Trans Hon Soc Cymmrodorion*, 31–74

Withers, C W J, 1995, Conceptions of landscape change in upland North Wales: a study of Llanbedr-y-cennin and Caerhun parishes, c. 1560–c. 1891, *Landscape Hist*, 17, 35–47

Chapter 8

Transhumance and Settlement on the Welsh Uplands: A View from the Black Mountain

Anthony Ward

It is suggested that the variation in scale and form of rectangular buildings recorded on the Black Mountain, which may be late medieval to early post-medieval in date, is indicative of a settlement dynamic in the uplands involving the use of satellite outstations. The use of outstations assists in managing the extra risk inherent in living in more marginal landscapes by diversifying the extraction of resources across contrasting environmental zones. Such out-stations may have been used as seasonal dwellings during transhumant cycles; locations from which higher altitude resources could be exploited on an intermittent but not necessarily seasonal basis; and as incipient farmsteads. The nature of particular episodes of settlement will reflect the interaction of various factors including wider social, political, economic and climatic conditions.

Introduction

This paper discusses transhumance as an explanation for aspects of activity in the Welsh uplands during the later medieval and early post-medieval periods. It is stimulated by a landscape survey on the Black Mountain in the Brecon Beacons during which many rectangular buildings were recorded. Such structures have usually been connected with seasonal exploitation of the uplands both in the Brecon Beacons (Crampton 1966a; 1968; Miller 1967a) and elsewhere in Wales (eg Allen 1979; 1993; Butler 1988, 956).

Following a short account of the local landscape and of the survey, the structures are briefly described and dating parameters considered. The historical background is followed by discussion of climatic change as an influence on land use. This prompts examination of some strategies which assist the regulation of the risks inherent in living in agriculturally more marginal landscapes such as hill country. One particularly important strategy is the exploitation of seasonally available resources across different environmental zones. This can give rise to the practice of transhumance, a ubiquitous explanation for activity in the Welsh uplands. The challenges of using this explanation in archaeological studies of settlement remains of the medieval and early post-medieval periods are considered. Finally, the dynamics of upland settlement are discussed and applied to the evidence from the Black Mountain.

The Black Mountain and the Field Survey

The Black Mountain is located at the western end of the Brecon Beacons. The massif rises in excess of 800m OD around Llyn-y-Fan. The area in which the fieldwork was carried out is at the western end of the Mountain, an area with maximum altitudes in excess of 600m OD (Fig 8.1). Here the massif comprises a north-facing escarpment made up largely of Old Red Sandstone with areas of limestone; a ridge crest mainly of Millstone Grit; and extensive southerly dip slopes coinciding with the northern edge of the Coal Measures. The slopes are broken by steep sided gullies and valleys which mostly drain to north and south. The varied soils are united by their poor drainage and stoniness. At altitude there is a covering of peat. The predominantly grassy vegetation provides pasture which is low grade by current standards.

The survey has been undertaken almost entirely on unenclosed common land which begins above altitudes of around 200m OD (Fig 8.2). Current hill farms regularly extend to above 300m OD elsewhere in the region. The chosen area, therefore, straddles a zone which elsewhere has often been enclosed and subject to recent or present day agricultural improvement. This had the advantage of extending the survival of field remains along a particularly substantial altitudinal gradient, although survey could, of course, be continued very usefully to still lower altitudes within the present day enclosure.

The fieldwork has produced evidence for activity of

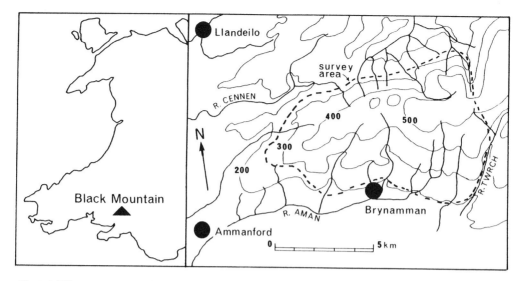

Fig 8.1 The survey area at the western end of the Black Mountain, Brecon Beacons (contours in metres).

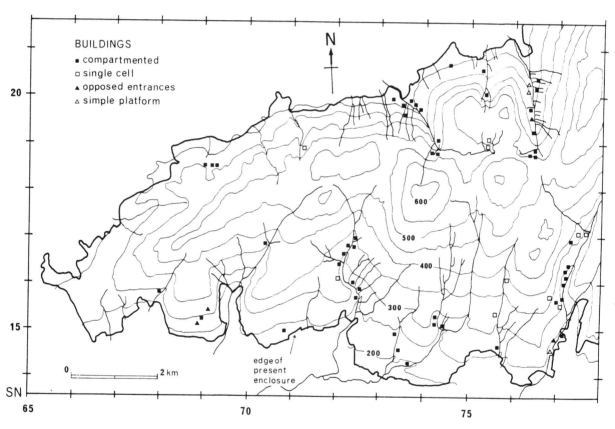

Fig 8.2 The distribution of different forms of buildings of likely medieval or early post-medieval date within the survey area (contours in metres).

both prehistoric and likely early historic date. There is also evidence for settlement, mostly in the form of rectangular buildings, of putative medieval or early post-medieval date.

The Buildings

In excess of 60 structures of likely medieval or early post-medieval date have been noted in an area of around 60 sq

km. They are located between 200m and 500m OD, with the majority in a 250m to 350m band. Most cluster in dispersed groups close to streams, often in deep cut gullies or valleys (Fig 8.2). A representative selection is illustrated in Figure 8.3.

The majority of structures are rectangular or sub-rectangular; they range from 10m to 30m in length. All are of drystone build. Most are subdivided into two or more

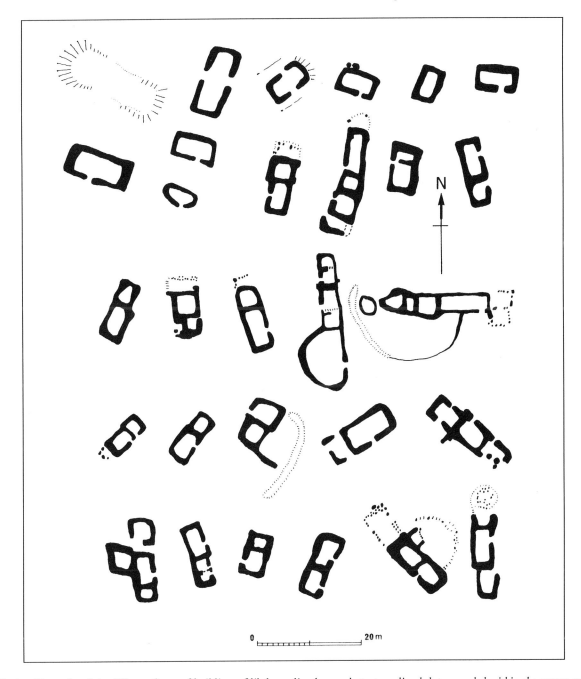

Fig 8.3 Examples of the different forms of buildings of likely medieval or early post-medieval date recorded within the survey area.

compartments. For the purposes of subsequent discussion elements of these buildings are assumed to have been used for human habitation. Often there are lesser structures close by which are presumed to be ancillary storage buildings, animal shelters and pens (Fig 8.4). A number of substantial, apparently, single cell buildings were recorded although, of course, they may have been subdivided internally by wooden partitions (eg Hook 1970). There are a few instances of buildings with opposed entrances but, mostly, obvious entrances are in one of the long sides. Sometimes compartments are connected internally.

The surviving walling ranged from around 0.3m to at least 1m in height. In some instances consistently low walling with minimal tumble suggests dwarf walls supplemented by turf or timber components. No fireplaces were noted, but floors were occasionally paved, and there were suggestions of the presence of drains under both internal cross walls and end walls of some structures. The buildings were not gabled and no stone or slate was seen which could have been used for roofing. There was only very limited evidence for remodelling or repair although it is allowed that this almost certainly occurred more frequently than can be detected by superficial examination. Discrete constructional techniques were noted, some of which were noticeably favoured within particular clusters of buildings. These include an end compartment defined by a single tier of

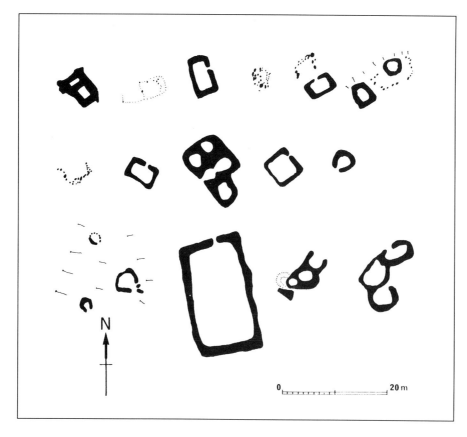

Fig 8.4 Examples of the foundations associated with buildings, apparently lesser ancilliary structures.

spaced, not contiguous, boulders; a pronounced orthostatic element in the construction; or walls faced by parallel slabs retaining a rubble core.

The majority of upstanding buildings are constructed on platforms, which vary in scale, and are set both at right-angles to and across the slope. There are also three or four examples of building platforms scarped at right-angles to the slope which have no visible signs of a superstructure. Around 35% of the buildings have associated annexes or plots. These are mostly small in area, with only a few being as much as several hundred square metres in extent. Only one building is accompanied by features which can be described as incipient fields. No outfield ploughing was noted close to the buildings although Mr Terry James of the RCAHMW (pers comm) has drawn attention to aerial photographs showing ploughing, which can almost certainly be linked to more recent structures, apparently connected with early industrial lime production. This is not visible under the conditions normally prevailing at ground level. Therefore, the possibility that aerial photography could produce further unrecognized evidence of cultivation in the vicinity of the rectangular buildings is accepted.

The range of variable structural detail noted could lead to an elaborate classification of the buildings. This, however, is avoided, not least because of a degree of confusion in the terminology previously used to describe similar sites, particularly when the presence or otherwise of a platform,

or its orientation in relation to the slope, is taken as a diagnostic feature. 'Platform house' was used by Lady Aileen and Sir Cyril Fox to describe a platform at right-angles to the contours on which there was sometimes visible evidence for a superstructure (eg Fox, A & C 1934; Fox, A 1939, 179–80; Fox, C 1940, 372–6). The Caernarvonshire *Inventories* used 'long hut' to describe all rectangular structures, regardless of the presence or orientation of any construction platform (RCAHMW 1956; 1960; 1964). Later, in one of the earlier Glamorgan *Inventories*, the definition of a 'long hut' was explicitly changed, its use being restricted to structures built across the slope. 'Platform house' was reserved exclusively for structures on platforms at right-angles to the slope (RCAHMW 1982, 43–4). However, a later Glamorgan *Inventory* concedes that a structure laid across the contours need not be a different type of building to one on a platform at right-angles to the contours (RCAHMW 1988, 5).

Consequently, a fourfold division is proposed for the structures recorded on the Black Mountain which gives weight to the general character of the superstructure rather than the presence of a platform and its orientation to the slope: firstly, the apparent single-cell building with one entrance; secondly, the apparent single-cell structure with opposed entrances; then, by far the most common building recorded, the compartmented structure; and, finally, building platforms without any trace of a superstructure.

Dating the Rectangular Buildings

There is minimal information with which directly to date these buildings on the Black Mountain. A sherd of Romano-British flagon found in a seepage close to one structure has been the sole artefact recovered. It at least serves as a reminder of a suggestion made in the context of settlement in north-west Wales that there could be an evolutionary relationship between prehistoric and protohistoric home-steads and compartmented linear buildings (Crew 1984). One building is partially overlain by spoil from an adjacent lime kiln; another has a lime kiln superimposed upon it. The kilns are examples of intermittent or 'field kilns' built to meet local agricultural requirements rather than large scale industrial production. An origin in the sixteenth century has been suggested for this type of kiln (Williams 1989, 12), but the form continues into the nineteenth century (Crossley 1994, 208–11) limiting utility of the structural sequence in indicating a *terminus ante quem* for the underlying buildings. Cartographic evidence drawn from estate records allows a pre-1700 date to be inferred for one cluster of buildings on the Black Mountain (Bowen Evans, pers comm).

Analogy with excavated upland-type settlement elsewhere in Wales is not hugely helpful. The paucity of securely dated sites is well rehearsed (Butler 1988, 956; Austin 1988, 153). The platform house (whatever that classification is worth) is the best dated of the upland house types but, unfortunately, the form seems to have had a long currency, from at least the twelfth century through until the fifteenth or sixteenth (Fox, A 1939; Knight 1984, 401–2; Kelly 1981–2, 875–82; Courtney 1991, 241–2). The single-cell structures in the Brenig Valley are firmly dated to the sixteenth century (Allen 1979; 1993). However, other excavated buildings are much less satisfactorily dated either on the basis of archaeological data, which is at least ambiguous, or by association with sparse documentary information. For example, the single-cell structure at Bwlch-y-Hendre, Cardiganshire, was thought to have been initially occupied in the sixteenth or early seventeenth centuries on the basis of land use considerations (Butler 1963, 405–6), while an origin firmly in the middle ages was suggested for a homestead in the Aber Valley, Caernarfonshire, on the basis of one sherd of pottery and a tentative mid fourteenth century documentary reference (Butler 1962).

Further afield in the north of England, a range of structures which look very similar to those on the Black Mountain have so far been dated by excavation to the later middle ages, and in the case of compartmented buildings, mostly to the sixteenth or seventeenth centuries, although with allowance for earlier origins (eg Ramm *et al* 1970, 9–39; Harbottle & Newman 1973, 154–8; 1977, 139–42). In south-west England analogous structural forms, such as those on Bodmin Moor, are assigned both to seasonal activity and to the 'long-house' tradition of permanent farmsteads which have origins in the middle ages, some continuing into the post-medieval period. Many of the houses on Bodmin Moor differ from those on the Black Mountain

through their association with fields (Johnson, N & Rose, P 1994, 80–98) and closely argued analogy between distant regions may not be reliable (Austin 1989, 237–8).

In conclusion, it is certainly premature to place the structures on the Black Mountain either within a very closely defined chronological bracket or to suggest a sequence for the different forms of building. Arguably, some structures are likely to predate 1500 but both construction and use beyond this date are probable.

A Historical Context for the Structures on the Black Mountain

The survey area is firmly within the Welshry. Mostly it lies at the southern boundary of the commote of Perfedd, clipping the western edge of the commote of Iscennen and adjoining the commote of Hirfryn (Fig 8.5), which were sub-units of Cantref Bychan (Lloyd 1935). Although Norman authority was established in Cantref Bychan late in the eleventh century with the foundation of a castle at Llandovery, this was very tenuous, and the area returned to Welsh rule before falling finally to the English during campaigns in 1276 and 1277. It was then incorporated into the Marcher Lordships (Davies, R R 1978, 29; Walker 1990, 90; Turvey 1990, 6–7). Perfedd became part of Llandovery, Iscennen part of Kidwelly (Evans, D L 1935, 208; Griffiths, R 1972, 14–17). To the south lay the Welshry of the Lordship of Gower and to the east Brycheiniog (Fig 8.5). Although the south-eastern boundary between Iscennen and Gower changed, probably in the late thirteenth or early fourteenth centuries (Rees, D 1988), the boundaries of Perfedd were largely stable for tenurial purposes through the middle ages into the post-medieval period as illustrated by mid eighteenth-century perambulations of the bounds (Morris 1985, 60–1).

In the early fourteenth century, Perfedd was populated largely by free tribesmen; it is recorded that the *maenorau* (see Longley p 41–2) were exclusively in the hands of free tenants of whom there were about 200 (Evans, D L 1935). Settlement foci would have been to the north west of the Black Mountain massif, at lower altitude in lands stretching to the River Towy (Davies, E 1936–7)(Fig 8.5). However, no systematic research seems to have been undertaken to identify the pattern of *gwely* lands held collectively by clans of free tribesmen and associated settlements.

In more recent centuries all landowners in the commote had common rights of grazing which included areas within the commote on the Black Mountain. These rights of common very likely derived from those held by tribal society under Welsh Law, a system which persisted in the area, albeit gradually disintegrating, to the beginning of the post-medieval period (Willis-Bund 1902, vii; Rees, W 1924, 217; Davies, E 1936–7, 56–7; Griffiths, M 1989, 233–4). The tenacity of Welsh customary law is attested by its continued operation in eastern Carmarthenshire in the early sixteenth century (Jenkins & Owen 1982, 24–5). Its extra-judicial application continued to impede effective husbandry

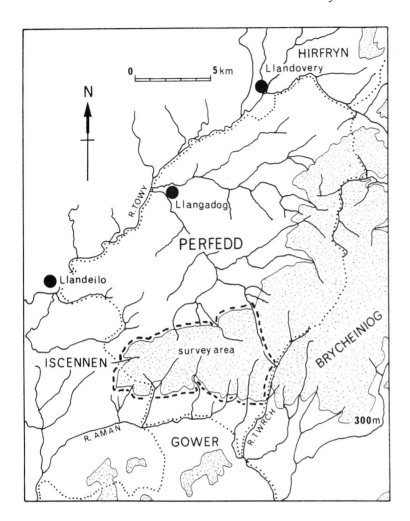

Fig 8.5 The commote of Perfedd in relation to other medieval administrative units. Land above c 300m OD stippled (after Morris 1985 and Rees, D 1991).

after the Act of Union by which it was formally abolished in 1536 (Owen, G 1892, 61; Colyer 1976, 3). The conservatism of remoter areas, in which category Perfedd seems to belong, should not be underestimated.[1]

It is not clear to what extent the present boundaries of the common land reflect those of former times. Some reduction in their extent might be expected through encroachment (Thomas, J G & Carter, H 1965, 145, 151–3; Griffiths, M 1989, 233–8) but at least along the southern edge of the commote, documentary sources suggest that the boundary between enclosed land and common has been reasonably constant since the sixteenth century (Bowen Evans 1991, 33).

There is little detail as regards population and settlement to supplement this very general account of Perfedd before records become fuller in the later seventeenth and particularly the eighteenth century. The very fragmentary historical information available for study at a local level across so much of the Welshry has encouraged general models of analysis and explanation which have emphasized some apparently widely applicable political, social, economic and demographic factors. These include *gavelkind*, the partible inheritance of the *gwely* lands by the sons which led to excessive morcellation into holdings which ceased to be

viable (Jones Pierce 1972, 341; Davies, R R 1978, 370–1; Jack 1988, 432); and then the decline of the *gwely* and the adoption of individual ownership, particularly from the later fourteenth century, although, as noted above, with allowance for local conservatism perpetuating the practice in remoter areas. There was also depopulation caused by plague and rebellion, particularly the Black Death in the mid fourteenth century and the Glyndŵr revolt of the early fifteenth century which accelerated the move from customary tenurial practices. Increasingly customary services were commuted for cash payment and a market in land was created. The agro-pastoral economy tended to place a growing emphasis on the pastoral end of the continuum, in which cattle, and increasingly sheep, were important; this was more manageable for a reduced workforce (Jones 1965; Davies, R R 1978, 425–55; Thomas, C 1975, 31; Jack 1988, 446, 493; Owen, D H 1989, 206–16). Also individually owned holdings were consolidated into small estates and the establishment of new farms encroached on common grazing, much of which had been a focus for summer grazing only (Griffiths, M 1989, 233–8). Additionally, climatic change has been seen as significant in the story of the upland areas in particular for much of the middle ages and early post-medieval period (Austin 1989, 234–8).

The Influence of Climatic Change

The short-lived phase of climatic amelioration, the 'Medieval Climatic Optimum', between *c* 1000 and 1300 has been cited as permitting the extension of both permanent settlement and cultivation to favoured locations within the upland zone (Parry 1985, 47). Such expansion has been identified in the Welsh uplands (Jones 1965). From around 1300, there was a climatic deterioration culminating in the 'Little Ice Age' between *c* 1550 and 1750. This deterioration has been held to contribute to a reduction in the viability of farming and settlement at altitude (Parry 1985, 47; Jones 1965, 50–1).

On the Black Mountain, palaeobotanical analysis indicates an increase in cereal cultivation in the regional pollen at the time of the Climatic Optimum, which may relate to arable activity hinted at in documentary evidence at Neuadd Wen on the floor of the Aman Valley to the south of the survey area in the Welshry of Gower (Rees, D 1991), this reducing thereafter, with an intensification of grazing of the local landscape through into post-medieval times (Cloutman 1983, 61).

However, it has been stressed that correlation of changes in the distribution and character of medieval and early post-medieval settlement should be approached with caution (Parry 1978, 144–5). Other factors, political, social and economic, may have been equally or more significant in modifying settlement patterns (Clarke 1984, 22–3; Bell 1989, 285–6). Further, there are likely to have been regional variations in the extent and speed of the impact of climatic change, both on account of topographical factors, and different balances in agricultural regimes (Astill & Grant 1992, 224–33). An actual significant retreat of upland settlement may only have occurred in areas where cultivation was especially important (Parry 1975, 12).

In Wales, it is very difficult to disentangle the effects of climate on settlement and land use from factors such as the English Conquest, depopulation caused by the Black Death in the mid fourteenth century, and the unrest and revolt which continued into the fifteenth century (Butler 1971, 254; Walker 1990, 168). The difficulties of generalizing about the impact of climatic deterioration is illustrated by examples from North Wales where arable farming, recorded at an altitude of 300m in the early fifteenth century, not only continued into the second half of the sixteenth century, but extended to still higher elevations at around 350m. On the other hand, while both summer and winter grazing is noted at around 400m in the early fourteenth century, by the mid sixteenth century winter grazing was not deemed possible at such altitudes (Jones 1965, 49–51).

It is, however, probably safe to argue that the instability inherent in climatic deterioration would have required still greater care in the management of resources in an upland zone, the economic potential of which was never more than modest, and where risks were certainly always higher than the favoured coastal and valley locations.

The Management of Risk in Upland Landscapes

The principle is simple: altitude will affect the nature of climate and its stability, which in turn affects soil, vegetation and animal life. Living in the upland zone carries with it higher economic risks than living at lower altitude. The risks are managed, and will always have been managed, in order to minimize the chance of failure in the subsistence base (Taylor 1965; 1980, 104, 110–11; Brush 1976, 127; Huss-Ashmore & Thomas 1988, 452–3).

Work by geographers and anthropologists has emphasized that, at a general level, there is a convergence of approach to the exploitation of upland landscapes by widely disparate contemporary peoples with an agro-pastoral subsistence base in order to minimize the uncertainty of food supply (Brush 1976, 125; Huss-Ashmore & Thomas 1988, 452). Sometimes there may be physiological responses in terms of acclimatization to altitude and climatic fluctuation or to the periodic availability of food (Harrison 1988, 26; Huss-Ashmore & Thomas 1988, 468). Frequently adaptations will be experiential, manifested in cultural attitudes, social organization and economic practices.

Relevant characteristics of risk management strategies in the more unpredictable environments, such as those of upland landscapes, include a conservatism in approaching decision making (Colson 1979, 24). Human judgement is an important feature in adaptation to fluctuating food supplies (Eyre & Jones 1966, 13–18), a cognitive input which is not obviously accessible via the archaeological record. However, comparative studies of processes of modern agricultural decision making have shown a deep distrust of innovation or experimentation with new crops or husbandry techniques amongst the farmers of the Black Mountain area compared with farmers on the climatically more favoured Gower Peninsula (Henderson & Ilbery 1974). This echoes the comments already made about the relative historical remoteness of the Black Mountain area.

Insurance relationships with other communities in different economic zones through trade or exchange (Brush 1976, 127, 130; Huss-Ashmore & Thomas 1988, 455) and co-operation within kinship units are seen as an effective and flexible response to fluctuations in food supply, facilitating, for example, redistribution of stored reserves (Huss-Ashmore & Thomas 1988, 464–5). Historically in the Welshry the latter can perhaps be seen in the organization of the *gwely*.

There is also an imperative to exploit the full range of viable ecological zones to even out the effects of both seasonal and unpredictable fluctuations in food production. Populations at higher altitude are likely to have mixed agro-pastoral economies which could have taken advantage of more than one ecological/economic niche. The nature of the regime is likely to be towards the pastoral end of the agro-pastoral continuum, which is recognized as well adjusted to the utilization of more marginal zones, such as the uplands (Johnson, D L 1969, 2; Jarman *et al* 1982, 42), on account of the capacity for stock both to store food and exploit different zones on the hoof (Huss-Ashmore & Thomas 1988, 460–1).

One common adaptation to ensure a spread of risk across different topographical and ecological niches is the morcellation of landholdings which encourages the equitable distribution of land with greatest potential. Often it is subtly regulated through social mechanisms in order to maintain viable holdings (Galt 1979; Bentley 1987). In the Welshry this adaptation can be seen in *gavelkind*, but ultimately, as noted, it tended to be maladaptive since the amount of cultivatable land in temperate uplands is often finite and eventually plots are subdivided to the point where they cease to be viable.

The diversity of an upland landscape can be exploited from a single location where the local environmental gradient is sufficiently steep so as to place various zones of production within ready access of a community. Movement is necessary when a community cannot exploit the required range of the environmental niches from a single base, extractive capacity decreasing with increasing distance (Brush 1976, 127–8; Higgs 1979, 160).

Estimates of the effective daily catchment area of an agro-pastoral community vary. It is calculated that English village settlements will have their territory within a radius of 4km (Chisholm 1979, 109), although a reduced figure of 2km has been argued for the catchment of early historic settlement (Ellison & Harriss 1972, 915–17). One hour's walking time, up to 4km, or as much as 7 or 8km in the case of stock management has also been proposed (Higgs 1979, 163–4). Obviously, local topographical considerations in hilly areas, the concentration of resources, and patterns of landholding affecting rights of access and passage will modify such theoretical figures which can only indicate very broad parameters (Netting 1976, 142; Galt 1979, 95).

However, when a community cannot exploit efficiently the required range of environmental/economic zones from a single base, movement in some form or other becomes necessary. Establishment of a satellite base is a well attested means of extending the range of exploitation of agricultural communities (Chisholm 1979, 110–14). This can be either for arable or pastoral production, or both, and involves the relocation of an element of the population. Alternatively, in the case of pastoral activities, what has been termed 'stock transference' can take place which involves much less social dislocation, perhaps only the movement of herders (Jarman *et al* 1982, 45–6). Where these activities are based on cycles of movement to allow the exploitation of seasonally available resources, they can be described as transhumant practices.

It is suggested that a rationale for transhumance in the Welsh uplands should be approached from this basis of risk management rather than from other oft-cited explanations, which are largely only secondary benefits, albeit perhaps important ones of the practice. These include sparing the cultivated land the depredations of grazing beasts; providing opportunities for the maintenance of the principal holding; or even allowing young folk time to themselves, euphemist-

ically speaking, in order to reinforce relationships between the kindreds. Perhaps the literature of *The Old Summer Pastures* promotes an excessively romantic view of transhumance (Sayce 1956; 1957).

Transhumance as an Interpretative Model for the Welsh Uplands

The frequency with which transhumance has been invoked as an explanation for land use in the Welsh uplands at various periods and by several disciplines is striking. Both prehistoric and later field remains have been explained in terms of the practice (eg Fox, C 1932, 66–7; Butler 1988, 956). Geographers too have drawn on the practice to account for past land use (eg Davies, B L & Miller, H 1944, 524; Bowen 1965, 272–3), Palaeo-environmental data has been interpreted in the context of transhumant activity (eg Moore 1981), while a broadly based ecological approach to past land use in South Wales has emphasized the potential importance of transhumance (Webley 1976). Historians of both the earlier and later middle ages have attributed an important role to transhumance in the agricultural economy (Davies, W 1982, 39–41; Rees, W 1924, 217), while social historians have explored the traditions of *hafod* (summer farm and pasture) and *hendre* (home farm and land holding) (Davies, E 1980; 1984–5).

It is also striking that transhumance is used as an explanation without much attempt at close definition. There has been the frequent, if not invariable assumption, of a single social and economic context for the practice following the model most frequently described in the European highland setting. This requires a seasonal vertical movement of both people and animals between climatic and ecological zones, from permanent lowland settlements to dwellings in summer upland pastures. There are also instances of 'inverse transhumance' where the movement is away from the uplands to milder, lower lying pasture (Galaty & Johnson 1990, 22–3). In a western and northern European context, movement is usually on a relatively limited scale of distance (Johnson, D L 1969, 18–19). Although this does not provide access to more distant complementary resources, compared with longer movements as described, for example, by Carrier (1932), it can be a flexible and sensitive response to the uncertainties of upland landscapes. Compared with more extended patterns of movements, less energy is expended in taking stock to upland pastures and bringing produce back to the settlement; there is less loss of stock as a result of accident and disease; and there can be a rapid response to fluctuations in local conditions (Jarman *et al* 1982, 203). This strategy involves the bi-polar movement of people between settlements, one of which is never entirely abandoned, the other, usually located on land held in common, being occupied on a seasonal basis only. The permanently occupied settlement is a focus for cultivation in an agro-pastoral economy which almost invariably is perceived as both family and subsistence based (Davies, E

1935, 97; 1941 155; Evans, E E 1940, 172; Graham 1953–4).

The paucity of historical data for the detail of the practice of transhumance in medieval and early post-medieval Wales is widely recognized. This is apparent from the two articles written by Professor Sayce in the *Montgomeryshire Collections* in the 1950s which are still frequently cited as standard syntheses for Welsh transhumance (1956; 1957). However, much of the argument has to comprise analogy with practices elsewhere in Britain, or in the Alps, or Norway (Sayce 1956, 120–1), areas which present rather different environmental parameters with both longer and steeper altitudinal gradients.

Transhumance closely defined means no more than 'the regularly recurring seasonal migration of the flocks and herds in search of pasture' (Carrier 1936, 59) or, in terms of a more recent expression, 'a form of livestock management making use of seasonal variation in the availability of pasture' (Cribb 1991, 19).

So defined, simply as a pastoral strategy, transhumance carries no implication of a particular social, economic or cultural context. World-wide, it is apparent from the briefest scan of the anthropological literature that transhumance can take place in the context of many different environments, societies and economies. It can be equally characteristic of, at one extreme, nomadic pastoralism, which has no direct involvement with sedentary agriculture, and also of more broadly based agricultural systems of various types which do include sedentary cultivation (Johnson, D L 1969, 11–12, 18–19; Cribb 1991, 19–20). Transhumance can be found along a goodly part of the agro-pastoral continuum; the social, cultural and settlement associations will reflect the particular point where it is found on that continuum.

It is important, therefore, not to assume a particular social or economic model for transhumant activity in Wales. Focusing on the broad medieval/early post-medieval periods, it can be questioned whether it was always part of a family based subsistence regime or necessarily involved significant displacement of the population. It is, for example, possible to argue for an element of stock transference where population dislocation is restricted (Jarman *et al* 1982, 45–6). Further, this could take place outside the context of a family based subsistence regime with population movement confined to specialist herders, who could be the owners of the beasts, but who could also be employed or bonded retainers, tending animals on pasture, either held in common or hired.

The potential for variability in the practice through time is supported by a close reading of such information as there is for transhumant activity in Wales and comparable areas of the British Isles. There are medieval references to temporary settlement on the summer pastures (eg Rees, W 1924, 217). While these imply that people stayed with the stock, it seems that the nature and scale of population dislocation is largely speculative. References to 'vaccaries' at which the cattle of nobles were tended by full-time herders (Davies, R R 1978, 115–16) indicate that stock transference

to seasonal pastures was likely, in addition to any transhumance practised through a family based subsistence regime. Support for this can be derived from recent, better documented transhumant practices in both Ireland and Scotland, where retainers or specialist herders are known to have resided at 'dairies' located on seasonally available pasture (Aalen 1964a 70; Miller 1967b, 167). In Wales, it has also been noted that the use of the word *lluest* denotes a summer location associated with the guardianship of sheep under the care of a single shepherd; the term *hafod*, however, is more often deemed to be a centre for family based dairying (Davies, E 1984–5, 86–7). The use of hired pastures on a seasonal basis, as opposed to those held in common, is a further potential variant on the transhumant theme. It remains current practice with animals transported by lorry from hill farms to better grazing during the winter. It is particularly germane to note that into the early decades of this century, sheep from the Black Mountain were actually driven to hired pastures in coastal Cardiganshire for overwintering (Davies, E 1936–7).

Transhumance and the Archaeological Record

The movement of animals to seasonal pastures has often been coupled in descriptions of more recent western European transhumant practices with movement of people from permanent settlement to temporary huts or camps (eg Galaty & Johnson 1990, 22–3). Archaeologists have eagerly seized upon the settlement dimension on account of its tangibility which has sometimes led to statements which seem almost to give priority to buildings and people over animals in consideration of the practice. For example, Noddle has written, 'transhumance involved the construction of houses' (1989, 39). Bradley writes of transhumance as 'the regular movement of all or part of a farming *community* from one economic environment to another' [emphasis added] (1978, 57).

In the Welsh uplands, archaeological and historical studies have endeavoured to complement each other, correlating settlement remains with settlement patterns, including seasonal activity, referred to by historical sources (Austin 1989, 235). The sources, however, give little indication of the likely character of the settlement which might be found. Gerald of Wales' 'wattled huts . . . strong enough to last a year or so' (Thorpe 1978, 251–2) are often assumed to be seasonally used structures (Jones 1972, 356; Davies, E 1984–5, 78; Butler 1987, 47–8). Many centuries later, Pennant's 'long low room with a hole at one end to let out the smoke' is explicitly a seasonally occupied building (Pennant 1883, 325–6). Such slight evidence has led to the conclusion that seasonal dwellings were never a clearly defined architectural form (Smith 1967, 722), a conclusion rather better substantiated elsewhere in the British Isles from more thoroughly documented transhumant activity which indicates a rich diversity of associated settlement structures (Ward 1994, 518–19). This is not surprising if the potential diversity of socio-economic contexts for transhumance is recalled –

the character of any structure reflects the social and economic context for the practice of transhumance.

It should also be noted that the over-ready association of relatively high altitude medieval settlement in Wales, exclusively with seasonal activity, has not gone unchallenged. Briggs has suggested that ploughing in the uplands with a putative medieval date can be taken as an indication of permanent occupation (1985, 302–6). Richard Kelly has argued more generally that the significance of seasonal movement during the middle ages and early post-medieval period has been over-emphasized; that many upland settlements could have been permanently occupied; and that daily movements of animals may well have been a more common occurrence than seasonal movements (1981–2, 885–7).

Sometime ago Butler proposed a three-fold division of Welsh upland settlement: firstly, the occasional nucleated hamlet; secondly, the isolated farmstead (with the apparent implication of all-year-round occupation); and finally the seasonal dwellings (1971, 257). A scan of the archaeological literature on excavated upland settlement sites in Wales, taking particular account of the criteria used to distinguish the permanent farmstead from the seasonal dwelling, is revealing. Criteria include siting, particularly with regard to altitude; the extent and character of cultural debris; and documentary evidence.

The buildings in the Brenig Valley, Denbighshire, sited about 400m OD, were claimed as *hafodydd*, in part because of a nearby *hafod* name though without any close documentary corroboration (Allen 1979, 3). There was a notably rich material assemblage including ceramics, a spur, a sword-hilt guard and a powder pan from a firearm. The absence of items such as hasps, swivel hooks, door pivots and hinges, is taken to support the claim of seasonal activity (Astill 1992, 45). The house platforms at Beili Bedw, St Hermon, Radnorshire, again with occupation in the fifteenth or sixteenth centuries, did *not* produce nearly such a rich cultural assemblage (Courtney 1991, 253). However, they were deemed all-year-round residences essentially on account of their siting at much the same altitude as an adjacent modern farm, *c* 330 to 360m OD (Courtney 1991, 249).

Opinion has been divided as to the character of occupation of the thirteenth- and fourteenth-century platform houses on Gelligaer Common, Glamorgan (Robinson 1982, 114). Lady Ailleen Fox considered the buildings excavated on Graig Spydydd to be permanently occupied on the evidence of ironworking (1939, 172). Peate, however, later argued that they were summer dwellings only, on account of a location at 400m and the paucity of finds (1946, 128). Butler appeared to support Lady Fox when describing the sites as farmsteads (1962, 35; 1971, 260), although latterly perhaps qualifying this view with a statement that the houses were occupied permanently before the Black Death (1988, 957), thereby leaving open the possibility of later seasonal occupation. At the platform house site of Cefn Graeanog, Caernarfonshire, the scale of the structures, the location at 150m OD, the range of cultural debris, and evidence for

the local cultivation of crops, were taken to indicate a permanently occupied settlement (Kelly 1981–2, 885–7).

Despite the absence of any material culture, a compartmented building on Bodafon Mountain, Anglesey (Griffiths, W 1955, 23), has been interpreted as a farmstead with implications of permanent occupancy (Butler 1971, 257). The 'slight occupation layer' at a compartmented building on Penmaenmawr, Caernarfonshire, coupled with an almost total absence of finds, was initially seen as, either an indication of a short period of occupation, or seasonal usage (Griffiths, W E 1954, 83). Subsequently, the site was categorized as a farmstead on the basis of limited historical evidence for sixteenth-century land use in the area (Butler 1971, 257). The building excavated at Bwlch-y-Hendre, Cardiganshire, has been termed a *hafod* because of the absence of finds and some historical data for seasonal land use in the region (Butler 1963, 402–6; 1988, 956), but it has also been included within the farmstead category (Butler 1971, 259). Seasonal usage was argued for the buildings at Aber, Caernarfonshire, located at about 180m OD, because of a correlation between the site and documentary evidence for summer pasturage, and general local land use considerations (Butler 1962, 32–6).

To summarize, a paucity of finds has sometimes been taken as an indicator of seasonal activity only (eg at Penmaenmawr and the Gelligaer sites), although paradoxically the rich cultural assemblage from the Brenig Valley sites did not preclude their interpretation as summer dwellings. However, relative material poverty has also not discouraged the interpretation of sites as farmsteads (eg Gelligaer, Bodafon and Penmaenmawr). Limited place-name, land use and documentary evidence has been used to bolster interpretations but very rarely can it be said with any assurance to relate specifically to the structure in question (eg Bwlch-y-Hendre and Penmaenmawr). Higher altitude location has been viewed as both a barrier, and no bar, to permanent occupation (Gelligaer and Beili Bedw), while lower altitude locations, say below 200m, have been seen as an indicator of permanent settlement (Bodafon and Cefn Graeanog), but, quite rightly, not necessarily excluding seasonal activity (Aber). Sometimes, as perhaps in the case of the structures of the Brenig Valley, interpretation as *hafodydd* may reflect the weight of historical tradition rather than specific information.

While the cumulative evidence of structure, siting, material culture and economic data can persuasively suggest a permanently occupied farmstead, as at Cefn Graeanog, the poor quality of the evidence from most other sites, and inconsistencies in the use of interpretative criteria, strongly argue against didactic conclusions regarding the character of settlement at similar structures, excavated or unexcavated. The ambiguity of interpretation regarding the permanence or seasonality of medieval upland settlement is, of course, not surprising in the context of the well rehearsed challenges of identifying seasonal episodes at any period through the archaeological record.

The Dynamics of Upland Settlement

The ambiguity may mirror a reality across the four or five centuries to which the structures under consideration could belong. It may be useful on occasions to make a distinction between *the extent* of settlement in upland landscapes and *its character*.

The idea that there is not a static frontier for settlement on what are today perceived as marginal landscapes, including the uplands, is unexceptional. Rather, there is a broader zone within which the extent of settlement can fluctuate according to the interaction of social, political, economic, technical and environmental factors. This is well illustrated by the late eighteenth- and early nineteenth-century expansion of Welsh hill farming settlement and its subsequent retreat (Thomas, C 1989, 254–7).

However, the complexities of the processes involved in the dynamics of medieval settlement on marginal land have been discussed (Dyer 1989), and it seems worth considering that sometimes it is not the extent of settlement which changes, but its character. There is a danger of unnecessarily polarizing a debate in seeking excessive continuity in the practice of either permanent or seasonal settlement.

Earlier the use of satellite centres was noted as an adaptive mechanism to extend the range of environments which can be exploited within the upland zone. Such outstations could have functioned in several ways.

Firstly, they could have been used on a strictly seasonal basis as is apparently implied when the terms *hafod* and *lluest* are used. The weight of tradition might suggest that this was the most usual form of satellite settlement.

Secondly, they could be used on an intermittent basis to extend the range of the principal holding, a flexible adaptation to special circumstances which might arise from time to time outside the usual seasonal cycle. There are references from Scotland to the occasional use of satellite centres, normally on a seasonal basis, for the overwintering of stock (Fenton 1977, 129–30). Exceptional usage may be prompted by larger than usual numbers of stock to be housed at the principal holding; inadequate fodder at the principal holding which needs to be eked out by whatever the satellite centre can supply; disease amongst stock or humans at the principal holding; or, indeed, exceptionally favourable climatic conditions (such as mild Novembers) which extend the grazing period at the satellite holding.

Finally, the satellite holding may form the nucleus of a permanently occupied farmstead in circumstances which encourage intake of land. Such settlement has been described as a 'natural growth point' for encroachment (Griffiths, M 1989, 238). The expansion of grazing grounds from the later middle ages onwards has been noted. It is very likely to have involved the adaptation of seasonal pastures which has been charted in Wales for later periods by Elwyn Davies through the use of estate records (1984–5, 83–6). The establishment of permanent farmsteads at the location of seasonal settlements is also noted in both Ireland (Ó Duilearga 1939, 297; Aalen 1964, 65) and Scotland (Fenton

1977, 124, 129; Miller 1967b, 200). The logic of the tactic is self-evident: it removes some of the risk factor through the use of a known location and landscape, perhaps with intermediate stages of experimental, intermittent overwintering.

A point here – the process can be reversed (Sayce 1957, 86; Ó Moghráin 1943, 165, 170–1; Miller 1967b, 201). Permanent settlement can turn or return to seasonal usage through a process of long term decline. However, a reversal may be much more rapid: an initiative to establish a permanent farmstead may quickly fail or be rapidly aborted because of external pressures or human misjudgment. This will blur distinctions between seasonal and permanent settlement, since historical information is unlikely to be available in sufficient detail to chart such relatively short-lived episodes. Equally, archaeology has been shown to be a blunt instrument with which to distinguish between seasonal and permanent activity, let alone more extended, but still relatively short term, episodes of occupation.

Returning briefly to one of the more informative excavations of a settlement of this type in Wales, that in the Brenig Valley, it is interesting that while the excavator assumes a seasonal pattern of usage over a period of perhaps a century, the pottery expert states that the ceramics could equally well be derived from a shorter rather than a longer period of use – 'the maximum period during which the pottery was in use at the *hafod* was about a century, but the span could have been very much shorter' (Greene 1979, 36). Why, therefore, is seasonal occupation over the longer time-scale assumed rather than a shorter, more intensive period resulting from either close-set episodes of overwintering, or, in view of the notable cultural assemblage from the site, a failed or experimental attempt at permanent occupation? The answer comes in the use of the word *hafod* in that sentence from the pottery report. Interpretation is constrained by a preconceived view of how the Welsh uplands were exploited particularly in respect of the use of satellite locations.

In conclusion, therefore, the study of land use and settlement in upland landscapes, such as the survey area on the Black Mountain, may best be advanced by taking a longer chronological perspective, looking at a broad continuum of diverse settlement activity, rather than seeking the absolutes of 'permanent' or 'seasonal' occupation at a given moment, absolutes which, in any event, are often unlikely to be sustained in terms of either the historical or archaeological records.

Back to the Black Mountain

Returning to the Black Mountain, interpretation of the structures should explicitly recognize that over an undefined period but perhaps one spanning several centuries:-

a) that transhumance is only *one* of a range of adaptations which may have been necessary for the exploitation of the area;

b) that the practice of transhumance may have involved a number of different social and economic models;
c) that usage of satellite outstations may have involved more than a repetitive seasonal cycle.

As previously noted, the commons of the survey area are at the southern and eastern margins of the commotes of Perfedd and Iscennen which allows the main settlement foci to be placed with confidence on the more viable land north and north west of the Black Mountain (Fig 8.5). Within Perfedd, the Black Mountain commons are presently up to 7km wide. Therefore, without even taking account of the possible reduction of the extent of the common, exploitation from lower ground to the north west could easily have involved return journeys of 8 to 10km, and more, depending on the precise location of the principal holding relative to the area of upland to be grazed. While such distances are perhaps just about possible, in theory for the daily return movements of livestock, the desirability and practicality of such daily travel is another matter. Expenditure of time and attrition to the animals is likely to have weighed against such practices when consistent grazing of the upland commons was necessary.

Outstations would have been advantageous and are most probably to be found in the rectangular foundations recorded during the field survey. The structures are variable in scale, complexity and associations in terms of ancillary buildings, plots and paddocks. These variations may reflect the range of practices involved in seasonal exploitation, as well as the role of the outstation in contemporary settlement dynamics.

The smaller buildings may relate to socially less complex stock transference. The larger, more elaborate, structures could involve greater social dislocation, either as regards numbers of people, or length of stay. In particular, the larger buildings, which are comparable with peasant domestic architecture in terms of scale with that excavated in nucleated settlement in the Englishry of south-east Wales (Robinson 1982), or in form with the house-and-byre or longhouse homesteads (Wiliam 1986, 17; 1992, 18; Smith 1975, 445), may have been used for overwintering or more extended stays, while not necessarily functioning as independently viable farmsteads. Some, perhaps those with pens and paddocks, could be regarded as incipient farmsteads which ultimately failed to flourish.

The viability of outstations in these landscapes, either in terms of overwintering or more extended stays, needs a little more consideration. Firstly, it should be remembered that support could have been forthcoming from the principal holding. Secondly, the potential of the landscape cannot be judged by modern day economic or husbandry criteria. However, it is worth noting that, even using modern criteria, the ridge flanks of the Brecon Beacons are regarded as nutritious for sheep at all times of year while even ridge tops have a more restricted year round potential (Crampton 1966b, 74–5). Cattle husbandry, with careful and labour intensive herding, is also possible all year round on high altitude pastures, albeit with a decreased stocking rate. While shelter is not normally necessary, supplementary fodder

usually is (Broadbent 1981; Hughes & Huntely 1988, 91). This can be in the form of hay or oats, either a crop grown in the vicinity of the outstation, which is attested (eg Sayce 1957, 66–9; Aalen 1964a, 67–8; Ó Danachair 1983–4, 36–8; Miller 1967b, 198–202), or it could be imported from the principal holding. Could those elements of buildings which apparently comprise no more than settings of non-contiguous boulders be supports for a fodder storage platform raised off the ground as a protection from damp? Finally, in relation to pioneering attempts to establish farmsteads, the utility of inverse transhumance to resources at lower altitude should be remembered.

In the absence of compelling and precise dating evidence, the temptation to explain these buildings on the Black Mountain, and the variations in the structures, as responses to particular historical phenomena noted earlier is resisted, although the fifteenth century, a period which has been described by historians 'as a century of transformation' (Davies, R R 1978, 425–6), is a tempting point of origin. All that is reasonable is to contemplate the range of potential stimuli which could have led to changes in approach to the exploitation of the more marginal landscapes during the later middle ages and early post-medieval period.

Acknowledgements

The help and encouragement of good friends has been much appreciated, particularly Muriel Bowen Evans, Heather and Terry James and the late Bill Morris. Thanks to Dyfed Archaeological Trust and particularly to the RCAHMW through the good offices of David Leighton for access to records of sites. The fieldwork in fact largely coincided with and was deliberately designed to complement a major landscape survey undertaken by the RCAHMW in the Brecon Beacons. This resulted in a valuable exchange of information and ideas. Fieldwork was funded at various times by the Cambrian Archaeological Association, the Carmarthenshire Antiquarian Society, the University of Wales Board of Celtic Studies and the University of Kent. Their generous support is gratefully acknowledged. Finally, this work formed part of a PhD dissertation undertaken at the Department of Archaeology, University of Nottingham. The guidance, of my supervisor, James Kenworthy, has been most valuable.

Notes

1 A convincing case can be made for the relative isolation of parts of upland Perfedd on both historical and, interestingly, genetic grounds during the middle ages and post-medieval period. Norman, and later, English influence was slight compared with coastal and valley locations in the region; there were no Cistercian holdings in the vicinity to influence husbandry practices; and there are instances of the late application of Welsh tenurial law in the area. The inhabitants of the Black Mountain have excited the interest of physical anthropologists throughout the present century on account of a rare, significantly higher than average frequency of blood

group B in the locality (Fleure & James 1916; Fleure & Whitehouse 1916; Mourant & Morgan Watkin 1952; Garlick & Pantin 1957). This is still taken as supporting the conclusion that the population is a product of continuity with little external genetic input (Potts 1976, 252–3).

References

Aalen, F H A, 1964, Transhumance in the Wicklow Mountains, *Ulster Folklife*, 10, 65–72

Allen, D, 1979, Excavations at Hafod y Nant Criafolen, Brenig Valley, Clwyd 1973–74, *Post-Medieval Archaeol*, 13, 1–59

Allen, D, 1993, Later history of the valley, in F M Lynch, *Excavations in the Brenig Valley. A Mesolithic and Bronze Age landscape in North Wales*, Cambrian Archaeol Monographs 5, Bangor, 169–82

Astill, G, 1992, Rural settlement – the toft and the croft, in G Astill & A Grant (eds), *The countryside of medieval England*, Oxford, 36–61

Astill, G, & Grant, A, 1992, The medieval countryside. Efficiency, progress and change, in G Astill & A Grant, (eds), *The countryside of medieval England*, Oxford, 213–34

Austin, D, 1988, Excavations and survey at Bryn Cysegrfan, Llanfair Clydogau, Dyfed, 1979, *Medieval Archaeol*, 32, 130–65

Austin, D, 1989, The excavation of dispersed settlement in medieval Britain, in M Aston *et al* (eds), *The rural settlements of medieval England*, Oxford, 231–46

Bell, M, 1989, Environmental change as an index of continuity and change in the medieval landscape, in M Aston *et al* (eds), *The rural settlements of medieval England*, Oxford, 269–86

Bentley, J W, 1987, Economic and ecological approaches to land fragmentation, *Ann Rev Anthropol*, 16, 31–67

Bowen, E G, 1965, The heartland, in E G Bowen (ed), *Wales, a physical, historical and regional geography*, London, 270–81

Bowen Evans, M, 1991, Dros y Mynydd Du in Frynaman, in H James (ed), *Sir Gâr. Studies in Carmarthenshire History*, Carmarthen, 23–35

Bradley, R, 1978, The prehistoric settlement of Britain, London

Briggs, C S, 1985, Problems of the early agricultural landscape in upland Wales, as illustrated by an example from the Brecon Beacons, in D Spratt & C Burgess (eds), *Upland settlement in Britain*, Brit Archaeol Rep, Brit ser 143, 285–316

Broadbent, P J, 1981, Cattle production in the hills and uplands, in J Frame (ed), *The effective use of forage and animal resources in the hills and uplands*, Proceedings of a symposium organised by the British Grasslands Society, vol 12, 83–4

Brush, S B, 1976, Introduction to cultural adaptations to mountain ecosystems, *Human Ecology*, 4, 125–33

Butler, L A S, 1962, A long hut group in the Aber Valley, *Trans Caernarvonshire Hist Soc*, 23, 25–36

Butler, L A S, 1963, The excavation of a long hut near Bwlch y Hendre, *Ceredigion*, 4, 400–7

Butler, L A S, 1971, The study of deserted medieval settlements in Wales (to 1968), in M Beresford & J G Hurst (eds), *Deserted medieval villages*, London, 249–69

Butler, L A S, 1987, Domestic building in Wales and the evidence of the Welsh Laws, *Medieval Archaeol*, 31, 47–58

Butler, L A S, 1988, Wales, in H E Hallam (ed), *The agrarian history of England and Wales 1042 to 1350*, Cambridge, 933–65

Carrier, E H, 1932, *Water and grass: a study in the pastoral economy of southern Europe*, London

Carrier, E H, 1936, *The pastoral heritage of Britain. A geographical study*, London

Chisholm, M, 1979, *Rural settlement and land use. An essay in location*, London

Clarke, H, 1984, *The archaeology of medieval England*, London

Cloutman, E, 1983, *Studies of the vegetational history of the Black Mountain range, South Wales*, unpublished PhD thesis, Univ Wales, Cardiff

Colson, E, 1979, In good years and in bad: food strategies of self-reliant societies, *J Anthropol Res*, 35, 18–29

Colyer, R J, 1976, *The Welsh cattle drovers. Agriculture and the Welsh cattle trade before and during the nineteenth century*, Cardiff

Courtney, P, 1991, A native Welsh medieval settlement: excavations at Beili Bedw, St Hermon, Powys, *Bull Board Celtic Stud*, 38, 233–55

Crampton, C B, 1966a, Hafotai platforms on the north front of the Brecon Beacons, *Archaeol Cambrensis*, 115, 99–107

Crampton, C B, 1966b, Hills, soils and grasslands in Brecknock-shire: a study of potential land use, *J Brit Grassland Soc*, 21, 70–9

Crampton, C B, 1968, Hafotai platforms on the north front of the Carmarthen Fan, *Archaeol Cambrensis*, 117, 121–6

Crew, P, 1984, Rectilinear settlements in Gwynedd, *Bull Board Celtic Stud*, 31, 320–1

Cribb, R, 1991, *Nomads in archaeology*, Cambridge

Crossley, D, 1994, *Post-Medieval archaeology in Britain*, Leicester

Davies, B L, & Miller, H, 1944, Carmarthenshire, in L Dudley Stamp (ed), *The land of Britain. The report of the land utilisation survey of Britain*, Part 39, London, 499–559

Davies, E, 1935, Sheep farming in upland Wales, *Geography*, 20, 97–111

Davies, E, 1936–7, The Black Mountain: a study in rural life and economy, *Trans Carmarthenshire Antiq Soc*, 27, 53–64

Davies, E, 1941, The patterns of transhumance in Europe, *Geography*, 26, 155–68

Davies, E, 1980, Hafod, Hafoty and *Lluest*: their distribution, features and purpose, *Ceredigion*, 9, 1–41

Davies, E, 1984–5, Hafod and *Lluest*. The summering of cattle and upland settlement in Wales, *Folk Life*, 23, 76–96

Davies, R R, 1978, *Lordship and society in the March of Wales 1282–1400*, Oxford

Davies, W, 1982, *Wales in the early middle ages*, Leicester

Dyer, C, 1989, 'The Retreat from Marginal Land': the growth and decline of medieval rural settlements, in M Aston *et al* (eds), *The rural settlements of medieval England*, Oxford, 45–57

Ellison, A & Harriss, J, 1972 Settlement and land use in the prehistory and early history of southern England: a study based on locational models, in D L Clarke (ed), *Models in archaeology*, London, 911–62

Evans, D L, 1935, The later middle ages (1252–1536), in J E Lloyd (ed), *A history of Carmarthenshire: vol 1, from prehistoric times to the Act of Union 1536*, Cardiff, 201–67

Evans, E E, 1940, Transhumance in Europe, *Geography*, 25, 172–80

Eyre, S R, & Jones, G R J, 1966, *Geography as human ecology*, London

Fenton, A, 1977, *Scottish country life*, Edinburgh

Fleure, H J, & James, T C, 1916, Geographical distribution of anthropological types in Wales, *J Roy Anthropol Inst*, 46, 35–172

Fleure, H J, & Whitehouse, W E, 1916, Early distribution and valleyward movement of population in south Britain, *Archaeol Cambrensis*, 6th series, 16, 101–40

Fox, A, 1939, Early Welsh homesteads on Gelligaer Common, Glamorgan, *Archaeol Cambrensis*, 94, 163–99

Fox, A, & C, 1934, Forts and farms on Margam Mountain, *Antiquity*, 8, 395–413

Fox, C, 1932, *The personality of Britain*, Cardiff

Fox, C, 1940, A croft in the Upper Nedd Valley, Ystradfellte, Breconshire, *Antiquity*, 14, 363–76

Galaty, J G, & Johnson, D L, 1990, Introduction: pastoral systems in global perspective, 1–32, in J G Galaty & D L Johnson (eds), *The world of pastoralism. Herding systems in comparative perspective*, London, 1–32

Galt, A H, 1979, Exploring the cultural ecology of field fragmentation and scattering on the island of Pantelleria, Italy, *J Anthropol Res*, 35, 93–108

Garlick, P J, & Pantin, A M, 1957, The *ABO, MNS* and *Rh* blood groups of the Black Mountain, Carmarthenshire, *Human Genetics*, 22, 38–43

Graham, J N, 1953–4, Transhumance in Ireland, *Advancement of Science*, 10, 74–9

Greene, J P, 1979, The pottery, 28–37, in D Allen, Excavations at Hafod y Nant Criafolen, Brenig Valley, Clwyd, 1973–74, *Post-Medieval Archaeol*, 13, 1–59

Griffiths, M, 1989, The emergence of modern settlement patterns 1450–1700, in D H Owen, *Settlement and society in Wales*, Cardiff, 225–48

Griffiths, R, 1972, *The Principality of Wales in the later middle ages: the structure and personnel of government, I, South Wales, 1277–1536*, Cardiff

Griffiths, W E, 1954, Excavations on Penmaenmawr 1950, *Archaeol Cambrensis*, 103, 66–84

Griffiths, W E, 1955, Excavations on Bodafon Mountain, 1954, *Trans Anglesey Antiq Soc Field Club*, 12–36

Harbottle, B, & Newman, T G, 1973, Excavation and survey on the Starsely Burn, North Tynedale 1972, *Archaeol Aeliana*, 5th ser, 1, 137–75

Harbottle, B, & Newman, T G, 1977, Excavation and survey in North Tynedale 1973–75, *Archaeol Aeliana*, 5th ser, 5, 121–54

Harrison, G A, 1988, Seasonality and human population biology, in I de Garine & G A Harrison (eds), *Coping with uncertainty in food supply*, Oxford, 26–31

Henderson, H J R, & Ilbery, B W, 1974, Factors affecting the structure of agriculture in the Amman and Upper Tawe Valleys, *Swansea Geographer*, 12, 61–6

Higgs, E S, 1979, The history of European agriculture – the uplands, *Philosophical Trans Roy Soc London*, B275, 159–73

Hook, D, 1970, Excavations at Caio, Carms, 1969, *Carmarthenshire Antiq*, 6, 101–3

Hughes, J, & Huntley, B, 1988, Upland hay meadows in Britain – their vegetation, management and future, in H H Birks *et al* (eds), *The cultural landscape – past, present and future*, Cambridge, 91–110

Huss-Ashmore, R, & Thomas, R B, 1988, A framework for analysing uncertainty in highland areas, in I de Garine & G A Harrison (eds), *Coping with uncertainty in food supply*, Oxford, 452–68

Jack, I R, 1988, Farming techniques: Wales and the Marches, in H Hallam (ed), *The agrarian history of England and Wales, vol 2, 1042–1350*, Cambridge, 412–96

Jarman, M R, *et al*, 1982, *Early European agriculture. Its foundations and development*, Cambridge

Jenkins, D, & Owen, M, 1982, Welsh Law in Carmarthenshire, *Carmarthenshire Antiq*, 18, 17–27

Johnson, D L, 1969, *The nature of nomadism*, University of Chicago Department of Geography Research paper 118

Johnson, N, & Rose, P, 1994, *Bodmin Moor. An archaeological survey Vol 1: the human landscape to c 1800*, London

Jones, G R J, 1965, Agriculture in North-West Wales during the later middle ages, in J A Taylor (ed), *Climatic change with special reference to Wales and its agriculture*, Symposia in Agricultural Meteorology Memorandum 8, University College of Wales, Aberystwyth, 47–51

Jones, G J R, 1972, Post Roman Wales, in H P R Finberg (ed), *The agrarian history of England and Wales, Vol 1 (ii), AD 43–1042*, Cambridge, 281–382

Jones Pierce, T, 1972, Pastoral and agricultural settlements in early Wales, in J B Smith (ed), *Medieval Welsh society*, Cardiff, 339–59

Kelly, R S, 1981–2, The excavations of a medieval farmstead at Cefn Graeanog, Clynnog, Gwynedd, *Bull Board Celtic Stud*, 29, 859–908

Knight, J K, 1984, Sources for the early history of Morgannwg, in H N Savory (ed), *Early Glamorgan: prehistory and early history*, Glamorgan County History, Vol 2, Cardiff, 365–409

Lloyd, J E, 1935, The physiographical background, in J E Lloyd (ed), *A history of Carmarthenshire: vol 1, from prehistoric times to the Act of Union 1536*, Cardiff, 1–21

Miller, R, 1967a, Shiels in the Brecon Beacons, *Folk Life*, 5, 107–10

Miller, R, 1967b, Land use by summer shielings, *Scott Stud*, 2, 193–221

Moore, P D, 1981, Neolithic landuse in Mid-Wales, in *Proc IV International Palynological Conference*, Lucknow (1976–77), 3, 279–90

Morris, W H M, 1985, Boundaries of the Lordship of the commote of Perfedd, *Carmarthenshire Antiq*, 21, 60–3

Mourant, A E, & Morgan Watkin, I, 1952, Blood groups, anthropology and language in Wales and the western countries, *Heredity*, 6, 13–36

Netting, R Mc C, 1976, What Alpine peasants have in common: observations on communal tenure in a Swiss village, *Human Ecology*, 4, 135–46

Noddle, B A, 1989, Flesh on the bones. Some notes on animal husbandry in the past, *Archaeozoologia*, 3/1.2, 25–50

Ó Danachair, C, 1983–4, Summer pasture in Ireland, *Folk Life*, 22, 36–41

Ó Duileargra, S, 1939, Mountain sheilings in Donegal, *Béaloideas*, 9, 295–7

Ó Moghráin, P, 1943, Some Mayo traditions of the buaile, *Béaloideas*, 13, 161–71

Owen, D H, 1989, The middle ages, in Owen, D H (ed), *Settlement and society in Wales*, Cardiff, 199–223

Owen, G, 1892, The description of Penbrokshire [sic], H Owen (ed), London

Parry, M L, 1975, Secular climatic change and marginal, agriculture, *Trans Inst Brit Geographers*, 64, 1–13

Parry, M L 1978, *Climatic change, agriculture and settlement*, Folkestone

Parry, M L, 1985, Upland settlement and climatic change: the medieval evidence, in D Spratt & C Burgess (eds), *Upland settlement in Britain*, Brit Archaeol Rep, Brit ser, 143, Oxford, 35–49

Peate, I, 1946, *The Welsh house*, Liverpool

Pennant, T, 1883, *Tours in Wales*, Vol 2, J Rhys (ed), Caernarvon

Potts, W T W, 1976, History and blood groups in the British Isles, in P H Sawyer (ed), *Medieval settlement, continuity and change*, London, 236–53

Ramm, H G, *et al*, 1970, *Shielings and bastles*, London

RCAHMW, 1956, *An inventory of the ancient monuments in Caernarvonshire, Vol I East*, London

RCAHMW, 1960, *An inventory of the ancient monuments in Caernarvonshire, Vol II Central*, London

RCAHMW, 1964, *An inventory of the ancient monuments in Caernarvonshire, Vol III West*, London

RCAHMW, 1982, *Inventory of the ancient monuments in Glamorganshire, Vol 2: medieval secular monuments, Part II: non-defensive*, London

RCAHMW, 1988, *Inventory of the ancient monuments in Glamorganshire, Vol 4, domestic architecture from the Reformation to the Industrial Revolution: farmhouses and cottages*, London

Rees, D, 1988, The changing borders of Iscennen, *Carmarthenshire Antiq*, 24, 15–21

Rees, D, 1991, Neuadd wen: changing patterns of tenure, in H James (ed), *Sir Gâr: studies in Carmarthenshire history*, Carmarthenshire Antiq Soc Monograph, ser 4, Carmarthen, 43–51

Rees, W, 1924, *South Wales and the March 1284–1414: a social and agrarian study*, Oxford

Robinson, D, M, 1982, Medieval vernacular buildings below the ground: a review and corpus for south-east Wales, *Glamorgan-Gwent Archaeological Trust Report 1981–82*, 94–123

Sayce, R Y, 1956, The old summer pastures. A comparative study, *Montgomeryshire Collect*, 54, 117–45

Sayce, R Y, 1957, The old summer pastures part 2: life at the hafod, *Montgomeryshire Collect*, 55, 37–86

Smith, P, 1967, Rural housing in Wales, in J Thirsk (ed), *The agrarian history of England and Wales, vol IV, 1500–1640*, Cambridge, 767–813

Smith, P, 1975, *Houses of the Welsh countryside*, London

Taylor, J A, 1965, Soils and vegetation, 95–127, E Bowen (ed), *Wales: a physical, historical and regional geography*, London

Taylor, J A, 1980, Environmental change in Wales during the Holocene period, in J A Taylor (ed), *Culture and environment in prehistoric Wales*, Brit Archaeol Rep, Brit ser, 76, 101–39

Thomas, C, 1975, Peasant agriculture in medieval Gwynedd: an interpretation of the documentary evidence, *Folk Life*, 13, 24–37

Thomas, C, 1989, Rural settlement in the modern period, in D H Owen (ed), *Settlement and society in Wales*, Cardiff, 249–67

Thomas, J G, & Carter, H, 1965, Settlement patterns – rural and urban, in E G Bowen (ed), *A physical, historical and regional geography*, London, 270–81

Thorpe, L (ed), 1978, Gerald of Wales: *The journey through Wales / The description of Wales*, Harmondsworth

Turvey, R K, 1990, Llandovery Castle and the Pipe Rolls (1159–62), *Carmarthenshire Antiq*, 26, 5–11

Walker, D, 1990, *Medieval Wales*, Cambridge

Ward, A H, 1994, *An archaeological field survey of part of the Black Mountain in south-east Dyfed: a contribution to the interpretation of economy and settlement in the region from prehistory to the early modern period*, unpublished PhD thesis, Univ Nottingham

Webley, D P, 1976, How the west was won: prehistoric land-use in the southern Marches, in G C Boon & J C Lewis (eds), *Welsh antiquity*, Cardiff, 19–35

Wiliam, E, 1986, *The historical farm buildings of Wales*, Edinburgh

Wiliam, E, 1992, *Welsh long-houses. Four centuries of farming at Cilwent*, Cardiff

Williams, R, 1989, *Limekilns and limeburning*, Princes Risborough

Willis-Bund, J W (ed), 1902, *The Black Book of St David's*, London

Chapter 9

Historic Settlement Surveys in Clwyd and Powys

Robert Silvester

The Clwyd-Powys Archaeological Trust has over the last four years been conducting rapid surveys of all the historic settlements in its area, and in December 1994 only villages in two districts of Clwyd – Glyndŵr and Delyn – remained to be completed. These surveys, utilizing a consistent methodology and prepared to a common standard, were designed specifically to assist in planning and development control rather than academic study. No substantive analysis of the data collected has been undertaken, though the opportunity may arise in the future. However, for the purposes of the conference a preliminary assessment of the small settlements in the local authority districts of Brecknock Borough and Radnorshire was conducted. An attempt was made to distinguish between early medieval Welsh foci and those settlements that could be classed as Anglo-Norman. In the light of this analysis the settlements in Brecknock Borough exhibiting relict earthworks were examined, and while there is no exclusive correlation, the majority of such settlements are either atypical or Anglo-Norman in origin.

Background and Methodology

In 1991 the Clwyd-Powys Archaeological Trust embarked on a survey of all the historic settlements in the Brecon Beacons National Park, in conjunction with the National Park Authority's own archaeologist. During the twelve months that followed, Brecknock Borough Council together with Cadw funded a comparable survey covering the remainder of the old county of Breconshire (the southern extremity of modern Powys). The concept of historic settlement surveys was one that was readily accepted by other district councils. In 1992/93 Wrexham Maelor Borough Council (Clwyd) and Montgomeryshire District Council (Powys) both commissioned studies; Colwyn Borough in north-western Clwyd, and Radnorshire followed suit in 1993/94, the latter completing the study of Powys. During 1994/95 surveys were conducted in Alyn and Deeside, Delyn, Glyndŵr and Rhuddlan, the four remaining districts in Clwyd, thus completing the assessment of the Trust's region.

In addition, two Powys towns – Brecon and New Radnor (see Silvester Ch 12) – have been examined in greater detail, and a number of abandoned and shrunken settlements in Brecknock Borough have been the subject of measured surveys (Jones 1993; see below).

The reports that resulted from these surveys were seen primarily as planning tools and were never envisaged as vehicles of academic research. It is not necessary to dwell on the organizational and methodological aspects of the surveys, but it is necessary to consider the background to the surveys and their fundamental purpose. The original project design drawn up for the Brecon Beacons National Park survey highlighted the then current *ad hoc* basis on which archaeological and indeed planning responses had been initiated with reference to specific developments within historic settlements. It signalled the need for a more structured approach to the understanding of historic settlements, and the preservation and management of what was viewed in essence as a fragile resource. Circulation by the government late in 1991 of the Welsh Office version of the *Planning and Policy Guidance Note: Archaeology and Planning*, generally known as *PPG 16 (Wales)*, acted as a further spur to the initiation of the surveys. It emphasized the responsibilities of local planning authorities in the conservation of the archaeological heritage and confirmed archaeological remains as a material factor in determining the outcome of planning applications.

Two principal objectives were defined for each survey: firstly, to identify, insofar as the evidence permitted, what was termed the 'historic core' of each settlement, and to compile a consistent level of data which could be used by Cadw, the regional archaeological curators and the relevant local authority; and secondly to define areas of potential archaeological significance within those historic cores where prospective developers might be required to undertake archaeological assessments or evaluations as a constituent of the planning process.

The approach adopted for the study of each settlement involved limited documentary research, focusing on the more easily accessible written sources: the county Sites and Monuments Records, the National Monuments Record held by the Royal Commission at Aberystwyth, listed building data and printed secondary sources including the main county histories and the relevant county journal. Early printed maps included Ordnance Survey editions, the road maps of Ogilby (1675), the county maps of Bowen and Kitchin (1762), and others of eighteenth-century date, while manuscript map sources comprised tithe, enclosure and estate maps. Vertical aerial photography held by some local authorities and the National Monuments Record and, where available, oblique aerial photographs of individual villages in the Clwyd-Powys Archaeological Trust archive were also examined.

Fieldwork concentrated on open areas within and around each settlement, the identification of earthworks that might signal earlier habitation or land use, and the morphology of the historic settlement core. In general, it was assumed that the church reflected an historic focus of activity and therefore the churchyard and its immediate environs were studied on a consistent basis.

With the fieldwork and documentary research complete, individual reports were produced. Each village study summarized the current state of knowledge under a standard set of entries, though for some of the larger settlements the historic background had to be limited to an outline. Each text also incorporated a set of recommendations covering specific planning issues, together with proposals for further archaeological survey and research. Every report was accompanied by a map scaled at 1:2500 depicting listed buildings and scheduled ancient monuments, an historic core boundary or 'envelope' utilizing whatever evidence had been assembled, and the definition of potentially significant areas where an evaluation might be required.

What must be stressed is that these were rapid examinations of a mass of disparate data, not in-depth analytical studies. This can be placed in perspective by noting that only twelve weeks – 60 working days – were scheduled for all aspects of the study of the 100 or so villages in Montgomeryshire, a time allotment which was by no means exceptional. From the Trust's point of view the reports provided a set of paper records with a circulation limited to Cadw, the sponsoring local authority and the Trust itself. They were primarily for consultation during development control and planning work, were prepared to a consistent level with standard recommendations for each settlement, and displayed a standard level of mapping. In essence they represent handbooks for the historic settlements in each local authority area.

It was never within the remit of this ongoing programme to analyse individually or collectively the historic settlements of Clwyd and Powys, or to produce an academic synthesis. Nevertheless, a significant amount of new information has become available over the last four years as a consequence of the fieldwork and map assessment. In the remainder of

this paper a preliminary attempt is made to pull just a few strands of the evidence together to demonstrate the potential. Two districts of central Powys have been selected, the old county of Radnorshire and Brecknock Borough covering the north-western portion of the old county of Breconshire.

The Historic Settlements of Radnorshire and Brecknock Borough

Brecknock Borough is hill country, dominated by the Cambrian Mountains to the north and Mynydd Eppynt to the south. Relatively narrow river valleys – the Elan Valley rivers in the north, the Irfon and its tributaries in the centre and the Usk in the south – thread their way through these hills. In contrast to this upland zone, Radnorshire reveals more topographical variety, with contiguous uplands and lowlands. The uplands lie to the west with the massif of Radnor Forest and the hills beyond the River Ithon, while further east are the open flats of the Lugg and Teme valleys and the Walton Basin. It is a border zone reflecting Anglo-Norman influence and the vicissitudes of intermittent warfare in the middle ages.

It also offers a superficial contrast in settlement which can be summarized by the well used aphorism of English nucleation and Welsh dispersal. This was a theme touched upon in relation to the area over 25 years ago in *The rural landscape of the Welsh borderland* (Sylvester 1969), and it is worthwhile trying to build on the base established in that volume to determine how clearly this dichotomy can be recognized in the physical evidence.

Churches, Churchyards and their Settings

Whilst the perceived relationship between churches and settlement raises its own set of questions, an examination of the former in their setting offers the most valid starting point for this study. It is now widely accepted that those churchyards displaying curvilinear characteristics offer useful pointers to early Welsh ecclesiastical sites (Edwards & Lane 1992, 5). What may be less readily appreciated is the extent to which later modifications and enlargements to the layout of individual churchyards have confused their original form, in some instances disguising their curvilinearity altogether. Trying to establish the earlier form through analysis of modern large scale Ordnance Survey maps alone can be positively misleading; map analysis needs to be complemented by fieldwork, and even subjective assessment based on analogy has a part to play.

Of course, many churchyards, whether rectilinear or curvilinear, retain what we can assume to be either their original or a very early form (Fig 9.1). Llanfaredd (Radnorshire) on the east bank of the River Wye below Builth Wells is typical of a number of very small churchyards, apparently unaltered over the centuries. Some larger yards, too, reveal no obvious modifications to their form, as for example Merthyr Cynog (Breconshire), traditionally the

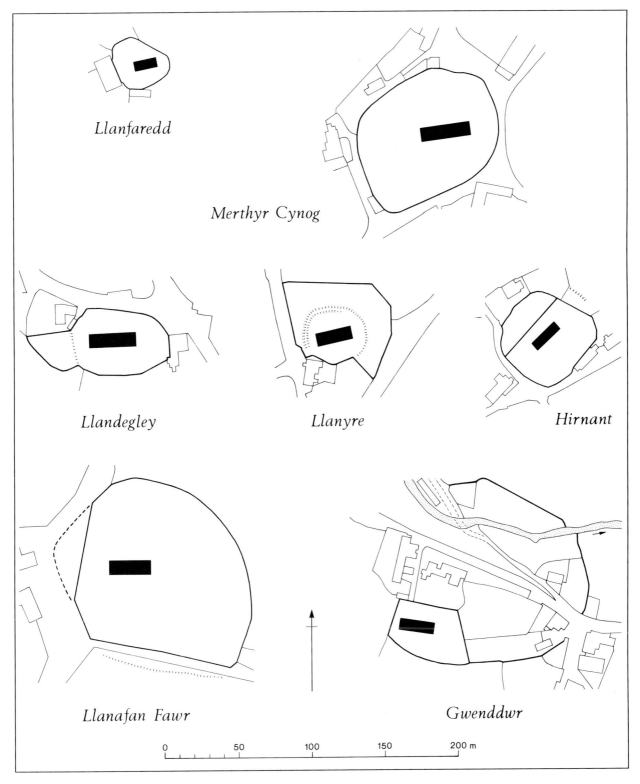

Fig 9.1 Churchyards and enclosures in Breconshire, Radnorshire and Montgomeryshire.

site of an early medieval *clas* foundation on the eastern fringe of Mynydd Eppynt (Rees 1967, pl 27). In other cases, an earlier perimeter can still be detected inside or outside the present churchyard. Llandegley (Radnorshire) offers an extreme example: a nineteenth-century extension which post-dates the Tithe survey and does not necessitate

a confirmatory site visit. At Llanyre (Radnorshire) across the River Ithon from Llandrindod Wells, the earlier bank is so pronounced that part of it is even depicted on modern large scale Ordnance Survey maps; the remainder is discernible as a scarp bank except where it converges on a noticeable disconformity on the southern side of the churchyard wall, the one point where the modern circuit still follows the earlier enclosure.

Demonstrable examples of shrinkage are less common, the clearest one being further north in western Montgomeryshire: at Hirnant, not only does a stone wall form a chord across the northern part of the churchyard, in order to provide a vegetable garden for the former vicarage, perhaps at the time of its rebuilding in 1749, but the original bank and ditch on the north-east side still show as low earthworks outside the present circuit. Further churchyard modifications are more conjectural though hardly inconsiderable in terms of numbers. At Llanafan Fawr (Breconshire) road alterations can be assumed to have influenced the western and southern sides of the churchyard, and indeed a low earthwork can be detected in the pasture field to the south of the road. It is conceivable, too, that this large enclosure is itself a later expansion from a smaller circular enclosure which can still

be seen as a platform around the church, or that there were two contemporary concentric enclosures at this remote location. The former morphology of Gwenddwr (Breconshire) in the hills on the western side of the Wye between Brecon and Builth Wells is more transparent. Here the fourteenth-century church of St Dubricius occupies a small rectangular churchyard, but a much more extensive curvilinear enclosure is implicit in the layout of boundaries to the east and north.

Overall, 43 of the 89 churchyards in Brecknock Borough and Radnorshire reveal some degree of modification, that is 48% of the total. Excluded from these figures are extensions that have been added to churchyards during the last 50 years. In a recent survey of Cornish churchyards, it was calculated that less than 10% had been altered prior to the occurrence of tithe mapping in the mid nineteenth century (Preston-Jones 1992, 106). The equivalent figure for this area of mid-Wales is much higher: 33 out of 89 churchyards

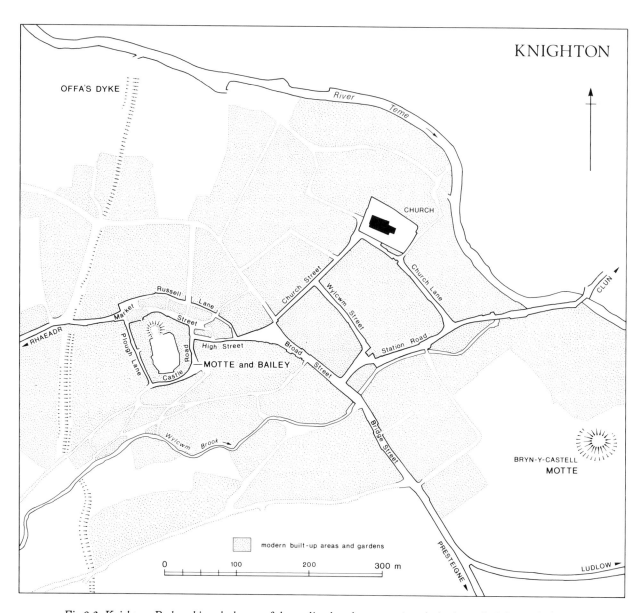

Fig 9.2 Knighton, Radnorshire: the layout of the medieval settlement against the backgound of the modern town.

(37%) show changes that are evidenced by fieldwork alone, and can be claimed to pre-date the introduction of widespread nineteenth-century mapping.

The number of churchyards revealing some degree of curvilinearity, either in their present form or as a relic of a former circuit, predictably becomes proportionately greater as one moves westwards from Radnorshire into Brecknock Borough. Nearly 60% of the churchyards can be so classified.

A second element that can be invoked to define early Welsh foci are dedications to Celtic saints, regardless of whether or not they are linked with a *llan* place-name, as, for example, with St Afan at Llanafan Fawr and St Tecla at Llandegley. At least 48 and possibly as many as 53 of the churches have (or had) Celtic dedications, in contrast to at least 40 with Anglo-Norman dedications. Yet no less than fifteen of the latter are dedicated to St Michael, and it seems quite probable that changes in political or ecclesiastical control, or local topography (Morris 1989, 53) may have led to the original Celtic dedication being abandoned in some places. Similarly, no less than fourteen of the medieval churches in the study area have dedications to St David: given that much of the area fell within the medieval diocese of St David's this is perhaps not surprising (Bowen 1977, 81). In several instances, rededications are documented. Llanynis (Breconshire) was originally dedicated to St Llŷr, now to St David, while the current dedication to St Matthew at Llandefalle (Breconshire) superseded that to St Maelog.

A third factor that can be taken into account is topographic location. Most indisputable early Welsh churches in this and adjacent areas of mid-Wales have an intimate association with water, whether they are set on river terraces, in valleys or on spurs above streams. Anglo-Norman churches on occasions exhibit a similar preference, but such associations appear less consistently.

Turning to well documented Anglo-Norman churches and settlements, these are fewer but nevertheless distinctive as nucleations, and are much more in evidence in Radnorshire than Brecknock Borough. Knighton (Radnorshire) appears in Domesday Book as 'Chenistetone' interpreted as 'farm of the servants' (Charles 1938, 179), a manor already in existence at the time of the Norman Conquest, though with no evidence of a settlement. Knighton (Fig 9.2) has two mottes on opposite sides of a valley. While the more easterly motte, Bryn-y-Castell, is isolated from the town by this valley, the early market place, consisting of a broad thoroughfare, lay on the north side of the smaller motte with a network of narrow streets linked to it (Soulsby 1983, fig 50). Subsequently, the area between this early settlement and St Edward's church, set in its rectangular churchyard above the River Teme, was developed with a regular grid of streets and the market place was moved downhill to the edge of this development. The date of these modifications is not chronicled, but anything other than a post-conquest origin seems improbable.

Knighton lies just to the east of Offa's Dyke, as does Norton (Radnorshire). Domesday Book has it as 'Nortune' or 'North Farm' (Charles 1938, 174). Motte and church

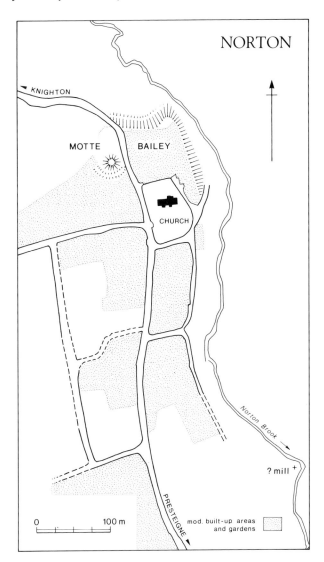

Fig 9.3 Norton, Radnorshire: the layout of the medieval settlement against the background of the modern village.

are set together (Fig 9.3), St Andrew's appearing to occupy part of the bailey which runs along the lip of the steepsided valley of the Norton Brook. From this focus the single street running southwards patently represents the core of the settlement, but even on modern maps there are hints of a broader pattern with parallel back lanes and continuous terminal boundaries to the plots. That the nineteenth-century inhabitants of Norton called it a borough and styled themselves burgesses (Lewis 1833) reinforces the view that the layout of the settlement may have been planned. On the south side of the village was an open-field system with three or four fields divided into furlongs. Quillets or strips were still in evidence at the time of the tithe survey in 1845 together with a few of the mere or boundary stones that demarcated the strips.

Painscastle (Radnorshire) has no church, but is only 2.5km from the Welsh foundation at Llanbedr in whose ecclesiastical parish it lay. Painscastle itself (Fig 9.4) consists of the eponymous earthwork, probably constructed by Pain

Fig 9.4 Aerial view of Painscastle, Radnorshire, from the north (Copyright Clywd-Powys Archaeological Trust, Ref no 87-MB-203).

Fitz John in the 1120s. A town had developed by 1231, with a weekly market and annual fair by 1264, and there is a record of 50 burgesses in 1309. A village market place or green survives in attenuated form and there are a number of early buildings, foremost of which is Upper House, thought to be have been constructed as early as 1410 as the residence of the Earl of Warwick's stewards (Beresford 1988, 571).

A conspicuous feature today of some of these Anglo-Norman settlements in Radnorshire is the number of functioning farms within the village. Painscastle has four; New Radnor and Kinnerton also have four; Evenjobb has three. In most cases the surrounding fields are or were covered by ridge and furrow. But not all of what can be classed as Anglo-Norman foundations now appear as nucleated settlements. Heyope (Radnorshire) for instance consists of the church of St David's in a rectangular yard, accompanied in the nineteenth century only by the Rectory, while the hillside church of St Mary's, Pilleth (Radnorshire) is now accompanied only by the farm known as Pilleth Court.

Correlation of these various elements – Welsh church settlements on the one hand, and their Anglo-Norman counterparts on the other – reveals a distributional pattern that can largely be anticipated (Fig 9.5): a spread of nucleated

settlements displaying Anglo-Norman characteristics along the border and extending up the more accessible valleys, Welsh settlements, often no more than an isolated church and adjacent house or farm in the hills. Inevitably some settlements fall into a hybrid class, displaying mixed characteristics. Anomalies in the pattern are created by Anglo-Norman foundations further west, such as Cefnllys in the Ithon valley near Llandrindod Wells, Rhayader and Builth Wells, though the first of these traditionally had a Welsh predecessor (Howse 1949, 266).

Historic Settlements with Earthworks

One of the curious aspects of the settlements in this part of mid-Wales is the significant number displaying earthworks in permanent pasture adjacent to the built-up area: up to thirteen in Brecknock Borough and perhaps eighteen in Radnorshire. These figures are in marked contrast with the other districts of Powys. To the south, in the Brecon Beacons National Park, it is difficult to recognize a single village with significant earthworks, while in Montgomeryshire only three or four places have revealed anything of interest. Subsequent land use may play some part in this dichotomy, but other factors must have some influence

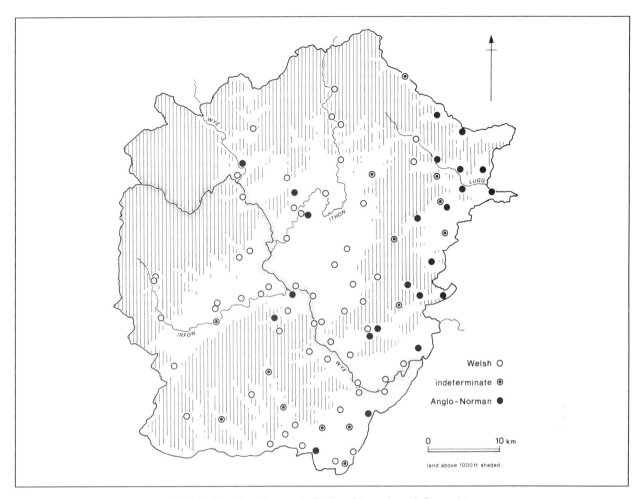

Fig 9.5 Church settlements in Radnorshire and north Breconshire.

including the obvious one that in many areas settlement shrinkage simply did not occur. The wider geographical implications cannot be considered here, but the presence of so many earthwork sites begs the question as to whether they influence the existing concept of Welsh dispersed and Anglo-Norman nucleated settlements in this region.

Earthworks some 3 ha in extent spread over several fields at Llanddew (Fig 9.6), little more than 2km north of Brecon. They include holloways, adjacent building platforms, and fishponds that are probably associated with the bishop's palace to the north west. A few miles east Llanfihangel Tal-y-llyn (Breconshire) has an area of about 2.5 ha, all in one field, consisting of holloways and at least thirteen platforms. At Gwenddwr (Fig 9.7), a field on the opposite side of the stream to St Dubricius' church reveals a minimum of ten platforms, trackways and lynchet banks. A second field to the east of the churchyard contains a further five platforms and a holloway.

But Gwenddwr may be atypical of the Brecknock Borough settlements. The name (though not necessarily the site) is documented in connection with a grange of the Cistercian abbey of Dore (Williams 1990, 43), as well as being the traditional site of an early medieval monastery (Jones & Bailey 1911, 13). Llanddew and Llanfihangel

Tal-y-llyn are both close enough to Brecon to have had their development influenced in the post-conquest period. Other, more remote Brecknock Borough settlements such as Crickadarn (Breconshire) have much more restricted earthworks: a couple of platforms and some field boundaries.

In fact four of the thirteen Brecknock Borough settlements – Alltmawr, Llan-y-Wern, Llanafan Fawr and Llanlleonfel – have earthworks which on closer inspection are not really consistent with settlement activity. Two more – Crickadarn and Garthbrengy – have sharply defined earthworks which could suggest a post-medieval origin, and Gwenddwr as already noted may be exceptional; and five either have distinctive Anglo-Norman characteristics – Alexanderstone – or fall within the intermediate group – Llanddew, Llanfihangel Nant Bran, Llanfihangel Tal-y-llyn and Llanfilo – whose attribution is uncertain. Only Llandefalle has been classed as a Welsh settlement in the preliminary analysis, and as this is only 8km from Brecon and has a known rededication, Anglo-Norman influences may have influenced its development in the post-conquest period.

Comparable detailed assessments are not yet available for Radnorshire but on the basis of a rapid examination of the eighteen settlements with relict earthworks, seven

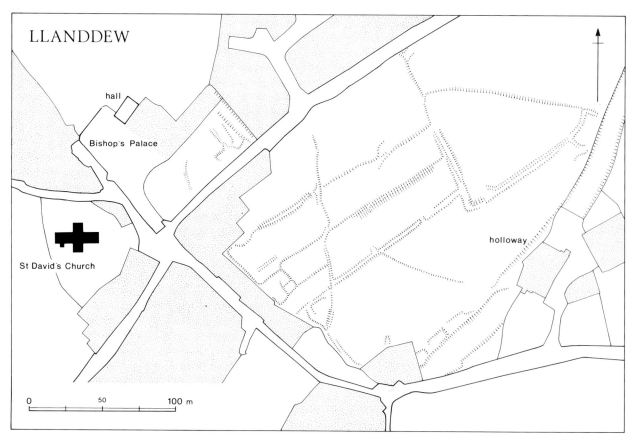

Fig 9.6 Earthworks at Llanddew, Breconshire.

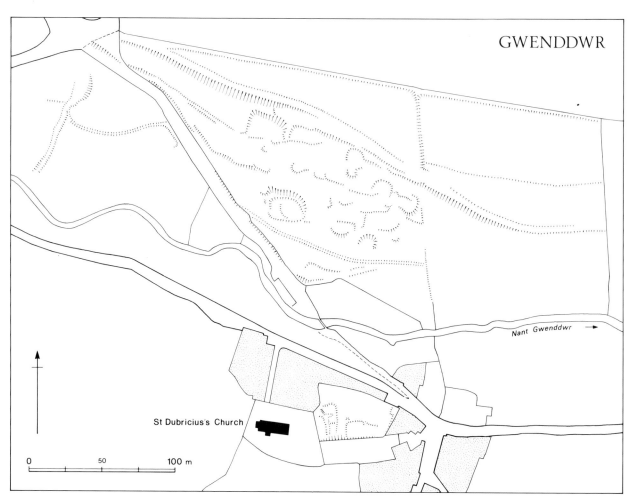

Fig 9.7 Earthworks at Gwenddwr, Breconshire.

including New Radnor (see Ch 12) are Anglo-Norman, three fall in the indeterminate grouping and at two places the earthworks look to be the remnants of farms of probable post-medieval date. This leaves no more than six in the Welsh group, most of them seemingly with no more than a couple of platforms, except for Glascwm.

On the basis of this preliminary examination not many of the obviously Welsh settlements have relict earthworks, and of those that do some appear to be atypical. Field evidence thus tends to favour the conventional view of dispersed Welsh settlement in the medieval era and the recognition of earthworks adjacent to so many settlements has not really overturned this view.

Conclusion

Much remains to be learnt of the origins, nature and growth of the hamlets and villages in central Wales. Indeed, to adopt a pessimistic viewpoint, many facets associated with these questions seem largely insuperable. Nevertheless, fieldwork has isolated some interesting aspects which deserve to be considered further. The survival of earthworks, normally in the form of platforms and tracks, does appear to indicate that some villages have either shrunk or perhaps more conceivably have experienced some degree of settlement shift. Llanfihangel Tal-y-llyn and Gwenddwr, and in Radnorshire, Llowes and Pilleth, offer the potential to throw at least some light on these problems through excavation. It is to be hoped that opportunities for further analytical assessment will emerge in the not too distant future.

Acknowledgements

The writer would like to thank Brian Williams for the line drawings.

References

Beresford, M, 1988, *New towns of the middle ages*, 2nd ed, Stroud
Bowen, E, & Kitchen, T, 1762, *The Royal English atlas*
Bowen, E G, 1977, *Saints, seaways and settlements*, Cardiff
Brown, A E, 1972, The castle, borough and park of Cefnllys, *Trans Radnorshire Soc*, 42, 11–22
Charles, B G, 1938, *Non-Celtic place names in Wales*, London
Edwards, N, & Lane, A, 1992, The archaeology of the early church in Wales, in Edwards & Lane (eds), *The early church in Wales and the West*, Oxbow Monograph 16, Oxford, 1–11
Howse, W H, 1949, *Radnorshire*, Hereford
Jones, N W, 1993, *Brecknock Borough historic settlements: earthwork survey*, Clwyd-Powys Archaeological Trust Internal Rep 83, Welshpool
Jones, T, & Bailey, J R, 1911, *A history of the county of Brecknock, Vol 3*, Glanusk
Lewis, S, 1833, *A topographical dictionary of Wales*, 2 vols, London
Morris, R, 1989, *Churches in the landscape*, London
Ogilby, J, 1675, *Britannia*, (facsimile, Amsterdam, 1970)
Preston-Jones, A, 1992, Decoding Cornish churchyards, in N Edwards & A Lane (eds), *The early church in Wales and the West*, Oxbow Monograph 16, Oxford, 104–24
Rees, W, 1967, *An historical atlas of Wales*, London
Soulsby, I, 1983, *The towns of medieval Wales*, Chichester
Sylvester, D, 1969, *The rural landscape of the Welsh borderland*, London
Williams, D H, 1990, *Atlas of Cistercian lands*, Cardiff

'God Made Nature and Men Made Towns': Post-Conquest and Pre-Conquest Villages in Pembrokeshire

Jonathan Kissock

This paper presents an overview of the morphogenetic approach to village origins. It outlines the variety of plan forms that exists and uses anthropological evidence to demonstrate that one particular form – the regular row village – is the result of deliberate village plantation. A range of examples of this type of village in Pembrokeshire is then discussed. It is proposed that these villages were planted in the wake of the Norman Conquest and subsequent Flemish settlement of the area. It is suggested that the Flemish lords, notably Tancard and Wizo, acted as loca-tores by deliberately establishing villages and bringing in communities to settle them. The immigrants seem to have been attracted to the area by the offer of burgess status; hence the new villages can be described as rural boroughs similar to those found elsewhere in Europe. Other villages have a radial form, with plots lying around the circum-ference of churchyards or other important centres. It is proposed that these villages are an earlier form with their origins lying in the systems of social organization to be found in pre-Norman Wales.

Methodology

In April 1992 the Dyfed Archaeological Trust commenced its Cadw funded *Historic Settlements Project* with the aim of listing the archaeological and historical resources of two districts of that county. Contrasting areas were selected for study: the coastal, agricultural lowlands of South Pembroke-shire, and the land-locked, partly industrialized, uplands of Dinefwr (see p 6). The material gathered for the Project formed the basis of an account of the development of the settlement pattern from the early medieval period onwards. This paper focuses on the part of the project which examined village origins in South Pembrokeshire and hence it also drew upon earlier work undertaken by the author (Kissock 1990; 1992). The author's previous research covered the whole of the former county of Pembrokeshire and was based on the belief that careful analysis of village morphology is one of the most effective ways in which village origins can be studied. Both the spatial extent and methodological approach are clearly evident in this paper.

As early as the late nineteenth century F W Maitland believed that village morphology was a fruitful subject for study and regretted that he did not have enough time to examine the subject in depth (1897, 368). Later, W G Hoskins briefly considered village plans and concluded that they were both 'interesting and tantalizing' (1955, 49). Their interest lay in the variety of forms, which he thought might underlie early cultural or historical differences. He found

them tantalizing because there was no way of knowing how they had changed over time or what the various plan forms meant.

In the late 1960s and 1970s Brian Roberts produced a classification of plans and has since used this technique to interpret the development of nucleated settlements (1987). Roberts uses a classificatory grid within which, he argues, a nucleated settlement of any shape can be placed. The grid is divided into two major columns: rows and agglomerations. The two columns are further subdivided into plans with or without greens. His four basic types are then divided into villages which are regular in shape and those which are not. Thus, at this stage, four types of both row and agglomerated settlement are recognized. The regular agglomerations can be separated into two categories: radial and grid settlements; again both can be found either with or without a village green. The irregular agglomerations have also been sub-divided into irregular grids and simple irregular agglomera-tions; these forms may or may not have a village green. Sometimes one village may comprise two or more elements each with a separate shape; these villages are classified as having composite plans. Roberts has used his grid to consider the patterns of village morphology in Warwickshire, Co Durham, Somerset and Cumberland. Furthermore, he has proposed that a morphological study be carried out in Pembrokeshire, which he sees as of considerable interest as a region of dated Norman settlement imposed on a Celtic landscape (Roberts 1985, 8).

The classification of the various village plans is only the first stage in understanding the evolution of the settlement pattern of any one area. Once all the villages have been analysed and described using the terminology of the grid they can be plotted on distribution maps. These maps form the interpretative aspect of the analysis and are used to compare the distribution of different types of plan with the other factors, for example the physical nature of the landscape or the past political structure of the region. The spatial correlation of the two is used to explain the origin of the villages. For example, the pattern of large nucleations in parts of Warwickshire is attributed to the early colonization of areas suited to large scale arable cultivation (1985, 16–17).

Roberts's grid has not received unqualified support. The most detailed criticisms have been made by David Austin (1985, 202–7), who has claimed that there are three major, closely linked, shortcomings in Roberts's work. First, whilst it is possible to elucidate simple, convincing early plans from complex modern ones, complex early plans cannot be deduced from modern simplicity. Second, it is noted that all typologies are subject to inherent chronological problems. Third, it is argued that the processes of change are not critically and methodically explored and hence the studies lack vitality. Indeed, Austin has gone so far as to describe the linkage of regularity and deliberate planning as 'a simple myth' (1990, 144). According to Austin, Roberts's means have become his ends, because he does not carefully separate morphology and typology. Thus there is a danger of the pattern explaining the process. Nevertheless, Austin has himself used morphological analysis in his discussion of the growth of the village of Thrislington (1989, 163–73). Here, however, he did rise to some of the criticisms he made by exploring alternative morphologies. One interesting solution to the third problem has been explored here: ethnographic evidence for village morphologies and foundation has been used in order to explore the links between processes and patterns, proving that regular morphologies are the product of planning. It must however be remembered that morphology is just one element in a 'tool kit' that also includes topography, survey and excavation.

Various ethnographers and geographers have studied settlement forms in a variety of regions which were subject to colonial rule and immigrant settlement. Evidence from Australia, sub-Saharan Africa and the Indian subcontinent can be assembled and used to show a clear link between these processes and regular settlement morphology. In the mid eighteenth century Germanic communities emigrated to Australia and Prussians, settling near Adelaide, laid out villages in which long, narrow, equal strips extended back from properties which fronted a street. These *Hufendörfen* types of settlement were designed to give every family an equal share in the land (Young 1987, 302–3). There is also evidence from west Africa for regular village morphologies being a colonial and conquest-related development. Hodder has discussed the changes which happened to the indigenous settlement patterns following European colonial activity

and remarks, 'The major change was simply in plan, the original, clustered, formless street plan gave way to a grid iron pattern (1979, 225). In the British colonies the growth of colonial townships and military garrison depots was common. For example, on the Indian north-west frontier, a formally laid out colonial cantonment was added to the agricultural and marketing town of Peshawar in 1849 (Kirk 1979, 50). In Cameroon and Togo the Germans deliberately forced some groups into nucleated settlements with the aim of acquiring easy access to supplies of forced labour (Morgan 1959, 59; Gleave 1963, 343). Changes of this nature seem to have been quite common. The imposition of colonial rule appears to have led to the formation of regular village morphologies. Hodder concludes that the specifically European nature of the impact was unimportant. What he considers to be important is that there was an invasion, and therefore what he sees in west Africa is nothing more than, 'common, universal and common sense responses to invasions by technologically relatively advanced peoples' (Hodder 1979, 227–8).

With the validity of the morphological approach briefly demonstrated, it is now possible to look at the methods used to gather the data for the morphological study. The shapes of all the settlements in the region were thoroughly examined using the second edition of the 25in Ordnance Survey county series maps. The original surveys for these maps were made between *c* 1860 and 1895, with revisions made immediately prior to their publication between *c* 1905 and 1920. There are several advantages in using this series of maps. They are widely available, they use standardized conventions and omit all the relatively recent accretions to the settlement pattern. Every nucleation was examined and its morphology recorded according to Roberts's terminology. Two particular types of village shape are of interest here: those with regular rows as an element in their plan and those which have a radial form. It will be argued that those which are regular in shape are post-Conquest foundations and those which are radial could be pre-Conquest in origin.

Village Foundation in the Post-Conquest Period

Templeton

Templeton is the most clear-cut example of a planned village in south-west Wales. It also provides some of the best evidence of a plan which has not changed for perhaps 450 years. The village stands astride the A 478, just south of the small town of Narberth, on a south-facing slope which is poorly drained at the foot. The village (Fig 10.1) overlies a co-axial field system, which might be prehistoric. This has been has described elsewhere (Kissock 1993, 195–6). Sentence Camp, a ringwork castle, stands in a peripheral position to the settlement as a whole. It lies beyond the village and is separated from it by the large boundary bank which lies to the rear of the western row.

The current morphology of Templeton – a series of cul-de-sacs running off the main thoroughfare – is relatively recent. This can easily be demonstrated by comparing the

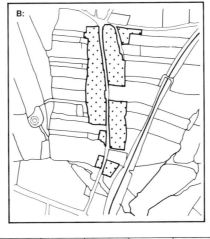

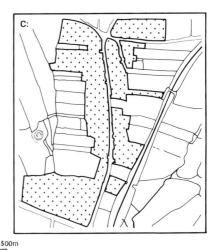

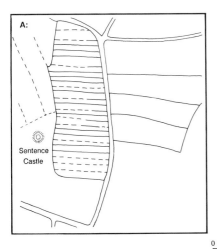

A: Templeton in the immediate post-Conquest period. 26 small and 4 large plots lie along the main road, Sentence Castle lies further west. A possible coaxial field system of an earlier date apparently disappears under the planted village.

B: Templeton in 1901. The basic plan is still clearly visible despite increased building (stippled areas) and plot amalgamation.

C: Templeton in 1993. The density of building has increased considerably and very few opportunities remain for the examination of earlier street frontages.

Fig 10.1 Templeton.

contemporary form with that shown on the 1901 Ordnance Survey 25in county series map (Fig 10.1, B, C). This map, together with earlier documentary material, can be used as the starting point for a reconstruction of the earlier plan (Fig 10.1, A). To the east of the main road, where the railway now runs, there were four large plots. All ran east-west from the street and terminated in the narrow valley some distance east of the street itself. A number of platforms were cut into the hillside along this side of the street. Some of them correspond to the proposed medieval boundaries. The Dyfed Archaeological Trust examined one of these and was able to demonstrate that it was constructed in the nineteenth century. Some of the platforms are, therefore, likely to have been constructed as the density of settlement increased in the nineteenth and twentieth centuries.

The western side of the street is also planned. A row of fourteen plots stood here in 1901. Some of the plots seem to have been merged with others and it is likely that there were once 26 plots, all of equal size and identical shape. All the plots have an area of just over a quarter of a hectare and are 18m wide and 180m long. There is some documentary evidence to support the idea that plots were once being amalgamated. In the late thirteenth century Sarah and Walter le Cole acquired two adjacent plots: those between the holdings of Robert le Skynnare and Philip Heylot (NLW Slebech MS 486). This may have been one of a series of transactions which led to the reduction in the number of plots in this row. The ability to perform a transaction of this nature at this date suggests that Temple-

ton might have been in decline in this period. This would be unusual as the late thirteenth century is generally thought of as a time of rising population. The agricultural depression of 1314 to 1321 and the plagues of 1349 and the 1360s could only have made the situation worse and increased the opportunities for plot acquisition and amalgamation.

Demonstrating that village plans have not changed appreciably in the interval between their origin and their first appearance in a detailed map is crucial to any discussion of morphogenesis. Templeton, it will be proposed, was founded at the end of the eleventh century but it was not mapped in detail until the late nineteenth. Hence there is a considerable 'leap of faith' involved in the morphological reconstruction: the morphology may have changed at any time between the two dates. Earlier maps of Templeton do not help in reconstructing the morphology – the tithe map is badly damaged and an earlier estate map is unclear. There are, however, two surveys which push the reconstruction of the village plan back to 1532 and thus considerably reduce the length of the 'leap' required. After the execution of Rhys ap Gruffudd in 1532 his lands in Narberth, including Templeton, were seized by the Crown. The rental roll for 1532 lists all the tenants (PRO SC6/Hen VIII/5262), the number of whom corresponds exactly with the number of plots in the early twentieth-century village. A second survey was carried out in 1609 (PRO LR2/206/118–86) and, once again, the number of tenants in that year is equal to the number of plots that existed three centuries later.

The name Templeton clearly suggests a link with the

Knights Templar; yet nothing is known of this. In the history of the Order in Wales, Templeton is dismissed as a mere 'hamlet' (Rees 1947, 32) and there is no known evidence which refers to the village as a Templar holding. Yet, the position of Templeton, in the extreme east of the lordship of Pembroke and so almost at the easternmost extremity of Anglo-Norman penetration into south-west Wales, is a most apt location for a manor held by a military order. This area remained a frontier until 1542, as the adjacent parishes of Lampeter Velfrey, Llanddewi Velfrey and Crinow all lay within the Welsh commote of Efelffre, part of the *cantref* of Gwarthaf.

Angle

Angle has developed in a sheltered valley which runs from east to west between two bays at the westernmost end of South Pembrokeshire. The name Angle is thought to derive from the Middle English for 'nook' or 'corner' and is an appropriate description of the locality. The tenurial history of Angle is most complicated: three ecclesiastical institutions (including an alien priory) had lands there, as did two secular lords. Settlement is now concentrated around the tidal mudflats at the eastern end of the valley, but the morpho-

logical analysis shows that this has not always been the case (Fig 10.2).

Detailed morphological analysis has shown that the village once lay further west and was probably restricted to the northern side of the street. The curved boundaries on the southern side contrast markedly with the perpendicular ones to the north and suggest that the southern row may have been laid out over open-field. The plot boundaries on the northern side are almost 210m long with the exception of a group of four shorter plots on the western end. It is possible that these are of a different date, possibly either a late addition to, or an early forerunner of, the main planned settlement. In the eighteenth or nineteenth century the focus of the settlement shifted eastwards as maritime activity grew to be the dominant factor in the village's economy. To the east of the planned element, and separated from it by a short distance, lay the church, the castle and the rectory. Groups of high-status buildings standing away from village cores have been noticed elsewhere (for example, at Letterston, see below) and the term 'magnate core' is proposed to describe this phenomenon. At some point, perhaps when the village began to grow at its eastern end, the magnate core shifted further east so as to preserve the spatial distance between the two social groups.

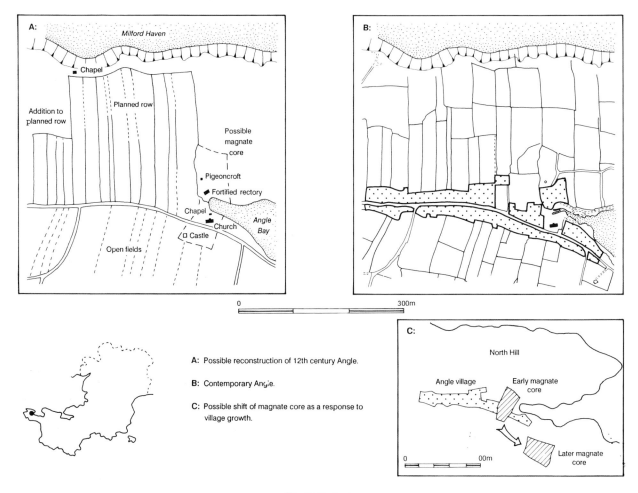

A: Possible reconstruction of 12th century Angle.

B: Contemporary Angle.

C: Possible shift of magnate core as a response to village growth.

Fig 10.2 Angle.

Letterston

At Letterston two long rows face each other across a street (Fig 10.3). The plots are over 250m long and vary from 20m to 100m wide; as at Templeton, it is possible that plots have been amalgamated as measurements in multiples of 20m are frequently found. It is possible that the south row resulted from expansion over former open-field; however the evidence is less clear than it was at Angle. In recent decades the village has extended eastwards 'leapfrogging' the A 40 and forming a second focus around the now disused railway station. Expansion to the north west around Greenplain has also taken place.

At the head of the road which runs between the planned rows of Letterston there now stands a large farm, Great Letterston Farm. Adjacent to it stands the rectory and, a little further west, two smaller farms – Court Farm and Heneglwys ('Old Church') Farm. This group of buildings, large farms and some ecclesiastical buildings, also form a magnate core. There was originally a gap between this group of buildings and the northern row of the rest of the village; it is now filled by a small row of post-war houses. Between the southern row and the magnate core lies the village green. Here too, it is as if the more important members of the community wished to preserve a spatial distance between themselves and the remainder, a spatial difference which reflected and may have helped to reinforce the social differences. This smaller group of farms could have existed long before the village did. They may have formed an element in the original, dispersed, Celtic settlement pattern of the area. The planned rows and the proposed magnate core are nevertheless clearly visible.

The Historical Context

Having reviewed the morphology of these three settlements in some detail, it is now necessary to put them into a historical context. The first Norman incursions into south-west Wales were begun in 1093 by Roger of Montgomery, earl of Shrewsbury, and William fitz Baldwin, sheriff of Devon. Although the first advances were easy, the Welsh soon regained the offensive and from 1094 onwards there was an uneasy balance as first the Normans and then the Welsh periodically gained and lost the upper hand (Rowlands 1981, 145). Southern Pembrokeshire was seized by Arnulf de Montgomery and the *cantref* of Penfro turned into the earldom of Pembroke. Like many a marcher lord de Montgomery had land in England too, and having established his claim in south-west Wales, he departed in search of other opportunities. The task of consolidating the conquest of Pembrokeshire was then left to local magnates, prominent amongst whom were members of the de Barri, de Brian, fitz Gerald and fitz Martin families. Their first objective was to defend what they had gained. This was done in three ways: castles were built, settlers were brought in to exploit and if necessary fight to retain the newly won lands, and key holdings were grouped into baronies entrusted to the most dependable men or to the Knights Templar

and Hospitaller. The influence of Arnulf de Montgomery and his lieutenants on the settlement pattern of the earldom cannot be underestimated. It is possible that some of the villages of the area were planted in the late eleventh century. The regular village morphologies of Cosheston and Redberth (both examined as part of the *Historic Settlements Project*) testify to an origin of this type (Fig 10.4).

After the failure of the Bellême rebellion and the flight into exile of Arnulf de Montgomery, the earldom of Pembroke was forfeit to the English Crown. This situation lasted from 1102 to 1138 and, during the early part of this period, Henry I seems to have made a major change to the settlement pattern of the region. He opened up lands to large numbers of Flemish settlers. There is plentiful historical evidence for the arrival of the Flemings in the early twelfth century and their settlement in the area between the earldom of Pembroke and the Anglo-Norman/Welsh border. It was here, in the former *cantrefi* of Rhos and Daugleddau, that Henry I is believed to have had them deliberately settled, perhaps to replace the followers of de Montgomery, who were likely to have fled along with their lord. The contemporary sources – Orderic Vitalis (Chibnall 1978, 443), *Brut y Tywysogyon* (Jones, T 1952, 27–8; 1955, 53), the *Annales Cambriae*, William of Malmesbury and Florence of Worcester – are unanimous on this matter. For example, William of Malmesbury made use of grand literary style when he wrote,

'The Welsh, perpetually rebelling, were subjugated in repeated expeditions by King Henry, who, relying on a prudent expedient to quell their tumults, transported thither all the Flemings . . . He settled them, with all their property and connections, at Ross, a Welsh province' (Stevenson 1854, 349–50).

Florence of Worcester was less dramatic when he stated that,

'Henry, king of England, removed into Wales all the Flemings and made them settle in the district called Rhos' (Forester 1854, 222–3).

The *Annales Cambriae* simply note, 'The year 1107 the Flemings came to Rhos' (Williams ab Ithel 1860, 34).

All sources agree that the focus of the settlement was Rhos and some sources state that settlers went to Daugleddau too. One settler, Wizo, is described as, 'prince of the Flemings inhabiting Daugleddau' (Darlington 1968, 134–5). Dates between 1105 and 1113 are given by all sources, except Orderic Vitalis who claims that the settlement took place in 1134 (Chibnall 1978, 443). It is also generally agreed that the settlers left Flanders after large tracts of land had been lost during severe flooding. But recent research has questioned this and it has been claimed that the Flemish migration was prompted by over-population and subsequent social unrest (Toorians 1990, 107). Population was certainly growing in Flanders and emigration was taking place in the second half of the twelfth century. It seems that after 1042 catastrophic inundation (frequent in earlier years) was much less common and large areas of

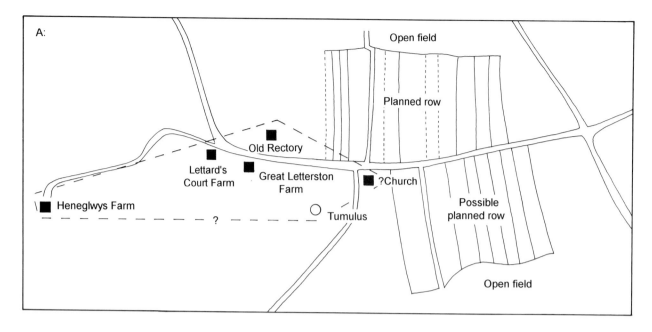

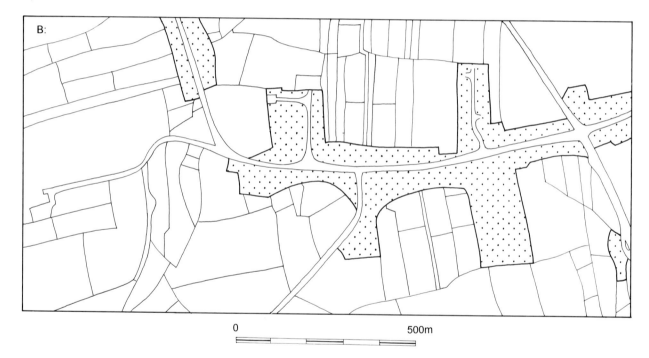

0   500m

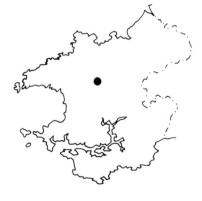

A: The medieval settlement at Letterston. A planned village of one, or perhaps
   two, rows stands adjacent to the magnate core. This may predate the village
   and be a remnant of a much earlier, less concentrated pattern. Reconstructed
   from early O.S., tithe and estate maps.

B: Contemporary Letterston. Considerable development has taken place within
   and to the east of the planned village; little development has occurred within
   the magnate core.

Fig 10.3 Letterston.

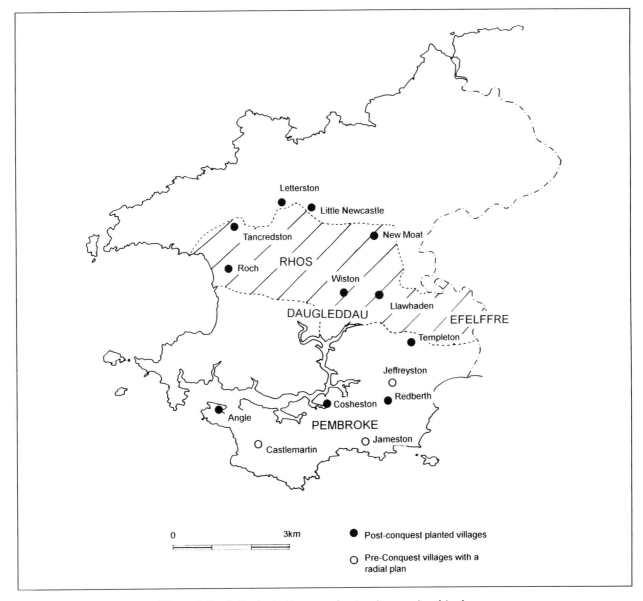

Fig 10.4 South Pembrokeshire: map showing sites mentioned in the text.

marshland were drained. Whilst more and more land was becoming available, much of it was too sandy, salty or wet to be productive and per capita yields were low (Nicholas 1992, 98, 108–9) – all factors which would have led to emigration. Regardless of the specific circumstances of emigration, Flanders and England had long been linked through dynastic bonds, commercial and cultural ties and ecclesiastical and military links; hence Flemish settlement within the English realm was nothing new (George 1926, 81–97; Hollister 1965, 187–9).

Village Plantation and the Role of the Locatores

Village plantation elsewhere in Europe has been studied in detail (Hoffmann 1989; Bartlett 1993), and the mechanisms of settlement are now well understood. They provide both a series of instructive parallels and a context in which the

Welsh material can be examined. There are four areas of planted settlement which will be taken into account here: the villages founded by the Germanic communities as they expanded into eastern Europe, the *bourgs ruraux* of Normandy, the rural boroughs of Ireland and the planted villages of northern Britain. Long-distance migration to new settlements was a common feature of European life in the twelfth and thirteenth centuries. Bartlett has provided a vivid description of it,

> 'Recruiting agents traveled in the overpopulated parts of Europe collecting emigrants; wagons full of anxious new settlers creaked their way across the continent; busy ports sent off ships full of colonists to alien and distant destinations; bands of knights hacked out new lordships' (1993, 2).

One of the largest movements of population in the medieval period was from the Germanic lands into eastern Europe

(Koebener 1966, 86; Aubin 1966, 471–2). The movement appears to have started as early as the last three decades of the eighth century, when Charlemagne directed the settlement of Frankish farmer-soldiers along the eastern border of the recently expanded Franconian empire (Nitz 1983, 171–3). This movement was at its peak in the twelfth and thirteenth centuries with the settlement of an area stretching from the Baltic coast to the Carpathian Mountains. The settlement of eastern Europe appears to have been well controlled. The whole process was under the direction of *locatores*, who acted in an entrepreneurial role as the 'middlemen' between lords and settlers. They were entrusted with the task of finding people and moving them to the new settlements. In many cases they were expected to bear the cost of the move, the maintenance of the settlers until the first harvest and the provision of houses, a church, mills and other facilities. *Locatores* received good rewards for the risks they undertook. These included a plot of land (usually much larger than that offered to the other colonists and sometimes tithe free); a proportion – varying between one third and two thirds – of the profits of the courts; and certain monopolies associated with the colonists' demands for access to markets. The ordinary settlers received favourable terms too. In the north they were guaranteed certain immunities, freedoms and personal protection. They were also exempted from the *ius ducale*, heavy burdens of services which the indigenous population were expected to perform for the monarchy, their overlords and the church (Knoll 1989, 160). The villages laid out by the *locatores* were linear and regular in plan. These *Hufendörfer* are the dominant form of village in many of the colonized areas (Mayhew 1973, 66–8).

The pattern of village foundation in Normandy – and in particular that of the establishment of *bourgs ruraux* – has been studied in great detail by Lucien Musset (1960, 86–94; 1966, 177–93). There are several types of *bourgs*; however, only one type, the *bourgs purement villageois*, is relevant to this analysis. About half of the 140 *bourgs* known by 1300 fall into this category; between 65 and 70 of recognized *bourgs*, '*se trouvaient dans des localités purement rurales*' (Musset 1966, 186). The role of the burgess as a cultivator, working the land for a lay or ecclesiastical lord, seems to have been well established in northern France in the later medieval period. At present, however, analysis of the morphology of the *bourgs ruraux* has proved impossible; apart from distribution maps, there are no maps in the French studies of *bourgs*, and maps with sufficient detail for a morphogenetic analysis appear impossible to obtain.

The concept of the Irish rural borough has been developed by Robin Glasscock (1971, 279–97; 1987, 223; see Murphy p 143). Burgess tenure, with its economic advantages, was widely used to induce settlers to migrate to Ireland. As a result there were a large number of small boroughs which were never more than villages, and which never had anything other than an agrarian economy, and yet also had an urban constitution. The immigrants were guaranteed low rents, usually of 1s a year, and the use of

hundred (rather than the more punitive manorial) courts to settle disputes. This, along with certain personal liberties and freedoms, gave settlers pecuniary advantages. These boroughs were not towns, in the economic, as opposed to the legal sense. Only limited and localized trade is likely to have occurred and frequently the burgesses owed some labour services on the lord's demesne. There is some evidence for the regular layout of the Irish rural boroughs. For example, Kiltinan, Co Tipperary, appears to have had a regular plan with roads now marked by well defined hollow ways. Burgesses are known to have resided there in 1308 and it is recorded in a list of Tipperary boroughs in 1437.

Brian Roberts (1972, 33–56) and June Sheppard (1974, 118–35) have argued that the planned villages of Yorkshire and Co Durham were deliberately planted after the 'Harrying of the North'. In the Fylde area of Lancashire A J L Winchester has noted a concentration of regular village plans; he believes that these were deliberately planned as 'a wave of colonisation' ran through the area between *c* 1150 and *c* 1300 (1987, 5–6). Roberts has examined the village plans of Cumberland and has argued that the numerous, regular row villages of the county date from 1092, when William Rufus ordered the resettlement of the area. Both Roberts's and Winchester's dates are open to critical examination. The settlement patterns of Cumberland and Westmorland were – so Roberts argues – deliberately created. Futhermore, he speculates, whether men, such as Gamel and Glassan (the founders, respectively, of Gamblesby and Glassonby), were deliberately employed as *locatores* (1989, 66). They appear to have included Flemings, for example Michael the Fleming and Turgis Brundis, lord of Liddel, both of whom received land from Henry I sometime after 1120. Planted villages also exist in southern Scotland. Some of the names of these villages include Flemish personal names (Barrow 1980, 35–46). These names include Wizo (in Wiston and, perhaps, Wyseby) and Tancard (in Thankerton; there are two settlements with this name in Lanarkshire). G W S Barrow argues that the Flemish settlement of Clydesdale may have taken place between *c* 1150 and *c* 1250 (1980, 111–12). A date early in this time range for this group of villages is supported by documentary evidence. Wizo donated the church of Wiston to the monks of Kelso sometime between 1153 and 1159 (Nicolaisen 1976, 38) and Tancard received his grant of land from Malcolm IV between 1153 and 1165 (Barrow 1980, 285). A brief study of the morphology of two of these villages was carried out but no conclusive results were achieved. The landscape around Wiston is extremely regular and the southernmost of the two Thankertons also has a regular morphology. Yet it must be noted that many Scottish settlements were replanned in the late eighteenth century (Millman 1975, 103–7).

Some clear parallels emerge from this discussion. Regular morphology is a common feature of the planted villages of eastern Europe; it appears to exist in northern Britain and Ireland too. *Locatores* were commonly used to plant villages in eastern Europe; men like Wizo and Tancard appear to have undertaken this task in parts of Britain. Finally, certain advantages, usually of an economic nature – exemptions from tithes, profits of courts, burgage tenure – were offered to both *locatores* and settlers. It is also possible to find evidence for all of these in south-west Wales.

The Role of Locatores *in south-west Wales*

Rowlands has speculated that the leaders of the Flemish communities in south-west Wales in the early decades of the twelfth century were *locatores* (1981, 148), but this is now possible to prove. In the foregoing discussion of settlement in northern England and southern Scotland the activities of two men – Wizo and Tancard – were described. Both appear to have planted villages there and both also worked in south-west Wales. The Flemish *princeps* Wizo founded Wiston *c* 1110. Tancredston, in Pembrokeshire, seems to have been founded by Tancard the Fleming in the early twelfth century. Tancard is also known to have held lands in another area of planted settlement, the North Riding of Yorkshire (Farrer 1914–16, 203–5). He sold these lands before *c* 1135 and soon afterwards founded settlements in Clydesdale. Both Wizo and Tancard were clearly *locatores* in that they were active in establishing villages, and then, once this had been successfully done, they moved on elsewhere with the aim of founding other villages.

It could, of course, be argued that there were several different men with the names Tancard and Wizo, all of whom happened to be founding villages in the early twelfth century and thus that the pattern is the result of chance rather than deliberate action. This argument would be strengthened if Tancard and Wizo were popular names at the time, but this is not so. Wizo is a known but rare name in Flanders in the period *c* 1060 to the mid twelfth century. Names containing the element Tanc- are also fairly rare in post-Conquest English records. The chances that several men called Wizo and also several men called Tancard were coincidentally figuring in related contexts are therefore slight, and it may be argued that the actions of two individual *locatores* are being witnessed.[1]

A recent appraisal of the careers of Wizo and his family has been made by Toorians (1990). This reviews what is known of Wizo's life and his presence in Pembrokeshire, especially his donations to the Welsh church. Reference is made to the actions of a Wizo in Lanarkshire, but despite the rarity of the name, Toorians dismisses him as 'a namesake'. He also assumes that Wizo 'must have died shortly before 1130' as nothing is known of his life in Pembrokeshire after that date (1990 110, 112). Indeed, this is what would be expected if Wizo were a *locator*; having established a community in south-west Wales and exhausted opportunities there, he would have moved on to found other villages elsewhere. Wizo does not seem to have completely severed his links with Pembrokeshire as he left a son, Walter, behind him. The reason for this is unknown. He may simply have abandonned his family when he went north. Alternatively, he may have entrusted his Welsh holdings to his son for the duration of his activities in Lanarkshire. Village foundation was a venture which carried with it considerable risks and hence retaining lands in Wales to return to, if all was lost, would have been a sensible precaution. Third, the successful management by a son of his father's foundations may have been a stage in a life cycle which formed a prelude (or one could even say apprenticeship) to the son eventually becoming a *locator* himself.

In eastern Europe two advantages are known to have been enjoyed by *locatores*: larger plots at little or no rent and certain privileges which may have included an exemption from tithes. There is evidence for both in south-west Wales. It is not too fanciful to envisage Lettard (an important Flemish settler) seizing the farms which formed the magnate core at Letterston (see above and Fig 10.3) for himself and, in so doing, dispossessing the original Celtic owners. He then arranged for a village to be planted near the farm to create a new settlement, the outline of which is visible today. Lettard may have been a *locator* too. Although there is no evidence for him or his work outside Pembrokeshire, his designation as 'Litelking' suggests a person of some importance (Rowlands 1981, 148).

The Flemish settlers, as a whole, were exempt from certain tithes. In *c* 1175 Gerald of Wales was, as he records in *De Principis Instructione*, required to collect tithes from those who had refused to pay (Butler 1937, 39). The Welsh paid reluctantly, but the Flemings of Rhos refused, claiming that they had been granted immunity from tithes on wool and cheese. This may have been one of the economic advantages used to attract Flemish communities to the area. Richter has proposed that this exemption was granted to them 'on their arrival' (1972, 18–19), as indeed might be expected if this mechanism was used to attract settlement to the area. A search for large areas of tithe free lands in planted villages has also been carried out. The results are equivocal. Certain lands which were exempt from tithes from the twelfth century onwards managed to keep this status until the tithe maps and schedules were compiled in the mid nineteenth century. Several areas of tithe free land were noted in the vicinity of the village of Angle. The tithe free lands include two large areas, the arable land of North Studdock Farm and the grazing land of Broomhill Burrows, as well as a few other miscellaneous plots. This may represent land granted to the *locator* of Angle as part of the reward for his services. Another explanation is, however, possible: many monastic orders were exempt from tithes. Three ecclesiastical institutions held land in Angle in the middle ages and it is probable that the tithe free land belonged to one or more of them rather than to a *locator*. Interestingly, the men of Angle claimed that they were also exempt from tithes. This was based upon their belief that – although not resident in Rhos or Daugleddau – they were of Flemish ancestry (Butler 1937, 44).

Rural Boroughs in South-West Wales

In only a few circumstances is there evidence to show that Welsh burgesses, like some of their Irish counterparts, owed agricultural labour services and that their borough is perhaps better considered as rural rather than urban. The question of the existence of rural boroughs in the study areas is fraught with difficulties. The first problem is that of definition; there is a need to specify exactly what is meant by a rural borough, and to do so in a way in which the limited evidence can be used so as to indicate which settlements did or did not fall into this category. There are also problems with the nature of the evidence – all of it post-dates the period of settlement, sometimes by several centuries. The paucity of the evidence and the confusing nature of some of it has led to the very rigorous definition of a rural borough which is used here. Unless proved otherwise a borough is taken to be an urban centre; only when evidence to the contrary exists are these centres taken to be rural boroughs.

In the earlier discussion of the Irish rural boroughs and the French *bourgs ruraux* one fundamental characteristic was referred to. This was the existence of an agricultural, rather than an urban, economic base. The examples cited were of communities of farmers (not manufactures or traders) who held land and owed services – often obligations of agricultural labour – to their lords. Hence the existence of relatively large areas of land attached to settlements which have an urban constitution will form the first part of the criteria used to determine whether or not any settlement was a rural borough. In some of the Welsh urban centres, burgesses were allowed to hold land. In Swansea – the largest urban centre – they were allowed seven acres each. Thus, in addition to land holding it will be necessary to demonstrate that the community had an agricultural rather than an urban economy. One way in which this can be done is by examining the service obligations which were placed on burgesses to see if they included agricultural labour. *The Black Book of St David's*, which records the holdings of the bishopric in 1326, notes the existence of burgesses in New Moat, Llawhaden and Letterston (Willis-Bund 1902). Whilst Letterston receives only a brief mention, New Moat and Llawhaden are described in considerable detail. At New Moat each burgage tenement had 8 acres (over 3 ha) of land attached and every burgess was obliged to spend one day per year ploughing, another harrowing and a third reaping for the lord. One important element of an urban economy is not found at New Moat; there is no evidence that a market was held here. No mention is made of a market in a charter which lists the bishopric's markets and fairs in 1290. There was only a three-day annual fair (6, 7 and 8 December) (*CChR* 1257–1300, 469). Thus it appears that New Moat was a rural borough; the burgesses held land and performed labour services, and the economy appears to have been based on agriculture rather than on manufacture and trade.

In Llawhaden there were 174½ burgage plots; each available at a 12d annual rent. These were held by 113 burgesses. Some of the holdings were large; the average size of a holding was over two hectares and the largest was nine. Service obligations on the lord's demesne also existed. The holder of a burgage was required to spend one day of each year ploughing for the lord, half a day harrowing and a further day reaping. The lord did not have the right to a market here either. As at New Moat, the only local trading opportunity was the two fairs which were held every year. Templeton may also have been a rural borough. The unusual, and not fully explained, tenure of burgesses 'of the wind' (*de vento*) existed here in 1283 (PRO C133/27/7).

New Moat and Llawhaden differ from the urban centres of Pembrokeshire in three crucial ways. First, the burgesses owed labour services – ploughing, harrowing and reaping – to the lord. Second, they do not appear to have had markets and hence were denied the opportunity to trade on a regular or a long-distance basis. Third, the communities were much smaller. In the early fourteenth century the burgesses of New Moat and Llawhaden numbered 44 and 113 respectively. This can be compared with 360 burgesses at Haverfordwest in 1324 and 247 at Tenby in 1307 (Beresford 1967, 255–6). The argument that New Moat and Llawhaden were rural boroughs has drawn almost exclusively on one very comprehensive source: *The Black Book of St David's*. There is no information of comparable quality or date for the rest of the planted villages. Nevertheless, it has been shown that two of the planted communities meet the attributes of rural boroughs, and it is possible to argue that other planted settlements fall into this category too.

The organization of planned settlement in south-west Wales shows clear parallels with the establishment of the French *bourgs ruraux*, the east European *Hufendörfer* and the planted settlements of the other parts of the British Isles. This section has argued that some of the new foundations were rural boroughs, that is villages with the inflated status of towns. This artificial rank brought with it economic advantages which attracted settlers to the new foundations. These rural boroughs were founded by *locatores* (men who made a career of establishing new settlements in frontier areas). Neither rural boroughs nor *locatores* were previously thought to have existed in Wales. The arguments presented here have directly challenged and refuted earlier views.

Pre-Conquest Villages

The *Historic Settlements Project* has demonstrated that only a limited amount of the settlement in south Wales was planted in the wake of the Norman Conquest. Villages are not restricted to the areas settled by the Normans and very few have regular morphologies. In only two areas of Pembrokeshire – the earldom of Pembroke and the *cantrefi* of Rhos and Daugleddau – this was not the case. A substantial proportion of the rural settlement of south Wales must therefore owe its origin to other processes and may have come into being at a different date. Therefore the evidence for pre-Norman nucleated settlement will now be examined. The thorough morphological analysis carried out in South Pembrokeshire as part of the Cadw project, has revealed a particular type of village – with a radial shape – which could be characteristic of pre-Conquest nucleations.

Jeffreyston

The morphology of Jeffreyston is most interesting (Fig 10.5). It is possible to discern, amidst the contemporary boundaries, traces of a radial settlement plan. The church stands at the centre of the settlement; the churchyard is raised and, allowing for a nineteenth-century extension on the western edge, is largely circular in shape. Both features are generally agreed to be indicative of early church sites (Edwards & Lane 1992, 5). At least two early Christian monuments have been found here, including a Class II cross-incised rectangular slab (Nash-Williams 1950, 186).

Close to the church there may have been a small lay settlement, or a community of clerics or both. Unfortunately (but not unexpectedly) any traces of such a settlement have been totally obscured by a millennium of successive building and rebuilding on the site. Around this nucleus there might once have been gardens and short strips arranged in a radial pattern. The gardens are likely to have been heavily manured and may have formed the infield portion of an infield/outfield system.

Castlemartin

Castlemartin also has a radial pattern (Fig 10.6). The principal elements of the contemporary village are the defended enclosure and the settlement which, in the main, clusters to the south of it. Other properties lie on the northern side of the road leading west, where expansion has taken place from the late nineteenth century onwards. The church stands some distance from the village centre in a sheltered valley. In the pre-Conquest period the enclosure seems to have been the focus of settlement. This circular, defended site is of uncertain date, but possibly has a prehistoric or early medieval origin; there is no inherent reason why it should be a post-Conquest castle. Radiating from the earthwork were a number of strips; these are now most clearly visible on the northern edge of the settlement where recent building has not taken place. Once radiating strips might have surrounded the whole circumference of the enclosure. The radial boundaries run from the edge of the earthwork out to a terminal boundary 200 to 250m away. This boundary runs beyond the limit of the strips on the west and south showing that strips surrounded at least a quarter of the enclosure. It is also possible that the pattern of radiating roads to the south and east preserve something of the pattern of boundaries in the opposite quadrant.

There is no documentary evidence for an early Christian site at the centre of Castlemartin. Indeed, as has been

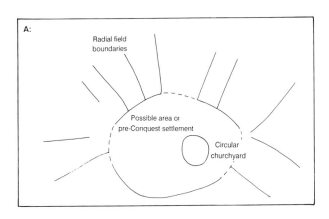

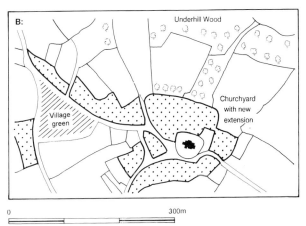

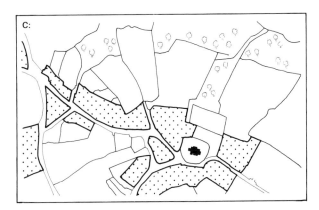

A: Tentative reconstruction of pre-Conquest Jeffreyston.

B: 19th and early 20th century Jeffreyston.

C: Modern Jeffreyston.

Fig 10.5 Jeffreyston.

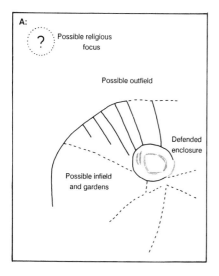

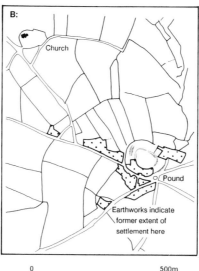

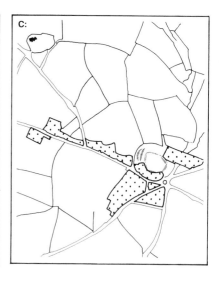

0   500m

A: Castlemartin in the pre-Conquest period. Gardens and infield radiate from a central enclosure. Some boundaries are preserved as later field boundaries, others may have followed roads and tracks. St. Michael's Church may lie over an earlier religious site.

B: Castlemartin in the mid 19th century. Settlement is concentrated around the former enclosure and has shifted or shrunk since the medieval period as the presence of earthwork sites shows. Where there is no building north and north-west of the enclosure the earlier pattern can clearly be discerned; the major terminal boundary can be traced further west and south.

C: Castlemartin in 1970.

Fig 10.6 Castlemartin.

noted, the church lies some distance away from the village. Castlemartin was a demesne manor of the Norman earls of Pembroke and, like many of the demesnes, may have originated as pre-Conquest *tir bwrdd* or 'table land' – land devoted to growing foodstuffs for the kings, their families and retainers (Davies, R R 1978, 109; see Johnstone p 57). Ken Dark has postulated (1994, 91), based on the discovery of a single bronze pin of sixth-century date and Irish type (Mathias 1927, 192), that Castlemartin could have been occupied in the period from *c* 400 to *c* 700. It certainly seems that Castlemartin could have been an important focus of activity in the years immediately before the Conquest and earlier, and perhaps, the site of a pre-Conquest village.

Jameston

At Jameston, near Manorbier, a radial plan village is laid out on one axis and the surrounding field system on another (Fig 10.7). The strips of the large co-axial system run on a north-south axis, whilst those which are associated with the village seem to run outwards from its centre. The chronological relationship between the two has been the subject of debate. Roberts argues that Jameston is a settlement of Celtic origin within a later, presumably Anglo-Norman, field system (1987, 64). Austin claims that the co-axial system is Bronze Age and that the village is a Norman plantation within an earlier framework (1988, 202). It appears to this author that Jameston was founded on top of an area of co-axial field, which is older than the village itself; however the village need not be a Norman foundation (Kissock 1993, 196).

Penally, 3km from Jameston, was certainly the focus of a pre-Conquest religious community and the reputed birth place of St Teilo is nearby. It has one cross and three shaft fragments all of ninth- or tenth-century date (Nash-Williams 1950, 200–3). *The Book of Llandaff* also mentions certain properties here, in an area which includes Longbury Bank, the best known early medieval archaeological site in this region. Copies of charters 77, 125b and 253 (Davies, W 1979, 95–6, 126) relate to lands near Tenby. All of the places mentioned lie on the River Ritec or south of it along the coast towards Manorbier. It is possible that the group of settlements listed in 77 formed the *territorium* of *terra Pennalun*. Campbell and Lane have argued for a group of properties lying along the Ritec and forming 'a coherent block of territory adjacent to the ancient monastery' (1993, 55–60). Both Jameston and Penally were in the same post-Conquest manor, Manorbier. It is possible therefore that Jameston was a part of an early medieval estate and the site of an early nucleation.

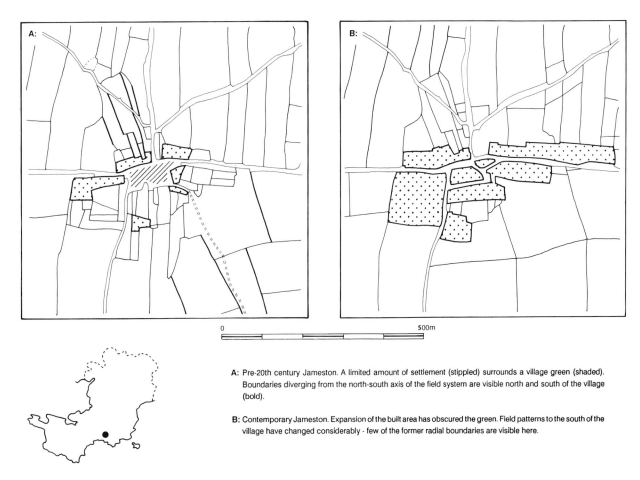

A: Pre-20th century Jameston. A limited amount of settlement (stippled) surrounds a village green (shaded). Boundaries diverging from the north-south axis of the field system are visible north and south of the village (bold).

B: Contemporary Jameston. Expansion of the built area has obscured the green. Field patterns to the south of the village have changed considerably - few of the former radial boundaries are visible here.

Fig 10.7 Jameston.

Similar radial forms are known elsewhere in Wales, for example at Llanynys, Denbighshire, and Llanfilo, Breconshire. This pattern is often found in those settlements which are thought to have been of ancient importance, perhaps those which acted as a focus for the wider community (Jones, G R J 1973, 346–7). In his evolutionary model for Llanynys, Jones proposed that a naturally high location was selected for an embanked enclosure, which became a place of burial and, eventually, the raised circular yard of a later church (1972, 348). At Llanynys, he considers that land arranged in this way was *tir corddlan* or nucleal land. Bond communities were settled on this land and their produce, and later their revenues, were assigned to support a *clas* community of an abbot and 24 others. Jeffreyston might parallel Llanynys as the location of an ecclesiastical community, Castlemartin could have been *tir bwrdd* and, at the moment, the exact status of Jameston is unknown. Nevertheless all seem to have been important in the pre-Conquest period, furthermore they all share a radial form. This form has been linked in north Wales with sites of ancient importance. In south Wales, whilst the processes underlying pre-Conquest village origins remain speculative, it is of considerable importance that settlements of this period have been recognized as elements within the contemporary landscape.

Conclusion

It has often been assumed that when the Normans conquered south Wales they brought the settlement pattern with them and that they imposed castles, market towns and villages with their open-fields upon an empty countryside. In exceptional circumstances this is true; it has been demonstrated that *locatores* deliberately encouraged the settlement of Flemish communities in rural boroughs in Rhos and Daugleddau. The formally planned settlements belong to this phase of village formation. These villages are not, however, the only ones in the region. Villages already existed in Pembrokeshire before the Norman conquest.

Acknowledgements

I wish to record the debts I owe to my former colleagues at both the Dyfed Archaeological Trust and the Department of English Local History, University of Leicester, and most especially to Neil Ludlow who made all the maps for this paper. Barbara Burkhardt kindly reminded me of the proverb of Marcus Terentius Varro that forms the title of this paper.

Notes

1   I am most grateful to Cecily Clarke for her comments on the comparative rarity of these names. They are discussed further in Marynissen 1986, 241–4.

References

Primary unpublished sources
National Library of Wales (NLW)
    Slebech MS 486
Public Record Office (PRO)
    C 133/27/7, 1283
    LR2/206, 1609
    SC6/Hen VIII/5262, 1532

Published sources
Aubin, H, 1966, Medieval agrarian society in its prime – the lands east of the Elbe and German colonisation eastwards, in M M Postan (ed), *The Cambridge economic history of Europe, vol 1, The agrarian landscape of the middle ages,* 2nd ed, Cambridge, 449–86

Austin, D, 1985, Doubts about morphogenesis, *J Hist Geog,* 11, 201–9

Austin, D, 1988, Review note: The making of the English village: a study in historical geography, *J Hist Geog,* 14, 201–2

Austin, D, 1989, *The deserted medieval village of Thrislington, County Durham, excavations 1973–1974,* Society for Medieval Archaeology monograph 12, Lincoln

Austin, D, 1990, Medieval settlement in the north-east of England – retrospect, summary and prospect, in B E Vyner (ed), *Medieval rural settlement in north-east England,* Durham, 141–50

Barrow, G W S (ed), 1960–71, *Regesta Regnum Scottorum,* 2 vols, Edinburgh

Barrow, G W S, 1980, *The Anglo-Norman era in Scottish history,* Oxford

Bartlett, R, 1993, *The making of Europe: conquest, colonisation and cultural change 950–1350,* Harmondsworth

Beresford, M W, 1967, *The new towns of the middle ages: town plantation in England, Wales and Gascony,* Woking

Butler, H E, 1937, *The autobiography of Giraldus Cambrensis,* London

CChR, Calendar of Charter Rolls, 6 vols, HMSO, 1903–27

Campbell E, & Lane, A, 1993, Excavations at Longbury Bank, Dyfed, and early medieval settlement in south Wales, *Medieval Archaeol,* 37, 15–77

Chibnall, M (ed), 1969–1981, *The Ecclesiastical History of Orderic Vitalis,* 6 vols, Oxford

Dark, K R, 1994, *Discovery by design: the identification of secular élite settlements in western Britain AD 400–700,* Brit Archaeol Rep, Brit ser 237, Oxford

Darlington, R R (ed), 1964, *The Cartulary of Worcester Priory (Register I),* Pipe Roll Society, new series, vol 38, London

Davies, R R, 1978, *Lordship and society in the March of Wales 1282–1400,* Oxford

Davies, W, 1979, *The Llandaff Charters,* Aberystwyth

Edwards, N, & Lane, A, 1992, The archaeology of the early church in Wales: an introduction, in N Edwards & A Lane (eds), *The, early church in Wales and the West: Recent work in early Christian archaeology, history and place-names,* Oxbow Monograph 16, Oxford

Farrer, W (ed), 1914–16, *Early Yorkshire charters,* 3 vols, Edinburgh

Forester, T (ed), 1854, *Florence of Worcester's Chronicle,* London

George, R H, 1926, The contribution of Flanders to the conquest of England, *Revue Belge de Philologie et d'Histoire,* 5, 1–97

Glasscock, R E, 1971, The study of deserted medieval villages in Ireland, in M W Beresford & J G Hurst (eds), *Deserted medieval villages,* Woking, 279–301

Glasscock, R E, 1987, Land and people c. 1300, in A Cosgrove (ed), *A new history of Ireland, vol 2, Medieval Ireland 1169–1534,* Oxford, 205–39

Gleave, M B, 1963, Hill settlements and their abandonment in western Yorubaland, *Africa,* 32, 343–52

Hodder, B W, 1979, The European impact on indigenous nucleated, settlements in western Africa, in B Burnham & H Johnson (eds), *Invasion and response: the case of Roman Britain,* Oxford, Brit Arcaeol Rep, Brit ser 73, 223–9

Hoffmann, R C, 1989, *Land, liberties and lordship in a late medieval countryside,* Philadelphia

Hollister, C W, 1965, *The military organisation of Norman England,* Oxford

Hoskins, W G, 1955, *The making of the English landscape,* London

Jones, G R J, 1972, Post-Roman Wales, in H P R Finberg (ed), *The agrarian history of England and Wales, vol 1, part 2, AD 43–1042,* Cambridge, 281–382

Jones, G R J, 1973, Field systems of north Wales, in A R H Baker & R A Butlin (eds), *Studies of field systems of the British Isles,* Cambridge, 430–79

Jones, T (ed), 1952, *Brut y Tywysogyon or The Chronicle of the Princes, Peniarth MS. 20 version,* Cardiff

Jones, T (ed), 1955, *Brut y Tywysogyon or The Chronicle of the Princes, Red Book of Hergest version,* Cardiff

Kirk, W, 1979, The making and impact of the British Imperial north-west frontier in India, in B Burnham & H Johnson (eds), *Invasion and response: the case of Roman Britain,* Brit Archaeol Rep, Brit ser 73, Oxford, 39–55

Kissock, J A, 1990, *The origins of the village in south Wales: a study in landscape archaeology,* unpublished PhD thesis, Univ Leicester

Kissock, J A, 1992, Planned villages in Wales, *Medieval World,* 6, 39–43

Kissock, J A, 1993, Some examples of co-axial field systems in Pembrokeshire, *Bull Board Celtic Stud,* 40, 190–7

Koebener, R, 1966, The settlement and colonisation of Europe, in Postan, M M (ed), *The Cambridge economic history of Europe, vol 1, The agrarian landscape of the middle ages,* 2nd ed, Cambridge, 1–91

Knoll, P, 1989, Economic and political institutions on the Polish-German frontier in the middle ages: action, reaction and interaction, in R Bartlett & A MacKay (eds), *Medieval, frontier societies,* Oxford, 151–74

Maitland, F W, 1897, *Domesday Book and beyond: three essays in the early history of England,* Cambridge

Marynissen, C, 1986, *Hypokoristische suffixen in Oudnederlandse persoonsnamen,* Gent

Mathias, A G O, 1927, South Pembrokeshire – early settlements, *Archaeol Cambrensis,* 82, 188–95

Mayhew, A, 1973, *Rural settlement and farming in Germany,* London

Millman, R N, 1975, *The making of the Scottish landscape,* London

Morgan, W B, 1959, The influence of European contacts on the landscape of southern Nigeria, *Geographical J,* 125, 48–64

Musset, L, 1960, Recherches sur les bourgs et les bourgs ruraux du bocage Normand, *Le pays bas-Normand*, 53, 86–94

Musset, L, 1966, Peuplement en bourgage et bourgs ruraux en Normandie du Xe au XIIIe siècle, *Cahiers de Civilisation Medievale*, 9, 177–93

Nash-Williams, V E, 1950, *The early Christian monuments of Wales*, Cardiff

Nicholas, D, 1992, *Medieval Flanders*, Harlow

Nicolaisen, W F H, 1976, *Scottish place-names: their study and significance*, London

Nitz, H-J, 1983, Feudal woodland colonisation as a strategy of the Carolingian Empire in the conquest of Saxony, in B K Roberts & R E Glasscock (eds), *Villages, fields and frontiers: studies in European rural settlement in the medieval and early modern periods*, Brit Archaeol Rep, Oxford, 171–84

Rees, W, 1947, *A history of the Order of St. John of Jerusalem in Wales and on the Welsh border*, Cardiff

Richter, M, 1972, *Giraldus Cambrensis: the growth of the Welsh nation*, Aberystwyth

Roberts, B K, 1972, Village plans in County Durham: a preliminary statement, *Medieval Archaeol*, 16, 33–56

Roberts, B K, 1985, Village patterns and forms: some models for discussion, in D Hooke (ed), *Medieval villages: a review of current work*, Oxford, 7–25

Roberts, B K, 1987, *The making of the English village: a study in historical geography*, Harlow

Roberts, B K, 1989, Nucleation and dispersion: distribution maps as a research tool, in M Aston, D Austin & C Dyer (eds), *The rural settlement of medieval England: studies dedicated to Maurice Beresford and John Hurst*, Oxford, 59–75

Rowlands, I W, 1981, The making of the March: aspects of the Norman settlement in Dyfed, *Proc Battle Conference Anglo-Norman Stud*, 3, 142–57

Sheppard, J A, 1974, Metrological analysis of regular village plans in Yorkshire, *Agr Hist Rev*, 22, 118–35

Toorians, L, 1990, Wizo Flandrensis and the Flemish settlement in Pembrokeshire, *Cambridge Medieval Celtic Stud*, 20, 99–118

William of Malmesbury, Stevenson, J, & Sharpe, J (eds), 1854, *The history of the kings of England and of his own times*, London

Williams ab Ithel, J (ed), 1860, *Annales Cambriae*, London

Willis-Bund, J W (ed), 1902, *The Black Book of St David's*, London

Winchester, A J L, 1987, *Landscape and society in medieval Cumbria*, Edinburgh

Young, G, 1987, Pioneer settlement patterns in the Onkapringa district council of south Australia, *Antiquity*, 61, 297–310

Small Boroughs in South-West Wales: their Planning, Early Development and Defences

Kenneth Murphy

This paper discusses and puts into context the results from numerous, often small scale, excavations and watching-briefs undertaken by Dyfed Archaeological Trust since 1975 in some of the smaller medieval boroughs of Dyfed. Despite the limited scope of much of this intrusive archaeological work, the information obtained, when combined with historical data and plan analysis, has greatly advanced our knowledge of the planning, development and, in some cases decline, of these boroughs from the early twelfth century to the fourteenth century. Two interrelated themes are discussed: planning and early development, and the role of defences. These are addressed by an analysis of the results of work in seven boroughs, though a large proportion of this paper is devoted to an examination of the relatively large-scale investigations in just two of these: Newport and Wiston, both in Pembrokeshire.

Introduction

Virtually every pre-industrial town in Wales was founded between the last quarter of the eleventh century and the first quarter of the fourteenth. Some of these foundations have flourished, grown and developed into our modern commercial towns, county towns and cities. Most, however, have not evolved beyond local market centres serving small hinterlands, whilst others went into decline and decay, either in the middle ages or more recently. This paper is devoted to these small, local market centres and decayed boroughs.

The many various archaeological investigations which Dyfed Archaeological Trust has undertaken in the smaller medieval boroughs of south-west Wales do not form part of an all embracing, coherent project, but have taken place in a piecemeal fashion over several years. Certain research themes were, however, pursued: town planning, early development and the role of defences. In the following discussions of individual projects it is not always possible to separate these themes, but for the ease of the reader this paper has been divided into two main parts: planning and early development, and the role of defences.

Much of the Trust's early work in small boroughs was small scale in character, often purely reactive, and based broadly upon the recommendations contained in the surveys undertaken by the Urban Research Unit in the mid 1970s (Delaney & Soulsby 1975; Soulsby & Jones 1977) and upon a Trust policy document (Dyfed Archaeological Trust 1975). More recently, numerous commercial and public building developments and small-scale infill housing schemes have enabled the Trust to conduct larger scale excavations

and surveys with an emphasis on the research themes introduced above: planning and layout, early development and the role of defences. Broadly speaking, within the orbit of building development two types of site become available for archaeological investigation. The first comprises open areas within decayed boroughs. These may have been open since the middle ages and can be quite extensive. A whole range of archaeological techniques can be employed: aerial photography, geophysical survey, topographic survey, plan analysis and, of course, excavation. The second type of site usually becomes available due to small scale infill development – a new house built on a single vacant burgage plot – or the rebuilding or renovation of an existing building. Clearly the form of the archaeological response in these cases is far more limited and usually involves small excavations or a watching brief. In addition to these site specific techniques it has, for many boroughs, been possible to conduct historical surveys and plan analyses; these have been carried out either to place the site specific investigations in a wider context or for local and regional planning purposes. In a few instances, Trust staff have undertaken historical surveys and plan analyses of boroughs out of personal interest; I am grateful to my colleagues for allowing me to use their information in this paper.

Planning and Early Development

Newport

The first project described here is by far the largest so far conducted by the Trust in a small borough. Newport,

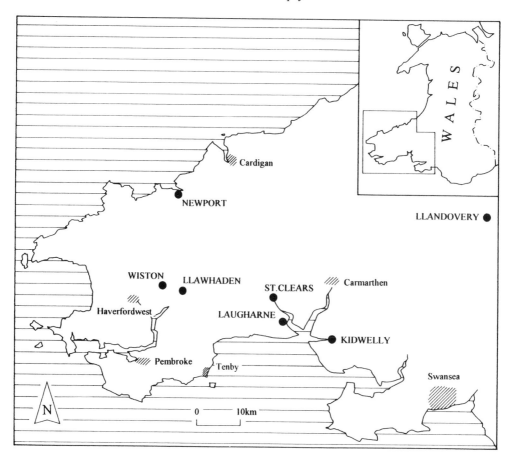

Fig 11.1 Location of sites mentioned in the text.

Pembrokeshire, is a small town situated on the south side of the sheltered Nevern estuary (Fig 11.1). Cemais, the lordship covering this part of north Pembrokeshire, was in the possession of Robert Fitzmartin by 1115 (Lloyd 1911, 425) following the Anglo-Norman conquest of South Wales. He established his stronghold at Nevern (King & Perks 1951), 4km upstream of Newport, on the site of an Iron Age fort and also, one suspects, an early medieval high-status site; it was certainly an important pre-Norman ecclesiastical centre. Nevern Castle was taken in 1191 by Rhys ap Gruffudd (Jones 1952, 74) during the reconquest of Dyfed. Cemais, however, was soon back in hands of the Fitzmartins, but Nevern was not refortified; instead a new castle and town were founded at Newport *c* 1197 (Murphy 1994, 58). Newport Castle was destroyed in 1215 by Llywelyn ap Iorwerth and again in 1257 by Llywelyn ap Gruffudd (Jones 1952, 91, 111). The disruption to the lives of the inhabitants during these uncertain early years of the town must have been have been considerable and it may be that the regranting of privileges in *c* 1241 (Charles 1951, 34) by the son of William Fitzmartin was an attempt to attract settlers back to the town following depopulation in the wake of the 1215 attack. It is argued below that it is still possible to detect signs of these and other troubles in the town's topography and in the archaeological record.

The present day town is centred around the A 487 coast road with modern development down to a village called The Parrog (Fig 11.2). Much of the medieval topography can still be detected in the modern town. This topographic evidence is strongly supported by rentals published by Charles (1951), one of 1434 and one of 1594. V E Bignall (unpublished 1991) has analysed these rentals as part of her undergraduate dissertation; I am grateful to her for allowing me access to her work. Figure 11.3 is a schematic plan of Newport based upon the 1434 rental in relation to modern topography. It is not possible to relate the burgage plot boundaries recorded in the rental to modern boundaries because of subdivision of some burgage plots and the merging of others, but the plan does show the correct number of plots as recorded in 1434. The status of the much eroded earthwork known now and in 1434 as 'Old Castle' is the first problem to be addressed when analysing the medieval topography of Newport. On morphological grounds it was classified as an Iron Age defended enclosure on the Dyfed Sites and Monuments Record (no 1468); its central position between two medieval streets and its name recorded in 1434 surely indicates its medieval origin – it is presumably the castle founded by William Fitzmartin *c* 1197. It is clear from the plan (Fig 11.3) that Long Street and St Mary's Street were laid out on either side of Old Castle, ran to the south for some 500m before crossing an ancient route – the present West Street/East Street/Bridge Street – and then

Fig 11.2 Newport from the north. Back-filled trial trenches in the shape of a cross in the lower centre of the photograph mark the site of the excavation (Copyright: Dyfed Archaeological Trust).

continued for a further 100m. The burgage plots on Long Street and St Mary's Street were contained to the east and west by canalized streams, Afon Felin and Afon Ysgol-heigion. Therefore the first phase of the town seems to have been packaged into a neat rectangle and included the burgage plots on Long Street and St Mary's Street and the Old Castle. The streams mentioned above are nothing more than shallow ditches and could never have served a defensive function.

A phase of expansion can be recognized on the plan with burgage plots spreading along West Street, East Street and Goat Street with a further phase of development represented by plots on Bridge Street. The rental of 1594 explicitly states that most of the burgage plots at the northern end of Long Street and St Mary's Street near to the Old Castle were unoccupied and several were merged into small fields. The recording of several plots in the hands of individual burgesses in 1434 may perhaps be an indication that this process of desertion in the northern area of the town was well established by the early fifteenth century. If this is so, then perhaps this process of desertion was prompted by the founding of the castle on its present dominating site at the southern end of the town following the Welsh attacks of 1215 or 1257. The record of a town in an advanced state of decay in the 1594 rental does not seem to have been the low point for Newport; this was probably reached in the late

eighteenth century (Fenton 1903, 303). Since then, the town has experienced slow growth.

Apart from the well known late medieval pottery kilns off West Street investigated earlier this century (RCAHMW 1925, 277), the first archaeological investigation in the town occurred in the mid 1980s during the building of a bungalow on Long Street (Stenger 1985). This salvage excavation revealed stone-built structures associated with medieval pottery. In 1991, a planning application was submitted to build a new primary school on a sports field in Long Street (see Fig 11.3 for approximate position) in an area of former burgage plots. A geophysical survey (conducted by Geophysical Surveys, Bradford) demonstrated the below ground presence of burgage plot boundaries, but, because of interference from wire fences and other objects, it was impossible to determine if building remains were present. Trial excavations revealed the presence of buildings along the street frontage of Long Street; full excavation followed. The street frontage of three burgage plots (marked A, B and C on Fig 11.4) was excavated, together with some burgage boundaries.

All burgage boundaries consisted of shallow ditches which, despite the heavy clay subsoil susceptible to flooding, served no drainage function. The earliest recognized boundaries lay on the north-south division between Long Street and St Mary's Street (Fig 11.4). In its primary phase this central division consisted of a segmented ditch, each segment about 14m in length and corresponding to the width of a burgage plot. Once established, this central division deviated little from its original line, though it underwent many rediggings and was eventually merged into one continuous ditch. No recognizable east-west burgage boundaries were present until after the establishment of buildings along the street frontage. At the street frontage these plots were of different widths: plot A was 18m wide, plot B 11m and plot C 18m. It is possible to recognize in these boundaries the means and methods by which the town was planned and laid out. The consistent 14m length, the depth and the shape of the ditch segments along the central boundary suggest centralized planning and a design which had to be adhered to; it was along this central division that the position of individual plots was pegged out. As plots were taken up it would have been the responsibility of individual tenants to form their own boundaries between plots to the north and south. These boundaries may initially have been simple turf baulks or insubstantial fences which were later translated into ditches and banks. The width of the plots at the east end against the central division was controlled by the 14m long pegged out segments of the boundary. But no such control existed along Long Street, and therefore, as the first plots began to be taken up, it was possible for occupiers to enclose more within their burgage than was originally planned; this seems to be the case with plots A and C which enclosed a greater area at the expense of B. Certainly, no buildings existed on plot B in the primary phase of occupation and when, finally, the plot was built upon, the burgage was found to be too narrow to

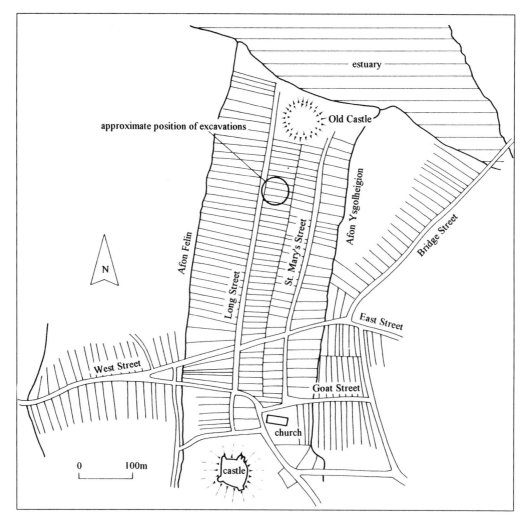

Fig 11.3 Schematic plan of Newport from a rental of 1434.

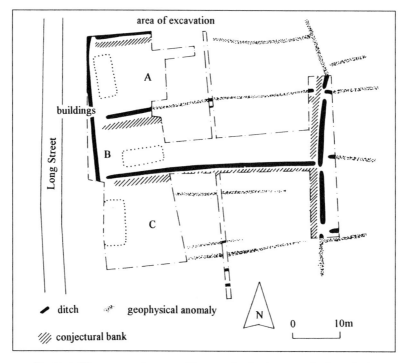

Fig 11.4 The excavated area at Newport showing burgage plot boundaries.

construct a house side-on to the street as in the neighbouring plots.

Except for a possible demolition layer associated with the final phase of building in plot A, evidence for buildings comprised drainage gullies and floor hollows cut into the clay subsoil (Fig 11.5). In plots A and C the buildings were the earliest recognized features on the street frontage and predated the burgage boundary ditches; the structure in plot B post-dated the digging of these ditches.

The building in plot C was represented by the most comprehensive set of remains: these comprised a rectangular floor hollow, 9.2 × 3.2m, filled with mixed soil and charcoal surrounded by a drainage gully, 12 × 6m. The floor hollow was divided into two halves with a hearth in the centre of the southern half. Analysis of charcoal associated with the hearth suggests that its source was waste material, perhaps from animal bedding or crop processing; presumably kindling for a domestic fire. Fragments of perforated local shale indicate that the building may have been at least partly roofed with tiles. A curving length of gully to the east of the building may mark the extent of a small yard. Drainage gullies ran from this building, then crossed plot B, predating the building within it, and emptied into the drainage gullies of the buildings in plot A.

At least three phases of building were present in plot A; all three were similar to the one described above in plot C. The last phase was also associated with a massive clay bank which seemed to have a break in its centre. This bank may be the remains of the west wall of this building. If this is the case, then it is important evidence in defining the nature of the building. The presence of this bank and the lack of other structural wall elements suggests that the walls of the last phase of the building in plot A, and probably all the other excavated buildings were earth built. As in plot C there was evidence of a yard to the rear of the building and some fragments of local roofing shale were also present.

As previously stated, the construction of the building in plot B was not coeval with those in the other plots; this structure post-dated both the digging of the drains that ran across the plot and the burgage plot boundary ditches. There is no stratigraphic reason, however, why buildings in all three plots were not standing at the same time. The form of the building in plot B is similar to those in the other plots but, because of the narrowness of the plot, for reasons outlined earlier, the building was constructed end on to the street.

All the excavated remains described can be placed into five phases of building and burgage boundary development. Apart from features associated with a mesolithic flint-working site, these five phases are stratigraphically the earliest recognizable features excavated. It is assumed that the five phases belong to a period immediately following the town's foundation c 1197, though absolute dating of them relies on the associated pottery assemblage. A total of 7337 sherds was recovered from the excavation programme, of which 1845 (Fig 11.6) came from the five phases of stratified

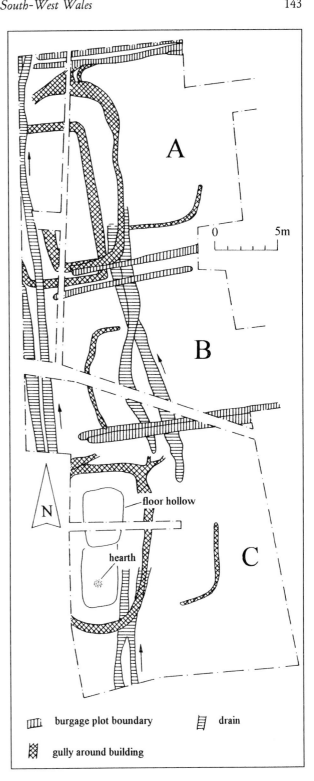

Fig 11.5 *The excavated building remains at Newport.*

deposits (Brennan & Murphy 1993–4). This stratified assemblage is dominated by local Dyfed Gravel Tempered Wares which account for over 92% of the total. The form and fabric of this ware changes little from the twelfth to the sixteenth century and no kilns have been identified, despite the suspicion that several centres of production were involved.[1] The dating of the assemblage therefore relies on

| Phase | Local Pottery | | English Pottery | | | | | | Cont Pottery | |
	Lung	Lgl	HGcp	HGgl	Min	NW	IC	Hmic	S	Total
III	118	42	1	6	-	1	-	-	-	167
IV	205	18	-	-	-	1	-	-	1	225
V	554	52	10	27	3	4	1	-	1	652
VI	281	67	11	4	-	-	1	1	1	367
VII	318	50	41	16	1	-	-	2	6	434
Total:	1476	229	63	53	4	5	2	3	9	1845
Percent	80%	12.4%	3.4%	2.9%	0.3%	0.3%	0.1%	0.2%	0.5%	100%

Key: Local pottery: Lung = unglazed wares, L.gl = local glazed; *English pottery*: HGcp = Ham Green cooking pots, HGgl - Ham Green glazed wares, Min = Minety type wares, NW = N Wiltshire wares, IC = uncertain Irish/Cornish wares, Hmic = Hereford micaceous ware; *Continental pottery*: S = Saintonge

Fig 11.6 Newport excavations. Table showing pottery from five phases of building and burgage plot development.

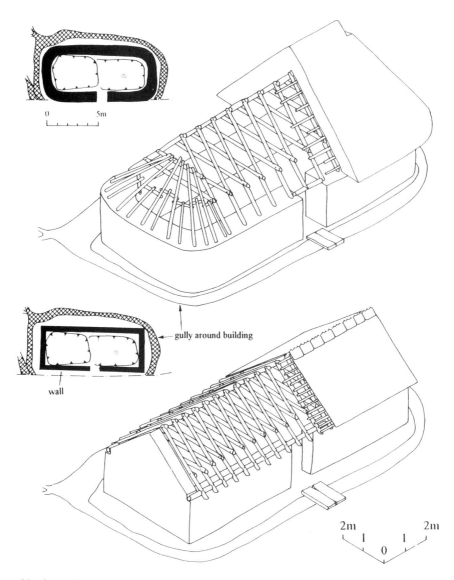

Fig 11.7 Two possible alternative reconstructions of a building based upon the excavated remains from burgage plot C at Newport.

the imports, namely Ham Green wares and other wares from the west of England. Broadly, the assemblage from the five phases described above accumulated in the first 75 years or so of the thirteenth century.

Following the abandonment of the buildings, the burgage plots were given over to agriculture. There are sufficient differences between the plots to indicate that during this period the boundaries were intact and that the plots continued to be held individually. There was no evidence for any industrial activity in the burgage plots, either when the buildings were occupied, or following their abandonment. A boulder placed alongside Long Street in perhaps the seventeenth or eighteenth century acted as a boundary marker for administrative purposes between plots B and C, even though by this period documentary evidence states that the burgages in this area had been merged into a small field or close.

Two suggested reconstructions of the building remains are presented here (Fig 11.7). Both are based upon the evidence of the building from plot C. The first features walls of earth, or 'clom' as it is still known in Pembrokeshire and Carmarthenshire, up to 1m thick. Walls of this thickness are known from extant examples in both Wales and Ireland (Evans 1969a; 1969b), and in the reconstruction shown here a 1m thick wall would allow a 0.2–0.5m space between the base of the wall and the surrounding drain. The building has rounded corners. Though it requires over twice the amount of building material of the square-cornered design, the round-cornered building sits more comfortably in the excavated plan. However, the majority of excavated examples of medieval clom buildings are thin-walled, usually about 0.5m, although these walls invariably contain internal timber stud work for additional strength, as with the examples excavated at Goltho by Beresford (1975) and at Wimborne by Field (1973). The square-walled reconstruction is shown with a tiled roof, but given the small quantities of tile recovered, perhaps a thatched roof with tiles around a smoke hole would be more appropriate. Because of the rounded walls the first example would necessarily have been thatched.

Clom is a building material ideally suited for use in a new town; the raw material is readily available at low cost, buildings can be raised quickly, and it is suitable for communal and periodic working. Generally it is considered that working in clom requires a large labour force with a few days' break between courses for the work to dry. McCann (1983, 5) recorded that earlier this century eight men working intermittently raised the walls of a two-storey clom-built house in three months.

Two questions are raised by the work at Newport: why were the burgage plots under examination abandoned after about the third quarter of the thirteenth century and why were the clom buildings never translated into timber- or stone-built dwellings? The answers to these questions are to be found in the documentary record: the 1434 rental not only provides a location for individual burgage plots and a record of burgage plot expansion, as described earlier, but also a record of abandonment and desertion. The relocation

of the castle from Old Castle near the estuary to its present site probably occurred, either in 1230 or in the 1270s, following its recapture by the English in the wake of Welsh attacks either in 1215 or 1257. This relocation changed the focus of the town and encouraged the growth of burgage plots around the new castle. The attacks of 1215 or 1257 may well have caused the abandonment of the three plots investigated. Therefore the expansion of burgage plots around the new castle at the southern end of the town was at the expense of, and not in addition to, reoccupation of the plots around Old Castle.

Wiston

A second borough in Pembrokeshire in which Dyfed Archaeological Trust has had a long interest is Wiston. There are several problem areas associated with this borough that are addressed here, but which have not been satisfactorily resolved. In the twelfth century, in the wake of the Anglo-Norman invasion of South Wales, Flemish settlers arrived in south Pembrokeshire (Jones 1952, 39–40). Foremost amongst these settlers was Wizo the Fleming, who gave his name to Wiston. Wizo arrived in Pembrokeshire prior to the year 1112 and disappears from the historical record *c* 1230 (Toorians 1990, 100; see Kissock p 131). The castle founded by Wizo was captured by Hywel ab Owain in 1147 and in 1195 by Hywel Sais (Jones 1955, 121, 175). The entry for the year 1220 in the *Brut y Tywysogyon* (Jones 1952, 97) contains the first reference to a town when both it and the castle were destroyed by Llywelyn ap Iorwerth. Toorians (1990, 103) considers that the castle was not refortified following this destruction but was superseded by Picton Castle 5km to the south. It is more likely, however, that the Wiston Castle continued in use, but that its status was downgraded, the *caput* shifting to Picton. The discovery, during recent excavations, of fourteenth-century pottery in the keep of Wiston Castle (Murphy unpublished 1995, 8) supports its continued use following the attack by Llywelyn ap Iorwerth.

There has been much debate concerning Wiston's borough status (see Kissock p 130), or lack of it. Most authorities (Soulsby 1983, 269; Beresford 1988, 570) dispute its borough status and no charter is known. However, in 1835 the Commissioners on Municipal Corporations (Green unpublished, Vol 19, 351–2), reporting under the Borough of Wiston, noted a mayor, alderman, burgesses and an annual fair. Earlier documents, such as an Inquisition Post Mortem of Sir John Wogan, 1577 (Green 1916, 199), record burgages. Documentary evidence for Wiston is, however, scarce; nothing like the wealth of material available for Newport exists and historical maps are few, the earliest being the tithe survey of *c* 1840. This cartographic evidence shows that Wiston in the early to mid nineteenth century consisted of the church, manor house and castle. The planning, development and decline of Wiston are, then, purely archaeological problems rather than the historical and archaeological problems existing at Newport. The

Fig 11.8 This aerial view of Wiston from the east shows the dispersed nature of the modern settlement. The church is centre left, the castle centre right (Copyright: Dyfed Archaeological Trust).

following is a record of how these problems are beginning to be solved.

Plan analysis and an examination of modern topography is the first step in attempting to resolve these problems (Fig 11.8). The village of Wiston (as it now is) is dominated by the massive bulk of the motte-and-bailey castle – the finest example of its kind in south-west Wales (Fig 11.9). The bailey of the castle is large, enclosing an area of about 1 ha. The entrance to the bailey faces east and is approached by a distinct hollow way, a feature which may be associated with the manor house, an Elizabethan structure largely demolished *c* 1850; just the rear wing survives. A drawing of 1740 (Oxford, Bodleian Lib Gough Maps 37, f 25[vp] [Lower]) shows the manor house and a gatehouse. It is unclear from the drawing whether this is the medieval gatehouse to the castle or a later structure associated with the manor house. St Mary's Church lies to the south of the castle on the opposite side of what is now the main road through the village. Earthworks, apparently of stone buildings, lie on a small green immediately in front of the church (Fig 11.9, A-A). These are the only definite building earthworks in the present village, although further earthworks on the south side of The Green are surely remains of the former town. A recent survey of The Green undertaken by the author has revealed possible remains of a planned element to the settlement, though the details of this work have yet to be analysed. There are no indications that the remains of the town as defined here were ever defended.

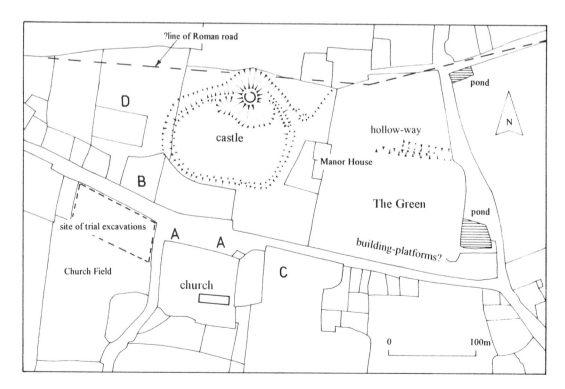

Fig 11.9 Wiston showing the positions of the trial excavation, earthworks (A-A) and watching briefs (B, C and D).

PERIOD	SOURCE	SHERDS	(% OF TOTAL)	VESSELS	(% OF TOTAL)
Roman	Non-local	5	(0.2)	5	(1.3)
Medieval	Local	2024	(91.6)	286	(69.8)
"	Non-local English	63	(2.8)	29	(7.0)
"	Contintental	2	(0.1)	2	(0.4)
Post-medieval	All types	118	(5.3)	88	(21.5)
TOTAL		2212	(100%)	410	(100%)

Fig 11.10 Table showing pottery from trial excavations at Church Field, Wiston.

It is possible that the castle was established on the site of an Iron Age hillfort. Certainly the size of the bailey, about 1 ha, is comparable with defended areas of Iron Age sites in south-west Wales. Other evidence for a pre-Norman presence in the area comes from survey and excavation currently being carried out on the Roman road west of Carmarthen. The course of this road has been traced from Carmarthen to a crossing point of the River Cleddau 5km east of Wiston (Fenton-Thomas unpublished 1994). Its route to the west is the subject of current fieldwork, but the evidence so far collected indicates that the road runs immediately to the north of Wiston Castle (Q Drew, pers comm). The presence of a pre-existing defensive circuit adaptable to the requirements of a motte-and-bailey castle, and a Roman road, the line of which may still have been used in the medieval period, are perhaps some of the reasons why Wiston was sited on a ridge away from river transport.

The first archaeological investigation at Wiston, a watching brief in 1979 during the building of a house (Fig 11.9, B), revealed medieval deposits which were interpreted as the remains of a timber building (Williams unpublished, n d). No other work was undertaken until 1990, when an application was made by the Church in Wales to develop Church Field (Fig 11.9). A geophysical survey of Church Field (undertaken by Geophysical Surveys of Bradford) detected what seemed to be building-plot boundaries, pits and likely areas of buildings. Some of the geophysical anomalies were then examined by narrow, hand-dug excavation trenches (Murphy unpublished 1994a). The excavations demonstrated that the interpretation of linear geophysical anomalies as building-plot boundaries was correct, and that these boundaries consisted of several phases of shallow ditches similar to the burgage-plot boundaries at Newport. Timber buildings along the street frontage preceded stone buildings, and further stone buildings on the eastern side of the site were also partly examined. However it was impossible to obtain either a convincing building sequence or information on the buildings' functions because of the narrow and widely spaced trial trenches. The positions of the trial trenches were guided very much by information from the geophysical survey. One trench was located over a distinct magnetic anomaly, interpreted as a pit by the geophysicists, and this proved to be correct. The pit contained layers of charcoal interleaved with burnt clay.

Plant macrofossil analysis revealed that the charcoal contained much grain, mostly oats, and this evidence, with the burnt clay, suggests the pit was filled with the demolished remains of a corn-drying kiln. A radiocarbon determination obtained from the charcoal of 1150±70 BP (CAR-1441) calibrates at two standard deviations to give a maximum date range of cal AD 680–1019.[2] Assuming the use of old wood, a date of usage for the kiln in the twelfth or thirteenth century rather than later in the medieval period is acceptable. This is compatible with a few sherds of Dyfed Gravel Tempered Ware which were mixed with the charcoal.

The pottery assemblage from Wiston (Fig 11.10) (Brennan in Murphy unpublished 1994a) bears a striking resemblance to that from Newport. Some 2212 sherds were recovered – a remarkable number considering only trial excavations were involved – of which 2024, almost 92%, were the locally produced Dyfed Gravel Tempered Ware. As with Newport, the assemblage is dated by the presence of imports; in the case of Wiston the pottery seems to have accumulated in the twelfth, thirteenth and early fourteenth centuries.

Since the 1990 trial excavations at Church Field, two further watching briefs have been undertaken in the presumed former area of the town. At C (Fig 11.9) (Murphy unpublished 1994b) what were assumed to be the tops of medieval pits were noted during house construction adjacent to a possible earthwork building platform. The new house is set back from the road and the pits, therefore, may have been located behind a medieval street frontage. At St Aidan's School, D, a watching brief (Murphy & Darke unpublished 1995) failed to reveal any evidence for medieval occupation.

Archaeological investigations have, then, started to flesh out the bare historical facts relating to Wiston. The former extent of the borough has started to be defined and information from excavations has begun to chart the settlement's planning, development and decline. Some problems have not, however, been addressed: for instance, the town as now defined does not seem to have been defended, but then little is known of the settlement in its earliest period, the twelfth century. Could it be that an early settlement was located in the castle bailey and that the excavated site and locations of the watching briefs formed part of a later, planned development?

Llawhaden

Intermittent and small scale archaeological investigations have been carried out at Llawhaden, Pembrokeshire, a former borough located 4km to the east of Wiston. Llawhaden was an estate of the bishop of St David's centred on Llawhaden Castle, a building of relatively minor significance until the late thirteenth century when Bishop Bek transformed it into a great fortified mansion. At the same time he established a hospice and created a new borough (Murphy unpublished 1993). This is a late foundation for Dyfed and must be regarded as infilling in a landscape crammed to capacity with small towns; Wiston, as mentioned above, lies only 4km to the west, Narberth 5km to the south-east and Haverfordwest 12km to the south-west. Initially, the borough seems to have been quite successful as 174½ burgages held by 126 burgesses are recorded in 1326 (Willis Bund 1902, xvii), but it was little more than a small village by the later middle ages. Its failure and that of Wiston are probably linked; the two boroughs are close together, both are on a ridge with no port facilities and both are close to larger, established and potentially better sited towns.

The original pre-borough settlement probably lay immediately outside the entrance to the castle, but with the foundation of the town, burgage plots were laid out on either side of the road from the castle to the hospice (Fig 11.11). Narrow strip fields are now the only testimony to the existence of these plots; other evidence having been obliterated in the seventeenth and eighteenth centuries by Llawhaden House, its ancillary buildings and gardens. Llawhaden was, however, a sizeable settlement; this is evidenced by a further row of burgage plots on a steep hillside by the side of a lane south west of the castle. These plots, most unusually, survive as a series of earthwork terraces and individual buildings, in the form of low platforms, may be present on these (see the historical section by H James

in South Pembrokeshire District Council 1989). The town was never enclosed by a defensive circuit.

Small scale excavations carried out on the hospice – an extant building – revealed some important evidence concerned with the layout of the town. A geophysical survey (by Geophysical Surveys of Bradford) carried out on open ground immediately to the west of the standing building detected what seemed to be building-plot boundaries. Small scale excavations demonstrated, but not conclusively, that these plots post-dated the remains of a stone building probably associated with the hospice (Murphy unpublished 1993). If this is the case, then we have evidence for town expansion after 1287 – the date of the foundation of the hospice and borough.

Llandovery

In all the examples so far given site specific, detailed archaeological investigations were either preceded by or carried out in conjunction with documentary research, topographic analysis and plan analysis of the relevant borough. This was not the case at Llandovery. Here an evaluation was carried out on the site of the former cattle market immediately north of the castle in advance of plans to build a new library and day centre (Murphy unpublished 1991) (Fig 11.12, A). The area of the proposed development was identified by Soulsby and Jones (1977) as archaeologically sensitive, but its history is poorly understood. It may have been an open area in the early fourteenth century, possibly enclosed by a defensive circuit, but whether these formed part of the castle defences or town defences is unclear (Murphy unpublished 1991). The results of the evaluation were negative; any stratigraphy that may have been present had probably been removed during construction of the cattle market earlier this century. However, without a historical and topographic study, it is simply not possible to place the

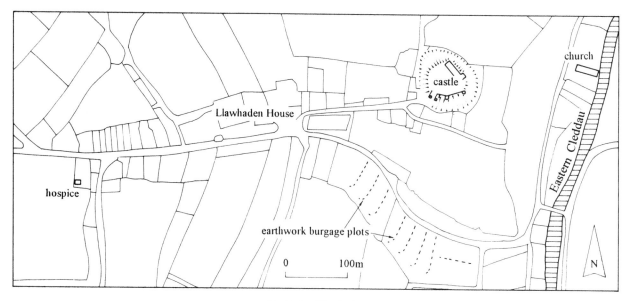

Fig 11.11 Llawhaden.

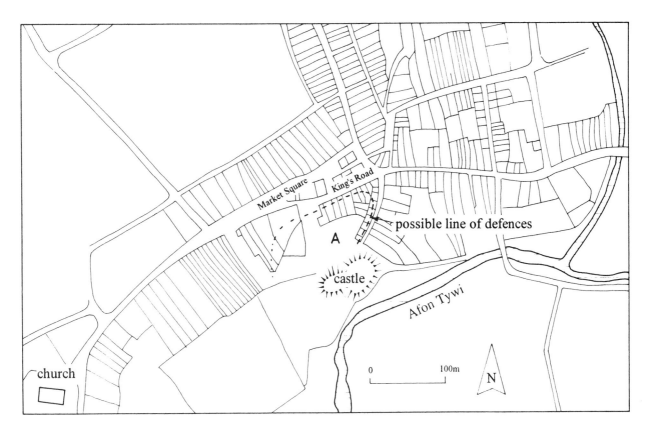

Fig 11.12 Llandovery.

evaluation results in context. For instance, the plan of the town seems to indicate that burgage plots were centred around Market Square and King's Road, with a further block of plots to the east. The former, according to Soulsby (1983, 162–3), might have been defended, but what of the site of the former cattle market? Was it originally part of the town, perhaps an early defended area, with the present town a later expansion? Or was it an outer bailey to the castle as the later medieval name of Castle Yard for the area would imply? Perhaps in the past it has served both functions, but without a fuller study of the town these sort of questions cannot be satisfactorily answered.

The Role of Defences

The examples so far discussed have been of work carried out in deserted boroughs or in towns where there is ample open space to undertake relatively large scale archaeological investigations. This is in contrast to archaeological sites that become available through the renovation of single buildings or the redevelopment of small plots in built-up and often busy little towns. Deeper and far more complex stratigraphy is often present than in the examples discussed above, but, because of the nature of the sites, it is a rare opportunity that allows for a thorough investigation and understanding of the archaeological evidence. A greater emphasis has to be placed on plan analysis and historical documentation of these smaller boroughs; ideally these

studies should be carried out prior to any excavation or other intrusive study.

Laugharne

One such study has been carried out at Laugharne, Carmarthenshire. Here the line of the former defences has been the subject of several studies (Avent 1987; Delaney & Soulsby 1975; Soulsby 1983, 158–60). All are agreed that permission to wall the town was granted in 1465, but some have expressed doubts that defences were ever constructed beyond gates with connecting earth banks. All show the route of the defensive circuit enclosing a considerable number of burgage plots (shown on Fig 11.13 by a pecked line), despite the fact that they were aware that Mary Curtis (1880, 89–90) had clearly indicated the locations of the town gates (Fig 11.13) in positions which would not be compatible with such a circuit. Figure 11.13 is based on the Laugharne Township tithe map of *c* 1840 deposited with Carmarthenshire Record Office. The location and number of burgage plots recorded on the tithe map approximately matches those recorded on a survey of 1592 (Laugharne Corporation, unpublished). Analysis of this survey, not only locates the position of burgage plots, but also the town gates (Murphy 1987). From this, it is clear that the defended area of the town was small, about 1.4 ha, and that, according to the 1592 survey, it contained only 25 burgages out of a total of 154. It may be argued, therefore, that this small defended area was

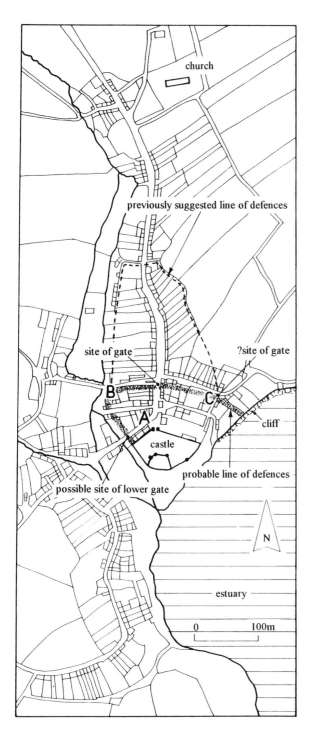

Fig 11.13 Laugharne.

the 1592 survey existed prior to the 1465 permission to enclose the town, and that no additions or extensions were added to the defences following the issue of the permission.

Even though long term excavations have been carried out in the castle, intrusive archaeological investigation in the town of Laugharne has been limited to a single watching brief (Murphy unpublished 1992) carried out during building demolition (Fig 11.13, A). Stratified medieval deposits were recorded, but it was not possible to obtain a building plan or a convincing stratigraphic sequence. Two future small scale building developments are planned on the line of the defences (Fig 11.13, B, C); it is hoped that useful information on the exact line and nature of the defences will be obtained from watching briefs during building work.

St Clears

St Clears, Carmarthenshire, 6km upstream from Laugharne, is a town in which it has been possible to obtain much useful information through small scale excavations and watching briefs. Don Benson, the director of Dyfed Archaeological Trust, has long had an interest in the town and is currently compiling an in-depth study on it (Benson forthcoming). I am grateful to him for supplying much of the following information. A castle seems to have been founded here in the late eleventh century, with the first

*Fig 11.14 An almost vertical view of St Clears
(Copyright: Dyfed Archaeological Trust).*

established in the early years of the settlement's history, perhaps soon after the foundation of the castle in the early twelfth century (Avent 1991, 167), and that the extra-mural burgages were developments of the thirteenth and fourteenth centuries. It is unlikely that the murage licence of 1465 was for permission to translate the existing earthen defences into stone walls and gates as by then only a fraction of the town's burgages was enclosed by them. We must therefore assume that stone gates located by Curtis and by

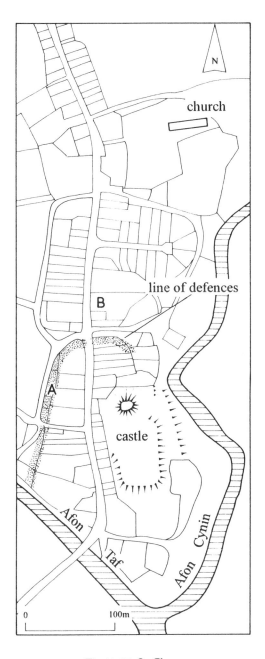

Fig 11.15 St Clears.

In 1979, a 90m length of defensive earthwork was identified on the western side of the town. Rescue recording of this was carried out in 1979, and in 1989 controlled excavation was undertaken on a short length of the earthwork (Fig 11.15, A). The defensive system was seen to consist of an external ditch, the material from which was upcast to form a bank, which seemed to be of two phases. No finds were recovered to assist in the dating of the defences, though three radiocarbon determinations (CAR 1342, 900±60 BP; CAR 1343, 1630±60 BP; CAR 1345, 840±60 BP) were obtained from charcoal incorporated in the buried soil beneath the bank and one from charcoal in the rampart core (CAR 1344, 1040±60 BP). CAR 1343 calibrates at two standard deviations to cal AD 241–611 and is presumably evidence of unspecified Roman or post-Roman activity in the area. The combined maximum date range of the three remaining dates, calibrated at two standard deviations, is cal AD 868–1289. Though not of assistance in firmly assigning the construction of the rampart to a specific century, these dates confirm the medieval nature of the defences.

Within the town, field evaluation in response to a planning application (Darke & Benson unpublished 1993) has been undertaken on a vacant plot, possibly originally two burgages, outside the defended area (Fig 11.15, B). The evidence from this excavation is difficult to interpret, but seems to show use of these burgages in the twelfth and thirteenth centuries, possibly with buildings alongside the street frontage.

Kidwelly

Detailed notes on the borough of Kidwelly, Carmarthenshire, have been published by Heather James (1980). Roger, bishop of Salisbury, founded a castle at Kidwelly soon after 1106. According to Fox and Radford (1933), the original castle was a ringwork with timber defences, the plan of which is reflected in the extant, mainly thirteenth- and fourteenth-century, stone castle. Avent (1991, 170) has questioned some of Fox and Radford's conclusions, based upon just ten day's fieldwork, though the presence of two defended enclosures roughly concentric to the castle and separated by a ditch would seem to support the case for a ringwork. The medieval borough is situated in the enclosure to the south west; the enclosure to the north east is further sub-divided and there is no evidence that it was ever built upon – medieval documents refer to gardens in the vicinity and post-medieval records to rabbit warrens (James 1980, 7).

The documentary and topographic evidence for the town defences has been previously reviewed (James 1980) and therefore no detailed discussion will be entered into here. The earliest murage grant was in 1280. The south-west gate of the town still survives and some lengths of the town wall; elsewhere it is possible to trace the course of the defences with a high degree of confidence (Fig 11.16). Writing in 1546, Leland states that Kidwelly had two further

mention of a town in 1248, while the charter dates to 1392. The history of the castle and town is poorly documented; great emphasis must therefore be placed on plan analysis and the archaeological record.

St Clears is situated at the confluence of the Cynin and Taf (Fig 11.14). To the west and north of the motte-and-bailey castle is a line of defence defined by the street pattern, which encloses an area, exclusive of the castle, of about 1 ha. It is unclear whether this was an outer bailey of the castle or a defended settlement, though from the apparent burgage plots shown on Figure 11.15 the latter seems more likely. A lobe of further burgage plots to the north, though well defined by the street pattern, does not ever seem to have been defended. The priory church lies to the north.

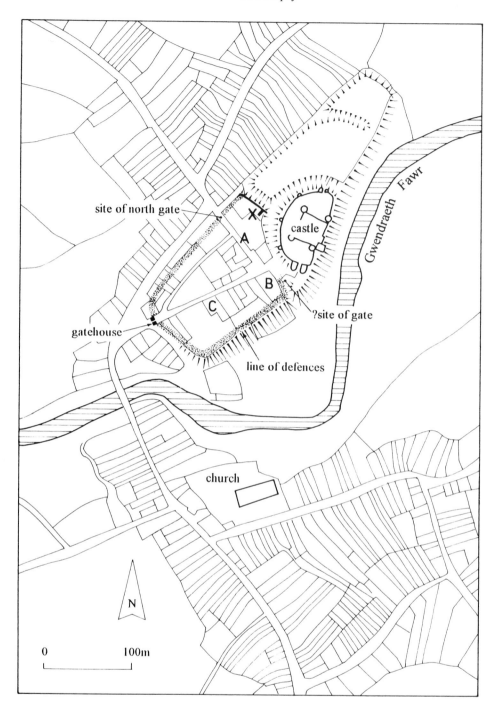

Fig 11.16 Kidwelly.

gates (Hearne 1744, vol 5, 20): the position of the north gate is fairly certain, that of the third gate less so. In total about 1.3 ha were enclosed by the defensive circuit.

In 1980, a small trench (Fig 11.16, X) was dug adjacent to a surviving section of the town wall (James unpublished 1980). This work clearly demonstrated that the wall sits on an earthen bank – part of a earlier defence circuit consisting of a bank and ditch. James (1980, 6) has noted that, even with extensive excavation, it would be difficult to prove that this circuit and the castle ringwork were constructed contemporaneously. If they were, they may be an indication

that the town was founded as a planned settlement dating to the early twelfth century, and was not the result of informal development outside the castle gates which was later defended and granted borough status.

By the fourteenth century, the majority of the burgages lay either just outside the confines of the defensive circuit or on the opposite side of the river around the priory church (Soulsby 1983, 152); this latter area forms the modern town centre. In the early sixteenth century there were just three burgages, seven tenements and eight cottages within the defences (James 1980, 13). The lack of late medieval and post-medieval development, coupled with the presence of much open space within the defended area, makes Kidwelly potentially a prime site for good preservation of stratified deposits of the twelfth to fourteenth century. Excavation has, however, generally failed to reveal such deposits. James' excavation (unpublished 1980) (Fig 11.16, A) found that nineteenth-century buildings had removed earlier deposits, whilst at site B (Murphy unpublished 1990) a series of rubbish pits of fourteenth-century date or earlier lay in a burgage plot behind the street frontage. No building foundations, floor surfaces or other structural evidence were present; it was considered that the rubbish pits lay behind medieval buildings on the street frontage, the evidence for which had been removed. In contrast, an excavation undertaken in connection with a small private museum (site C) revealed stratified deposits associated with buildings and possible industrial activities. Unfortunately, the results of these excavations were never reported upon; some of the finds are in Carmarthen Museum.

Conclusions

It often seems to be forgotten that in Dyfed, as in a good part of Wales, in the late eleventh, twelfth and thirteenth centuries, the vast majority of towns functioned as frontier towns and were, on occasions, subjected to attacks, sieges and other deprivations. On other occasions, they may have experienced rapid growth; for instance, when they functioned as garrison towns. The oft cited model for medieval settlement right across Europe of steady growth followed by decline from the mid fourteenth century with recovery at the end of the middle ages is applicable to Wales, but with modifications to allow for the local conditions outlined above. For instance, work at Newport has demonstrated that both decline and recovery during perhaps the 75 years following the town's foundation in the late twelfth century are still reflected in the town plan and are archaeologically detectable. Detailed plan analysis, coupled with archaeological excavation in other towns, may reveal similar patterns. For example, at Kidwelly it would be of great interest to know if the deserted enclosure to the north east of the castle was ever occupied, and if it was, whether it was conceived as part of a defended settlement contemporaneous with the early ringwork castle.

The economic and political reasons for the foundations of towns have been discussed by others (eg Beresford 1988, Soulsby 1983) and it is not intended to reiterate them here. Two points only may be mentioned. The first concerns the close distribution of small boroughs in south-west Wales. This is probably a result of the nature of the Anglo-Norman conquest, which led to a fragmentation of the area into numerous small lordships, with the lord of each either encouraging or actively founding a borough or small town. The second point relates to the above, but is concerned with research in Ireland. In Ireland the term 'rural borough', has been applied to settlements endowed with burghal status but their function was to attract settlers and so increase

the revenues of feudal lords (Graham 1985, 26–31; see Kissock p 130). It is uncertain whether the founders of these boroughs intended or expected them to develop into full-blown towns; most were never more than villages. In south-west Wales such boroughs as Wiston, New Moat, Llawhaden, Templeton (all in Pembrokeshire) and Abergwili and Dryslwyn in Carmarthenshire may have been founded simply as mechanisms to attract settlers and so maximize revenues, as in the rural boroughs of Ireland. South-west Wales, and in particular Pembroke, acted as a springboard for the late twelfth century Anglo-Norman conquest and colonization of south and central Ireland. Perhaps the inspiration for the Irish rural boroughs came from the Anglo-Norman feudal lords' experiences of settlement and borough creation in south-west Wales.

In this paper the discussion of planning and early development has been nominally separated from that of the role of defences. In reality no such distinction can be made; early defensive circuits often dominated the plan and development of later medieval towns, as at Kidwelly, and later defensive walls may have been designed to accommodate planned extensions to towns, as perhaps at Tenby. Many settlements – later transformed into boroughs – that grew under the protection of Anglo-Norman castles were provided with defensive circuits, though it is not clear whether these were contemporaneous with the castle defences, or later additions.

There is also the possibility that early settlements were established in the baileys of castles. Soulsby has hinted that this may have been the case at New Moat, Pembrokeshire (1983, 198–9) and Walker (1989, 134) has suggested a similar situation at Pembroke. Wiston may be another example. Certainly, the approximately 1 ha area enclosed by the defences at Wiston Castle is comparable in size to the defended areas of the towns of Laugharne (1.4 ha), Kidwelly (1.3 ha) and St Clears (1 ha), though in the last example it is unclear whether the defensive circuit enclosed an outer bailey or the town. In this case perhaps any distinction is unnecessary, though it raises the interesting problem of who controlled space: was it under seigneurial or civic administration? Certainly, the question of possible non-military settlements within castle baileys is one that can only be answered by excavation.

Further defensive circuits encompassing small, early settlements may yet be discovered beneath some towns. In a recently published study of the walls of Tenby, Thomas (1993, 3) recognizes that the walls follow the course of an earlier earthen rampart, but no mention is made for the possibility for a yet earlier line of defence (Fig 11.17). The defensive circuit as described by Thomas encloses a large area including a substantial planned element of the town; a date after 1187 is suggested for its construction. It seems likely, however, that an earlier circuit cutting off a small portion of the headland on which Tenby is situated was constructed to defend a settlement which grew up near the castle in the early twelfth century. Certainly, at Pembroke the plan of the town indicates several successive lines of

Fig 11.17 Tenby. The remains of the castle stand on the promontory, top left, the parish church is in the centre and the town walls run from the lower left towards the top right. A planned element to the street pattern can clearly be seen between the town walls and the church, while the less regular plan between the church and the castle suggests earlier, unplanned growth (Copyright: Dyfed Archaeological Trust).

defence prior to construction of the town walls in the late thirteenth or early fourteenth century (Ludlow 1991).

The figure provided by Beresford (1988, table VI.2) that 86% (72 out of 84) of medieval new towns in Wales were provided with some form of defence may be an underestimation in light of the above observations. It is, however, clear that a small number of towns were not defended; Newport is a good example. The reason why this town was not provided with defences is open to speculation. Perhaps at the town's foundation *c* 1197 it was perceived that a period of peace lay ahead. The decision may have been political: the provision of a defensive circuit would have been seen as tantamount to an admission by William Fitzmartin that he was unable to control his lordship. Alternatively, it may have been economic: there may simply have been insufficient resources, notably labour, to build defences. Whatever the reason, the town must have suffered badly during the attacks of 1215 and 1257.

An aspect of town planning that has not been touched upon in the discussion of individual boroughs is the relationships between the castle, the borough and the church. It is clear from the plans discussed here that the church is often separated from the borough; this is certainly the case with Llawhaden, Laugharne, St Clears, Kidwelly and Llandovery. To these may be added Cardigan and possibly Carmarthen, Pembroke and Tenby. The explanation for some of these examples has been well rehearsed: the castles and towns were located near to pre-existing churches; it was not, therefore, considered necessary to construct new places of worship within the towns. Llawhaden, Llandovery, Carmarthen and possibly Laugharne fit into this category. The remainder seem to be the result of a deliberate Anglo-Norman policy of separating the church from the castle and associated settlement.

Towns are arguably the most lasting and important contribution of the Anglo-Normans to the modern Welsh landscape, and to modern Welsh life. Their planning, their early history and their development are beginning to be understood by detailed historic surveys, plan analyses and archaeological investigations. But much remains to be done, and it is clear from this short review of recent work that the subject is more complex than was suspected ten or twenty years ago.

Acknowledgements

Thanks are due to my colleagues in the Dyfed Archaeological Trust for allowing me access to their unpublished work and for their advice and comments on this paper. In particular, I would like to thank Neil Ludlow, Heather James and Don Benson.

Notes

1 For a full review and discussion of Dyfed Gravel Tempered Ware and other medieval pottery from Wales see Papazian and Campbell (1992).

2 A computer programme *Radiocarbon Calibration Program 1993*, devised by the Quaternary Isotope Lab, University of Washington, was used to calibrate the radiocarbon determinations in this paper.

References

Unpublished sources

Dyfed Archaeological Trust, 1975, *Dyfed historic towns*, Dyfed Archaeological Trust policy document

Bignall, V E, 1991, *Newport (Trefdraeth) in west Wales. An analysis of the origins, planning and development of a Norman new town*, Undergraduate dissertation, University of Wales, Lampeter

Darke, I M & Benson, D G, 1993, *Report on the archaeological evaluation of land at Parc-y-Drain, High Street, St Clears*, Dyfed Archaeological Trust

Fenton-Thomas, C, 1994, *The Roman road west of Carmarthen*, Dyfed Archaeological Trust

Green, F, The Francis Green collection of documents, Haverfordwest Public Library

James, H, 1980, *Castle Farm car park, Kidwelly*, Dyfed Archaeological Trust

Laugharne Corporation, *The Castle Lordship and Manor of Tallaugharne otherwise Laughan with the Members*

Murphy, K, 1990, *Kidwelly Castle car park extension, Archaeological assessment, Jan 1990*, Dyfed Archaeological Trust

Murphy, K, 1991, *An archaeological assessment on the site of the proposed branch library and day centre, Llandovery, Dyfed, January 1991*, Dyfed Archaeological Trust

Murphy, K, 1992, *The Butcher's Arms House, Laugharne – archaeological watching brief and recording, November 1991*, Dyfed Archaeological Trust

Murphy, K, 1993, *Assessment, survey and excavation at Llawhaden Hospital, Dyfed, November 1992*, Dyfed Archaeological Trust

Murphy, K, 1994a, *Trial excavation at Church Field in the medieval borough of Wiston, Dyfed, 1990*, Dyfed Archaeological Trust

Murphy, K, 1994b, *Cawdor Farm, Wiston, Dyfed, November 1994 – watching brief 29537*, Dyfed Archaeological Trust

Murphy, K, 1995, *Wiston Castle: archaeological recording 1995*, Dyfed Archaeological Trust

Murphy, K, & Darke, I, 1995 *Extension to the school playground: St Aidan's V. A. School, Wiston, Archaeological, watching brief*, Dyfed Archaeological Trust

Oxford, Bodleian Library, *Gough Maps 37, fol. 25ᵛᵖ (Lower) The north view of Wiston Castle, July 9th 1740*

Williams, G, n d *Building site adjacent to Wiston Castle (PRN 8510; SN 021 186)*, Dyfed Archaeological Trust

Published sources

Avent, R, 1987, The siege of Laugharne Castle from 28 October to 3 November 1644, in R Avent & J Kenyon (eds), *Castles in Wales and the March*, 185–204

Avent, R, 1991, The early development of three coastal castles, in H James (ed), *Sir Gâr: studies in Carmarthenshire history*, Carmarthenshire Antiq Soc mon ser 4, 167–88

Benson, D G, forthcoming The topography and archaeology of medieval St Clears, *Carmarthenshire Antiq*

Beresford, G, 1975, *The medieval clay-land village: excavations at Goltho and Barton Blount*, Soc Medieval Archaeol mon

Beresford, M, 1988, *New towns of the middle ages*, 2nd ed, Gloucester

Brennan, D F M, & Murphy, K, 1993–4, The pottery from excavations in three burgage plots in the town of Newport, Dyfed, 1991, *Medieval and Later Pottery in Wales*, 14, 1–8

Charles, B G, 1951, The records of the borough of Newport in Pembrokeshire, *Nat Lib Wales J*, 7, 33–45, 120–37

Curtis, M, 1880, *The antiquities of Laugharne, Pendine and their neighbours*, 2nd ed, London

Delaney, C, & Soulsby, I N, 1975, *Historic towns in Carmarthen District*, Urban Research Unit, Dept Archaeol, Univ Coll Cardiff

Evans, E E, 1969a, A Cardiganshire mud-walled farmhouse, *Folk Life*, 7, 92–102

Evans, E E, 1969b, Sod and turf houses in Ireland, in G Jenkins (ed), *Studies in folk life*, London, 79–90

Fenton, R, 1903 *A historical tour through Pembrokeshire*, 2nd ed, Brecknock

Field, N H, 1973, The Leaze, Wimborne, an excavation in a deserted medieval quarter of the town, *Proc Dorset Nat Hist Archaeol Soc*, 94, 49–62

Fox, C, & Radford, C A R, 1933, Kidwelly Castle, Carmarthenshire; including a review of the polychrome pottery found there and elsewhere in Britain, *Archaeologia*, 83, 93–138

Graham, B J, 1985, *Anglo-Norman settlement in Ireland*, Irish Settlement Studies 1

Green, F, 1916, The Wogans of Pembrokeshire, *West Wales Historical Records*, 6, 169–203

Hearne, T, 1744, *The itinerary of John Leland the antiquary*, 9 vols, 2nd ed, Oxford

James, H, 1980, Topographical notes on the early medieval borough of Kidwelly, *Carmarthenshire Antiq*, 16, 6–17

Jones, T (trans), 1952, *Brut y Tywysogyon (Peniarth MS. 20 version)*, Cardiff

Jones, T (ed & trans), 1955, *Brut y Tywysogyon (Red Book of Hergest version)*, Cardiff

King, D J C, & Perks, J C, 1951, Castell Nanhyfer, Nevern (Pemb.), *Archaeol Cambrensis*, 101, 123–8

Lloyd, J E, 1911, *A history of Wales*, 2 vols, London

Ludlow, N D, 1991, Pembroke Castle and town walls, *Fortress*, 8, 25–30

McCann, J, 1983, *Clay and cob buildings*, Aylesbury

Murphy, K, 1987, Notes on the topography of Laugharne, *Carmarthenshire Antiq*, 23, 62–5

Murphy, K, 1994, Excavations in three burgage plots in the medieval new town of Newport, Dyfed, 1991, *Medieval Archaeol*, 38, 55–82

Papazian, C, & Campbell, E, 1992 Medieval pottery and roof tiles in Wales AD 1100–1600, *Medieval and Later Pottery in Wales*, 13, 1–107

RCAHMW, 1925, *An inventory of the ancient monuments in Wales and Monmouthshire, Vol 7, County of Pembroke*, London

Soulsby, I, 1983, *The towns of medieval Wales*, Chichester

Soulsby, I, & Jones, D, 1977, *Historic towns in the borough of Dinefwr*, Urban Research Unit, Dept Archaeol, Univ Coll Cardiff

South Pembrokeshire District Council, 1989, *South Pembrokeshire local plan: Llawhaden village inset no 11*, planning document, Planning and Technical Dept, South Pembrokeshire District Council

Stenger, C M, 1985, Long Street, Newport, *Archaeol Wales*, 25, 43–4

Thomas, W G, 1993, The walls of Tenby, *Archaeol Cambrensis*, 142, 1–39

Toorians, L, 1990, Wizo Flandrensis and the Flemish settlement in Pembrokeshire, *Cambridge Medieval Celtic Stud*, 20, 99–118

Walker, R F, 1989, Henry II's charter to Pembroke, *Bull Board Celtic Stud*, 36, 132–45

Willis-Bund, J W (ed), 1902, *The Black Book of St Davids*, Cymmrodorion Record Ser 5, London

Chapter 12

New Radnor: The Topography of a Medieval Planned Town in Mid-Wales

Robert Silvester

New Radnor in central Powys is a good example of a planned settlement that failed to expand. Established in the earlier part of the thirteenth century if not before, it was granted borough status, became a shire town in 1536, but gradually went into decline during the post-medieval era as other towns in Radnorshire grew more prosperous. New Radnor's decline has, however, permitted the survival of a range of features relating to the medieval settlement: its earthwork castle, town defences and the remnants of a street pattern relegated to back lanes and holloways, as well as sporadic house platforms in pasture where there were once burgage plots. Overall, New Radnor offers the best opportunity in the region for further examination of a planted town.

To Harold Carter, New Radnor (formerly in the historic county of Radnorshire, now in Powys) was a 'town of stunted or retarded growth'. . . 'one of the best examples where the reactions of weak growth on physical form are clearly apparent' (Carter 1966, 180). To other writers it is simply a typical example of a medieval planned town with a characteristic grid layout (eg Butler 1976, 38). Yet the failings highlighted by Carter are without question the reason why the town is so interesting to the landscape historian: the fossilization of features of its medieval design and form are here more pronounced than in many contemporaeous settlements in this region of Wales.

New Radnor (SO 212608; Fig 12.1) lies at the western end of what has become known as the Walton Basin, a low-lying flattish plain that carries the Summergil and Hindwell Brooks to their meeting with the River Lugg as it flows eastwards into the Herefordshire lowlands (Fig 12.2). West of the town the valley narrows rapidly but still offers access to the district of Elvel and the hills of central Wales. In terms of accessibility it lies on the margin between the border and the Welsh heartland.

Origins and Development

The origins of the town are clouded. A late Saxon *burh* has been tentatively postulated (J Spurgeon, unpublished notes; see also Musson & Spurgeon 1988, 107) dating to *c* 1063 and following Harold Godwinson's successful campaign against Gruffudd ap Llywelyn in north Wales (Stenton 1971, 576). An alternative view is of a late Saxon motte-and-bailey castle (Howse 1989, 9, following earlier writers).

On present evidence neither seems particularly convincing. There is no documentary evidence that points to the pre-conquest emergence of New Radnor, for Domesday Book contains the simple statement 'the king holds Radnor. Harold the Earl held it [in the time of Edward the Confessor]. Here are 15 hides, it is and was waste' (Thorn & Thorn 1983, I, 65), thus introducing a complication over the name 'Radnor' which was to continue in use without a qualifying prefix for another two centuries. Nor has anything of significance come from recent excavations in the town (see below). More telling, at least as far as the *burh* hypothesis is concerned, is the location: defensively a more exposed setting for a town could hardly have been selected, overshadowed as it is by the prominent knoll now occupied by the castle of New Radnor.

The earliest reference to New Radnor is in the *Taxatio* of Pope Nicholas IV in 1291 (*Taxatio* 1802), though as Old Radnor is mentioned by name in 1252–3 this implies that New Radnor was by then in existence (*CIM 1* 1904, 58; King 1983, 415, n 40). Documents naming only Radnor (eg *CPR, Henry III, Vol 4* 1908, 508) have been claimed as evidence of a stronghold at Old Radnor (SO 250590), 4km to the south east. Early in the nineteenth century, Sir Richard Colt Hoare's diary proclaimed that Old Radnor was the settlement referred to in these early documents (Thompson 1983, 201), and a century later the Royal Commission on Ancient and Historical Monuments in Wales opined that New Radnor came into existence only in the early thirteenth century (RCAHMW 1913, xviii). Admittedly Old Radnor does have a church of some architectural significance, but it lacks a castle worthy of the

Fig 12.1 Aerial view of New Radnor, Radnorshire, from the south west. The town defences can be seen in the centre and right foreground, the castle mound and bailey in the centre background (Copyright Clwyd-Powys Archaeological Trust, Ref no 86-MB-262).

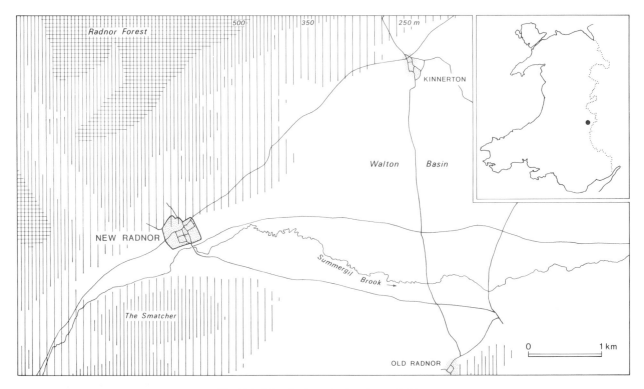

Fig 12.2 New Radnor: its location and siting.

name and the case advanced by the Royal Commission for Castle Nimble, a curious and puny ringwork in the valley below the village, inspires no confidence. And as a small, hillside settlement Old Radnor is hardly likely to have been important enough in 1188 for Baldwin, Archbishop of Canterbury, accompanied by Gerald of Wales, to have used it as a starting point for his perambulation of Wales, preaching the First Crusade (Thorpe 1978, 75–7).

On the other hand, Jonathan Williams, the Radnorshire antiquary and contemporary of Colt Hoare, dismissed the arguments for Old Radnor in his manuscript history of the county (Davies 1905, 179); and much more recently Jack Spurgeon (pers comm) has also argued that most if not all the post-Conquest references to 'Radnor' relate to New Radnor.

Circumstantial evidence clearly favours New Radnor. Radnor Castle features frequently in the documentary record: sacked by Rhys ap Gruffudd in 1196, refurbished by William de Breos and occupied by his ally Llywelyn ap Iorwerth, captured and destroyed by King John in 1216, sacked by Llywelyn in 1231, rebuilt by the earl of Cornwall in 1233, and destroyed by Llywelyn ap Gruffudd and Simon de Montfort in 1264 (Remfrey 1994, 12–18). Throughout the twelfth century it had been intimately associated with the family of de Breos, marcher lords who were responsible for constructing other great earthwork castles at Builth Wells in Breconshire (20km to the south west) and Painscastle and Colwyn in Radnorshire (15km to the south and 12km to the south west respectively). It is a reasonable assumption that New Radnor's impressive motte is the de Breos stronghold referred to in the records; it may even have been thrown up as early as 1096 by Philip de Breos, one of the original marcher lords.

Dating the town's establishment poses more difficulties. Some time before his death in 1135 Philip de Breos, lord of Radnor, granted a burgage in Radnor to St Peter's Abbey at Gloucester. The document recording the gift was witnessed by numerous burgesses in the town, thirteen of whom are named. This grant has also been attributed to the late twelfth century though this conflicts with the span of Philip's seigneurage (Beresford 1988, 573). Overall, there can be little doubt that New Radnor had emerged as a settlement in the first half of the thirteenth century if not earlier. In 1235 the Charter Rolls refer to the de Breos lands including 'Radnor Castle and the town of the castle' being granted to the earl of Pembroke (*CChR I*, 1903, 192).

The town received its first murage grant in 1257, with subsequent grants in 1280, 1283 and 1290 (*CPR, Henry III, Vol 4* 1908, 508; *Edward I, Vol 2* 1893, 69, 377; Turner 1970, 243). A weekly market was operating early in the fourteenth century, and a charter for a yearly fair was acquired in 1306 (*CChR III* 1908, 68). At the beginning of the fourteenth century it appears to have been one of the twelve most populous towns in Wales (Soulsby 1983, 21).

As a border plantation accompanying a strategically sited stronghold that guarded one of the few natural routeways westwards, it was initially successful. But as a market centre it had little to recommend it. In time other, better placed Radnorshire settlements, notably Knighton and Presteigne, expanded at New Radnor's expense. Owain Glyndŵr sacked the town in 1401, leaving ruins which were still obvious to John Leland nearly a century and a half later (Smith 1964, iii, 10). It was 'metley well wallyd, and in the walle appere the ruines of iiii gates . . . the buildynge of the towne in some parte meatly good, in most part but rude, many howsys bwinge thakyd [thatched]'. An Act of Parliament in 1544 described it as a decayed town (Howse 1989, 18), yet eight years previously it had been elevated to the rank of a shire town in the Act of Union. W H Howse, the Radnorshire historian, speculated somewhat wryly, that this was primarily because it had the only castle in the new county which was still in a sufficiently complete state to function as a prison. Certainly Bishop Lee, President of the Court of the Council of the Marches, had come to New Radnor in 1535 and wrote to Thomas Cromwell that the castle was 'not to be repayred, but only a prison house amended, which must neds be doon' (quoted in Howse 1989, 15).

The early years of the seventeenth century witnessed the publication of John Speed's atlas entitled *The theatre of the empire of Great Britain* (1611), each county map accompanied by at least one inset town plan. As the county town of Radnorshire, New Radnor was depicted in detail for the first time. Though there is undoubtedly a stylized element to the plan, the overriding impression is of a town in decline, with dwellings sparsely spaced on those streets away from the main thoroughfares and large open areas within the walls (Silvester 1994b, 21). When Ship Money was levied in 1636, the whole borough of New Radnor was taxed at only £6, a clear measure of its decay for nearby Presteigne had to find £28 (Howse 1989, 18). Later in the century John Ogilby, in his *Britannia* (1675) reported it 'at present a poor town consisting in about 40 houses, yet hath 3 fairs annually; one good inn of accommodation; sending one burgess to Parliament'.

New Radnor had borough status (though its first extant charter dates only from 1562), it had its own recorder, coroner, receiver and sergeants-at-mace, and was governed by a corporation of 25 'Capital Burgesses' (Howse 1989, 24). It held Quarter Sessions for the county, and had a gaol which was relocated to Broad Street with the continued deterioration of the castle. Yet this administrative gloss cannot disguise the economic failure of the town. By the beginning of the nineteenth century, Jonathan Williams could note,

'its deserted streets, several of which have no buildings and others of which are now only footpaths, . . . not more than 50 dwelling houses, and most of those of mean appearance . . . the barn-like appearance of its supreme Court, where its chief magistrate is sworn into office, and its representative in Parliament elected, the desolate site of its once formidable and frowning castle . . . of which one stone is not left upon another... [and] the decrease of modern population amounting to 36 persons in the course of 77 years . . . to 1800' (Davies 1905, 180).

Fig 12.3 New Radnor at the time of enclosure in 1811 (based on a manuscript plan by permission of the National Library of Wales).

The twentieth century has seen a gradual infilling of vacant plots within the town. Upwards of 24 new houses appeared between the first edition of the Ordnance Survey 25 inch map surveyed in 1887 and its modern equivalent of 1982, excluding the small council estate of fourteen semi-detached dwellings in the south-east corner of the walled town. Yet for a small town these developments are relatively insignificant and it seems likely that the modern population of New Radnor has not yet matched its medieval peak. A considerable amount of open space remains within the walls, signalling the potential of New Radnor for the townscape historian.

Archaeological Excavation

The Clwyd-Powys Archaeological Trust's involvement with the town commenced relatively recently. In 1988 a corn-drying kiln of late medieval or early post-medieval date was unearthed on the street frontage of Hall Lane (Dorling 1988), one of New Radnor's minor streets (Fig 12.4, A). Three years later, in response to a proposed housing development, more extensive excavations were carried out just within the western town defences on a one-acre plot fronting onto Church Street (Fig 12.4, B). The banks of a post-medieval croft apart, the field was almost completely featureless, a fact which had not aided the previously-argued case for scheduling. Geophysical survey proved uninformative, but excavation revealed medieval activity in what may have been two burgage plots, though there had been considerable disturbance, presumably as a result of post-medieval cultivation. The most obvious features were more than a dozen large latrine or rubbish pits, one with well-constructed drystone walls. Most had highly organic fills, though lacking large quantities of material debris. One plot contained the fragmentary stone walls of a rectangular building with a small oven built into the wall angle; the other plot revealed a post-built structure later replaced in stone, with evidence of smithying. Post-medieval activity was largely absent (Jones 1992; in prep).

The Townscape of Medieval Radnor

The archaeological potential of the open ground in New Radnor has been amply demonstrated by these excavations. The townscape gives an additional dimension. Documentary evidence is sparse when compared with many English market towns: a number of fourteenth-century extents, the first of which is dated to 1301 (*CIPM Vol 3* 1912, 160), have yet to be examined, but entries in the various Calendars of State Papers usually refer to the castle, less frequently the town.

However, there is a valuable and, by mid-Wales standards, exceptional set of early maps for New Radnor (Silvester 1994b), starting with Speed's map in 1611. Exactly 200

years later, an Enclosure Act was passed for New Radnor, and a manuscript map depicting the entire parish embodies a detailed representation of the town (Fig 12.3; based on NLW Harpton Coll no 4). Copied from this but incorporating new information was a plan of New Radnor in Williams' *History of Radnorshire* which was originally proposed for publication in 1818, but appeared only as a series of articles in the 1850s in *Archaeologia Cambrensis* and then in abridged form. Add to the group the Tithe survey of 1846 and the first edition of the 1:2500 Ordnance Survey map published in 1889 and these offer an unusually strong, early map base.

Four elements of the townscape are worth examining in more detail: the castle, the town defences, the roads and gates, and the street pattern.

New Radnor's motte is sculpted from a natural hillock overshadowing the town. Part of the keep and a length of curtain wall reportedly survived into the last century (Davies 1905, 179), and the site was subjected to at least three episodes of excavation in the later eighteenth and nineteenth centuries (Howse 1989, 9). In addition, it is documented

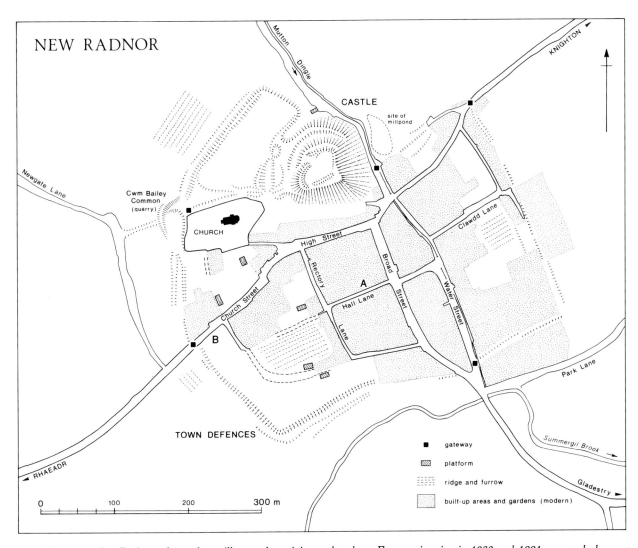

Fig 12.4 New Radnor: the modern village and surviving archaeology. Exacavation sites in 1988 and 1991 are marked A and B respectively.

that sometime after 1791 the local squire modified the earthworks to produce a 'wide promenade', probably to be equated with a ledge which runs around the north and east slopes of the motte below its crest. Today only earthwork foundations are visible on the motte summit. The large sub-rectangular bailey to the north west has earthworks backing on to its bank, but it is no more than supposition that these represent structures contemporary with the medieval occupancy of the castle. New Radnor owes its existence to the castle - without it the town would never have been founded, at least not in this location. Indeed, the two are closely integrated, for the castle defences effectively form the northern perimeter of the town, and the main entrance to the castle probably lay adjacent to the churchyard boundary on the northern edge of the town.

The town defences are likely to date from the thirteenth century for the first murage grant appears in the Patent Rolls of 1257 (*CPR, Henry III, Vol 4*, 609). An earthen bank and ditch form the primary elements of the defensive perimeter, but at some point the former was faced with a drystone revetment wall, the small, flat slabs of which are still visible in places on the south-west and south-east sides. William Camden in 1610 claimed that a wall also surmounted the bank (Howse 1989, 18) – and we may note that Speed's map records 'the ruines of the old wall' (Silvester 1994b, 19) – although no remains of such a feature now exist.

The defences are best preserved on the south side, the bank up to 2.7m high, and the ditch in places 1m deep. Their course on this side adopts an irregular line explained by the fact that to save effort the builders utilized the edge of the river terrace of the Summergil Brook, which in the vicinity of the town is a substantial scarp bank a metre or more high. Elsewhere the defences appear in a variety of guises, whether as a low spread bank in the primary school playing field at the south-east corner of the town or a deep, stream-eroded gully south west of the churchyard. Notwithstanding these variations, and the recognition that particularly on the north-east side of the town the defences have suffered denudation since the compilation of the early nineteenth-century maps, almost the complete circuit can still be traced, a rarity amongst the medieval defended towns of central Wales.

One error has been perpetuated on the early maps. Created on the 1811 Enclosure map and copied on Jonathan Williams' plan, the 'town wall' is depicted as swinging abruptly north in the north-east corner of the town to link with the northern defences of the castle bailey, thereby giving some illusion of symmetry to the overall plan. But detailed fieldwork and an appreciation of the local topography demonstrate the fallacy of this depiction, for the defences as shown would have followed the deep, steep-sided valley of Mutton Dingle. Whether sited along the bottom of this valley or on the top along its lip, such a line would have been a defensive liability as well as involving the construction of an extra 200m of earthwork for the protection of only a mill and mill pond. Needless to say no ground evidence exists to lend support to this early nineteenth-century invention.

In the 1530s Leland noted the remains of four gates to the town (Smith 1964, iii, 10). None now survives but their positions can be readily determined. The West Gate or High Gate at the end of Church Street looked toward the pass that followed the upper reaches of the Summergil Brook and led around the southern edge of the Radnor Forest massif into the hills of central Wales. Traces of a sinuous hollowed track can be seen edging the modern road just outside the defences, but most of its line has been removed by the main A 44 road. The South Gate at the bottom of Water Street led to a network of tracks in the hills between New Radnor and Gladestry, and also served what is now known as School Lane (but in the last century, Park Lane), a green track running due east along the upper edge of the river terrace for several kilometres. In places it doubles as a parish boundary and as a routeway it probably predates the foundation of New Radnor. Northeastwards, the East Gate led onto the road to Knighton and Presteigne and this too shows as a holloway for a short distance before converging with the modern B 4372. Finally, there was the North Gate facing towards Radnor Forest, its track passing beneath the castle and now followed by a metalled lane.

There was also a fifth gate to the north west, which, in view of Leland's failure to mention it, had probably fallen into disuse by the sixteenth century. It is recalled in the name Newgate Lane, a deeply incised holloway running down off Radnor Forest towards the north-west corner of the town. At the bottom of its descent, it adopts a new alignment nearly parallel to the town defences. This was almost certainly a late medieval or post-medieval modification designed to feed traffic through the West Gate, and is indicative of the 'New Gate's' abandonment at a relatively early date, for it served the castle rather than the town. Originally Newgate Lane ran eastwards – it can still be seen as a broad hollow leading to what on nineteenth-century maps is termed Cwm Bailey Common and which has the appearance of a hornwork to the town and castle defences. However, what the maps fail to reveal is that this is a large quarry, fringed by both spoil and an embanked trackway, which interrupted the line of Newgate Lane adjacent to what must have been the 'New Gate' through the town defences. The track then led eastwards towards the castle, still recognizable as a hollow beside the churchyard wall, and beneath the bailey earthworks.

The medieval grid plan of New Radnor is clearly reflected in the street network today. The major streets – Broad Street, High Street and Water Street – are still in use and form the foci for modern housing. But as a material representation of the decay of New Radnor, several other streets have now been wholly or partly abandoned to pasture or green ways. An extension of Hall Lane, west of Rectory Lane, and an unnamed street south of and parallel to it are now no more than grassy hollows, the former some 4m wide and little more than 0.2m deep, the latter considerably wider at 12m and deeper too. Both of them fed into a lane that met Church Street at right-angles and ran on to the church itself. South of Church Lane, this 'lost' lane now gives access only to a modern dwelling and a field; to the north it has disappeared altogether except for a field access beside Church Cottage.

These contractions in the street pattern occurred not in the late medieval or early post-medieval era, but as recently as the nineteenth century. The Tithe Map of 1846 depicts the complete network of lanes while the first edition of the large scale Ordnance Survey map 50 years later shows it in its attenuated form. Other changes are equally recent in origin but more subtle inasmuch as they have left no traces on the ground. Broad Street and Water Street now meet beyond the line of the town defences, but originally must have converged further north before exiting through the South Gate: the modification is likely to have taken place when the grounds of a large house known as The Laurels were laid out in the nineteenth century. Early in that century an intra-mural lane led from Water Street to a farm called Clawdd, which had gone by 1846, and then turned northwards to link with the present Clawdd Lane. This has all but disappeared. Finally we should note an anomaly on Speed's map, a fork at the northern end of Water Street. The resultant triangle is shown as completely filled with houses and is such an obvious feature on the map that it is difficult to dismiss it simply as a cartographic error. Yet there is no independent evidence, either cartographic or topographical, to confirm it, and probably only excavation will be able to clarify the confusion.

Despite these modifications to the pattern, the grid is a reasonably typical layout of a medieval plantation, not perhaps quite as regular as Llanidloes (Montgomeryshire) but better than many. The main axis of this grid is Church Street extending into High Street, a former track skirting the uplands of Radnor Forest that pre-dated the foundation of the town. Equally early perhaps was Park Lane which followed the river terrace on the northern side of the Summergil Brook. At some point its course was adjusted to converge on the South Gate of the town: the mostly likely occasion was the construction of the defences. Prior to this the track probably maintained its position on the terrace, and perhaps joined the main routeway, discussed above, less than 200m beyond the later town. If this is the case, the southern arm of Rectory Lane should probably be recognized as a relic of the pre-urban landscape; it might also explain why this relatively minor back lane survives as an exceptionally wide holloway in pasture, only Broad Street being of comparable size; and it would also resolve its alignment, slightly skewed from the rest of New Radnor's street plan.

It is these features pre-dating the emergence of New Radnor that have precipitated the anomalies in the town's grid pattern. Natural factors, too, have played a part, for the divergence of the upper end of Water Street is due primarily to the course adopted by the stream running down Mutton Dingle.

Only one house within the town is considered to have medieval origins: 8 Church Street incorporates the framework of a fifteenth-century cruck-built dwelling (1993 Schedule of Listed Buildings of New Radnor). But, given that relatively large areas of New Radnor remain undeveloped, it must be anticipated that the stratified remnants of medieval dwellings could exist within open pasture. Certainly fields in the south-west sector of the town, and also the field immediately south of the church, contain earthworks. These, however, cannot be dated with any precision. Several rectangular earthwork banks may represent the foundations of post-medieval buildings though only one can be equated with a structure depicted on early maps. One or two of the platforms could conceivably signal medieval sites, but the 1991 excavations near The Porth demonstrated the degree of attenuation on medieval occupation sites. That cultivation, perhaps late medieval and certainly post-medieval, has occurred within the defences is evidenced by the perceptible traces of ridge and furrow in a field to the west of Rectory Lane.

The 262½ burgage plots recorded in an *Inquisition Post Mortem* in 1304 (*CIPM Vol 4* 1913, 160) plainly fell within the town walls and might be expected to have left some mark upon the pattern of modern enclosures and crofts. Modern and indeed late nineteenth-century Ordnance Survey maps are, however, arguably of less value than the Enclosure Map of 1811 (Fig 12.3). Most of these maps depict intermittent tenement strips fossilized on both sides of High Street; the map of 1811 in addition shows a continuous though slightly sinuous boundary on the west side of Broad Street. At its widest the block of land so defined matches that between Broad Street and Water Street, and again there are hints of a few surviving burgage boundaries. It is hardly surprising that the two main streets of the town should reveal the most cogent evidence, yet the large number of burgage plots evinced in the 1304 *Inqisition* points to much more of the intra-mural area being divided up and utilized.

Conclusion

Among the towns of central Wales, New Radnor is of particular interest and significance. Contracting from its *floruit* in the fourteenth century, rather than being totally abandoned, it is the best example of a shrunken plantation in the region, and almost certainly one of the best in Wales. It has the best preserved town defences in Powys, more readily intelligible than those of Montgomery which is the only comparable centre. Its fine castle earthworks are unencumbered with later buildings in contrast to the other great Radnorshire castles of Colwyn and Painscastle. Its street pattern, though partially abandoned, is a classic of its type. Overall, as an archaeological resource it has a remarkable potential for further examination, and as a settlement its elucidation is facilitated as much by fieldwork and early cartography as by the standard procedures of documentary research and excavation.

Acknowledgements

This study originated in a survey (Silvester 1994a) prepared
for and funded by Cadw, Welsh Historic Monuments as an
assessment of the archaeological resource at New Radnor
to supplement the excavations at The Porth, New Radnor
in 1991/92. The writer would like to thank Dr Sîan Rees
of Cadw for her support as well as the farmers in New
Radnor who allowed access to their land within and around
the town. Thanks are also offered to the organizers of the
Bangor conference for inviting the writer to contribute this
paper, and to Brian Williams for drawing the plans.

References

Unpublished Sources

National Library of Wales (NLW) Dept of Maps and Prints,
   Harpendon Coll, no 4

Published Sources

Beresford, M, 1988, *New towns of the middle ages*, 2nd ed, Stroud
Butler, L A S, 1976, The evolution of towns: planned towns
   after 1066, in M W Barley (ed), *The plans and topography of
   medieval towns in England and Wales*, CBA res rep 14, London,
   32–48
Carter, H, 1966, *The towns of Wales: a study in urban geography*,
   2nd ed, Cardiff
CChR, Calendar of Charter Rolls, London, 1903–27
CIM, Calendar of Inquisitions Miscellaneous 1, London, 1904
CIPM, Calendar of Inquisitions Post Mortem, London, 1904–
CPR, Calendar of Patent Rolls, London, 1891–
Davies, E, 1905, *A general history of the County of Radnor compiled*
from the manuscript of the late Reverend Jonathan Williams,
   Brecon
Dorling, P, 1988, Hall Street, New Radnor, *Archaeol Wales*, 28,
   76
Howse, W H, 1989, *Radnor old and new*, Kington (reprint of
   1944 ed)
Jones, N W, 1992, *New Radnor – The Porth, Powys*, Clwyd-
   Powys Archaeological Trust Rep 39, Welshpool
Jones, N W, in prep, Excavations at the Porth, New Radnor
King, D J C, 1983, *Castellarium Anglicanum*, New York
Musson, C R, & Spurgeon, C J, 1988, Cwrt Llechryd, Llanel-
   wedd: an unusual moated site in central Powys, *Medieval
   Archaeol*, 32, 97–109
Ogilby, J, 1675, *Britannia* (facsimile, Amsterdam, 1970)
RCAHMW 1913, *An inventory of the ancient monuments in
   Wales and, Monmouthshire, vol 3, County of Radnor*, London
Remfry, P M, 1994, *Radnor Castle 1066 to 1282*, Malvern
Silvester, R J, 1994a, *New Radnor: a topographical survey*, Clwyd-
   Powys Archaeological Trust Rep 101, Welshpool
Silvester, R J, 1994b, New Radnor on old maps, *Trans Radnorshire
   Soc*, 64, 15–24
Smith, L T (ed), 1964, *The itinerary of John Leland in or about
   the years 1535–1543*, 5 vols, London
Soulsby, I, 1983, *The towns of medieval Wales*, Chichester
Stenton, F M, 1971, *Anglo-Saxon England*, Oxford
*Taxatio, Taxatio ecclesiastica Angliae et Walliae, auctoritate P.
   Nicholai IV., circa A.D. 1291*, Record Commission, London,
   1802
Thompson, M W (ed), 1983, *The journeys of Sir Richard Colt
   Hoare through Wales and England 1793–1810*, Stroud
Thorn, F, & C (eds), 1984, *Domesday Book: Herefordshire*,
   Chichester
Thorpe, L (ed), 1978, *Gerald of Wales. The journey through
   Wales/The description of Wales*, Harmondsworth
Turner, H L, 1970, *Town defences in England and Wales*, London

Chapter 13

Medieval Settlement in Wales: A Summing Up

Christopher Dyer

The organizers of this conference deserve congratulation for putting together such a full and comprehensive programme of papers, which give us an overview of the settlement history of the Principality over a thousand years, from the end of the Roman province up to the fifteenth century and beyond. In summing up the proceedings, I will firstly consider why the study of medieval rural settlement is a subject of compelling importance, and then pick out from the conference papers themes of chronology, organization, the market, and agriculture, before making some concluding comments about future work.

Medieval settlements are worth studying for a number of reasons. Firstly, we can only begin to understand the experiences of medieval people of all kinds if we can visualize the structures and spaces within which they lived and worked. One approach is to reconstruct the medieval settlement hierarchy, ranged in size from towns to hamlets and isolated farms. The hierarchy can also be seen in its varying degrees of organization from the highly regulated plans of boroughs and villages to the apparently haphazard arrangement of farms along the edge of a common pasture. In fact these do not represent contrasts between planning and its absence, but more a question of different types of planning, because creating even the most irregular hamlet involved some decision making about the placing of boundaries and houses. Settlements also formed a social hierarchy, reflected strongly in the Welsh evidence, from royal sites to the hamlets of serfs.

A traditional and still valuable way of approaching medieval settlements is to relate them to methods of production, and so a second reason for studying them is to gain insights into the economy. Large villages are usually located in the midst of arable fields, and they were likely to be committed to corn growing, while hamlets and isolated farms often had a more pastoral orientation. The buildings themselves (barns and byres notably) and the surrounding gardens and paddocks contributed to the efficiency and variety of production. The building techniques and materials of the houses and their contents provide information about rural crafts, and the settlements were often sited in places which allowed their inhabitants to take advantage of non-agricultural employments in fishing or woodland industry.

In addition to these material considerations, a third advantage of studying settlements lies in the insights that they provide into social attitudes. One clue as to social relations between the aristocracy and the rest of society is provided by their tendency to live either apart or together, and one sees in different periods and among the various types of lords sometimes a tolerance of peasant settlements at their gates, and sometimes an anxiety to live in a remote place – perhaps for reasons of security, or for access to hunting grounds – but also presumably because the close proximity of the lower orders proved irksome. We can also learn something about the relationship between individuals and the group from the organization of settlements, where often each household had its space strongly delineated by walls, ditches or hedges, but where there were also communal facilities – greens, drove ways, churches etc. Of course the scattering of farms could be associated with a strong community, because the isolated households still belonged to villages and parishes, and were often dependent on common pastures which were subject to collective regulations.

In short then, settlements were artefacts, but can tell us about ideas – dominance, compliance, deference and co-operation are only some of the factors behind the location and form of settlements. The creation of every place involved making decisions, about the placing of boundaries and buildings, and about the movements of inhabitants over long distances, or more modest relocations within smaller spaces. Our problem as observers of these sites lies in our need to reconstruct the thinking that lies behind them, for example the ideas which led to one village plan type being borrowed and imitated in a number of neighbouring settlements. We lack any clear and detailed contemporary record of the process.

All of these decisions took place within the context of restraints imposed by the natural environment of soils, terrain and climate, and in a society with many man-made restrictions. Therefore a fourth reason for investigating settlements must be to help us to appreciate the constant fluctuations in those natural and political restraints, and to unpick the relationship between the wider changes and the shifts in the number and form of settlements.

The final importance of settlements lies in the tangible and visible link that they provide with the past, which helps scholars to plan and analyse their layout, and gives us an immediate educational visual aid which has much greater impact than any verbal description. But it is precisely the attraction of old places which encourages modern commuters to wish to live in or near them, that faces us with dilemmas of controlling development so that it does not destroy the last traces of the medieval period.

Some Themes in Welsh Settlement Studies

Lying behind the papers delivered at this conference are four major issues which need to be addressed directly and which represent some of the major problems in Welsh settlement studies, though of course they are often questions which concern those investigating the subject throughout western Europe.

Chronology

We need to set our studies of settlements within an overall chronological framework of the growth or shrinkage of population and the cultivated or exploited area. These are not necessarily related, because although it used to be believed that population levels provided the key to understanding the degree to which settlement was organized and nucleated, we now realize that the two factors are not causally connected. It is still useful, however, to have some notion of the overall trends in population, because they will help us to see how the growth and decline of settlements fit into a larger picture of expansion and contraction.

The most controversial period in population history must be that between *c* 400 and 1000. The shortage of good evidence from every part of Europe tempts us to argue that there was a massive drop in population levels and economic vitality in that period, or at least in the first two or three centuries. This is a naive view because the absence of material evidence cannot be regarded as an accurate reflection of the amount of human activity. In England no one would guess from the relatively small number of surviving churches of the eleventh century, or the occasional finds of datable eleventh-century pottery or coins, that the whole country was densely populated and thoroughly exploited, but this is revealed by Domesday Book.

However, it would not be surprising to find that in the centuries following 400, with the withdrawal of the stable political rule and the commercial infrastructure of the Roman province, that there would be some insecurity and economic recession with a consequent drop in population. This would be most marked in the most thoroughly romanized areas in south-east Wales, but would have repercussions, with a reduced demand for cattle or minerals on the uplands. In the examples presented to this conference there seems to be clear evidence for this contraction in the neglect of the drainage system in the Gwent Levels and the consequent loss of land to the sea.

The next period for which we have concrete evidence, the twelfth and thirteenth centuries, clearly saw an expansion in the area of reclaimed land in the Gwent Levels, the foundation of new settlements in the form of nucleated villages in Pembrokeshire, and new boroughs scattered over the whole Principality. It so happens that this is also a period of known expansion in the rest of western Europe, but it is dangerous to expect every region to have an identical experience. Indeed, a good deal of scepticism has been expressed about the assumption by French historians in particular that this period saw the dramatic advances in cultivation which they call the *grands défrichements*. In the special circumstances of Wales, we cannot view this period simply as one of continuous *internal* growth, because the new boroughs and villages were founded as part of a programme of colonization by migrants and were designed as a framework of conquest under new political rulers. Indeed, we find that some of the grandiose plans for new boroughs did not always work: the excavation of Newport has revealed evidence for decline at the end of the thirteenth century, when most towns and settlements elsewhere were still expanding.

We should also presume that Wales shared in the retreat of settlement in the fourteenth and fifteenth centuries: this is well recorded both in documents and in the archaeology. In the cases reviewed at this conference, the desertion of Deri in Anglesey, and the shrinkage of the border villages, provide evidence for contraction. However, the story is not one of universal abandonment, because there is good evidence for the establishment of new permanent settlements on upland pastures, which is very much parallel to discoveries in England of the building of new farms and cottages, usually in upland or woodland locations at this period.

In Wales, as elsewhere in western Europe, we are faced with the problem of explaining this period of contraction, either in terms of internal crises of the social and agricultural system, or attributing it to the worsening climate and epidemics which acted as exogenous factors.

Organization of Settlement

The second problem confronting Welsh settlement history as indicated both by recent publications and the papers at this conference, concerns the degree to which settlement was directed and organized. There is perhaps more evidence in Wales for settlement being ordered into regular patterns within estates, and for deliberate creation of settlement, than in any other part of Europe. We have the Welsh laws, with their ideal type of rural society organized in royal centres and peasant hamlets; and archaeological and topographical evidence for settlements of the pre-Conquest period with circular or curvilinear perimeters which must have been the result of some coherent plan. Among the post-Conquest settlements are the regularly planned nucleated villages, similar to the linear or row settlements in parts of

England and western Europe, which were set up for colonists who would replace the rebellious Welsh with a more compliant population, and provide bases for political control.

I have always tended to be a sceptic on the matter of the planning of settlement by lords and the state, and feel that one should always allow for some impetus towards the creation of settlements from below, as well as direction from above. One notes from the reports at this conference, resulting from village surveys, a healthy scepticism about the old assumption that Welsh peasants lived in dispersed settlements and English in nucleated ones, so perhaps settlement forms did not depend entirely on political direction. It is always a pleasure to observe, as in the case revealed by the excavations at Newport, that people did not stick to the plan originally assigned to them. The three burgage plots as originally laid out changed as two tenants developed their holdings at the expense of their neighbours, no doubt reflecting disparities in wealth and status. And even when lords unquestionably planned villages and towns, and set out the plots for migrants, their success and failure depended very much on the willingness of settlers to take advantage of the opportunities offered.

The Market

Historians sometimes like to draw a sharp divide between rural and urban settlements, though in the case of the Welsh boroughs this is clearly a difficult matter. We must regard some of the boroughs as essentially rural settlements in which migrants were encouraged to take up land by being granted the advantages of privileged tenures. But that did not guarantee that they became traders and craftsmen separated from agricultural production, because there is ample evidence that they held lands and pastoral rights in the countryside and were really little more than high-status villagers.

The most striking evidence for the development of the market in medieval Wales comes from the emphasis on pastoral farming, which only makes sense in the context of an export trade in animals and animal products. The transhumance systems, and the management of herds and flocks on upland pastures from the temporary *hafod* settlements, all show the systematic exploitation of pastoral husbandry. The settlements established on the pastures when *hafod* buildings were occupied permanently, and when new farms were established on the hills in the fifteenth century, are good evidence for the ability of people to live mainly from the profits of trade rather than from consuming the foodstuffs that they grew themselves: the people who lived in the uplands must have obtained their grain by exchange or purchase. In the lowland too, the work on the Gwent Levels has shown the shift from arable to pastoral farming in the later middle ages and it is suggested that dairy products from that district were carried by boat to Bristol. The well-documented trade in live cattle in the midlands and south east of England shows how the surplus animals from the Welsh pastures helped to satisfy the growing demand for beef in the later middle ages. In the already complex commercial world of the middle ages, the food preferences and purchasing power of London artisans influenced the lives of peasants in the upland pastures of north Wales.

Agriculture

A number of the contributions showed how settlements made use of varied resources, and particularly how they balanced the exploitation of the arable land of the lowlands with the more extensive upland pastures. We need to learn a lot more about the territories used by the settlements. For example, there is clear evidence of varying degrees of communal control of such assets. The Gwent settlement of Whitson was based on long individual strips of land rather than extensive communal fields, but clearly in Pembrokeshire we find areas of intermixed common field of the type more frequently found in England and western Europe. Hill pastures were clearly shared by large numbers of communities who travelled considerable distances with their livestock.

Welsh upland settlement provides us with a great opportunity to investigate the marginal land hypothesis – the idea that in times of population expansion and land hunger, settlement advanced into marginal uplands, and then abandoned that territory in times of contraction. In fact the Welsh evidence, like that from some other regions, seems to contradict that view, because of the market demand for pastoral products in the later middle ages. Even though the population was contracting, we find a continued exploitation of the resources of the uplands, and clearly we cannot make a simple equation between population levels and the degree of management of pastoral resources. The history of Welsh farming is a great antidote to the view that the expansion and contraction of corn growing is the main key to understanding the history of settlement and agriculture.

Future Work

The contributions to this conference show very well the value of interdisciplinary work, based on every available type of source material, and using the retrogressive technique by which research begins with the patterns of settlements and fields shown on nineteenth-century maps, which can then be traced back to earlier phases of landscape development. Research needs to be conducted on a number of different scales – there is a case both for superficial surveys over whole counties and regions, and for more detailed studies of individual settlements and their territories. It is important though that the territory should be considered as well as the settlement. One realizes why it is necessary for planning purposes to emphasize the 'historic cores', but in those areas where the majority of people lived in irregular and dispersed settlement outside the 'historic cores', it is clearly desirable to include in any study all the surroundings as well as the village centre itself.

In addition to studies of areas, both large and small, there is a place for thematic investigations of princely sites, churches, boroughs and upland settlement, because work of that kind, comparing similar sites in different environments and periods, can provide new perspectives. One would like to see this work extended to other types of settlement, such as castles and monasteries, and indeed further work on boroughs could embrace their rural hinterlands as well as the street patterns of the towns themselves.

Research into rural settlement has a practical and immediate importance because of its implications for modern planning policy. Modern inhabitants are attracted to live in the countryside partly by the link with the past that the village or hamlet represents, but we must ensure that they do not destroy that connection by insensitive building which swamps the 'historic core' of medieval settlements. Similarly, in towns, the boundaries between plots and the relationship between houses and streets that we know to be of twelfth- or thirteenth-century origin, must not be swept aside by the crude logic of modern shopping centres and redevelopment. This damage is caused not by wilful vandalism, but simply by ignorance of the earlier settlement history and the nature of boundaries. It is our job as settlement historians to make sure that those who frame planning policy are aware of the historical and archaeological dimension.

Index